Organic Gardener's Basics

by Barbara P. Lawton and

George F. Van Patten

Printed in the United States of America

Van Patten Publishing

ISBN: 1-878823-01-9 Trade Paperback
ISBN: 1-878823-14-0 Hard Cover

Publisher's Cataloging in Publication

(Prepared by Quality Books Inc.)

Lawton, Barbara Perry
    Organic gardener's basics/ Barbara P. Lawton, George F. Van Patten
    p. cm. -- (Organic gardener's series ; 2)
    Includes index
    ISBN: 1-878823-01-9 (trade paper)
    ISBN: 1-878823-14-0 (hardcover)
    1. Organic Gardening. I. Van Patten, George F. II. Title. III. Series
    SB453.5.L39 1993   635'.048'4
          QB193-20013

Jacket/cover design by Peter Callis, Linda Provost
Cover photo: Rosalind Creasy
Back cover photos: Larry Turner
              US Department of Agriculture
Technical Editor: Stevie O. Daniels
Copy Editor: Bruce Taylor
Artwork: Hart James
        Ann Woods
        Dyann Alkire
        Jon Shane
        Jin Kwon
        Merrillyn Clarke
Layout & Design: PC Design
Typesetting: Microline Graphics

10 9 8 7 6 5 4 3 2 1

Distributed by **Login Publisher's Consortium**
1436 West Randolph Street
Chicago, IL 60607
1-800-626-4330

Drawing page 17, courtesy TroyBilt Inc.
Drawing page 52 courtesy Ames Tools
Drawing page 109 courtesy Safer's
Map on page 170 and chart page 177 courtesy
The Lawn Institute, Pleasant Hill, TN

Drawings and text on pages 61-67 adapted from
Weeds of the North Central States
University of Illinois
Agricultural Experiment Station
Urbana, Illinois 61801

Table of Contents

Foreword

This book, *Organic Gardening Basics,* by Barbara Lawton and George Van Patten is probably more comprehensive than any other basic organic gardening book that I have ever read. This literary pair has touched upon just about everything that one might want information about when one deals in the arena of organic gardening. As I digested the text, I was amazed at the amount of good solid practical information that came forth on every page.

Barbara and George seemed to have thought through every facet of practical organic gardening from earthworms to soil testing, growing cover crops, and leaky pipe irrigation. Information about integrated pest management, organic pesticides, and beneficial insects was clearly outlined in the text. One of the things that I was delighted to see was that perennials, biennials, ornamental grasses, and wildflowers found their place in this book.

I was also pleased to see that evergreens, shade trees, ornamental trees, shrubs, vines, and roses had their place, too.

With all the nuances in the world of gardening, I was pleased to see that fundamentals like hand weeding had not been overlooked. This book by Barbara and George will be a dynamic addition to any gardener's library.

Bob Thomson,
Host of The Victory Garden

Introduction

Through the centuries we gardeners have worked hand in hand with Mother Nature to fulfill our needs. Plant breeders have used their ingenuity to select and transform ancestral corn, potatoes, and many other food crops into the plump, tasty, and nutritious vegetables, fruits, and grains that we enjoy today. Small farms practicing crop rotation and soil building once fed entire villages, but production and transportation methods changed that. Modern megafarms that feed entire cities find it profitable to grow cash crops that require high nutrient levels to sustain production. They often use only chemical fertilizers on the land, concentrating on the profits from each crop. Especially during the years between World War II and the 1970s, farmers did little to return organic matter to the soil. They seemed to have little concern for tomorrow. Fortunately, in recent years, there has been a return to concerns for the soil and for the future of the cultivated land. Agricultural science has proven the value of organic matter in the soil and farmers are responding. The natural equation can get out of balance when you ignore the future of the soil and don't learn to build healthy soil.

Following World War II, there also was a surge in the development and use of pesticides, many of which turned out to be toxic to people, fish, and wildlife. In recent years, there has been significant reduction in the excessive use of chemical pesticides that had come to be commonplace. We have seen pesticides and other chemicals promoted as having minimal risk if used properly become banned as toxic hazards.

It is not always the fault of the chemical. Many common substances, such as table salt, are harmful to plants and animals in mega-doses. Too often, agricultural and home garden chemicals are used too much, unwisely, and in the wrong way. Soil can be made lifeless by excess chemical build-up. Poor soil management also can cause precious topsoil to be washed away.

The expense of poor land management cannot be measured on an income statement. The cost is carried on to future generations.

Modern science can teach us about Mother Nature. We can learn to grow bigger apples, longer cucumbers, and redder roses. We can study the natural equations of building healthy soil, attracting natural predators to eat the pests, and practicing organic weed control. With this knowledge, we can create beautiful, productive gardens that are interesting, safe, easy to care for, and fun.

If you have ever dug manure, peat moss, and leaf mold into a garden bed or knocked aphids off rose buds with the garden hose, you have taken the first steps toward organic gardening. Combine these procedures with a few other organic principles and you will see why organic gardening is so popular and fruitful. In addition, it is less expensive than the alternatives.

A sign of our times and an endorsement of organic gardening is that the United States Department of Agriculture in Beltsville, Maryland has changed the name of its road from "Chemical Way" to "Organic Way"!

In writing this book, we have called upon our own experience plus that of many lettered and unlettered experts in the fields of gardening and horticulture. We have provided the best information possible so that our book can serve as your basic gardening resource. Our book is a guide to sound and sensible gardening methods. You will learn more through experience than any book can teach you, but this will give you a healthy boost in the right direction. For details on aspects of gardening we have not included, see the list in the Appendix for books that you may wish to buy or borrow from your local library.

Most of all, we hope this book will help you enjoy gardening as much as we do.

Barbara Perry Lawton
George Van Patten

Chapter One

Soil

About Soil

Whether your yard is a slippery mud puddle or a frozen cement-like slab in winter and a water-guzzling dust bowl or rock-hard weed patch in summer, you can transform it into a rich vibrant garden with a little management, compost, and organic fertilizer.

Compost is easy to make and free. It is simply plant and other organic refuse that has been biologically decomposed until it is relatively stable. Compost made from partially decayed plant refuse from your garden is a good organic soil amendment. Organic fertilizer is the term used for animal manures, composts, and plant waste used as plant nutrients in place of chemical fertilizers.

Don't feel alone if your soil is poor; most of the world's soils have less than perfect structure, and fail to provide ideal nutrient balances. Many gardeners with soils worse than yours have transformed them to provide a good nutrient balance and texture.

As you learn about your soil, also learn as much as you can about your weather. Good weather information sources are your local local weather from the TV, newspapers, airport weather department, the forestry department, and the county agent for your Cooperative Extension Service. Be sure to ask about the average length of the growing season and the average last day of frost. Soil and weather will have more bearing upon the kinds of plants you can grow than any other factors.

Air, water, minerals, and organic matter are important non-living elements of soil. Air and water flow through the spaces between soil particles, so the texture of your soil is important. The mineral and organic elements serve as plant nutrients, and must be in soluble form for roots to draw them into the plant's manufacturing system. Solubility of the minerals and organics will depend on soil pH, the measure of acidity or alkalinity.

Organic matter is derived from living matter, For gardeners, the most important organic sources are plants and manures from cows, horses, and other herbivores.

Humus, the dark substance that remains when organic matter has thoroughly decomposed, is the binder that helps build good soil structure. Its fibers are sticky, and bind small particles together into larger crumbs that reduce the soil density and allow space for air and water to flow. It makes the soil loose and spongy, and able to hold nutrients and moisture.

The premise behind the organic method is simple: feed the soil and the soil feeds the plans. Healthy organic soil promotes strong, vigorous plants that are better able to resist insect and disease problems. Though organic matter may make up only 3 to 5 percent of the soil volume, it has a dynamic effect on soil structure, nutrient and water retention, and air pore space. An ideal loamy soil contains 25% air, 25% water, 45% minerals, and 5% organic matter.

Organic matter feeds the soil's bacteria. Heat, air, and water are also necessary for active bacteria; all are promoted by good soil structure and texture. When the soil warms in the spring, bacterial activity increases, and changes the nutrients into compounds that can be absorbed by plants.

First, determine what kind of soil you have, then decide the easiest way to transform it into rich organic earth teeming with life.

The texture of soil is based on the relative proportions of sand, silt and clay particles. Sand has large blocky particles (.05-2 mm.). Silt particles are smaller (.002-.05 mm.). Clay particles are the smallest of the three main types of soil particles (.001-.002 mm.) and, because of their small size, tend to pack together.

You may want to dig a hole to look at the profile or layers of your soil. The top layer is often darker and more fertile because of air and water penetration, and the accompanying decomposition of organic material. Deeper soil is usually lighter and less fertile.

To get the feel of your soil's texture, scoop up a handful of moist soil and rub it through your fingers. Clay soil feels and looks slippery. Sandy soil feels and looks gritty. Silty soil, in between clay and sand, feels almost greasy, but less slippery than clay.

The majority of soils include all three particle types – sand, silt, and clay. The most desirable soil is loam,

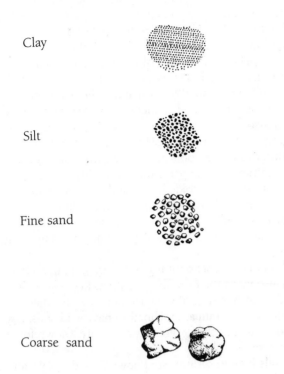

Clay

Silt

Fine sand

Coarse sand

combination of all three. When organic matter is added to loam so that it comprises about 5 percent of the total, the result is an ideal garden soil.

Few soils are all clay, all silt, or all sand. They are usually in combinations of the basic soil types. The quality of topsoil changes from one location to another. Soil on one side of your yard may have different characteristics than soil from the other side.

Use the "soil triangle' as an illustration —the one that shows graphically the proportions of sand, silt and clay in different types of soil.

Clay Soils

Clay soils, sometimes known as "adobe" or "heavy" soil, consists of mostly fine particles packed tightly together. About 100 particles of fine clay soil would fit into this period (.). Clay soil is very dense and is heavier than sandy or silty soils. It is slow to warm in the spring but will hold warmth into the fall. Water does not drain well in clay, and there is little room for air, so root growth is inhibited. The finer the particles, the heavier the clay and the slower the drainage.

Heavy clay soils are difficult to work when wet; they stick to tools and clump into rock-hard clods when dry. Clay soils hold fertilizers well but their water content is difficult to manage. Organic matter, such as compost and leaf mold when added to clay

soils, adds millions of tiny air pockets and improves water movement (irrigation and drainage), which in turn promotes root growth. Perfecting the structure of heavy clay soil will take several years of adding compost or other organic matter.

Heavy soils produce poor root crops because root growth is restricted. Other vegetables, whose useful parts are produced above ground, such as beans and broccoli, can flourish in moist clay soils. To improve clay soils, add compost or other organic matter to the top 12 inches. Contrary to popular belief, adding small amounts of sand to clay is not the way to obtain better drainage; the grains can bind with the clay to form a cement-like consistency.

Adding as much organic matter as possible and incorporating it into the soil through double digging (see illustration) is the quickest way to improve heavy soils. "Green manuring" growing a crop and tilling it under – should also be considered. (See details in Chapter 2)

Sandy Soils

Small, medium, and large blocky particles in sand allow plenty of air space and excellent root penetration. Light, sandy soils are generally easy to till even when saturated with water. Sandy soils warm quickly in the spring and produce early crops. Sandy soils do not hold fertilizers well — when they are overwatered, dissolved nutrients leach out of the soil with the water.

Compost, blended with sandy soil, binds the large particles together so that they hold water and soluble nutrients. The compost is soon "eaten" by bacteria and other soil organisms and becomes humus. Organic matter breaks down rapidly in hot climates. The more often the soil is cultivated and the hotter the climate, the more often organic matter should be added.

A mulch consisting of straw, leaves, or other insulating material spread on top of sandy soil, keeps it cooler and reduces evaporation. Winter cover crops or green manures plowed into the sandy soil improve water retention, prevent runoff, and promote soil life. Compost and cover crops, such as alfalfa, clover, and ryegrass, are good materials for improving sandy soils.

Loam Soils

Fertile loamy soils are ideal for gardening. They are easy to work and hold air and nutrients well. Coarse loam contains large soil particles and has plenty of room for root growth and air, and enough clay to retain moisture. Loam soils are easy to maintain and keep fertile. Loams are commonly found in old river beds, lake beds, and old gardens.

Loam consists of 20 to 30 percent clay, 30 to 50 percent silt, and 30 to 50 percent sand. Soil classifications also include sandy loams, clay loams, and silty loams, each having higher percentages of the named soil. Anything from artichokes to zucchinis will grow with ease in fertile, loamy soil.

As you gain more experience in gardening and caring for your soil, you will become more aware of the fact that the plants themselves are an important factor in improving your garden soil. They add a considerable amount of organic matter to the soil and their roots help keep the soil aerated.

Loam is the ideal concentration of sand, silt, and clay and becomes perfect for gardening when you add about five percent organic matter. This kind of soil combines the advantages of clay (moisture retention and fertilizer retention) and sand (quick warming, good drainage, and easy to work).

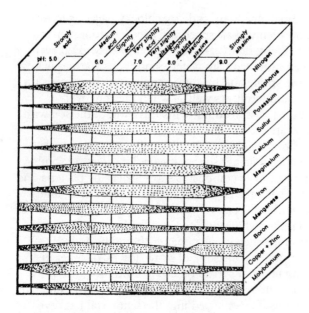

The pH chart shows the availability of various nutrients at different pH values.

About pH

The pH of a soil is the scale from 1.0 to 14.0 that measures the acid-to-alkaline balance. One (1.0) is the most acidic, 7.0 is neutral, and 14.0 is most alkaline.

The pH scale is a logarithmic scale, which means that a soil with a pH of 8.0 is 10 times more alkaline than a soil with a pH of 7.0. A soil with a pH of 5.0 is 10 times more acid than a soil with a pH of 6.0.

The pH of a soil is one of many conditions that affect plant growth. Plants can only take up nutrients that are in water soluble form and if the pH is too high or too low, the needed elements and compounds may be in insoluble forms. Most vegetables grow best in a slightly acidic soil with a pH between 6.0 and 6.8. Within this range, roots can absorb and process available nutrients. If the pH is too low (acid), manganese can concentrate to toxic levels, and the availability of calcium, phosphorus, and magnesium is limited. In an alkaline soil, with a pH above 7.0, the availability of phosphorus, iron, copper, zinc, boron, and manganese is limited.

Soil pH is dependent upon the underlying rock and also upon the prevailing weather. Regions such as northeastern and northwestern United States that receive a lot of rain are inclined to have acid soils. Dry regions such as the desert Southwest are known for their alkaline soils.

Soils high in sodium are known as sodic soils, and they are impermeable to water because of the high sodium content. Add 30 to 50 pounds of gypsum per 1000 square feet of sodic soil and cultivate it into the soil. The gypsum treatment is for sodic soils only, and can't be used to improve the structure other soils.

There are several ways to measure pH: pH soil test kit, litmus paper, or electronic pH tester (the easiest to use), all of which may be found at most garden centers. When testing for pH, take two or three soil samples and follow the manufacturer's instructions carefully.

Types of Lime

Lime can be an important addition to soils in wet climates. It reduces acidity, and improves the structure of clay soils, making them easier to work. Lime also helps make sandy soils compact better, and it neutralizes excess compounds of aluminum and iron as well as stimulates other chemical actions which in turn release locked-up nutrients. Adding lime generally creates a favorable environment for microorganisms that decompose organic matter.

Soil pH is comparatively easy to change. Adding some form of lime to acid soil will increase the pH, lessening acidity. Adding too much lime however, will make some nutrients unavailable or burn plant roots. First of all, get a soil test from Cooperative Extension Service or another soil lab in order to know what your soil pH is. Check with your local Cooperative

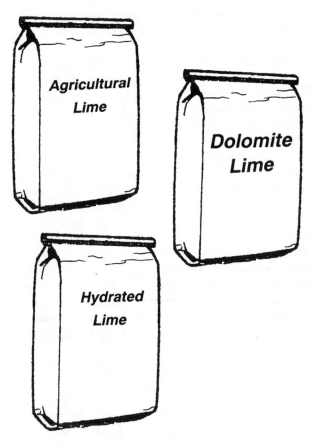

There are three types of lime that are readily available: agricultural lime, dolomite lime and hydrated lime .

Types of Lime

Agricultural or ground limestone (calcium carbonate) is one of the most common forms of lime and an excellent choice for adjusting pH. It is slow acting and will remain in the soil for several years.

Dolomitic lime (calcium magnesium carbonate) combines calcium with magnesium to form an excellent pH-altering substance, and adds two needed nutrients as well. Always buy slow-acting dolomite in the finest form available so it begins acting immediately following application. Even the finest grade will remain in the soil for up to five years.

Ground oyster shells contain calcium carbonate and small amounts of phosphorus; they are commonly available at feed stores. Oyster shells are very slow in decomposing.

Hydrated lime (calcium hydroxide) is quick acting and caustic to plants and microorganisms — not recommended for garden use.

Quicklime (calcium oxide), manufactured by searing or burning limestone, is fast acting, but caustic and may burn or kill plants and soil microorganisms — not recommended for garden use.

Wood ashes are a source of lime as well as phosphorus, potassium (potash), boron, and other elements. Hardwood ashes are about twice as alkaline as softwood ashes.

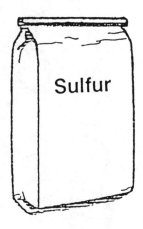

Elemental sulfur is the most common element used to lower pH. However if added in large quantities, it can increase to toxic levels. Check with your local garden center or Cooperative Extension Service for more specific guidelines on lowering the pH of alkaline soil.

Extension Service for recommendations on the amounts of lime you should apply to your soil.

Since the amount of lime needed to raise the pH of soil is dependent upon many factors, including temperature, moisture, soil type, and amount of organic matter, we have not included a table for lime application. In general, where lime is needed to raise the pH of naturally acidic soils, it should be added in small amounts every year and monitored with regular soil tests.

For best results, use the finest grind of lime and apply it in the fall so that it will affect the pH by the following spring. Do not apply lime to a freshly manured soil or it will combine to form ammonia gas and release needed nitrogen into the air.

It is possible to lower pH by adding liberal amounts of compost, peat, or organic matter to the soil. If a soil has a pH over 8.0, build a raised bed on top of the soil at least 12 inches high, so that the alkaline salts and water stay below the level of most feeder

Application rate of sulfur to lower pH of various soils

Lower soil pH to 6.5 and increase the acidity of soil by adding sulfur as follows.

If soil is 8.5, 46 pounds/1,000 square feet for sandy soil, 57 pounds/1,000 s.f. for loam, 69 pounds/1,000 s.f. for clay

If soil is 8.0, add 28 pounds/1,000 s.f. for sand, 34 pounds/1,000 s.f. for loam, 46 pounds/1,000 s.f. for clay.

If soil is 7.5, add 11 pounds/1,000 s.f. for sand, 18 pounds/1,000 s.f. for loam, 23 pounds/1,000 s.f. for clay.

If soil is 7.0, add 2 pounds/1,000 s.f. for sand, 4 pounds/1,000 s.f. for loam, 7 pounds/1,000 s.f. for clay.

roots. If you can see white alkaline salts on the surface, water very heavily to leach the alkaline salts deeper into the soil. Heavy watering may have to be repeated every spring.

Two Common Soil Problems

Hardpan and compacted soil are two similar soil problems. They both make it difficult to grow just about anything. Compacted soil is caused by heavy equipment or foot traffic. In the case of compacted

pathways, you might be wise to give up growing grass and just make the path official with brick or other pavers.

If compaction is severe from heavy equipment, you may have to have the soil aerated or loosened with a chisel plow. Hardpan is a condition whereby a layer of soil beneath the soil surface is hard and impermeable to both water and roots. Caliche is a hardpan common in the Southwest. It consists of a layer of calcium carbonate (lime) located below the topsoil. The texture of caliche varies from granular to solid cement-like rock and can be from a few inches to many feet thick.

To plant trees or shrubs in any hardpan area, you must bore clear through it to provide drainage. Use an auger to bore or dig with a pick and shovel completely through the hardpan. All other planting techniques remain the same as for other trees, shrubs, and bedding plants. (See also Chapters 7 and 10 for planting techniques.) Space drainage holes from 5 to 15 feet apart for flower and vegetable beds and hedge rows. Discard the hardpan bored out of the hole and replace

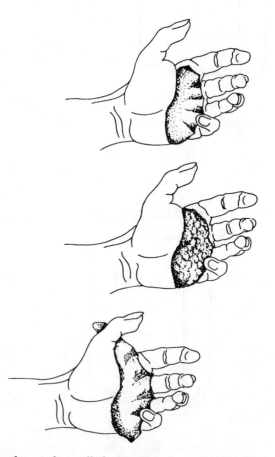

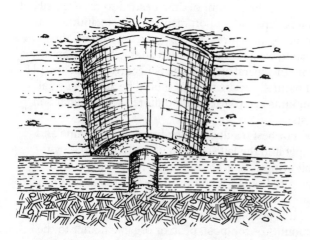

Bore a hole through the hardpan to provide drainage for roots.

The soil is ready to till if a handful of moist soil breaks apart fairly easily. If the soil sticks firmly together, let it dry out a few more days. After tilling in compost and organic fertilizers, the dark, moist soil should crumble freely.

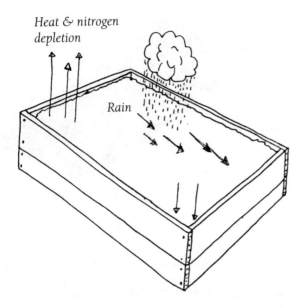

Heat & nitrogen depletion

Rain

Bare soil loses heat and nitrogen, promotes runoff, lessens water penetration, and provides no fodder for soil life.

it with compost or high-quality garden soil. This process is sometimes referred to as vertical composting.

Raised beds and container gardens may be used to overcome problems caused by compacted soil or hardpan.

Garden Beds

The first planting in garden beds can be made as soon as the ground can be worked in spring. Raised beds, whether double dug or not, dry out the soonest, and can often be worked first. Sunken beds, used to combat the heat of the desert, are ready when the weather warms. The popular flat-bed row gardens are often the last to become ready. The more compost added to any bed, the sooner it can be worked and planted. No-till garden beds are just what their name implies. They do not need to be tilled and are ready to plant as soon as the weather warms.

Before planting, fertilize the entire bed and add organic matter to the soil at the same time. One organic recipe for fertilizing loam is to apply a one- to two-inch layer of compost and ground alfalfa hay at the rate of four bales per 1,000 square feet. Work this into the soil to a depth of 4 to 6 inches by hand or with a rotary tiller

Established garden beds to which organic matter is added every year can be planted in the spring as soon as they can be worked. New garden beds that have

Using a broadfork is much faster and easier than a shovel to cultivate a garden bed.

been heavily amended and those which have freshly tilled-in cover crops should sit for about two weeks to allow decomposition of the organic matter to begin.

Raised Beds

Raised beds allow soil to drain better, warm up earlier in the spring, and stay warm longer in the fall. They allow you to plant vegetables two to four weeks earlier in the spring and harvest two to four weeks longer in the fall. Plants can be spaced more closely together, which increases the yield in a small space and crowds out weeds, lowering maintenance.

You can let sloped earth form the sides of the bed or use cedar, redwood, or black locust — all rot-resistant woods — to form the sides of the bed. Pressure-treated wood is another option. If you want to treat the wood yourself, Cuprinol 10 or products that contain copper napthenate will preserve wood for several years. Be sure to use rust-proof galvanized nails or lag bolts. Once made, raised beds seldom need to be deeply worked as long as you add organic matter annually.

The length is up to you but if you plan to frame the bed with wood, consider the length of your boards. Eight feet is the usual length of milled lumber in retail stores. You could also frame the bed with bricks, cinder blocks, or other masonry, eliminating the need for preservatives.

Constructing a Raised Bed with a Frame

Step One: Mark out the bed using four stakes. Stretch twine between the stakes to form a square or triangle. Dig out the high spots of soil under the string so that the ground is fairly level.

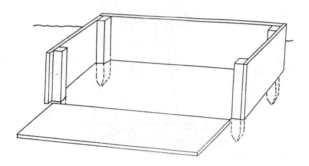

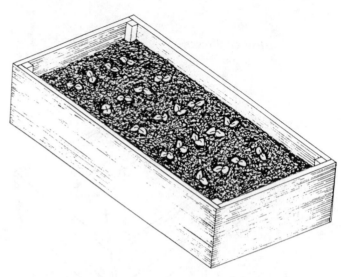

Step Two: Cultivate or double dig the area.

Step Three: Plant 4 x 4 wood posts at each corner and sink 2 x 4s every four feet along the inside of the twine. Bury the corner posts at least one foot deep. The 2 x 4s need only be about half that depth. In length, each post and 2 x 4 should be the planned height of the bed above the soil surface plus the depth it will be in the ground. A small portion of concrete set around each post will slow rotting and greatly increase stability. Use 2 x 6 boards to frame the raised bed.

Framed raised beds are beautiful: the sides make a wonderful base for a cold frame and trellises are easily attached to them. The negative points include: They are difficult to relocate and to till, and slugs like to hide along the inside of the frame.

Most wood preservatives are toxic to plants. Use only copper naphthenate-based preservatives, linseed oil, or latex paint on raised bed frames, compost boxes, and cold frames.

Sunken Beds

Desert climates, with sandy soils that heat up quickly and drain well, present conditions opposite to those that make a raised bed so productive. So it makes sense to reverse the raised bed, creating a sunken bed that stays cooler and functions as a catch basin for water.

To make a sunken bed, simply shovel out a 4-foot-wide trench up to a foot deep, pitching the soil onto the pathways.

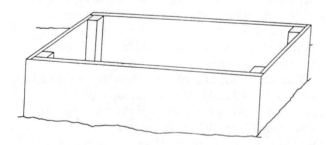

Step Four: Secure the sides and ends to the outside of the posts with galvanized box nails or lag bolts. Drill holes for bolts. For added stability in 12-inch or taller beds, stagger the end-seams of the 2 x 6's.

Step Five: Fill the raised bed with a mix of 50% mix of rich topsoil, 50 percent composted organic matter which includes, by volume, roughly ¼ well-rotted manure. Mix thoroughly, and water heavily to settle the mix. If the organic matter is not very decomposed, wait two weeks before planting.

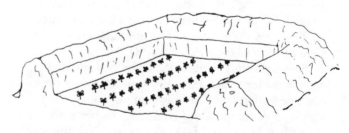

A sunken bed helps conserve water.

Use mulch, soaker hoses, and drip irrigation to conserve water just as you would in a raised bed. You will find that these beds stay cooler than flat beds and retain moisture.

In sunny, arid deserts of the West, organic matter is sparse. Instead of using only vegetative matter to improve the soil, layers of newspaper can be substituted to smother weeds.

Flat Beds

Traditional flat-bed gardens are popular among many gardeners. They are at the same level as the surrounding lawn, walkways or patio are easy to cultivate and maintain.The crops are planted in rows or wide strips spaced from 6 to 24 inches apart.

If the soil is loam, sandy loam or sandy, flat beds may be the best option for your garden. If most of your gardening efforts are spent on ornamental trees, shrubs, and flowers, flat beds often provide the easiest and most logical planting option. The beds can be formed to flow from the lawn area, along pathways, and around buildings.

Flat garden beds should be prepared as carefully as raised or sunken beds. If the area has not been cultivated, study the soil texture and structure in order to know how to condition it.

Attractive designs for ornamental gardens often include combinations of flat, raised, and sunken beds. Changes in garden levels can be very aesthetic.

Double Digging

Double digging is a traditional English way to prepare soil. The basic theory is simple: roots grow deeply into the soil so if you cultivate the soil to a depth of two feet or more below the surface of a raised bed, plants will grow better and be stronger and healthier. In double-dug beds, plants can be spaced closer than usual, resulting in dramatic increases in yield per square foot.

Intensive raised-bed, double-dug gardens with dense plantings have higher overall yields per square foot than conventional gardens. Vegetable gardeners who grow intensively often cull out the small, weak crops and eat them while waiting for the balance to mature.

While the above refers to vegetable gardening, there's no question but that double digging also results in healthier, more vigorous ornamentals as well.

Sandy soils are usually low in nitrogen and humus. Double digging and intensive gardening may intensify

these problems. Be wary of double-digging in hot climates with sandy soil; sunken beds will probably be a better alternative in hot, arid, desert climates.

Remember that double digging is hard work, especially in heavy clay soils. Unless you have help, don't take on more than you or your back can handle.

Double Digging Step-by-Step

Step One: Lay out the dimensions with stakes and a string. Typically beds are 4 to 5 feet wide and up to 25 feet long.

Step Two: To remove the sod or vegetation, cover the area with a piece of black plastic and secure it around the perimeter with weights or soil. The opaque plastic deprives the weeds of light and moisture, and substantially raises the surface temperature. In 30 to 60 days or less, depending on daily temperatures, most of the weeds will die. Some perennial weeds and grasses that are deep rooted may not die. If any remain, dig them up, getting out as much of the root as possible. The sod can be dug with a rented sod cutter. A sharp, flat-blade shovel also works well to cut strips about a foot wide within the perimeter of each bed. Next, using the shovel, cut 3-4 inches below the sod and turn each strip over. Haul the sod strips off to the compost pile, or use as fill.

 Double dug topsoil

 Old subsoil

 Double dug subsoil

 Old topsoil

Step Three: If soil is not moist, water the new bed area thoroughly.

Step Four: Dig a trench 18 to 24 inches wide and 12 inches deep across one end of the bed. Haul the soil from the trench to the opposite end of the bed.

Step Five: Step into the newly dug trench and loosen the subsoil with a spade or broadfork (page ##) to a depth of 12 inches. The first foot of topsoil has up to 50 times more soil life than the next 3 to 4 feet of soil. Mixing topsoil with subsoil does not bring new life to the subsoil, the surface life in topsoil simply dies when buried too deeply.

Step Six: Fill the first trench with soil removed from a new trench that is dug next to the first trench.

Step Seven: Repeat steps four through six until all of the soil in the bed has been double dug. Fill the last trench with the soil taken from the first trench.

Step Eight: Let the soil settle for a few days, then add soil amendments and fertilizer. Till them into the top layer of soil.

Step Nine: Wait a few more days, then plant the new bed.

A simple alternative, but not a substitute for double digging, is to cultivate the subsoil, the soil below the topsoil, along with the topsoil with a broadfork.

No-Till & Low-Till Gardens

No-till gardening is for gardeners who like to make the most efficient use of their time as well as those who can't or don't want to do heavy gardening work. The principles are simple. Rather than cultivating the soil, create fertile soil by adding layers of compost and mulch to the soil's surface.

In low-till gardening, you may start with a cultivated bed, one that has been well tilled and the soil amended by the addition of both organic and inorganic materials. Once that has been done, however, you proceed to apply compost and mulch as follows and do not cultivate again.

The nutrients in the compost leach downward, creating fertile topsoil. The roots and the earthworms do the cultivation work.

Deep roots break up the subsoil and pump minerals deposited in the subsoil to the surface. When the plant is finished producing, the roots are left in the soil to decompose, which further aerates the soil and adds more nutrients. Earthworms, bacteria, fungi, and other sub-soil life forms always have plenty of food from the decaying vegetation. Earthworms are most active during the cool months of fall and winter, and reproduce mostly in the spring.

A covering mulch of straw, leaves, or other insulating material will prevent rapid temperature fluctuations. Although the sun bakes the surface of bare soil, increasing the temperature significantly, the surface temperature of soil protected with mulch will not

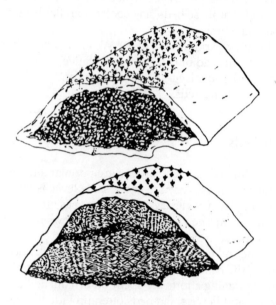

The no-till garden bed on top includes a layer of wood chips in the middle and below to help aerate the bed. The no-till bed on the bottom is made from shredded grass clippings and leaves with no wood chips for aeration.

increase as much. This buffering of the ambient temperature protects feeder roots near the surface. To achieve warmer temperatures for germination in cool spring weather, just pull the protective mulch aside so the sun can warm the soil. After the seedlings grow a few inches tall, brush the mulch back around them.

Moisture evaporation is slowed dramatically by a protective layer of mulch on the surface. Water soon evaporates from the surface of unmulched soil, but is retained much longer when a heavy layer of mulch/compost is used.

Sprinklers and rain pelt the soil's surface with droplets of water. This constant pounding creates a crusty surface layer on bare soil which encourages runoff, and keeps water from effectively penetrating. In a mulched garden, you can water with little or no runoff. The mulch absorbs the water, letting it seep slowly downward, penetrating the soil.

Weeds are smothered by successive layers of mulch and only an occasional weed will need to be pulled. Once a regular mulching program is underway, few weeds get a chance to sprout.

Insects and diseases are kept in check by natural predators that find favorable conditions for life in a surface-mulched garden. Of course, the gardener helps the garden keep its low-care option by practicing crop rotation and planting disease- and pest-resistant varieties. For more information on no-till garden-

Chapter Eight) many crops can be grown all winter using the heat provided by decomposition.

Bark chips make an excellent covering for garden paths. They provide heat, smother weeds, and keep mud from forming on paths.

ing see: *The Ruth Stout No-Work Garden Book,* Rodale Press, 1971.

To make a no-till garden, pile up organic matter, as you would to make a compost pile, lay down 2-4-inch base of wood chips, pile compost from several inches to a couple of feet high and 4-5-feet wide to form a raised bed. The top of the bed is 2 or 3 feet wide, sloping down to a 4-5-foot base. The fresh compost can easily be piled on grassy or weedy ground; the thick layer of fresh organic matter smothers weeds and grass.

Dig a path 2-4-inches deep and 2 feet wide along both sides of the compost. Pitch the soil from the path to the top of the raised compost bed. When the compost is covered with 2 to 4 inches of fine soil, you can plant in it. Apply 2 to 4 inches of organic mulch whenever the mulch has decomposed and become thin.

The "no-till" concept of organic gardening is built around the principle of no digging and continually adding organic matter, compost, and mulch, to the soil surface (See Side Bar). If you have a problem with excessive heat from the composting process, wait for two or three weeks and the temperature will drop.

As the compost decomposes, heat and nutrients are released to warm and fertilize the young plants. By the time the roots penetrate deep into the compost below, it will have cooled enough to form a perfect environment.

Sow seeds or plant transplants in the layer of soil on top of the raised bed. The compost pile provides heat and nutrients as it decomposes.

These methods are similar to sheet composting. The layer of soil on the top of the compost into which seeds and transplants can be immediately planted sets it apart from sheet composting. The soil is necessary to keep the seedlings from damping-off.

The no-till garden bed creates a good deal of heat that can be trapped under a plastic hoop house to extend the growing season. Seedlings can be put outside earlier when started in a no-till bed under a tunnel of plastic. In Zones 8-9 (See USDA Zone Map in

Forest Floor Inspiration

Creating no-till beds by sheet composting and continuously mulching mimics the process of soil building that occurs on forest floors. The lower soil layer, called subsoil, contains mineral-rich earth that incorporates a large amount of rock. The next layer, the topsoil, is the rich, fertile zone teeming with bacterial activity and nutrients. On top is a layer called the "duff," or leaves, needles, branches, chips, bark, moss, and whatever else falls from the forest growth.

The soils that form as a result of this debris buildup contain all the nutrients that will be available to the trees and undergrowth. These layers gradually merge together, and any definitive line between them gradually disappears. Water and nutrients move freely between the layers.

New topsoils are built by laying additional organic matter on top of older layers of organic material.

Transforming Compacted Soil

The no-till technique can be used to transform compacted stone-ladened soil, or even roadways, into a very fertile garden plot.

"The compacted soil was so hard that I had to use a pick and shovel to break it up" said Steve Rogers, a market gardener from Portland, Oregon. "I got tired of hard work, so I decided to use what I learned by examining the soil in the forest."

Rogers filled a compacted roadway with organic matter. First, he laid down a 12-inch layer of bark chips. Next, he piled various forms of organic matter, including leaves, grass clippings, and conifer needles, to a height of five feet. When the pile "cooked down," he piled more organic matter on top. He repeated the process five or six times over a period of three years. Crops were also grown in the compost piles during the three-year period. The compost was then moved and used as a top dressing-fertilizer for another bed. When Rogers removed the compost and inspected the soil below, the rocks were still present in the old hard-packed roadway, but the worms and microorganisms had turned this infertile hardpan into rich, crumbly, worm casting-packed soil. All without tilling!

When the weight of the top layer of "duff" decomposes and is compacted by subsequent layers, it forms rich humus which becomes part of the topsoil. In effect, the floor of the forest forms a giant compost pile. The top layer is continually built up by falling organic matter, just as a gardener would build a compost heap.

Water and minerals located in the subsoil are continually transported into the topsoil by the roots. The nutrients are manufactured into foliage and branches, then returned and redistributed throughout the top layer of the "duff" formed by fallen leaves and branches.

Mother Nature builds soil by continually adding layers of organic matter to the surface instead of tilling and incorporating organic matter into the soil. The worms, microorganisms, and roots work to bring these nutrients up from lower levels to distribute them

The Carbon & Nitrogen in Compost

Organic matter was once living and is composed of many elements, including carbon and nitrogen. During decomposition, soil microorganisms feed on the organic matter. They use carbon as an energy source and nitrogen as a building block for their bodies. The relationship between the amount of carbon and nitrogen found in all compost material is called the carbon/nitrogen (C/N) ratio. The best compost materials have a C/N ratio of 1/30, expressed simply as 30. For example, barnyard manure has a C/N ratio of 15, and sawdust about 400. Manure composts rapidly, while sawdust may take two years or more to decompose. A high C/N ratio indicates a high the carbon content.

The closer to 30 the C/N ratio, the faster the compost will heat and break down. This natural balance is upset when organic matter with a high carbon and low nitrogen content, such as sawdust, is introduced into the soil. More carbon provides extra food for the microorganism population. These microorganisms also need more nitrogen to grow. If they cannot find enough nitrogen in the organic material or nearby, they perish.

A nitrogen content of 1.5 percent is sufficient for organic material to take care of its own decomposition without affecting the soil's nitrogen. So, any organic material with a C/N ratio of 1/30 or less will decompose without adding extra nitrogen.

Look for green organic materials such as grass clippings or fresh leaves to ensure the fastest composting. Dry leaves are mostly carbon. Do not use meat products, which will attract scavengers. With the proper materials supplying adequate organic nitrogen, materials such as manures or fresh alfalfa hay, a compost pile can be started any time of the year, even in the middle of winter.

C/N of Compostable Materials

± 6:1	± 12:1	± 25:1	± 50:1	± 100:1
Bone meal	Vegetables	Summer grass	Cornstalks(dry)	Sawdust
Meat scraps	Garden weeds	Seaweed	Straw (grain)	Paper
Fish waste	Alfalfa hay	Legume hulls	Hay (low quality)	Tree bark
Rabbit manure	Horse manure	Fruit waste		Bagasse
Chicken	Sewage sludge	Hay (top quality)		Grain chaff
Pig	Silage			Corn cobs
Seed meal	Cow manure			Cotton mill

throughout the topsoil. Bacteria, insects, and enzymes further work on the top organic layer to break down, cultivate, aerate, and make nutrients available. The process goes on day and night all year round!

Compost

Every garden should have a compost pile. It can be started any season of the year. The average American throws away almost four pounds of garbage every day, up to half of which could be turned into compost.

Composting can be easy, rewarding, and profitable. In fact, smart gardeners often plant on top of compost piles. See "No-Till Gardens" above. The basics are simple: Collect organic matter, pile it up, and let it rot. All you do is keep microorganisms and bacteria in the pile well supplied with the proper proportions of air, food, and water.

As you will see, there are many ways to compost and to build compost piles, and to garden conservatively by recycling nutrients and organic matter back into the garden soil. There are two basic types of compost piles — hot and cold. They are described in this section.

The benefits of compost are numerous, It builds good soil structure; enables soil to retain nutrients, water, and air; recycles biological wastes; protects against drought; helps maintain a neutral pH, and feeds earthworms and microbial life in the soil.

Compost has an extraordinary buffering effect; it will lock out many undesirable elements and compounds that appear in the soil.

Organic gardens that take compost from landscapers and tree services trimmings are unable to control or accurately know if the materials were sprayed or fertilized with synthetic substances that may leave

The smaller the particle size, the faster it decomposes. Grinding or chopping increases usable surface area. Smaller particles provide more surface area for the bacteria to attack and decay. It also bruises and punctures branches and leaves, which allows bacteria to easily enter and decompose them.

harmful residues. And many of the leaves they receive are piled on city streets. Cars travel these streets, polluting the leaves with petroleum ladened debris, carbon monoxide, lead, and other heavy metals. The heavy machinery that removes this debris is often covered with petroleum oils.

Organic matter from outside sources, may contain traces of manufactured fertilizers, toxic chemicals, and heavy metals including cadmium and lead depending on where it comes from. When these "contaminated" materials are composted, most, if not all of the toxic substances are either leached out, broken down and changed into beneficial organic compounds, or bound in a molecular form that renders them harmless.

Hot compost piles are fueled by nitrogen-rich organic matter, air and moisture that provide an environment for microorganisms to change the compost into humus. A critical mass of at least 3 feet by 3 feet gives the compost pile the insulation and volume to "cook" rapidly. At the same time, compost piles should be no more than 5 feet high. Any higher and there is a risk of too little oxygen inside the pile. Too little oxygen causes anaerobic decomposition, which may produce in unpleasant odors. Turning a smelly pile will get more air into it and help to restore aerobic decomposition. With the correct mix of ingredients and regular turning, decomposition will be so fast that finished compost is ready in 2-4 weeks. Hot piles have to be turned every 2 to 3 days to keep them cooking — then the material will be ready in a month or less.

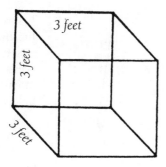

A "critical mass" of at least 3 feet square will provide a hot compost pile with enough insulation to retain heat.

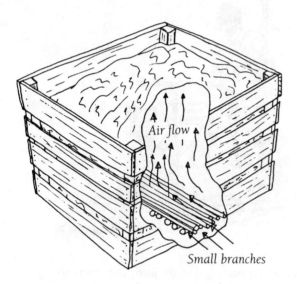

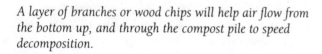

Small branches

A length of 4-inch perforated drain pipe, a tube of wire mesh, bundled cornstalks or bamboo inserted down into the center of the compost pile forms a ventilating stack, which will help aerate the pile.

A layer of branches or wood chips will help air flow from the bottom up, and through the compost pile to speed decomposition.

Cold compost piles lack adequate amounts of air, moisture, nitrogen-rich material or the critical mass of 3 feet square. Decomposition is slow but steady, taking a year or longer. Turning the pile adds air, speeding decomposition.

Sheet composting is a form of cold composting that is very easy. Refer back to no-till gardening for a useful application of sheet composting. To sheet compost,

spread organic matter out on the ground in a "sheet" or layer 4-12 inches thick and leave it to decompose as if it were a deep mulch. You can mulch on top of the sheet compost or not, as you wish. The organic matter can be left on the surface, as in no-till gardening, or tilled under, before or after it has fully decomposed. Weeds seeds that are not unearthed from below do not have a chance to sprout in sheet-composted gardens. Weed that grow through the mulch are either mulched again or hoed.

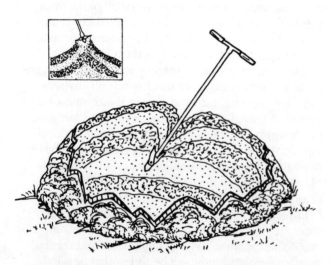

This compost aerator is easy to insert into the compost pile. The tines at the tip are hinged to help mix and aerate the inside of the pile.

Special long thermometers are available to check the temperature deep inside the compost pile.

Air

A layer of wood chips or dry brush below the pile helps air to circulate under the heap, where it is most needed. This chip base is eventually eroded and integrated into the compost pile and must be replaced from time to time. A 2-4-inch layer of dry organic matter sandwiched between green matter every 12 inches supplies sufficient aeration. Varying the size and texture of the organic matter also creates an environment that enhances air circulation.

To maintain a compost pile that requires the least work, don't bother turning the pile. Enough air for decomposition can be supplied when the organic matter is of varying sizes and textures. The outer layer of debris on the pile forms a seal around the pile. Disagreeable odors usually stay inside the heap.

When air is inadequate, decomposition becomes anaerobic and the pile starts to smell. Turning the pile is more work but will aerate the compost heap faster and encourage speedy aerobic decomposition. Turning also rearranges the decaying material. With a little care, you can move the outer, less decomposed portions of the pile to the center to heat up.

Heat

Heat speeds decomposition. The temperature in the center of the compost heap should be at least 55° F. Temperatures from 140 to 160° F kill almost all plant diseases, harmful insects, weed seeds, and roots. A "hot" compost pile will generate temperatures of up to 170° F for up to a week or more. Check the temperature of the compost pile by inserting a thin metal into the center of the pile for a few minutes. If the rod is warm when removed, it's probably hot enough. A soil or food thermometer will give an exact reading at different locations of the pile.

Compost piles shrink up to 70 percent as they "cook." This "cooking" takes place in a wide range of temperatures, moisture ranges, and other conditions. Each change in condition kills millions of microorganisms, grubs, and bacteria. Their decaying bodies release nitrogen (food) for other soil microorganisms that quickly multiply under the new temperatures and conditions.

Moisture

For best results, the moisture content of a compost pile should be between 40 and 60 percent. Moisture level is easy to check: The pile will have the consistency of a wrung-out sponge, or "glisten" with wetness.

Place a sprinkler on a dry compost pile for several hours during dry weather to add moisture and speed decomposition. Making a concave dip in the top of the pile will allow it to catch rainwater more efficiently.

Steam rises from the pile as heat builds. So much water is used that the center of the pile may become dry. Insert a probe into the pile to test for heat and moisture. Ideally, the probe should come out warm, moist and with no foul odors. Add water to the pile if necessary.

A crispy pile could be too dry and might become full of ants. The surface layer can be dry, but the inside of the pile should be evenly moist. Too much moisture can cause poor air circulation, anaerobic decomposition once again, and is signaled by a dank smell and slimy compost. An overabundance of flies also can signal excess moisture.

Turn the pile and add dry matter to aerate. A plastic cover or layer of soil will also keep it from smelling and will deflect excess rainwater.

If very dry material is used, add water while building the heap to ensure even moisture distribution throughout the pile. In dry parts of the country, you might want to make the top of the compost heap slightly concave to direct rain and supplementary water inside the compost pile.

Location

Build compost piles on a level ground surface with good drainage. Cultivate the soil below to break it up, so it will absorb nutrients and provide a safe haven for earthworms when the pile gets too hot. Easy vehicle access is important if you expect to have grass clippings and other chopped green matter delivered by landscapers or neighbors.

A compost pile should be convenient to access. Locate it close enough to the house so that adding kitchen scraps is easy. Collect the kitchen scraps, excluding meat and fish products, in a gallon plastic container with a lid that seals. Dig the kitchen scraps into the center of the pile so they do not attract scavengers.

The heap can be unsightly, and occasionally smell, if not properly maintained, so locate it out of view.

Do not move the compost pile from place to place. The soil below builds up a population of beneficial bacteria and microbes that will migrate into the pile. Decomposition progresses faster when these microbes and bacteria are readily available.

Finished Compost

Finished compost, (humus) is fertile, dark, and crumbly with a sweet, earthy smell. The finished compost will have a C/N ratio of 15 to 20. Finished compost can be applied to all crops, any time of the year, as a soil amendment/fertilizer or as a mulch/fertilizer sidedressing. Don't worry about overdoing it!

Even though finished compost is "stable" and will not break down rapidly, it keeps better when covered to prevent leaching out of nutrients. Use the finished compost within six months or many of the beneficial qualities will be lost. Compost is ready to use when it cools to below 100° F. However, compost that has aged and completely broken down will be the same temperature as the surrounding soil. Compost can also be used before it is completely finished. Many gardeners use partially decomposed compost that is only one or two months old. At this stage, properly balanced compost has enough nitrogen to feed the earthworms, bacteria, and other microorganisms and yet not take nitrogen from the plants.

Composting Materials

Note: All organic matter decomposes faster when bruised and/or chopped into small pieces. The greater the variety of organic matter the better. Diverse compost materials maintain good air circulation and keep matting to a minimum. Grass clippings are one of the best all-round, nitrogen-rich compost materials. They contain plenty of nitrogen and decompose very quickly. Fresh composting grass clippings often reach temperatures in excess of 170° F! Many of your neighbors will be happy to dump their grass clippings on your compost pile.

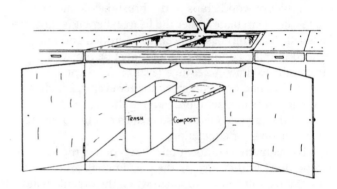

A covered container under the sink makes a perfect receptacle to collect kitchen wastes for the compost pile.

Note: Grass clippings may develop dry or wet pockets and should be mixed with more coarse debris.

Kitchen waste: Coffee grounds, egg shells, oyster, and crustacean shells, vegetable scraps, anything organic, especially from plants. Fish and meat scraps should be avoided because they attract scavengers, and can smell.

Leaves break down faster if green and chopped. Dry autumn leaves decompose much more slowly. City maintenance crews pick up leaves each fall. Call your local city maintenance department to get the specifics on how to get a load of leaves delivered to your house.

Conifer foliage: Pine, fir, and cedar needles break down fairly slowly, but make a good layer to provide aeration.

Weeds are okay if the pile gets hot enough in the center to cook the roots and seeds to a nonviable state. But avoid adding to cold compost piles any of the perennial weeds that have strong, sprouting underground root systems.

Fair Compost Materials

Ash: Wood and paper ashes add potassium (potash) but these leach out quickly and provide few long-term benefits.

Lime (dolomite): An occasional dusting "sweetens" and stabilizes the pH. Microbes work the best in a pH that is just below the neutral 7.0.

Greens and and granite dust add potassium.

Paper: Shredded newspaper and recycled paper break down a little faster than new, unshredded paper. Do not use slick, wax or ink-colored paper; the inks may contain heavy metals. Newspaper comprises about 14% of all landfill waste.

Peat moss tends to form dry pockets.

Rock phosphate and bone meal add phosphorus.

Sawdust robs the compost pile of nitrogen, needed for decomposition. If used, add nitrogen to compensate for the nitrogen loss. Weathered sawdust, like weathered straw, decomposes faster than fresh.

Sod and soil add weight.

Wood chips, hedge clippings, and small branches should be cut into small pieces or run through a chipper if possible. Add in small amounts for aeration. Wood chips break down slower and take longer than other, faster decomposing ingredients, and are best added directly to the surface as mulch.

Plant Poisons. Some plants contain, or produce during decomposition, substances which make it undesirable for their use in composting. This is called allelopathy and merely means the harmful effect that one plant can have upon another. For instance, black walnuts produce juglone, a substance that can hinder or even prevent growth of some plants. Giant foxtail, yellow nutsedge, and leafy spurge are other plants that produce growth-inhibiting substances. It is better not to use plants such as these in compost or mulch.

Do Not Compost These Materials

Charcoal briquettes do not break down. Furnace coal contains excessive amounts of sulfur and iron.

Chemical fertilizers are not all good compost activators. If you wish to use chemical fertilizers, mix them into the compost just before you dig it into the soil.

Insecticides, herbicides, rodenticides, if concentrated, may kill any life in the heap. But grass clippings treated with herbicides, such as Weed 'n Feed, create no problems in hot, active piles.

Cooked kitchen scraps putrefy and attract scavengers, and should be covered with soil if used.

Diseased plants with anthracnose, club root, dry rot, leaf spot or blights should be avoided.

Potato stems and leaves can be carriers of blight. Peony foliage is often a carrier of fusarium wilt and botrytis.

Dung: Cat, dog or any meat-eating animal's feces can transmit parasites harmful to humans.

High-cholesterol greases and fats break down slowly and attract scavengers.

Metal: Aluminum, plastic, greasy, painted metals could contain toxic materials that should not be added to compost.

Mud, sand, and gravel have no nutrient or bacterial value and add weight. Coarse materials can aid in aeration.

Perennial weeds: Crabgrass, dandelions, and other weeds that sprout from roots, are okay to add if the compost pile is hot enough to "cook" them to death.

Quicklime (calcium oxide) destroys humus.

Soapy dishwater could contain sulfates, but biodegradable soaps, such as Ivory, cause no harm.

Soil does not enhance compost and slows aeration, but can be effective in thin layers.

Sources of Organic Matter

Compost sources are everywhere. The following list will just give you a few ideas; there are many more. Let your imagination flow and you will be pleasantly surprised at the sources of compost you find. When reviewing the following list, think of different ways that you can get compost delivered to the utility area of your garden. Getting it delivered is much easier than hauling it yourself!

1. Some of the best sources are neighbors who throw away lawn and garden clippings.
2. Call landscapers and tree services that advertise in the Yellow Pages and local newspapers; ask them to dump their trimmings on your compost pile. Landscapers pay dearly to dump compostable debris at landfills. They are happy to conform to your specifications to save landfill fees. Take care that the landscapers are reputable and ask them not to dump unchipped brush or non-biodegradable materials.
3. Large amounts of grass clippings are usually found at golf courses, schools, and parks. Ideally, you can contact the maintenance crew and have the grass debris delivered.
4. Supermarkets are great places to collect compost materials. The produce manager is usually glad to save leftover produce for you to compost. Or ask if it's OK for you to scavenge the dumpster for food for the compost pile.
5. Tree services often have truckloads of wood chips that they will deliver free. Wood chips make a good mulch for flower beds, under trees and shrubs. They also make attractive garden paths. Once the chips decompose, they can be added to the garden. Like sawdust, wood chips contain little nitrogen and will pull this vital element from the soil as they decompose, so plan to add nitrogen-rich material or fertilizer.
6. City governments typically remove leaves from city streets each fall. Call the city to ask to have loads of leaves dumped at your garden.

Compost Activators

One of the best compost activators is a bucket of compost from a friend or neighbor's compost pile. Compost activators provide protein and bacteria. The right bacteria usually exists in a "cooking" compost pile and are unnecessary to add.

New compost piles: To speed decomposition in new piles, borrow a couple of handfuls of compost from the center of a neighbor's pile to spread on your pile. Several commercial compost activators are also on the market. Natural activators include alfalfa meal, blood meal, bonemeal, well-rotted compost, cottonseed meal, fish meal, fish waste, seaweed, hoof meal, horn meal, manure, and organic soil. Sprinkle activators over the compost pile when building it, then cover with more layers of compost.

Managing the Odor

A foul-smelling compost pile can make you unpopular in your neighborhood. Compost that smells bad lacks adequate air. A poorly aerated compost pile usually smells like ammonia or rotten eggs and has a high pH. It is full of anaerobic bacteria that do not digest organic matter as fast as their aerobic cousins. Odor and flies can also become a problem if you fill your compost heap with high-nitrogen materials such as grass clippings and kitchen waste, then neglect it. You should have high-nitrogen materials and high-carbon materials (fall leaves, twigs, chipped wood) in about equal quantities by bulk. That's where the recent garden composting slogan came from — half green and half brown."

To keep compost from smelling bad:

1. Build the compost pile on a base of wood chips or situate it on top of a platform, such as a pallet, that allows air to circulate from the bottom up through the heap. A 6-12-inch high base of wood chips allows air to circulate and water to drain.
2. When building the compost heap, do not walk on it. Stepping on the pile compacts the debris and forces out air required for decomposition. Let an outer crust stay intact to form an odor barrier. The crust also helps shed rain.
3. Turn the heap with a fork or tiller and incorporate a few wood chips, sawdust or dry organic matter. The heap will smell during the time that you are turning it and for one or two days afterward. To help diffuse the smell, turn the pile when the wind is blowing or during or just before a rainstorm.
4. Keep a small pile of sawdust or wood chips next to the compost pile, when large amounts of fresh grass clippings are added, incorporate a few shovelfuls of sawdust to balance out the C/N ratio in the mix.
5. The fastest way to stop a compost pile from smelling is to contain the odor by covering the pile with wood chips, straw, soil, or plastic. A 1-2-inch layer of wood chips, straw, or soil allows air to penetrate and traps most of the foul odor inside of the heap. A sheet of plastic will contain the odor, but allows less air to reach the pile.

Making Potting Soil From Compost

There are a number of ways to use well-rotted compost to make potting soils. Screened compost will work best in potting media.

For plants that require an organic, fertile soil, mix 1 part compost, 1 part good garden soil, and 1 part agricultural perlite or vermiculite. You could also use 2 parts compost and 1 part perlite or vermiculite.

For a very light-weight potting medium for hanging baskets of bedding plants, you could use 1 part compost and 1 part perlite or vermiculite.

For plants such as cacti that require a low-fertility, sandy soil, use 1 part compost and 3 to 4 parts builders' sand. You will have to water the lighter planting media more often, especially during hot, windy weather.

Step One: place a heavy duty one half-inch mesh framed screen over a large container such as a wheelbarrow.

Use a wheel barrow to collect the sifted compost.

Step Two: Shovel compost on to the screen and sift. The sifted compost falls into the receptacle below. Resift, mixing half compost and half rich soil and/or other additives such as listed above.

Step Three: Once mixed and screened, the compost/soil mix is ready to use.

Building a Compost Bin

Compost piles can be a free standing heap of organic matter or contained in a compost bin. The compost bin can be constructed of rot-resistant cedar or cypress. If these components are not available, use pine or fir painted with linseed oil, epoxy, Cuprinol 10, copper naphenate-based product or latex paint.

Compost bins with removable sides make it easy to add or remove compost.

A garbage can with the bottom cut out makes an excellent container to compost kitchen scraps.

Do not use creosote or tar preserved boards; they will hinder decomposition.

Two or three compost bins can be built next to one another. Use the first bin to hold fresh organic matter, the second bin for compost in process and the third bin for completed compost. Every few days, when you turn the contents of the second bin, material from the first bin can be added. When the second bin is near completion, turn its contents into the third bin to hold until you need it in the garden.

1. A bin of freight pallets is very easy to construct. Acquire four or five pallets of the same size. Set four of the pallets upright to form a box. Bind the corners of the pallets together using nylon rope. Use one of the pallets as a gate for the front, using the nylon rope for a hinge. Tie a bow knot on the side opposite the hinge to act as a hasp. The fifth pallet can be used as a platform below. Tie the upright pallets to the platform with nylon rope. The platform will provide an air space below the pile.

2. A galvanized wire basket, fabricated from hog wire or rigid wire mesh also makes a fine compost bin. The wire is easy to bend into any size circle and provides air circulation through the sides. The bottomless wire basket is easy to remove, providing access to finished compost. Hog wire or snow fence combined with steel fence posts make a fine compost bin.

3. The classic compost bin is made of wood with no bottom. Three sides of the bin are stationary with no front or a removable front to facilitate moving the compost. Use rust-proof, galvanized box nails or lug bolts to fasten the bin together. For most average yards, a 4-foot square bin is adequate. Use 2 x 4s for the corners and secure 2 x 6s on the sides leaving a one- or two-inch gap between them for air circulation.

4. To make a compost bin for kitchen scraps that is secure from scavengers, use a garbage can that has a secure lid with the bottom cut out. Cut some holes in the sides of the can for air circulation. When the can is full, just move it to another location and cover the existing compost with leaves or other dry debris.

5. Straw bales make an excellent compost bin and the walls are biodegradable. When the walls get too thin, just run a tiller over the pile and walls, mixing the two together.

6. Cinder blocks are also a good construction material for compost bins. The blocks are simply stacked up to form the desired structure. The cinder blocks also retain heat longer when the temperature cools at night.

University of California Quick Compost

1. Chop or shred all of the organic matter to increase its surface area.
2. Layer or mix manure and organic matter
3. Pile debris four to five feet high.
4. Turn every 2-4 days
5. Finished compost in 14 days

Piles of Grass:

1. Pile up enough fresh, finely-chopped grass to form a 3- to 5-foot pile.
2. Add an equal volume of coarser brown material for the needed carbon portion.
3. Turn the pile every 2 to 3 days if you want it to cook, otherwise just let it sit for several months before checking its progress. Keep the pile moist.
4. The hot compost pile will be ready when the heap cools to 100° or less. Cold compost piles will be ready in varying amounts of time depending upon the air temperature.

Piles of Leaves

1. Call the local government agency responsible for removing leaves that are piled up by residents each fall. Ask for a truckload of leaves to be delivered to your home.
2. If a truckload is too much, get your neighbors to donate leaves to your compost pile.
3. Shred the leaves before adding them to the compost pile. Shredding will speed the composting process by several months. Add equal volumes of green materials — such as grass clippings and leaves — to provide nitrogen for the cooking process. Keep the pile moist.
4. If you want fast compost, turn the pile every few days to keep it cooking evenly. Otherwise let it alone — it will probably cook on the inside and just slowly decompose on the outside.
5. After 4-6 months, check the pile. It's probably ready to use as compost. If not yet done, it still can be used as mulch.

Piles of Miscellaneous Debris

1. Lay down a 6-12-inch layer of brush or wood chips, a one foot pile of grass, weeds, or whatever else is handy.
2. A two- to four-inch layer of wood chips or dry organic matter is sandwiched between another foot or two of green organic matter. Another layer of dry organic matter is added, then green matter until the pile is four to five feet high. The layers of wood chips decompose slower than the rest of the pile and allow good air circulation to the middle of the pile.
3. The high nitrogen content of the green organic matter helps break down the dry wood chips that contain little or no nitrogen. If this pile is turned every few days, it will cook evenly and be ready for use as compost sooner. If not, it will still decompose, but unevenly. The process will take longer to cold compost, the length of time depending upon how hot the weather is.

Slow Composting

1. Throw everything that will decompose into your compost pile. Ask your neighbors to chip in too.
2. If possible, chip or shred everything that goes into the compost pile. This will speed composting by several months.
3. Once the pile grows to 6-10 feet in diameter and is 4-5 feet tall, plant a vining squash in the heap to shade it.
4. Let the pile decompose for up to a year.
5. No turning is necessary.

Compost in a Bag

1. Fill a plastic garbage bag(s) with organic matter.
2. Set the bag out in the sun for up to two weeks.
3. Every few days, pick the bag up and give it a few good shakes.
4. Anaerobic bacteria in the bag will break down the organic matter.
5. Open the bag(s) after 2-3 months. Expect a very foul odor from the almost totally broken down material. This odor, created by the anaerobic bacteria will soon dissipate.
6. Spread the mushy mix around the garden and cover with soil.

Sheet Composting

Sheet composting is a form of cold composting that is very easy. To sheet compost, spread organic matter out in a "sheet" or layer 6- to 12-inches thick and leave it to decompose. This "sheet" of compost can be spread over bare soil or laid on top of weeds.

The layer of compost provides food for earthworms and soil bacteria and smothers undesirable weeds. Keep it moist and let it compost for two to twelve months. The organic matter can be tilled under before or after it has fully decomposed.

Sheet composting is an excellent way to make your fall cleanup easier. Instead of removing plant residues from the garden, simply spread them out over the plot. If you should decide to till under the organic matter before it decomposes, nitrogen necessary to decompose the materials is tied up during the winter months, and it will not be washed away by rain and snow. Nutrients will be released again in the spring after the soil warms when most of the decomposition is complete.

Sheet composting can also be combined with a green manure crop. Start by spreading out the layer of compost and till it into the soil. Next plant a legume such as lupines or alfalfa that fixes nitrogen. In the spring, before the legume cover crop blooms, turn the cover crop under, incorporating it with the composted soil layer to form rich, well structured soil for planting.

The Wonder of Worms

Only a few of the 3,000 species of worms contribute to soil structure and fertility. The "night crawler," imported from Europe, is the largest and best known. These large earthworms thrive in the humid clay soils of the northern states. They are also

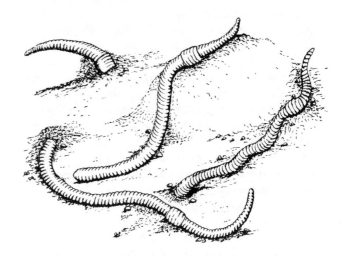

Night crawlers work day and night to cultivate and fertilize your garden.

found in well-irrigated sandy soils. Night crawlers prefer soils derived from limestone and rich in organic matter.

The "common field worm" is about two-thirds the size of the night crawler. Most common in warmer southern states, it can survive where soil fertility is too low for the night crawler.

A smaller worm, known as the "slim worm" is found in soil that will not support the common field worm. The holes and casts of the slim worm are small and have little effect on the soil.

The "manure worm" also called the "red wiggler" and the "rubellus worm" are common to compost piles and are occasionally found in soil. The red wiggler has alternating yellow and maroon rings tip to tip. They also squirm and wiggle a lot when handled. The red wiggler is often sold as a "hybrid worm." The rubellus worm is dark maroon in color. Neither worm adds much to the soil.

To find out how many earthworms you have in your soil, dig out a square foot of soil, about seven inches deep. Spread the soil out on a concrete slab and count both mature and young worms. The sample should contain at least ten earthworms for the soil to benefit significantly. The more, the better; some fertile soils have as many as 50 in the sample. If you have less than ten earthworms, add organic matter (worm food), and grow a cover crop or cover bare soil with compost to promote worm growth.

To some gardeners, night crawlers may be a nuisance, especially in lawns, since they leave earthy deposits of soil on the surface. These earthy deposits are easy to spread out and are a major contribution to healthy soil.

As an earthworm munches its way through the soil or a compost pile, it passes rich, dark, fertile "castings." The bigger the worm, the more castings it can produce. In humid soil, an earthworm will produce its own weight in castings each day.

Earthworms form an interconnected maze of channels filled with rich castings. The castings allow rain to penetrate quickly, and they make room for air pockets and root growth. They increase soil fertility by increasing availability of mineral nutrients and releasing nutrients found in organic matter. These gel-coated castings bind soil particles and greatly increase the soil's water-holding ability.

Worm castings are about five times richer in nitrogen than the average garden soil, the available calcium is twice as rich, seven times richer in soluble phosphorus, and eleven times richer in available potassium. Earthworms also neutralize the soil pH with calcium carbonate secretions. Earthworms cannot process nitrate and ammonium, common sources of nitrogen in chemical fertilizers; they need a constant food supply of organic matter and mineral particles found in the soil. In bare earth, they starve or migrate to greener pastures, especially during the fall and winter. Earthworms are not fussy, they will eat just about any organic matter you put in front of them.

Bare earth creates a downward spiral in soil quality. Lack of vegetation starves worms, erodes and compacts top soil, slows moisture penetration, and leaches away nutrients. Bare soil continues to get depleted.

With a little management, the bare earth spiral soon reverses. Rich organic soil, covered with plants, supports numerous worms, absorbs more moisture, and holds nutrients better.

Mother Nature shows us by example that bare soil is undesirable. Whenever the soil is bare, numerous varieties of weeds begin to cover it. The soil below begins to teem with life, water is held, nutrients are not flushed away, and erosion becomes minimal.

Soil can be fertile and contain no earthworms. The three basic soil qualities needed for fertility are: moisture, air space for root growth, and available nutrients. Gardeners should know that earthworms enhance all of these qualities. Worms do not till the soil like a rotary tiller or spade. To loosen the soil, tillage is much faster than earthworms. But this mechanically prepared looseness is short lived, especially in poor soils. Rain will soon compact the soil and the benefits of tillage are lost. The properties of the soil dictate its water-stability, or ability to stay loose.

Earthworms seldom need to be artificially "planted" in the soil. To increase earthworm populations, simply manage the soil better. The life cycle of earthworms is easy to understand and control. In the fall, juvenile earthworms become very active during wet, cool weather. They feed on decaying harvest debris and mineral particles in the topsoil. On moist nights and cloudy days they venture out of their holes in search of new, food-rich turf.

This activity continues during the fall, winter and spring, whenever the weather allows. They need food provided by mulch, compost, or other decaying organic matter. Without food, earthworms migrate or die. In the winter and spring, the mature earthworms lay eggs. As the soil dries in summer, they become dormant and may die. Their decaying bodies add available nitrogen to the soil during the time of peak need. Mulching and keeping the soil moist will keep the earthworms more active during hot summer months.

Bare ground freezes with the onset of cold weather and quickly kills earthworms. Protect and feed earthworms in areas where the ground freezes by planting a cover crop or mulching the soil. This will let the temperature drop slowly and gradually the earthworms adapt to the colder temperatures. Soil teeming with earthworms does not freeze as deeply because the multitude of fast draining channels carry the excess water deep into the soil before it has a chance to freeze.

Earthworms grow best in soil with a near neutral pH of 7. As the acidity of the soil increases, earthworms tend to disappear.

Crop Rotation

Crop rotation is easy. It's simply a method of planting annual crops in new locations each growing season to break up the life cycles of pests that spend one part of that cycle in the soil. Although it is most often applied to agriculture and to vegetable gardening, crop rotation does have some application to ornamental gardens. If ornamental plants, annual or perennial, do not do well in a site, replace them with unrelated plants. Sometimes, as is the case with roses, the soil becomes infested with diseases specific to that plant group and depleted of the nutrients on which that group depends. Then the soil is said to be, for instance, "rose tired." As a rule, perennial plants are not rotated unless they dwindle or die.

The basic rule of crop rotation for vegetables is to grow unrelated crops in an area in subsequent seasons, and to wait at least three years before replanting the crop in the same area. There are many different crop rotation schemes that range from 1 to 7 or more years in duration. For the sake of simplicity, only the 3-year plan will be addressed here.

Different crops have different nutrient needs, and do not always share diseases or attract the same species of insects.

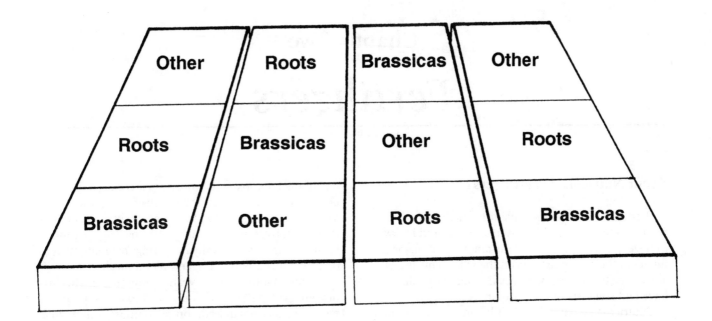

This simple crop rotation scheme rotates crops on a three year schedule.

When the same crop grows year after year in the same soil, many of the same nutrients are used up. This causes nutrient depletion, and after several years it becomes impossible to grow that crop in that location. Repeating the same crop allows associated insects, which have wintered over in the soil, to resume activity with each planting, and thrive perhaps to epidemic proportions.

The crop rotation schedule above divides vegetables into four categories: roots, brassicas, others, and perennials. The perennials, such as artichokes, asparagus, and rhubarb, are grown in the same bed for many years and do not participate in the rotation scheme.

Root crops require little nitrogen and should follow brassicas, which are some of the heaviest feeders. Finally, all others are grouped into a single category. To carry out this plan, follow the diagram.

If this 3-year plan is too much trouble, simply alternating root crops with above-ground crops will help garden fertility, disease, and insect control immensely.

Note that, when planning crop rotations, garden soils should stay in the same beds and not be mixed with other beds. If the soils from different beds are mixed as when rotary tilling, insects and diseases will be distributed throughout the entire garden bed, causing rotation to be useless.

Chapter Two

Fertilizers

About Nutrients & Fertilizers

Fertilizers are blends of plant nutrients. The law requires that packaged fertilizers are required by law to have a label that specifies the amounts of major elements in their formulations on the label. This is an advantage to gardeners, especially those who already have had soil tests of their garden done.

Nutrients essential for plant life include at least elements, 16 of which have been identified as the most important. Plants absorb three of these — carbon, hydrogen, and oxygen — from the air and from water. The balance are absorbed mainly from the soil.

The primary, or macro-nutrients — nitrogen (N), phosphorus (P), and potassium (K) — are the elements that a plant uses the most. The labels on fertilizer bags specify the N-P-K ratings of the contents. The numbers represent the percentage by weight of those three elements. Secondary nutrients include calcium, sulfur, and magnesium. The remaining nutrients (iron, copper, manganese, zinc, molybdenum, boron, and chlorine), called trace elements, are necessary in minute amounts. A complete fertilizer contains all three of the primary nutrients. Formulations with N-P-K ratings of 10-10-10, 5-10-5, and 20-10-5 would indicate the presence of all three primary nutrients. Some complete fertilizers labels list varying amounts of secondary and trace elements.

Incomplete fertilizers lack one or more of the macro-nutrients. Examples include super phosphate (0-20-0), blood meal (12-0-0), and bonemeal (0-12-0).

Importance of Nutrients & Fertilizers

The more you learn about gardening basics, the more you realize that the soil's nutrient content is as important as its texture and structure. The plants don't care whether nutrients come from organic matter or are part of a manufactured product. But to the gardener, the advantage of using organic matter is that it improves the soil structure.

The nutrient content of compost varies widely. Since the average gardener cannot tell by the look or feel of the compost what nutrients it contains, many choose to use manufactured fertilizers with known formulations. In addition to so-called chemical or synthetic fertilizers, manufacturers also package organic fertilizers, that is, naturally occurring materials such as dried manures, bonemeal, and blood meal.

In the first four to five years of building the health of your garden's soil, you may need to add supplementary nutrients in addition to compost and organic matter. A soil test will help you to determine what is necessary. The recommendations will usually be for synthetic fertilizers, but you can substitute naturally occurring materials. Many of the Cooperative Extension Centers have brochures to help you make the substitutions.

Primary Nutrients

Nitrogen (N) is mainly responsible for growth, and for overall size and vigor. It is most actively used by young buds, shoots, and leaves. Most forms of nitrogen are water soluble and are quickly washed, or leached, from the soil. Consequently, nitrogen is required often. To calculate "actual" nitrogen, multiply the (N) percentage on the fertilizer label by the weight of the fertilizer. For example, blood meal is usually marked as 12-0-0 which means that it is 12 percent nitrogen by weight. Therefore, 5 pounds of blood meal times 12 percent nitrogen is 0.5 pounds, the actual weight of nitrogen in the substance. Soil that is cold and wet, or acidic releases nitrogen very slowly because the microorganisms that release the nitrates do not flourish under these conditions. But warm, moist soil fosters microorganism growth which enables the nitrogen to be released rapidly. This is why it is necessary to fertilize more often in hot climates.

Nitrogen deficiency causes older leaves to turn yellow, growth to be stunted, and new leaves to be smaller. Older leaves at the bottom of nitrogen-deficient plants start turning yellow and may drop.

Excess nitrogen causes plants to grow fast. Stems become spindly and the leaves, lush green. But the

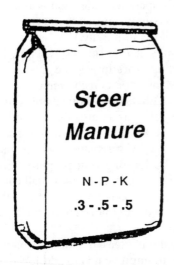

All packaged fertilizers have the nitrogen (N), phosphorus (P), and potassium (K) percentages listed on the label. The label also will tell you if the nutrients are slow-release or immediately available. Organic fertilizers are nearly all slow acting, though their labels don't usually tell you this.

plant tissue is soft, weak, and more susceptible to damage from insects, disease, drought, heat, and cold. Flowering and fruit set is delayed.

Phosphorus (P) is associated with overall vigor, and flower and seed production. Highest levels are required during germination, and during seedling growth and flower development. Decomposing organic matter and the weathering of soil release phosphorus and other elements.

A lack of phosphorus is often confused with a nitrogen deficiency because both have many of the same symptoms. One way you can distinguish between them is that phosphorus-deficient plants will have dull green leaves, and often the stems will turn shades of purple. Overall growth is slow, maturity is delayed, and flower and fruit development are retarded. Stone fruits, such as peaches, nectarines, and plums, may have an unusually intense bright color and fruits may ripen earlier. Phosphorus-deficient citrus fruits are stunted and have puffy skins. Phosphorus in soils and in fertilizers or other soil amendments is generally in forms that have low solubility. Therefore these materials, such as rock phosphate, should be thoroughly blended with the soil before planting. Because bacterial activity is reduced in acid soils, it may need more phosphorus because less is able to be "fixed." It is uncommon for phosphorus to leach out of the soil.

Excess phosphorus is unlikely.

Potassium (K) or the compound potash (K_2O) increases foliage chlorophyll and helps plants make better use of light and air. It encourages strong root

growth and is associated with disease resistance and water intake.

A lack of potassium makes plants grow slowly and is not easy to detect; leaves have mottled yellow blades and fringes; older leaves may appear scorched on the edges; new growth may die back. Do not confuse these symptoms with salt or fertilizer burn, which causes burned leaf tips that may curl under.

Excess potassium is very unlikely. About one percent of the potassium in the soil is available to plants. Insoluble potassium is found in organic matter and minerals. It moves within the soil slowly. Weathering, the wearing away of soil, releases potassium into solution. Potassium and other plant nutrients must be in soluble form to be available to roots.

Secondary Nutrients

Magnesium (Mg) is found in every chlorophyll molecule and is essential to the absorption of light energy. Magnesium aids in the utilization of nutrients. It also neutralizes soil acids and toxic compounds produced by the plant. Add dolomite lime as a long term solution and Epsom salts (magnesium sulfate) to your fertilizer mix at the rate of 2 teaspoons per 3 gallons of water for a quick fix.

Calcium (Ca) is essential to cell manufacture and growth. Plants must have calcium at the growing tip of each root. The easiest way to supply calcium is to add steamed bonemeal, colloidal phosphate or dolomite lime to the soil.

Sulfur (S) is an essential part of plant proteins; it is available in varying amounts in soil humus. Another source is the dissolved sulfur oxides in acid rain. Sulfur also is available in its pure form.

Trace Elements

Trace elements are essential for plant growth and must be present in minute amounts, but little is known about the exact amounts needed. They also function as catalysts to plant processes and nutrient utilization. Trace elements include iron (Fe), manganese (Mn), boron (B), molybdenum (Mo), zinc (Zn), chlorine (Cl), and copper (Cu). Trace elements are usually present in most soils. However, extreme acidity or alkalinity may make them unavailable to plants. Liberal applications of compost or organic matter of all kinds will often remedy this problem.

Many seaweeds, bat guanos, and fish fertilizers offer a full range of trace elements. Adding these components to your fertilizer mix will help assure a balanced amount of trace elements.

In Conclusion

Nutrient uptake can be immediate, providing the plants are fertilized with a soluble food that is absorbed through the leaves. Foliar feeding can be a "quick fix" for acute nutrient deficiencies.

The easy and inexpensive organic way to provide nutrients to plants is to feed the soil with a complete organic fertilizer, add compost, and let the soil "process" its nutrients for the plants. This slow-release method promotes good overall plant vitality.

Compost supplies organic matter and creates a soil environment in which microorganisms thrive, thus helping to break down and make soluble the nutrients plants need, but it doesn't really substitute for fertilizer. Based on a soil test, add needed supplemental nutrients by using fertilizers. Compost that contains high levels of nutrients can be used as a fertilizer once it is completely decomposed and able to pass through a quarter-inch screen.

Root hairs at the tips of the roots are where nutrients are absorbed into the plant. The majority of the root system is a support structure with conducting tubes. The roots must continually grow and expand to form new root hairs to take in nutrients, air, and water.

Soil Tests

If your soil has excellent texture and structure and is loaded with earthworms, you probably don't need a soil test. If plants are growing vigorously and vegetables are producing lush, tasty crops, you probably should just keep on doing whatever you are doing and not worry about testing. If, on the other hand, you are starting your first garden or have had poor results, you will want to have a soil test done. The soil test will give you a base line from which to work, and you will know what the soil needs in order to be productive. A soil test will tell you the pH, what nutrients are in good or short supply, how much organic matter the soil has, and other information vital to good gardeners. The test comes with recommendations for correcting soil problems that may exist. Some private labs and many Cooperative Extension offices offer advice on how to convert the chemical fertilizer recommendations into organic equivalents.

You can buy a commercial soil testing kit and do the tests yourself, but the results will not be as accurate as those from a soil lab. Private soil labs offer different options for soil analysis, from simple to extensive. Their costs will begin at about $30. Cooperative Extension Service offices in each state will usually provide soil analyzes at a reasonable fee. Contact your Cooperative Extension Service office for costs and procedures. (Cooperative Extension is a part of each state's university system, so if you can't find the phone number, call the university.)

The results of your soil test will only be as good as your sampling procedure, so be sure to collect the soil properly. Many experts recommend soil testing every three years. Others don't bother unless unusual circumstances, such as an area that is producing poorly, call for it. To learn more about your specific soil, call the U.S.D.A. Soil Conservation Service and request an index map for locating your property. From this map and others, the soil conservation staff can determine your soil type and classification. They will be able to provide and explain information about the properties of your soil.

Usually, no matter what kind of soil you have, the easiest way to improve it is to add lots of organic matter to compensate for poor properties such as bad drainage or poor water-holding and nutrient-holding ability. As described in the previous chapter, adding organic matter improves sandy soils as much as it does heavy, clay soils and all degrees of texture in between. Compost also acts as a buffer in helping to correct nutrient deficiencies. Chemical or Synthetic

Fertilizers

The advantage of synthetic fertilizers is that you know exactly what major nutrients are included and you can easily figure out from the label exactly how much to apply. A major disadvantage of chemical fertilizers is that they do not improve the soil structure. When applied incorrectly, some fertilizers may burn the plants or plant roots. Some fertilizers, both organic and chemical, will acidify the soil.

In many people's eyes, another disadvantage of chemical fertilizers is that they are made primarily from non-renewable resources such as petroleum, natural gas, and coal.

If only chemical fertilizers are used and no organic matter is added, the soil will gradually lose its organic matter and microbiotic activity. As organic matter is used up, the soil structure will deteriorate and become less able to hold water and nutrients. The result is obvious — you will have to use more and more fertilizer.

Chemical fertilizers come in several forms, including dry, soluble, liquid, powder, pellets, granules, and slow-release. The choices are subjective. Some gardeners prefer slow-release because they don't have to fertilize as often. Some prefer liquid fertilizer because it is easier to use with hanging baskets and containerized plants.

There are several ways to apply chemical fertilizer. You can top-dress a garden bed by applying fertilizer evenly over the entire area. You can side-dress plants by applying fertilizer around the bases of plants or along planted rows. You can broadcast fertilizer over an area by hand or with the aid of a mechanical spreader. You can foliar-feed plants by spraying a liquid fertilizer solution on the foliage. The method you choose will depend upon the kind of fertilizer, the needs of the plants, and convenience.

Many gardeners today use a mix of organic and non-organic gardening. They realize the importance of maintaining high soil quality through regular additions of organic matter. At the same time, they occasionally use chemical fertilizers to compensate for a nutrient deficiency or to give plants a fast start.

When using synthetic fertilizers, it's extremely important to read the labels carefully and follow directions. The initials W.I.N. and W.S.N. on labels stand for "water insoluble nitrogen" and "water soluble nitrogen." W.S.N. dissolves readily and so is considered a fast-release nitrogen source. W.I.N. does not dissolve easily, is often an organic form of nitrogen, and so is considered a slow-release nitrogen source.

If you choose to use chemical fertilizers, be sure to also maintain a regular program of amending the soil with organic matter.

Organic Fertilizer

Organic fertilizers, unlike many chemical fertilizers, continually build the soil and promote better structure as well as nourish soil life.

The growth or yield attained by using either chemical or organic fertilizers is about the same. However, in the long run, many organic fertilizers are much more productive than chemical ones because they improve soil structure and increase the soil's ability to hold moisture and nutrients. The chemical fertilizers do not build soil and can build up to toxic proportions after continued use. Organic fertilizers on the other hand, continually build the soil, promote better structure, and foster soil organism growth. The addition of organic fertilizers over a long period enhances the soil life, another plus for the great majority of garden plants.

The nutrients in organic fertilizers may vary greatly depending upon source, age, erosion, or climate. The figures given in the following list are approximations. For exact nutrient content, consult the supplier's specifications.

Read the labels and literature on the organic fertilizers you plan to use. Keep in mind that the plants must convert the nutrients to a chemical form before they are useable, no matter what the source.

Organic Fertilizer Costs

The cost of 100 pounds of (0-2-0) colloidal phosphate is $5 to $15. And the cost of a 100 pound sack of (0-12-0) bone meal is $40 to $50. But when you consider the cost of each in relation to the amount of available phosphorus, the "actual" cost is $20 to $25 per pound for bone meal and $7 to $8 per pound for colloidal phosphate. Twenty pounds of colloidal phosphorus is equal to one pound of bone meal.

Organic fertilizers are a little more expensive than their chemical counterparts but the price has been coming down. To fertilize a vegetable garden chemically costs less than one cent per square foot. Organic fertilizer for a square foot will cost from two to three cents. That's $20 to $30 for the average 1, 000 square foot garden. The extra cost, when wisely combined with a regular soil amendment program, will be made up in the taste of the produce, not spraying pesticides, and knowing your little piece of the earth is a better place.

The cost of cover crops and crop rotation are difficult to determine. Cover crops cost very little — a pound of seed ($2-5) covers 100-500 square feet of ground — and crop rotation is free! One ingenious gardener gets organic fertilizer and numerous garden services for free. Local landscapers deliver grass clippings, piling them neatly on his compost pile. For the privilege of dumping their clippings on his pile, they take turns cutting his lawn and doing other occasional odd jobs.

The grass clippings compost into a perfect compost/fertilizer, the landscapers do not have to pay a dump fee and Mother Nature is very happy!

Alfalfa hay contains about 2.5 percent nitrogen, 0.5 percent phosphorus, and 2.0 percent potash. Rich alfalfa hay is one of the best mulches available. Purchase alfalfa hay directly from the grower or at feed stores where, it is also available as pellets or meal. Bales of alfalfa hay are easy to store and spread. It can also be run through a shredder before being applied as a mulch. Alfalfa meal is easier to work into the soil if you want to use it as an organic amendment and fertilizer. Store hay in a dry place to guard against mold.

Blood (dried or meal) is collected at slaughterhouses, dried, and ground into a powder or meal. It is an excellent source of fast-acting soluble nitrogen (12 to 15 percent by weight), about 1.2 percent phosphorus, and under one percent potash. Apply just before planting or as a side dressing to stimulate green leafy growth. Blood meal attracts meat-eating animals, so always cultivate it into the soil and water well if using it as a side dressing. A good helping of blood meal can snap a very sick plant out of a prolonged illness. Note, however, that blood meal can burn foliage if applied too heavily.

Bonemeal is an old time fertilizer rich in phosphorus, approximately 12 percent. Bonemeal used to be a reliable source of nitrogen as well, but in modern processing methods it loses most of this element. The age and type of bone determine the nutrient content of this pulverized slaughterhouse product. Older bones have a higher phosphorus content than young bones. Use bonemeal in conjunction with other organic fertilizers for best results. Bonemeal is most commonly used as a phosphorus source when planting fall bulbs. It's lime content helps reduce soil acidity; it acts fastest in well-aerated soil. Since phosphorus doesn't move around in the soil to any great degree, you should till the bonemeal into the soil to a depth of 6 to 8 inches.

Fatty acids in raw bonemeal require longer to decompose. Steamed or cooked bonemeal is made from fresh animal bones that have been boiled or steamed under pressure to render out fats. The pressure treatment causes nitrogen loss and an increase in the percentage of phosphorus. Steamed bones are easier to grind into a fine powder and the process helps nutrients become available faster. The finer bonemeal

is ground, the faster acting it will be. Apply bonemeal to the soil as a seasonal source of phosphorus when planting, or to enhance flowers and fruit set as a mid-summer top dressing cultivated into the soil and covered with mulch.

Canola meal is readily available in British Columbia, Canada, and is becoming more available in the United States. Canola meal is the byproduct of canola seed oil production. High in available phosphorus, potassium, and trace elements.

Cottonseed meal is made from shelled cotton seed that has had the oil extracted. According to the National Cottonseed Products Association, virtually all chemical residues from commercial cotton production are dissolved in the oil. This acidic fertilizer contains about 7 percent nitrogen, 2.5 percent phosphorus, and 1.5 percent potash. It can be mixed with fish or kelp meal to make a more balanced fertilizer blend. Cottonseed meal is an excellent food for acid-loving plants.

Chicken manure is a favorite of many gardeners because it is so high in nitrogen. Manure from caged laying hens is generally higher in nitrogen than that from broiler chickens. If you can find a good source of chicken manure, get as much as you can. Pile it up next to the compost pile, let it rot for a couple of months, then cover it with a tarp to slow decomposition. Use it as a compost activator, a top or a side dressing. If the manure comes from a commercial chicken ranch that uses growth hormones, let it compost at least a year so the hormones are washed out or "fixed."

Many times, chicken manure is full of feathers that contain as much as 17% nitrogen, an added bonus. The average nutrient content of wet chicken manure is: N - 1.5%, P - 1.5%, K - 0.5%. Dry chicken manure: N - 4%, P - 4%, K - 1.5% Both have a full range of trace elements. Beware of using fresh chicken manure as a fertilizer because it can burn the plants.

Coffee grounds are acidic and encourage acetic-acid-bacteria in the soil. Drip coffee grounds are the richest, containing about 2 percent nitrogen and traces of

other nutrients. Add to the compost pile or scatter and cultivate in as a top dressing around acid-loving azaleas, blueberries, camellias, and rhododendrons.

Cow manure is sold as "steer manure" but may be collected from dairy herds. Gardeners have used cow manure for centuries and this has led to the belief that it is a good fertilizer as well as a soil amendment. Modern day "steer manure" that is collected from animals in the tight quarters of feed lots may have a high salt content. Some tests on bagged steer manure showed 5 to 9 percent soluble salt content by dry weight. If applied heavily, that's enough salt to stunt or even kill plants. In high rainfall areas this salt content is less of a problem . Manure collected from outdoor stock yards, where rain has had a chance to leach it, contains less salt and is preferable. In desert regions where salts tend to remain in the soil, excessive use of "steer manure" compounds the problem. The solution is to leach out the salt with generous sprinklings of water.

Steer manure is most valuable as a mulch and a soil amendment, holds water well, and maintains plant fertility for a long time. The nutrient value is quite low

and should not be relied upon as the main source of nitrogen. The average nutrient content of cow manure ranges from 0.6-0.3- 0.3 to 2-1-1 and also includes a full range of trace elements. Apply at the rate of 25-30 pounds per square yard.

As an amendment to broadcast on lawns, apply cow manure at the maximum rate of 12 cubic feet per 1,000 square feet. And as a conditioner, use no more than 8 cubic feet per 100 cubic feet of soil. Water the amended soil after a heavy application.

Diatomaceous earth (DE), which is the fossilized skeletal remains of microscopic salt water organisms called diatoms, contains a full range of trace elements. Although most often used in pulverized form as a non-chemical insect control, it can be applied to the soil when cultivating or as a top dressing. As an insecticide, it abrades and damages the soft bodies of crawlers such as slugs, larvae, and cabbage worms. Once the skin is damaged, body fluids can leak out and they die of dehydration. See page ## for more information.

Dolomitic lime adjusts and balances the pH, and makes phosphates more available. This ground lime adds calcium and magnesium, secondary nutrients which are generally needed in acidic soils. It is generally applied to "sweeten" or deacidify soil. See page ## for more information.

Feathers and feather meal contain 12 to 15 percent nitrogen that releases slowly. Feathers included in barnyard chicken manure or obtained from slaughterhouses are an excellent addition to the compost pile or as a fertilizer. Feathers are steamed under pressure, dried, then ground into a powdery feather meal. Feather meal contains a slow-release nitrogen of about 12.5 percent. Apply in the fall with cover crops for nitrogen-rich soil the following spring.

Fish meal, a solid by-product of the fishing industry, is dried fish ground into a meal. It is rich in nitrogen (about 8 percent) and contains around 7 percent phosphoric acid, and many trace elements. It has an unpleasant odor and should not be used indoors. Apply to the soil as a relatively fast-acting side or top

Fish meal and fish emulsion can contain up to 10 percent nitrogen. The liquid generally contains less nitrogen than the meal.

dressing; make sure to cultivate it into the soil or cover with mulch after applying. Always store in an air-tight container to avoid attracting cats, dogs, and flies. It is also a great compost activator.

Fish emulsion, a liquid by-product of the fishing industry, is an inexpensive soluble liquid high in organic nitrogen, trace elements, and some phosphorus and potassium. This natural fertilizer is difficult to over-apply and is immediately available to plants. Fish emulsion may be diluted with water and used as a foliar spray, but may clog small nozzles if mixed too rich. To prevent clogging, strain after mixing. Mix fish emulsion with water at label-recommended rates to make a soluble tea or use as a foliar spray. Even deodorized fish emulsion smells, so always store it in an air-tight container so it will not attract dogs, cats, or flies.

Fruit pomace, a byproduct of the food packaging industry, is rich in nutrients and is a major ingredient in many organic fertilizers.

Goat manure is much like horse manure but more potent. Compost this manure and treat it as you would horse manure.

Granite dust or granite stone meal contains up to 5 percent potassium and several trace elements. Nutrient release takes place slowly over several years. Always use the finest (pulverized) grade of this rock powder so that it will release nutrients as soon as possible. Granite dust is an inexpensive source of potash and does not affect soil pH. Apply as a top dressing at the rate of ten to fifteen pounds per 100 square feet. Combine granite dust with rock phosphate and manure for a complete fertilizer mix to start crops in the spring.

Greensand (glaucomite) is an iron potassium silicate that gives the minerals in which it occurs a green tent. Mined from an ancient New Jersey sea bed deposit of shells, it is rich in iron, phosphorus, potash (5 to 7 percent), and numerous micronutrients. Some organic gardeners do not use greensand because it is

such a limited resource. Greensand does not burn plants, slowly releasing its nutrients in about four years. Apply liberal amounts of greensand as a top dressing or blend with soil at the rate of 15 to 25 pounds per 100 square feet any time of year as a long-term source of potassium and trace elements.

Bat guano consists of the droppings and remains of bats. It is rich in soluble nitrogen, phosphorus, and trace elements. The limited supply of this fertilizer, known as the soluble organic super bloom, makes it somewhat expensive. Mined in sheltered caves, guano dries with minimal decomposition. Bat guano can be thousands of years old. Newer deposits contain high levels of nitrogen and are capable of burning if applied too heavily. The more popular older deposits are high in phosphorus and make an excellent fertilizer for flowering plants. Bat guano is usually powdery and used any time of year as a top dressing or diluted in a tea and used as a foliar spray. Do not breathe the dust when handling; it can cause nausea and irritation. Bats are too often associated with rabies and horror movies. Only ten cases of rabies have been reported in the United States from bat bites. Some bats eat thousands of insects nightly, others subsist on rotting fruit. Bats are invaluable to the ecosystem and should be protected as our friends. Bat guano may be difficult to find at retail stores.

Sea Bird Guano is high in nitrogen and other nutrients. The Humboldt Current along the coast of Peru and northern Chile keeps rain to a minimum and, therefore, decomposition of the bird guano is minimal. South American guano is among the world's best. The guano is scraped off the rocks of arid sea islands. The average dose for garden use is 1 tablespoon per gallon of water. Guano is also collected from many coastlines around the world.

Gypsum, hydrated calcium sulfate, is used to lower soil pH and improve drainage and aeration of salty soils. It is also used to hold or slow the rapid decomposition of nitrogen. It is not recommended for soils with a pH of 5.8 or lower.

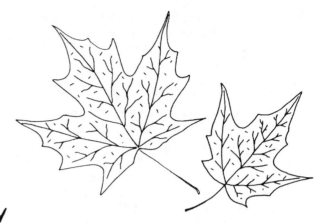

Hoof and horn meal is a coarse granular substance that is an excellent source of slow-release nitrogen. The drawback is that it can attract flies and encourages maggots. For that reason, it should be thoroughly worked into the soil. Soil bacteria must break it down before it is available to roots. Apply two to three weeks before planting. It remains in the soil for six months or longer. Hoof and horn meal contains from 6 to 15 percent nitrogen and about 2 percent phosphoric acid. Finely ground horn meal, on the other hand, makes the nitrogen available quicker and thus creates less of a problem with fly maggots.

Horse manure is readily available from horse stables and race tracks. Use horse manure that has straw or peat for bedding. Compost horse manure for two months or more before adding to the garden. The composting process kills weed seeds. Straw bedding may also use up much of the available nitrogen. But the straw makes a lot of air space within the manure so it can be piled quite high without adding other materials to provide ventilation. In fact, stomping the manure down as you stack it will drive out extra air spaces so that it will hold more water for composting. The nutrient content of horse manure is: N - 0.6%, P - 0.6%, K - 0.4%, and a full range of trace elements.

Pigeon manure has a high concentration of nitrogen but is more difficult to find than most organic fertilizers. Use it in the same fashion as chicken manure.

Rabbit manure is also excellent fertilizer but is difficult to find in large quantities. Use rabbit manure as you would chicken or pigeon manure.

Leaf mold is a form of compost or mulch. Decomposing leaves have a pH near neutral and offer one of the best soil amendments available. Many city governments collect leaves each fall. Give your city a call to ask them if they will deliver leaves to your garden. Call a couple of months before the leaves start to fall in case you need to sign a release. The leaves are generally delivered by the truckload which ranges in size from 5-15 cubic yards. Run the leaves through a shredder or chipper for faster decomposition.

Oyster shells are ground and normally used as a calcium source for poultry. They contain up to 55 percent calcium and traces of many other nutrients that release slowly. Add the ground shells to your compost pile or mix in small amounts with other fertilizers to add to your soil if it needs extra calcium. A handful or two on a new layer of compost or in a bucket of fertilizer is a good rule of thumb.

Paper ash is an excellent water soluble fertilizer high in potassium. Do not use ash from paper with colored inks or inks containing lead or other heavy metals. Paper ash contains about 5% phosphorus and over 2 % potash. Do not apply in large doses because the pH may be quite high.

Colloidal phosphate is a natural clay phosphate deposit that yields 2 percent phosphate by weight the first season and a total of 18 percent over the next several years. Colloidal phosphate is a natural clay phosphate deposit that contains just over 20 percent phosphorus (P_2O_5), calcium, and many trace elements. Colloidal phosphate is an excellent value; it will not burn, and is available to plants as needed. It is also a good soil builder that encourages earthworms and beneficial soil microbes. Cultivate soft phosphate into the soil annually at the rate of five pounds per 100 square feet of soil or turfgrass in conjunction with lime and nitrogen-rich manures and seaweed meal. Or till in 15 to 20 pounds of soft phosphate per 100 square feet along with lime every four years.

Rock phosphate is a calcium or lime-based phosphate rock that is usually ground to the consistency of small crumbs. This rock powder contains over 30 percent phosphate and a menagerie of trace elements. It does not leach out of the soil, remaining unchanged until taken up by roots. Apply at the rate of ten pounds per 100 square feet of soil or turfgrass every four or five years several months after applying annual manure.

Inorganic potash is added to organic fertilizers by some manufacturers as a good source of potassium. Muriate of potash is normally produced chemically by treating rock powders with sulfuric acid, but one company, Great Salt Lake Minerals and Chemicals Company produces a concentrated natural form. The muriate of potash is extracted from the Great Salt Lake. It requires little processing and is sold partially purified as a fertilizer that contains about 50 percent potassium.

Rock potash supplies up to 8 percent potassium and may contain many trace elements. It releases very slowly and stays in the soil for several years. Rock and gravel powders and dusts are being marketed as excellent sources of a broad range of minerals. These fine-textured materials will add elements needed by plants that may be lacking in garden soil. Rock dusts should be added to garden soil in combination with compost.

Seaweed meal or kelp meal is harvested from the ocean or picked up along beaches, cleansed of salty water, dried, and ground into a powdery meal. It contains potassium (potash), numerous trace elements, vitamins, amino acids, and plant hormones. The nutrient content varies according to the type of kelp and its growing conditions. Seaweed meal is easily assimilated by plants and contributes to soil life, structure, and nitrogen fixation. It may also help plants resist many diseases and withstand light frosts. Apply the dry powder at the rate of one or two pounds per 100 square feet of garden soil or lawn in the spring for best results, but it can be applied any time. Allow several weeks for soil bacteria to make nutrients available. Kelp meal also speeds compost decomposition and eases transplant shock.

Seaweed (liquid) contains nitrogen, phosphorus, potash, plant hormones, and all necessary trace elements in a chelated form (water-soluble and mobile in the soil). Apply a dilute solution to the soil or use as a foliar spray for a quick cure of nutrient deficiencies.

Liquid seaweed is also great for soaking seeds, and for dipping cuttings or bare roots before planting.

Sheep manure is high in nutrients and makes a rich manure tea — add water to ¼ bucket of manure and let it sit from one day to a month — see also liquid fertilizers. The resulting "tea" is good for watering plants that need a nutritious boost. The average nutrient content is 0.8- 0.5-0.4 with a full range of trace elements. Sheep manures are hot because they contain little water and lots of air. They heat up readily in a compost pile. Cow and swine manures are cold because they hold a lot of water and can be compacted easily, squeezing out the air.

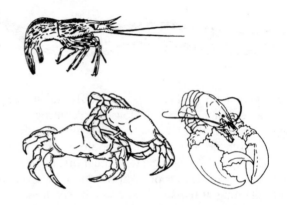

Shrimp and crab wastes contain relatively high levels of phosphorus and calcium. They should be composted before using or dug down deep into the garden.

Sludge (activated), the solids that remain after sewage treatment, contains about 5 percent nitrogen, 3 percent phosphorus, and numerous trace elements. The treated sewage is inoculated with microorganisms (activated) and aerated. Then it is filtered, dried, ground, and screened. It is commonly used as both a soil amendment and a fertilizer on ornamentals and lawns only.

Swine manure has a high nutrient content but is slower acting and wetter than cow and horse manure. The average nutrient content is 0.6-0.6-0.4 with a full range of trace elements.

Wood ashes (hardwood) supply up to 10 percent potash and softwood ashes contain about 5 percent. Potash leaches rapidly, so collect ash soon after burning and store in a dry place. Apply in a mix with other fertilizers at the rate of five or ten pounds per 100 square feet. The potash washes out of heavy layers of wood ash quickly and causes compacted, sticky soil. Avoid using wood ashes, which are highly alkaline, around azaleas, blueberries, camellias, rhododendrons, and other acid-loving plants. Do not use wood ash from treated lumber. Wood ash is an excellent material to compost.

Worm castings are the digested humus excreted by earthworms that contain varying amounts of N-P-K. They are an excellent source of non-burning, readily available nitrogen. Worm castings also promote fertility and soil structure. Mix with potting soil to form a rich, fertile blend. See "The Wonder of Worms"

Zoo Doo is the trademarked name of a fertilizer made from the composted manure and bedding from grazing animals at city zoos. The best and most abundant zoo manure, found in the elephant cages, is similar to cow manure in nutrient content. If you get fresh manure from a zoo, compost it until it has heated and cooled to keep weed seeds from sprouting and to keep it from burning plants when it is applied.

Material	N	P	K	Notes
Alfalfa hay	2.5	0.5	2	good mulch
Blood (dried or meal)	12-15	1.2	1	soluble
Bone meal (unsteamed	2-4	15	25	calcium, trace elements
Bone meal (steamed)	2-3	18-25	0.2	20% Ca, trace elements
Canola meal	0	0.2	1.3	iron, trace elements
Cottonseed meal	7	2	2	acidic
Compost	1-2	1	1	trace elements
Cow (steer) manure	0.5-2	0.3	0.5-1	excess salts
Coffee grounds	2	0.3	0.7	acidic
Feathers (dry or meal)	12-15	0	0	some trace elements
Fish meal	8	7	2	soluble
Goat manure	0.5	0.4	0.4	trace elements
Granite dust	0	0	4-5	some trace elements
Greensand (glaucomite)	0	1	5-7	iron, Mg., trace elements
Guano (bat)	2-5	8-10	1-2	soluble, trace elements
Guano (seabird)	10-15	5	2	soluble, trace elements
Hoof & horn meal	6-15	2	0	trace elements
Horse manure	0.6	0.4	0.4	trace elements
Paper ash	0	0.1	2-3	high pH
Potash rock	0	6-8	0	some trace elements
Poultry manure (wet)	1.5	1.5	1	soluble, trace elements
Poultry manure (dry)	3-4	2-4	1-2	soluble, trace elements
Soft phosphate	0	18-24	0	calcium, trace elements
Seaweed (liquid)	0.5	0.5	0.3	soluble, trace elements
Seaweed (meal)	1	1	1	soluble, trace elements
Sheep manure	0.8	0.4	0.5	trace elements
Swine manure	0.6	0.4	0.2	trace elements
Wood ash (hardwood)	0	1.5	7-10	soluble
Wood ash (softwood)	0	0.8	5	soluble
Worm castings	3.5	1	1	trace elements
Zoo Doo	1.0	0.6	0.5	trace elements

Note: This list shows only average nutrient amounts. The actual percentages will vary with the source. Consult suppliers for exact content.

Four Basic Organic Fertilizer Mixes

The following are excellent organic fertilizers that you can mix yourself. These are dry blends of high-nutrient materials. Since they come in a variety of textures and particle sizes, be sure to mix thoroughly before applying to the garden.

2-4-3
1 part bone meal
3 parts chopped hay
2 parts greensand

3-3-4
3 parts fine granite dust
1 part blood meal
1 part bone meal
5 parts seaweed meal

4-5-4
2 parts blood meal
1 part soft phosphate
4 parts hardwood ashes

4-6-4
2 parts cottonseed meal
1 part soft phosphate
1 part fine granite dust

All measures are by volume, not by weight. Dolomitic lime can be added to offset the acidity of many seed meals; it also contains calcium and magnesium. Mix the fertilizer with a shovel until it is a well blended and a uniform color.

A high nitrogen formula is just the same as the above mix, except add 3 or 4 parts blood meal.

An all purpose organic fertilizer mix is: 1 or 2 parts blood meal, 1 or 2 parts bone meal, 2 or 3 parts wood ashes, and 5 parts of compost. This mix should give you an overall N-P-K of about 2.5-5-2.5.

For seedlings and transplants, mix blood meal, greensand, and soft (colloidal) phosphate together in equal portions.

Liquid Fertilizers

Organic fertilizer tea concoctions may contain just about any soluble organic nutrient diluted in water. Fish emulsion is the most readily available commercial organic tea. Liquid seaweed is an essential source of trace elements. Soluble worm castings and manures are high in nitrogen and bat guano is high in phosphorus. These materials and others make excellent U-

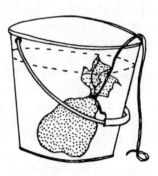

Organic tea bags are filled with fertilizer and soaked in water to form a liquid organic tea.

mix organic teas singly or in combinations. Mix the organic nutrient(s) in water and let them sit from one day to a month. Stir the solution again, then strain out the large particles by pouring the solution through cheesecloth or an old nylon stocking before applying.

A high-nitrogen soluble fertilizer, such as fish emulsion, will green up a tired garden. A dilute liquid seaweed application can solve most trace element deficiency problems. If this remedy fails to cure the problem, seek professional advice. Use a siphon mixer or small spray bottle to apply soluble teas.

Plants can only absorb nutrients in a soluble liquid form; applying liquid fertilizer makes nutrients imme-

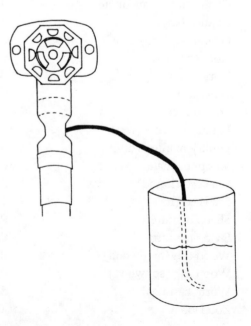

A siphon-X makes applying liquid fertilizers, fungicides, and pesticides very easy.

diately available. However, liquid fertilizers provide only a short term effect and leach out of the soil rapidly.

For a quick cure of unknown nutrient deficiencies, foliar feed your plants by spraying the leaves with a diluted liquid seaweed solution. The leaves can absorb it immediately, taking in all the nutrients that are available.

Application of Organic Fertilizers

Most organic fertilizers must be spaded into the soil in order to become available to plants.

Incorporate well-rotted manures and organic matter into the soil when cultivating beds. When sowing seed or transplanting seedlings, dig the hole several inches deeper than necessary, add a handful of a complete fertilizer mix, then cover it with soil before inserting the seed or transplant. Do not side dress seeds or new transplants with fertilizer or the roots will tend to stay on the surface or grow upward toward the fertilizer. If growth slows later in the season, apply a side dressing or liquid fertilizer. Regular applications of soluble teas will keep vegetables growing well.

There is no simple rule of thumb about how much fertilizer to apply. It depends on the plants, soil, water, temperature, and, of course, the fertilizer.

Those who garden in regions with acid soils may have to apply lime every year to "sweeten" the soil. Most vegetables and ornamentals require a soil pH of 6.5 to 6.8, slightly acid. Those living in regions with basic soils may have to apply sulfur regularly to lower

the pH. The practice that will most improve both acid and basic soils for most gardens is to add plenty of organic matter to the soil and to see that the garden gets adequate water.

When using organic fertilizers, which are mostly slow-release materials, the timing of fertilizing is not as critical as it is when using fast-release chemical fertilizers. Plan to work fertilizer into garden beds every spring as soon as the soil can be worked. Highly productive plants, including vegetables and annuals should have regular monthly applications of organic fertilizer.

Gardeners in areas that have cold winters, should not fertilize perennial and woody plants, including roses, fruit trees, and shrubs, after the first week in July. The reason for this is that mid- to late-summer feedings encourage lush soft growth which may be injured by early or sudden cold snaps.

Except for water soluble nutrients, most organic fertilizers must be mixed with soil so that the bacteria can break them down, making them available to plants. Make sure that meals, rock powders, and manures are well blended with the soil. Large chunks of some organic fertilizers will putrefy if not properly blended.

Slow-release organic fertilizers are difficult to over-apply. Most organic compounds release their nutrients gradually so precise application is not as crucial as it is with chemical fertilizers.

One important rule of thumb is to always apply liquid fertilizers when the soil is moist to avoid scorching tender feeder roots.

General Fertilizer Rules to Follow:

1. Always follow directions on fertilizer package.
2. Apply a complete N-P-K fertilizer 7-10 days before planting.
3. Apply a high-nitrogen supplemental fertilizer to stimulate leaf growth every 2-4 weeks.
4. Apply a phosphorus fertilizer to boost flower and fruit development.
5. Apply a biweekly weak liquid fertilizer to container plants.

Fertilizing Ornamental, Shade & Fruit Trees

Do not fertilize trees and shrubs during the first year after they have been planted. If trees are thriving and have healthy foliage and good color, you may not need to fertilize unless there is heavy competition from lawn, other woody plants, or garden beds. If you choose to fertilize, you can follow the regime below.

Apply an annual top dressing of a complete fertilizer mix to perennials, ornamental shrubs, and trees each spring. A good all-round mix includes rotted manure, colloidal phosphate, wood ashes, granite dust, and bone meal. Cultivate the fertilizer into the surface of the soil within the drip line of the tree. Add a fresh layer of mulch after the soil has warmed in the spring or summer.

Apply about one gallon per inch of trunk diameter of well-rotted compost or manure within the drip line of small trees and shrubs. This application functions as a soil amendment, mulch, and light fertilizer.

Trees absorb most fertilizers in the first two to four feet of soil. Deep feeding below this level is difficult and more trouble than it is worth.

Treat tree roots as if they are shallow vegetable roots. Be careful not to till fertilizers any deeper than 3 to 6 inches into the soil under shallow-rooted trees because this action can damage feeder roots. Be especially careful around top-feeding woody perennials like azaleas and rhododendrons.

If trace elements appear to be lacking (according to a soil test or general expert description of your region), apply a light dressing of liquid seaweed or seaweed meal. Nitrogen is important but trees do not need as much as vegetables.

Because there is such a wide range of species and because the nutrient values of organic fertilizers are so variable, it is not possible to give a general rule on amounts of fertilizer to use. For specifics, check with your local Extension agent or refer to a quality text on your plant varieties.

Since organic fertilizers tend to have a lot of bulk per pound of available nutrient, it is safe to say that no more than 2 to 4 inches of total finished compost, fertilizer and mulch should be put under trees at any one time unless it is to be worked into the soil. If materials under woody plants accumulate much more than that, the grade of the land will be changed, adversely affecting the root masses of the trees.

Spring-Flowering Bulbs

Apply a complete fertilizer in the hole when planting bulbs, and apply as a side dressing in the early spring before flowering.

The conventional wisdom used to be to use nothing but bone meal in bulb beds. There are three reasons for changing that advice.

Years ago, bone meal included a considerable amount of nitrogen and potassium from the blood and meat still on the bones. Today's bone meal has been steamed and processed to such a degree that it includes little more than phosphorus. Secondly, when dogs sniff around bulb beds fertilized with bone meal, they sometimes start digging for the "ghost" bones. Finally, the example for bulb care has always been Holland where they use a great deal of cow manure to improve soil structure and add moderate amounts of nitrogen and other nutrients.

The Dutch recommend using well-composted cow manure or a blended food for bulbs like the trademarked Bulb Booster which have the right proportions of nitrogen. Too much nitrogen is not good for bulbs or other flowering plants because it causes too much green growth.

Roses

Feed monthly during the growing season with a complete fertilizer as soon as new growth begins. Fish emulsion and manure tea will help roses develop vigorous growth and flowers.

In areas with cold winters, discontinue fertilizing in early summer to avoid having soft, tender growth develop late in the season.

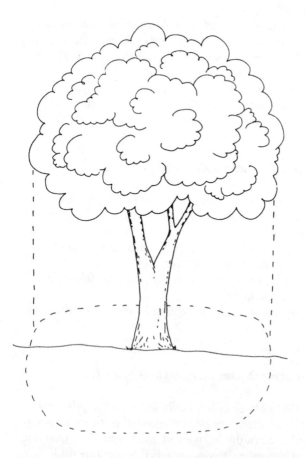

Apply fertilizers within the drip line of plants and lightly cultivate them into the soil.

Acid-Loving Plants

Feed azaleas, blueberries, camellias, rhododendrons, and other acid-loving plants with cottonseed meal (7-2-2) which will maintain soil acidity. Water with manure tea, fish emulsion, or some other liquid organic fertilizer every 3 to 4 weeks through the fruiting season.

Common Fertilizer Problems & Solutions

Burn. Fertilizer burn, injury of plant tissues, and even death, can occur if highly concentrated dry fertilizer is applied on plants or their roots. Follow application directions carefully. Be sure to water in the fertilizer well after application.

Chlorosis. When soil pH (potential hydrogen — a measure of soil acidity and alkalinity) is too high (too alkaline), nutrients including iron are transformed into insoluble mineral salts and thus are unavailable to plants. This lack of available iron causes chlorosis, a loss of the green pigment of foliage. Symptoms of chlorosis include slow growth and leaves that are yellow between the veins. The veins remain green. Applications of sulfur or cottonseed meal to the soil will lower the pH. Commercial fertilizers labeled for azaleas and rhododendrons will feed the plants as they lower soil pH.

Dry Soil. When soil is too dry, the ability of plants to take up nutrients is impaired since nutrients must be in solution to be usable. Add organic matter to the soil to increase its ability to hold moisture and nutrients. Do not fertilize when soil is extremely dry.

pH Problems. Most plant nutrients are insoluble form and thus available to plants when the soil pH is between 6.0 and 7.5 (7.0 is neutral, below that is acid and above is alkaline). When soils are outside of this range, plants will dwindle and eventually die from lack of nutrients. When soil pH is below 6.0, nitrogen, phosphorus, and potassium are less available to plants. Above 7.5, phosphorus, manganese, and iron are less available. Some plants require soils that are acid, others require alkaline. Fortunately, most garden plants are tolerant of a variety of soil types. You can either choose plants to fit the soil type or modify the soil, making it more basic by adding lime or more acidic by adding sulfur or cottonseed meal. It is more difficult to make soil more acidic, therefore, you would be wiser to choose plants that will thrive at a somewhat higher pH.

Wet Soil. If soil is too wet, there will not be enough air in the soil pores. Without air for their roots, plants can not metabolize nutrients, therefore fertilizers in such a soil are useless. Beware of overwatering. Add organic matter to clay soils to improve their draining quality. Correct drainage problems or move the plants.

Organic Soil Conditioners

Most soil amendments are added to improve the structure of the soil, to increase the organic content so that the soil is more capable of holding nutrients and moisture. When these organic materials are added to soil, they also act in varying degrees as fertilizers, providing a mix of nutrients to plant roots in usable forms.

Canola Seed Meal is a Canadian product that promises to become better known. A good source of nitrogen, phosphorus, trace minerals and vitamins, canola meal promotes plant growth as it adds organic matter to the soil. Spread 5 quarts (by volume) over each 100 square feet. Work it into the soil to a depth of 6 to 12 inches and water thoroughly.

Compost is the favorite soil amendment for most gardeners. Compost can be made from many organic sources (see Chapter One). The great advantage of composting is that, once you learn a bit about composts and about nutrients, you can match the two to provide needed elements and compounds for your plants while you build a a rich friable soil.

Mushroom compost is an excellent soil amendment, mulch and fertilizer.

Mushroom compost, the material that has been used by mushroom growers to grow their crops, is a mixture of horse manure, peat moss and other organic matter. It is a weak fertilizer, but is useful as a soil amendment and is a superb top dressing for trees and shrubs. The average nutrient content is low: N - 0.7%, P - 0.3%, K - 0.3% plus a full range of trace elements.

Mushroom compost that has been discarded by mushroom growers, starts as a mixture of horse manure, peat, straw. Frequently, gypsum is added, especially in areas of high-saline soil, to help bind soil particles together.

Mushroom compost is often chemically sterilized so that only mushrooms will grow in it. The law usually requires that after mushroom growers discard the rich compost, it must sit fallow for one or more years before it can be sold. The fallow time allows for any harmful chemicals to leach out and for microbiotic life to increase. The best mushroom compost comes from wet climates where the rain leaches out the undesirable chemicals. Mushroom compost is nearly at the humus state since it has been allowed to decompose for many years. Check at your local nursery or Cooperative Extension Service for a good source.

Seaweed, usually a meal made of processed kelp, is a wonderful soil conditioner that is rich in available trace elements. It also contains growth-promoting hormones. As a soil additive, seaweed helps release nutrients that are otherwise unavailable. Kelp's high concentrations of organic alginic acid and simple sugars do not immobilize nitrogen as they decompose, making kelp excellent for attracting bacteria and binding soil particles to one another. If you gather your own seaweeds (kelp, rockweed, and the like), be sure to rinse the salt water varieties thoroughly with fresh water to remove surface salt before composting or grinding fresh into the garden. Nutrient content: N - 0.3%, P - 0.1%, K - 1.0% and a full range of trace elements. Apply kelp meal at the rate of about 3 pounds per 100 square feet in early spring as soon as the soil can be worked. Perennial crops should have an application of kelp meal at the end of their dormant season.

Activated sewage sludge is processed and sold by a growing number of city sewage treatment facilities. It is aerated, inoculated with bacteria to speed decomposition, heated to 200° F., and is free of germs. It contains from 4 to 6 percent nitrogen and has the benefit of adding organic matter to the soil. Recommended for ornamental plants only. Do not use on fruits or vegetables. The material is dry and smells very similar to finished compost made in your yard. One particular product is known as Milorganite™. Coupled with lime, Milorganite™ is a good organic lawn fertilizer. It provides not only nitrogen, but many trace elements as well, and greatly improves the structure of the soil.

There continues to be some discussion as to whether or not Milorganite™ and the other activated sludge products contain heavy metals which may be taken up by plants and be harmful to your health when you consume them. In spite of the fact that plants process many dangerous elements and compounds into harmless substances, it is still wise to use this material only on ornamental plants. Wear gloves when working with it and wash hands thoroughly after applying.

Animal Manures are most useful both as fertilizers and as amendments to improve soil structure after they are composted. Composting will kill any weed seeds in the manure. It also will allow "hot" manures to cure — hot manures include high ammonium forms of nitrogen that can burn plant foliage and roots. Cow (steer), horse, chicken, sheep and other animal manures from non-meat-eating animals are good choices for the organic gardener.

Manure's' nitrogen content is valuable for maintaining a hot compost pile. (See also Chapter One on composting.)

Green Manures / Cover Crops

Green manuring, also known as cover cropping or catch cropping, is the practice of growing a crop and tilling it in to enrich the soil. The crop that is turned under adds organic matter to the soil. This process greatly improves the structure of soil and its tilth (ability to be easily tilled).

Green manuring has been used by farmers and gardeners for centuries to increase soil fertility. Green manures will attract earthworms by providing food, moisture and cover. Cover crops slow erosion, add and retain nutrients and moisture, slow weed development, and improve overall soil structure when turned under.

Normally, garden beds planted with a cover crop, rather than left bare, experience less nutrient loss. In fact, most nutrients are lost during the winter through leaching, when there are no crops to retain them. Fall-seeded cover crops reduce weeds by competing successfully with them.

Having one crop immediately follow another will not only keep your garden smaller and thus more manageable, it will use less fertilizer, lime, and compost. It will also require less weeding and overall work.

Tall green manure crops should be mowed or chopped finely before tilling under. Shorter green manure crops can be cut with a shovel or simply covered with a heavy layer of mulch when they are young and succulent and decompose rapidly. Soil microorganisms are provided with nutrition and energy, in turn, release nutrients for plant growth.

Chop tall green manure crops as finely as possible before incorporating into the soil. In small areas, an edging tool is easy to use. Larger areas are more of a challenge and may call for some kind of disk tiller or a composting mower. Shorter crops can be cut with a shovel or simply tilled in by hand or mechanically.

It's much easier to plan ahead by planting green manure crops to supply nutrients than hauling hundreds of pounds of manure to the garden. The green manures provide organic matter rich in nitrogen, which means that nitrogen is not drawn from the soil as they decompose into rich humus.

Green manures improve soil structure by helping soil organisms and organic matter to cement minute soil particles into soil crumbs (aggregates), thus stabilizing the physical structure. Soils that are well-aggregated — have good structure — have more pores to hold air, water, and nutrients. They are also better able to withstand the sometimes compacting effects of tillage and erosive quality of heavy rainfall.

Deep-rooted green manure crops such as lupines, sweet clover, and alfalfa can even break up compacted or hardpan soils and draw minerals up from the subsoil making nutrients available to other plant root systems in the topsoil level. Alfalfa, buckwheat, and mustard dissolve and absorb the mineralized forms of phosphorus in the soil and later the roots actually put phosphorus back into the soil.

Advantages of Green Manures

Using green manures in the garden will:

1. Provide organic matter
2. Enrich the soil with nutrients
3. Improve soil structure
4. Increase soil biological activity
5. Diminish nutrient leaching
6. Suppress weeds
7. Diminish disease and insect problems
8. Prevent soil erosion
9. Improve soil tilth and makes tilling easier
10. Moderate soil temperature
11. Moderate soil moisture
12. Help break up compacted soil

By shading the soil, green manures moderate extremes in both temperature and moisture. However, the plants also transpire water, which under dry conditions can cause a net loss of soil water.

Nutrient leaching is lessened by planting cover crops. Nutrients, especially nitrates, are trapped in the plant tissue and preserved for future use by subsequent crops.

Weeds are suppressed by a thick cover of vegetation. Weeds are slow to penetrate a green manure that successfully competes for sunlight, water, and nutrients. Weeds that are common in compacted soil will not grow as well when the soil becomes more friable with the addition of a green manure.

Green manures can also provide an inhospitable climate for destructive insects and diseases. Green manure choke out undesirable weeds that may foster disease and pest growth, disrupting their life cycles.

After plants have taken up nutrients from the soil, they can be recycled by composting, mulching, or cover cropping. For example green bracken ferns contain from 25 to 50 percent potash which can be reused by other plants if the bracken is composted or used as mulch.

Some winter cover crops include grasses, rye, winter oats, and wheat. To establish these green manure crops before winter frosts, sow from mid-August to mid-September. Plow them under the following spring.

Spring cover crops include fast-growing cowpeas, garden peas, sweet clover, and grasses. Sow in the early spring so they can be harvested or turned under before summer flowers and vegetables are planted.

Summer cover crops that thrive in hot weather include buckwheat, rye grass, millet, Sudan grass, and sunflowers. Cultivate the type that best suits your purpose. In no-till gardens, cut or simply brush succulent cover crops aside to sow flower and vegetable seed and lay mulch over remaining cover crops.

When turned under, green manures need plenty of air to decompose rapidly and provide the most benefit. Turn green manures under only to a depth of 2-6 inches so that they do not decompose under anaerobic conditions. In light sandy soils, they will still have enough air to decompose well if turned under to a depth of 4-8 inches. Mow the dense foliage of cover crops before turning under to break the foliage into smaller pieces and hasten decomposition. Green manure crops fit into two general categories: legumes that "fix" nitrogen and nonlegumes.

Nitrogen-fixing Legume Cover Crops

Nitrogen is "fixed" or converted by many leguminous plants, including peas and beans. Legumes gather nitrogen from the air and "fix" it through the bacteria-containing nodules on their roots. Legumes should be tilled under before they form flowers in order for this nitrogen to be deposited in the soil.

An inoculate bacteria (Rhizobium) colonizes the root nodules of leguminous plants so that nitrogen-fixing can take place. Numerous strains of this bacteria live in the soil, but to ensure its presence, it should be added to the soil when growing legumes. Purchase the inexpensive inoculant along with the nitrogen-fixing cover crop seeds at the nursery. Normally the dry, powdered inoculant is mixed with moist seeds before they are planted, or dissolved in water and applied

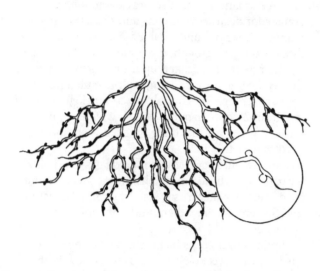

Legumes fix nitrogen from the air onto nodules located on their roots.

directly to the soil after the seeds are placed but before they are covered with soil. The packets contain several different Rhizobium bacterium that will inoculate numerous varieties.

For subsequent crops to take full advantage of the nitrogen fixed in the soil, they must be grown as a cover crop and tilled under before they bloom. A common misconception is that nitrogen fixed by legumes stays in the soil after harvest. The legumes use most of the nitrogen that they produce to grow. To deposit nitrogen in the soil, legumes must be tilled under before they use up the nitrogen.

ALFALFA or LUCERNE (*Medicago sativa*) is a deep-rooted perennial legume that grows up to three feet tall. Both irrigated and dry land varieties are available. It provides much green matter, fixes a good supply of nitrogen, and brings some calcium, magnesium, and potassium to the topsoil. In cooler, northern climates sow in the spring and till under in the fall. For a winter cover crop in mild climates, sow at the rate of ½ to 2 pounds per 1,000 square feet in late summer or fall and till under early the next spring.

AUSTRIAN PEAS (*Dolichos lignosus*) are large-seeded legumes that like well-draining, fertile, loamy soils. They will build tilth (good soil structure) as they add organic matter and thus humus to the soil. An excellent cover crop, the succulent growth is exceptionally heavy and lush. Simply cover the peas with a heavy layer of mulch or till it under before the plants bloom. Seed at the rate of 1 pound per 200 square feet.

SOYBEANS (*Glycine max*) thrive in all but the most alkaline soils and can withstand drought. Inoculate seed and sow late-maturing varieties in spring to summer for best results. Soybeans produce a good amount

of green growth. Save the seeds for future cover crops. Sow 2-3 pounds per 1,000 square feet.

FAVA BEANS (*Vicia faba*) (English Broad beans), a close relative of garden peas, are an excellent nitrogen fixer with deep roots. Plants grow five to eight feet tall and will winter-over in mild climates. They produce beautiful black and white flowers and attract beneficial insects. The beans can be shelled and eaten fresh or saved for the next cover crop. Sow up to 1 ½ inches deep in rows or broadcast 2-5 pounds per 1,000 square feet.

VELVET BEANS (*Mucuna deeringiana*) grow well in poor, sandy soils and are a good cover crop in the South. Roots grow to 30 feet long and vines can sprawl over 50 feet long. Sow at the rate of 2-3 pounds per 1,000 square feet when the soil is warm in the spring. Medics (*Medicago* spp.), close relatives of clover, grow vigorously in neutral to alkaline, reasonably fertile soil.

Selected varieties grow in drought to moderate-rainfall conditions. Medics are a good choice for soils that will not support clovers. Sow scarified inoculated seed ½ to 1 pound per 1,000 square feet during the fall in the South and in the spring in the North.

ALSIKE CLOVER (*Trifolium hybridum*) flourishes in fertile soil and can tolerate wet, alkaline conditions which other clovers cannot. A favorite in warm climates, it grows best in sandy or clay loams with good drainage. Sow in late spring at ½ pound per 1,000 square feet.

CRIMSON CLOVER (*Trifolium incarnatum*) produces bright, showy crimson spikes on 18-inch plants in the spring. It will grow on most any soil and is tolerant of both shade and medium acid soil. Grow in mild Northern climates southward. Sow ½ to 2 pounds per 1,000 square feet during mid-summer in heavy frost areas, and in the fall in milder climates.

WHITE DUTCH CLOVER has white flowers on low-growing foliage. A perennial, it will tolerate regular mowing and foot traffic once it is established. It forms a "sod" or "living mulch" and is often used in pathways between rows for this reason. Best on silty loams and clay soils with a pH of 6.0 to 7.0. A favorite winter cover crop in cool, moist climates, white clover grows well if irrigated in summer. This clover spreads rapidly to choke out weeds. Sow + pound per 1,000 square feet.

PERSIAN CLOVER (*Trifolium resupinatum*) is grown in warm southern and Pacific regions. It prefers moist, clay soils. Seed ½ to 1 pound per 1,000 square feet in the fall and till under the following spring.

RED CLOVER (*Trifolium pratense*) is a low-growing crop with an extensive root system that is popular in the North but will grow in all climates. Used extensively for soil renovation, red clover is extremely adaptable. It can grow on heavy to light textured soils and in soils with moderate acidity. Sow 1 pound per 1,500 square feet in the spring to late summer in well-drained soil.

SWEET CLOVER (white, *Melilotus alba;* and yellow, *M. alba var. annua*) will grow in any climate with well limed soil. The white type is a biennial which develops a long, fat taproot which breaks up compacted soil. It needs more than 17 inches of rainfall and can grow 2-6 feet tall. Sow at the rate of ½ to 1 pound per 1,000 square feet. The yellow-flowering type is an annual variety that is fast-growing. Sow in the spring and turn under before fall, or sow in fall for a winter cover. It will winterkill in the north and form a mat which can be tilled under in spring. Sow ⅔ pound per 1,000 square feet.

CROTOLARIA (*Crotolaria juncea*) is a tropical, pea-like plant used in the South. If the seeds are soaked in warm water prior to planting, they will germinate sooner. Sow 1-2 pounds per 1,000 square feet

Cowpeas (*Vigna unguiculata*), also known as field peas, are grown all over North America in all soils. They grow best on well-drained, sandy loams and can tolerate drought fairly well. Revered for their soil-building qualities and strong roots that penetrate hardpan. They will smother weeds and are shade tolerant. Inoculate seed of this fast-growing legume before sowing for the first time. Sow 2 to 3 pounds per 1,000 square feet when the soil has warmed in spring in the North. Plant in the fall in the South.

Lupines (*Lupinus* spp.) are tall and extremely deep-rooted perennial flowers that add nitrogen as well as phosphorus to the soil. They grow in all types of soil except poorly drained, heavy adobe. Seed must be inoculated for best performance. Sow 2 to 4 pounds per 1,000 square feet in the spring and till under in mid summer, or sow September through mid November in the spring in northern regions.

VETCH (*Vicia* spp.) is viney and available in many varieties for different regions. Common vetch not particularly winter hardy. This annual vine-type legume is best for well-draining soils and not tolerant of wet soils. Vetch is considered a noxious weed by most gardeners. If you should decide to plant it, make sure you can cultivate it in at least twice, or completely smother it with a heavy mulch.

HAIRY VETCH is perennial, tall with a large root system, and hardy to 0° if planted early enough in the fall to get established. It also grows well during spring and summer. Many times vetch is combined with rye or tall wheat grasses to support the vines. Hungarian vetch is better adapted to heavy, poorly drained soils than other vetches.

PURPLE VETCH is the least winter hardy but the most vigorous. The viney plants smother weeds both summer and winter. Tolerates low fertility and pH. Sow cold-tolerant vetches at the rate of 1 to 3 pounds per 1,000 square feet in late summer and turn under in early spring.

Non-Legume Cover Crops

Non-legume cover crops are mostly fast-growing grasses. They are valued for their ability to protect soil from erosion and to provide organic matter and nutrients. You should note that grasses do not "fix" nitrogen and are more difficult to turn under than clovers.

BARLEY (*Hordeum* spp.) needs rich, loamy soil and is a poor performer in acid or sandy soils. It is most commonly grown in Northern states. Plant winter hardy varieties in cold climates. Sow 2 ½ pounds per 1,000 square feet.

BUCKWHEAT (*Fagopyrum* spp.) is a large and vigorous annual with a huge root system. It is one of the best hot-weather cover crops. An excellent choice to choke out weeds, it creates plenty of organic matter and is a good bee and hoverfly attractor. Buckwheat tends to accumulate phosphorus which also helps to build up the soil when it is plowed under. It is an excellent choice to rebuild acidic and poor soils. Sow buckwheat in the late spring or summer after the ground has warmed. Two or three 60-day crops that grow up to 3 feet tall can be squeezed into one season in some parts of the country. Seed at the rate of 2 pounds per 1,000 square feet.

FIELD BROMEGRASS (*Bromus unioloides*) grows in many soils and is cultivated in Northern states. More hardy than rye, it is an excellent winter cover crop. Sow in the spring or late summer at the rate of 1 pound per 1,000 square feet.

MILLET (*Panicum* spp.) is an excellent choice for poor soils in arid South and Southwest climates. Sow 1 pound per 1,000 square feet in the spring or summer.

MUSTARD (*Brassica* spp.) is a very fast-growing, short and shallow, but heavily rooted cover crop. A bonus is that it produces lots of edible green matter. A good weed suppressor, it outgrows weeds and is a fast cover crop if you can only spare the garden space for a month to six weeks. Sow ½ to 1 pound of seed per 1,000 square feet in spring or summer and turn under before flowering. Mustard is a soil cleanser that stimulates microorganisms.

OATS (*Avena sativa*) grow in cool, moist climates on just about any soil in the United States. Winter oat varieties, sown in late summer or fall, are a good green manure in mild climates. Sow 3 pounds per 1,000 square feet. They grow quickly; large amounts of green matter can be tilled in after 6 to 8 weeks.

RYE, AND ITALIAN ANNUAL RYEGRASS (*Secale* spp.) are fast-growing grasses that produce an extensive root system and bulky green matter. They tolerate most soils and grow throughout the United States. Till the majority under leaving a few plants to collect seed from for the next cover crop. Plant annual ryegrass at a rate of 1 pound per 1,000 square feet as a fall-seeded cover crop. It germinates rapidly and continues growing at low temperatures. Plow it under in the spring. Plant fall (cereal rye) as early as August — it also germinates quickly and grows well in cool weather. Sow at a rate of 2 ½ pounds per 1,000 square feet.

SUDANGRASS (*Sorghum sudanense*) is the king of organic matter cover crops. It tolerates all but the wettest soil and grows vigorously with little irrigation throughout America. This crop matures in 85 to 105 days and tops out at 6 feet if well irrigated and the weather is hot. Sow 1 to 2 pounds of seed per 1,000 square feet in the spring and turn under one to three months later.

WEEDS are fast-growing and well adapted to local growing conditions. Some weeds make excellent cover crops. Many weeds, such as chickweed, have extensive root systems that break up the soil and the foliage provides a good deal of green matter. Chickweed, for example, grows in the Maritime Northwest during the winter to provide an excellent cover crop that is easy to remove or cover with more compost in the spring. Promote weeds, such as chickweed, that have qualities — it is free, self-seeding and easy to till under or remove with a bow rake or potato fork.

WHEAT grows best in fertile soil that is slightly alkaline (7 to 8.5 pH). Various varieties grow in summer and winter all across America. Sow winter wheat in early September and summer varieties during the spring. Sow 2 ½ pounds per 1,000 square feet.

Perennial shrubs that are members of the pea or legume family are able to fix nitrogen on their roots. Broom is a well-known shrubby legume. Wisteria, which can be either a vine or a shrub, is another.

Chapter Three:

Water

About Water

Plants and animals must have water to live. A large percentage of living tissue is made up of water. Some plants, such as lettuce, are more than 90 percent water.

Plants absorb water from the soil through their roots. They take in the nutrients that they need in water-soluble form. Water is also necessary for microbial soil life, and it circulates in the pores between soil particles, making it easier for plant roots to grow into the soil. Moist garden loam contains approximately 25 percent of its volume as water. About half of that water is available to plants. The need for extra water application, in addition to natural rainfall, depends on the soil, climate, time of year and plants being grown. Learning how to apply the proper amount of water is one of the trickiest challenges new gardeners face.

Because circumstances are so variable, it is difficult to explain in a general way how much water to apply. The guidelines for watering are many times contradictory, but there are some basic rules of thumb that will help you learn when and how to water wisely.

Learn to recognize the need for water by studying both plants and soil. Most plants that are near early stages of dehydration begin to look droopy and have less intense colors in their foliage. They may look grayish. The leaves will begin to get limp and may fold or turn away from direct rays of the sun.

To check the soil to see if supplementary water is necessary, scoop up a handful of soil three or four inches below the soil's surface. If it falls apart easily or, in the case of heavy clay soils, is hard, it has 75 percent or less of the volume of water it should have for growing healthy plants. Until you learn the relationship between your soil and water, check the soil twice a week to see if it is moist to a depth of three to six inches. Remember that most plant roots, even those of large trees, grow in the top six to eight inches of soil.

In northern states, soil moisture is usually adequate until May or June, so little watering is necessary. Ground moisture in southern states may dissipate by March or April. However, some areas have regular rainfall and need only small amounts of supplemental watering. Gardeners in those areas are most fortunate.

In most parts of the country, about one inch of water is lost by evaporation each week during the warm months of May and June. The warmer days of July, August, and early September usually see about 1.5 inches of water loss per week. September water loss is back to an inch, and by October water loss is usually practically nil.

Plants use water night and day as long as they live. At the same time they lose water through both transpiration and evaporation. Water loss is highest at noon and lowest at night. Wind and sun increase plants' water losses by increasing the rate of evaporation. Low humidity also increases water loss through evaporation.

Average annual rainfall in the United States ranges from a low of 0 to 8 inches in the desert Southwest to a high of over 100 inches in the Pacific Northwest. As you go south, more water is needed to grow crops because of increased evaporation in higher temperatures. In cooler climates, crops can be grown with less annual rainfall.

You can generalize about climate and weather, but you can't always count on it to produce the amount of rain needed for your garden. Both droughts and deluges can occur with devastating results. Too much water is often as bad as too little, since it can be so difficult to drain soggy land.

If there are extensive droughts, such as have occurred in both the Northeast and Northwest, your entire garden plan may have to be adapted to dry conditions. Water conservation often becomes mandatory. You may have to seek plants that are more drought tolerant. Make sure your soil has enough organic matter and is adequately mulched to help it hold moisture.

The Plains states often have strong prevailing winds that will dry soils already low in moisture. Wind is another climatic factor that may be of major importance in planning gardens. Organic soil content, and a regular program of mulching, will help moderate the effects of wind. Windbreaks of trees and shrubs will also protect your garden from drying winds.

Soils &Water

A water meter gives you a way to measure how much moisture your garden is receiving. Once you get a feel for watering, you will be able to check the soil moisture with your finger or by inserting a shovel into the soil to check the moisture at a deeper level.

Depending on the texture and structure of the soil, an inch of rainfall per week should be enough for many gardens, as long as the temperature is moderate. If it does not rain, you probably will have to water clay soils once a week, sandy soils about twice a week, and loam soils every 4-5 days. This is an approximation — the exact timing will depend on many factors, including amount of rain, temperature, day length, wind. Water should soak into the soil quickly to prevent evaporation and runoff. The humus functions like a water bank. Water is deposited and held when plentiful, then withdrawn by the plants when needed.

By now, you have learned that gardening is not an exact science, but rather one that calls for a reasonable awareness of plant needs combined with a common sense approach to meeting those needs.

Wise Watering Guidelines

* A 6-inch wide irrigation furrow, or ditch, will moisten an area 9-15 inches wide.

* Night watering works well. But do not water in the late evening and turn the water off for the night. This leaves foliage damp and promotes fungus and disease. If watering at night, water all night or very early in the morning. Watering all night will continually wash the foliage of problem-causing fungal spores and bacteria. Night watering is more efficient because the water does not evaporate as fast in cooler night temperatures.

* Tailor watering to the age of your crop. Be careful when planting seed or seedlings in summer heat. Small seedlings need frequent surface watering because the root systems have not yet developed. They

will need more water and shading until established during hot weather. Older, more mature plants benefit from deep watering.

*Water mature plants deeply and less frequently to promote deep root development, as opposed to watering often but only a little at a time. Most mature plants require 1 to 2 inches of water per week to sustain healthy growth. For example, a 100-square-foot bed will use from 10 to 25 gallons of water per day or about 1 ¾ inches of water per week. A ⅝ to ¾-inch watering hose will deliver about one inch of water over a 5,000-square-foot area in four to five hours. Most mature vegetables and annual flowers require about 1 inch of water per week during hot summer weather to sustain healthy growth.

* Wind dries soil rapidly. It also causes plants to lose much more water. Mulch slows evaporation from the soil's surface.

* Water late in the day or early in the morning in dry climates to decrease moisture loss from evaporation. However, do not water just before sundown. Water should evaporate from the foliage and the soil's surface before nightfall to help prevent fungal diseases. Morning watering regimens are best for wet climates where mold and fungus are more prevalent.

* Hoses that are the most durable and easy to handle are made from rubber, but they are also the most expensive. The best value are hoses with reinforced vinyl exteriors and rubber interiors, which cost about half as much as all-rubber hoses. The standard hose sizes include ½-, ⅝- and ¾-inch-diameter. The ⅝-inch diameter hose is considered the best value. It is lightweight and carries adequate water for most gardening needs.

Water Conservation

Each year, millions of gallons of water are wasted by unwise watering, by watering plants at the wrong time and in the wrong way. When there is ample rain and reservoirs are full, that's not too serious. We should make the point, however, that if there is ample rain, there is no need to add any supplementary water! During droughts, water waste is more than unwise. In some communities, it is literally a crime. Soil that is deeply cultivated, to a depth of 12 to 15 inches, improved by the addition of ample compost, and heavily mulched will use about one fourth as much water as it did before amendments were added. It will yield more vegetables and produce stronger and more prolific flowers. Shrubs and trees grown in this kind of soil will require less maintenance. Rich soil has up to 50 percent more pore space, thanks to the actions of bacteria, worms, fungi and roots.

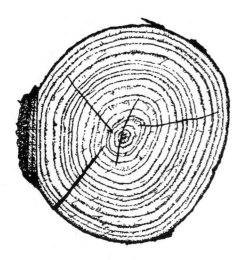

The wide growth rings of this cross section of a tree trunk demonstrate wet years; narrow rings show the years when less water was available to the tree.

Remember that a layer of mulch will not only moderate soil temperature, it will also conserve soil moisture by cutting down on evaporative water loss.

Soil usually can recover from one year of less-than-normal rainfall by the following year. However, if one dry year follows another, the soil does not quite recover all of the ground moisture. And if two dry years are followed by a third dry year, the soil and vegetation are in for some drastic changes in growth. Trees and shrubs grow less and lose their leaves sooner in the fall. Crops that are normally not irrigated must be watered to survive. Early spring transplants that normally can rely on spring rains to get established are stunted by the continuing drought.

Learn about the alternative methods of adding supplementary water when rainfall is less than required for the plants you are growing. Then you will be more able to use water wisely by using the method most practical for your particular situation.

A simple way to gain more water for your garden is to put rain barrels under down spouts. For centuries, hot, dry areas of Europe and Africa have featured houses with systems arranged to gather rain from the rooftops and store it in large cisterns. We would be wise to follow that example in many parts of our country.

Wise Plant Choices

In dry regions, xeriscaping (from the Greek xeros meaning dry) is an efficient way to conserve water and use it wisely. Xeriscaping calls for improving soil, mulching, limiting lawn areas, irrigating efficiently and using plants adapted to dry regions.

Plants that are succulent (thick, fleshy leaves and stems) are good choices for dry gardens. Cacti and sedums are good examples of succulent plants for dry places.

Many of the common garden herbs will adapt well to dry conditions. In fact, herbs are more fragrant and tasty when grown in comparatively poor soil that is on the dry side.

Native plants and plants that are native to dry areas should be top choices for xeriscapers. Check with your county's Cooperative Extension Service to learn what plants will adapt well to your region. Remember that even the toughest plants will need enough water to become established.

Water Application

When extra water is needed and water must be conserved, choose an appropriate method for your garden from among the ones we describe in this chapter. Monitor the soil so that you know when the soil is moist to the desired depth, 9 to 12 inches or more, depending on the plant varieties.

You can monitor soil moisture by digging with a shovel or trowel. Some people recommend using a stick or metal rod as a probe. This is difficult to judge — if soil particles stick to the probe, the soil is moist and if they don't, the soil needs more water. You might say that clay soils are easier to judge for moisture by using a probe — if you can't get the probe into the soil, it needs more moisture. That's a condition many gardeners may find in unimproved soil.

A moisture meter is the least intrusive method for checking on the depth of adequate soil moisture. Use it before and after watering, and it will tell you how long you need to water to get the desired results. If you use sprinklers, you can easily measure the equivalent of one inch of rain. Place a straight-sided pan, dish, or coffee can in the area to be watered. When it has an inch of water in it, you've reached your goal. Again, once you've done this a few times, you will learn how long you must water to get the equivalent of an inch of rain.

Underwatering

The results of too little water are many and affect all parts of the plants. Without soil moisture, the roots can't take up nutrients needed to grow, and to develop foliage, flowers and fruit.

When plants don't get enough moisture, first they wilt. Then the tips and edges of the leaves may begin to look scorched. If lack of water continues, the scorch spreads. Leaves droop and then they begin to drop. These are, of course, signs indicating damage taking place underground in the root systems.

Left unwatered, lettuce turns bitter, cauliflower heads do not grow, squash become fibrous, tomatoes, cucumbers and peppers are small.

If your carrots are woody or petunias blossoms don't last, they may have been underwatered. Many flowers and vegetables may wilt temporarily and look fine the next day, but the wilting is a big shock and they never completely recover. Root crops may not wilt or show signs of water-stress but the roots will be tough and woody.

Low soil moisture causes flowers to be smaller than normal and fewer in number. Both annual and perennial plants will be smaller and less healthy if they have too little water. Similarly, shrubs and trees will have less growth under drought conditions. In appearance, they will be droopy and will have poor color. In extreme droughts, there may be considerable die-back of foliage and branches of woody plants.

Overwatering

Overwatering is just as harmful as underwatering. Frequent, light watering leaves the soil moist to a depth of only an inch or two — the deeper soil can remain bone-dry. The opposite extreme, overwatering, reduces soil fertility by leaching away nutrients to below the feeder root zone. Although overwatering is more common in house plants, gardeners should beware of overwatering in gardens, especially in heavy clay soils.

There is a fertilizer (Oxygen Plus) made for gardeners who tend to overwater house plants. This fertilizer contains hydrogen molecules that will aerate the soil when it is overwatered.

Overwatering fills soil pores, causing a lack of oxygen in plants' root zones. With the exception of those adapted to bogs and water, all plants must have oxygen available in the soil. When water fills the soil to the exclusion of air, the plants drown.

An early sign of too much water is wilting. Lower leaves may begin to drop. If the soil remains wet too long, the plant will collapse and die.

Hand Watering

Hand watering is time consuming, but it gives you a chance to inspect the garden. It is best to use a water

Watering by hand is more time consuming, but it gives you a chance to look closely at your garden.

wand with a breaker. Breakers are the devices that go on the end of the hose or wand to break up the water and lower water pressure.

Brass fittings are superior to plastic fittings that can crack or scar when dropped or dragged across concrete or asphalt.

Watering cans are great for watering seedlings and individual plants, and for applying liquid fertilizers. Well-balanced plastic or rust-proof metal cans that do not splash are the best for hand watering. There are also watering cans made especially for hanging plants.

A water wand is one of the best choices for hand watering. When equipped with a pressure-breaking head, it slows water velocity so that it more easily goes into the ground without washing away the soil.

Brass or plastic twist-type nozzles emit a fine spray that graduates to a heavy stream of water and are more versatile than pistol-grip nozzles. Fogger nozzles change the water stream into a fine mist without reducing the volume. Bubblers are nozzles that mix air with the water so that it flows gently.

Bubblers are useful for soaking one spot at a time as in the case of newly planted trees and shrubs. Simply place the bubbler near the base of the plant you want to water.

There are numerous accessories for watering that may be useful in your garden. They include easy hose-mending kits and hose holders that will hold coiled hose neatly out of the way on reels, hooks or other gadgets. Quick-connect attachments at faucet and on hose ends are very handy.

Root waterers — steel tubes with holes at the bottom and a hose connection at the top — good choices, particularly in areas of compacted soil, for deep watering and fertilizing the root areas of trees and shrubs. Shutoff valves are hose-end attachments that allow you to turn off water without having to go back to the spigot when you want to change nozzles. Shutoff valves are best when made of brass.

Flood Irrigation

Flood or basin irrigation is one of the oldest irrigation methods in the world. Although flooding leaches salt buildup, it may carry away nutrients if the basin area overflows. It uses water very inefficiently. The water will flow about 2-4 inches laterally through sandy soil and up to 15 inches laterally in heavy clay soil. If roots are located 6 inches away from a flood irrigation ditch in sandy soil, they do not receive water.

The land that is being irrigated by this method must have a very slight incline to carry the water even-ly to all portions of the ditch before it soaks into the soil. If the incline is too great, the plants on the uphill end will receive less water than the plants further downhill. Flood irrigation also leaves clay soils muddy for days after application. When the clay finally dries out, an impenetrable surface crust generally forms. Flood irrigation is relatively efficient only when used around the base of trees and shrubs.

If you put straw or compost in an irrigation furrow, it will slow the water and greatly diminish runoff. Since the straw or compost slows the velocity of the water, it penetrates further into the soil.

Soaker Hoses, Leaky Pipe & Slow-Watering Devices

Soaker hoses deliver water from small openings along the length of the hose. They are made from nylon, vinyl, polyester, polyethylene, and rubber, and are resistant to rot and fungal attack. Canvas hoses, the original soaker hoses, are susceptible to rot and mold damage. Daily draining will protect them. Soaker hoses, especially the inexpensive vinyl kind, can rupture if used with high water flow and pressure. If your water pressure is high, do not turn the water fully on. You also can install a pressure/flow reducer to prevent excessive pressure. Breaks in hoses can be mended with a friction coupling.

Weave soaker hoses in between vegetables, on top of the soil mulch so that you can easily move them as the crops change throughout the season. For maximum efficiency, install enough soaker hose to cover each bed. In ornamental gardens, you may wish to

Building a small dike around a tree and flooding the bowl is an excellent method of flood irrigation.

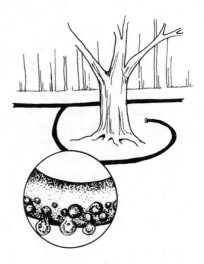

Soaker and leaky pipe hoses are very efficient ways to irrigate.

Homemade drip watering devices can be made from plastic containers.

place soaker hoses under the mulch for esthetic reasons.

If irrigation water is high in mineral salts, soaker hoses can become clogged with salt buildup. To flush, turn the water on full blast for a few minutes. Be careful when running water at full flow through soaker hoses, they tend to split under the increased pressure. Be careful when cultivating so that you do not puncture the hidden soaker hoses.

The "leaky pipe" soaker hoses made from recycled tires are wonderful! Each year hundreds of thousands of old tires are transformed into soaker hose. This unique hose releases water slowly through thousands of tiny pores. This is the most durable and absolutely the best soaker hose available. It may be stiff when you first use it but it should loosen up when warmed by the sun.

Homemade slow watering devices include pitchers, inverted bottles and plastic containers. Gallon milk jugs are good choices. Punch a small hole in the bottom of the plastic container. Set it alongside the plant you want to water. Fill the container with water. The water will drip out the hole and water the plant.

Sprinklers are more effective than hand watering but less effective than watering with soaker hoses. Overhead sprinkling is the easiest way to apply water though not necessarily the best. Besides losing water to evaporation, it wets foliage which can lead to fungal infections in susceptible plants. When water is full of chlorine and other salts, sprinklers promote salt buildup on leaves and in the root zones.

Sprinklers that throw small, light droplets are best for flower and vegetable beds. Large water droplets constantly pound the soil's surface. This can compact the soil, forming a concrete-like crust that is difficult for seedlings to penetrate and slows water absorption. You can use high-output sprinklers with big droplets on lawns because a crust does not form on the sod.

Typically, a sprinkler with average water flow will wet sandy loam to a depth of a foot or more each hour. However, sprinklers do not all deliver the same amount of water and different soils absorb water at distinct rates. Adjust the water so that the volume is just enough for the soil to absorb the water without running off.

Sprinklers are usually rated by the area they will cover. Many sprinklers throw a circular pattern of water but gardens are usually square or rectangular. Oscillating sprinklers and sprinklers that throw a square or rectangular pattern are more expensive, but may offer the best overall value.

Professional plantsmen often use impulse or impact sprinklers, also called "rainbirds" after the most common brand. These will cover partial or full circles up to 100 feet in diameter. An impulse sprinkler has a small nozzle that shoots the water out which is then deflected by a spring-loaded arm. This arm breaks the stream of water into droplets as it bounces back and forth, moving the sprinkler head slightly with each bounce. These are the sprinklers

There are many different hoses and water wands on the market. Compare them for flexibility, high-quality construction and capacity. As always, it pays to read the labels.

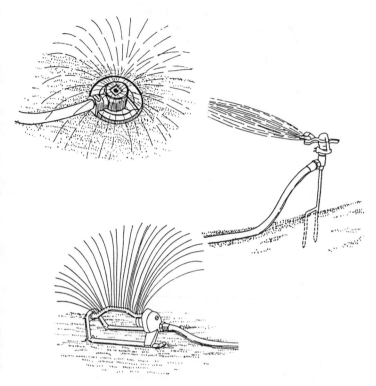

Water loss through evaporation is high on hot days with low relative humidity.

Drip Irrigation

Drip irrigation cuts water use by 30 to 50 percent. Water is applied in droplets through a network of low-pressure tubing over a long period of time. The water soaks into each plant's root zone slowly. Evaporation from sprays, runoff, and standing water (puddling) are eliminated.

When using drip irrigation, only a fraction of the soil surface gets wet, which reduces surface evaporation and makes it difficult for weeds to get started. Powdery mildew, leaf spot, and other fungal diseases are virtually nonexistent since no water touches the foliage.

Generally speaking, drip irrigation is more useful in vegetable than ornamental gardening. In ornamental gardening, you may find that a combination of watering methods will best serve your needs. Drip irrigation is less convenient in areas surrounded by lawn or without easy access to water.

Water applied slowly will penetrate sandy soils up to one foot within 15 minutes. Some drippers can be regulated to run very fast or closed down to run slower. The drip emitters let water out one drop at a time and are rated at delivering ¼ to over one gallon per emitter per hour. Drip emitters are sometimes connected to microtubing, spaghetti or transfer tubing.

In cold climates, some drip systems must be removed and stored indoors each fall to protect them from becoming brittle after prolonged freezes. Be sure to check the instructions for precise information about proper care.

You may wish to control drip systems with manual shut-off or automatic valves. A "Y" valve fitted at the faucet makes it possible to run two drip lines independently.

Antisyphon valves are required on permanent systems by health and safety codes to prevent water from mixing with the house water system. An in-line filter and regular flushing will remove debris and salt buildup that could clog emitters.

With all of the hose, tubing and attachments, drip systems are more expensive than a single hose and a sprinkler. However the initial cost is far outweighed by the time and water saved. Once installed, the drip system is easy to maintain, to turn on and off, and to use to add fertilizers.

Start small with your first drip system. The complete kits undoubtedly contain parts that you will never use. The most important components are the filter, pressure regulator, feeder hose, drip tubing, and emitters. Generally, these components are all that are necessary for even large drip systems.

When first watering with a drip irrigation system, dig down to see how deep the water penetrates. Check

you often see on golf courses and large public lawn and garden areas.

Sprinklers should be thoroughly drained and dried before storing for winter. Check sprinkler holes periodically and clean them if clogged. This will assure an even spray. Most oscillating, arc-type sprinklers pause too long at the turn around point, giving the ends more water than the middle. High-angle sprinklers loose a lot of their spray to evaporation and are affected by wind, which can blow the spray. Low angle sprinklers apply water more efficiently but cover less area. Sprinklers with large water outlets clog less and throw a fine spray of water.

Impact-type or rainbird sprinklers may put down too much water near the sprinkler. The center ground may stay too wet and the perimeter too dry. These sprinklers have a screw arm or adjustment to even out the water coverage.

Check your sprinkler's coverage by placing three cans in the water coverage area. Place one can near the sprinkler, one at the perimeter, and another in between. Leave the sprinkler on for one hour, then measure the amount of water in each can. If there are drastic differences between the volumes of water in the cans, you may want to use a different kind of sprinkler. Average all three to calculate the sprinkler's precipitation rate per hour. It should be somewhere between two and four inches.

the soil after one, two, and three hours. Then you will be able to water wisely, knowing how deeply the moisture will go in a given period of time.

Drip emitters apply exact amounts of water depending on their size. They are made for various volumes of application. For example, a more generous emitter can be placed on the uphill side of a plant to keep it as evenly watered as the downhill side.

Since clay soil has more lateral water movement, spaghetti tubing or drip emitters can be spaced further apart than on fast-draining sandy soil.

The root growth of most plants, including trees, is contained primarily within the top six to eight inches of soil. This is the area that is critical for plants to take up moisture and nutrients. Watering more deeply occasionally will flush or leach salt buildup in the soil.

A few useful facts about drip irrigation are:

* If gardeners skimp on the number of emitters, plant roots tend to develop heavily near these few emitters. That's why it's important to arrange drip irrigation emitters so that water is spread uniformly throughout the irrigated area.
* A green manure crop cannot be tilled under if drip tubing is buried in the soil.
* Drip tubing is easy to cut with a shovel or pierce with a spade.
* A few weeds will grow around the drip emitters. Tubes on top of the soil are easier to weed beneath.
* Drip systems are great for perennial shrubs, herbs, and trees. The irrigation system operates at low pressure and the compression fittings require no glue or hose clamps. Self-seating fittings seal themselves and seal better as the pressure rises.
* Drip tubing has a bad habit of "walking around" when the hose is turned on and off which changes the pressure in the line. Anchor drip emitters with a stake or bury them below the soil.

Underground Watering Systems

Now that plastic piping has come of age and is so much more reliable and durable, underground watering systems are not as prohibitive in price. Outlets are placed and aimed so that they will water specific areas of the garden. Pop-up sprinkler heads make it easier to do garden maintenance jobs without destroying the irrigation system. Timers make the system nearly foolproof.

However, installing an underground watering system properly is not a job for the average gardener or handy homeowner. It calls for some careful engineering to make it work properly. The better choice is to check around for a professional company experienced in this kind of installation. Get references and check them out before hiring a company to install an underground watering system.

Chapter Four

Weeds

About Weeds

A weed is an undesirable plant, nothing more, nothing less. It is said that there are many pounds of weed seeds in every garden bed. These undesirables should be stopped while they are still small, before they get a good start. Older, desirable plants usually can easily compete with weeds by shading them. But if weeds are left unattended until late spring they may be growing out of control by early summer. Poisonous or rash-causing plants such as poison ivy, poison oak, poison sumac, and stinging nettles can be removed manually. Of course, you must make sure to wear protective clothing to prevent the foliage from touching your skin and creating a painful rash. Slick clothing and gloves provide the best protection from the irritating oils of the first three and the minute prickers of the nettle.

Cut canes and branches of these plants off at ground level with a lawn mower, weed whacker, ax or shovel. Continue to cut the foliage as long as it resprouts. Do not touch the tool blades as the irritating plant oils will be on them.

After using tools on plants such as poison ivy, wash them thoroughly in soapy water. Cover the area with 6-8 inches of wood chips to smother the plants.

An alternate method is to dig the entire plant, making sure to remove as much of the root as possible, since even tiny root slivers can sprout. This is possible with smaller plants but may be extremely difficult in the case of old established plants.

Dry foliage from these plants may cause as much discomfort as fresh; do not handle it with bare skin, even after it is dry. Do not burn the foliage of poison ivy, poison oak, or poison sumac. The irritating oils are carried in the smoke and can cause internal and external rashes.

Some garden weeds help attract beneficial insects, and some produce aromas that confuse destructive insects. But do not let the garden become overrun with weeds. An excess of weeds will rob desirable plants of valuable nutrients, water, and sunlight. Plants grown in a weed-free bed will yield more than those grown in a weedy plot.

Weeds make great compost. Make sure that they get buried or turned into the middle of a hot compost pile so that all the seeds are cooked and killed. Experts recommend not adding weed seeds to a compost pile unless you are an expert hot composter.

Bindweeds (wild morning glory), thistles, and nightshades should not be permitted to go to seed. Thistles store so much water and nutrients in their tissues that they can develop viable seed even after a mature plant has been cut down. Bury thistles deep within the compost pile and make sure they cook completely.

There is a natural order to weed control. Once you learn to work within this natural order, weed control becomes more tolerable. Simple ways to control weeds include:

* Deprive weeds of sunlight
* Manually remove weeds
* Never let weeds flower and go to seed
* Once a bed has been prepared, don't disturb weed seeds that are buried two inches or deeper in the soil. If they surface, they could sprout.

Preparing a New Garden Bed

If you decide to dig a new bed, remove as many weed roots as possible, especially the roots of perennial bindweeds, grasses, docks, blackberries, kudzu, and anything that spreads by root cuttings.

Remove as much as possible of foliage, stems and roots and destroy them with thorough hot composting. These tenacious plants will sprout from the smallest piece of root left in the soil. Some gardeners have good luck composting these weeds by first letting them dry out completely in the sun for a couple of weeks. Then they put the dead weeds in a hot compost pile. It may take several years to rid the soil of some of these pernicious weeds.

A "cleaning" crop such as potatoes will help rid the soil of weeds by shading them out with their dense canopy of leaves. The added bonus is that the potatoes are edible.

Don't let weeds get a strong start in new garden beds. Removing all the roots from a garden bed before planting is tedious, time-consuming work, but it saves hours of weeding over the life of the garden bed.

Toss annual weeds that have not gone to seed on the compost pile. If they have gone to seed, make sure they are soon covered with more compost so that the seeds will be "cooked" in the compost heap to render them inviable.

Chapter One, which is all about soils, includes more specific instructions on preparing new garden beds. If you do till deeply or double dig your garden beds, you are quite likely to expose weed seeds. As described below, regular attention to weed removal will soon reduce that problem.

An excellent no-till option when preparing a new bed is to leave the weeds and smother them with layers of newspaper ten to fifteen sheets thick. Only use newspaper with black ink; color inks may include heavy metals. Water down the newspaper immediately so that it won't blow away while you are working on the next step. Cover the newspaper with a mix of equal parts compost, leaf mold, manure, and top soil.

Pile this rich, fertile mix 6 to 12 inches deep, then top dress the bed with two to four inches of a good shredded bark mulch. This method will work even better if you cut the weeds short and just let the cuttings lie on the ground before you put down the newspaper.

The weeds will not be able to grow through the newspaper and soil mix. The newspaper will be adequately decomposed by the time new roots need to penetrate it.

Competitive Planting

In both vegetable and ornamental gardens, you can beat the weeds by planting fast-growing plants that shade the weeds so much that they can't grow. Most persistent weeds thrive in full sun, as you probably have observed.

Some of the cover crops or green manures are excellent at competing with weeds. For instance, alfalfa is an extremely vigorous grower that will compete successfully with even the toughest weeds, such as thistles.

Mow or cut the weeds to the ground in the spring, then rake the soil surface and plant alfalfa seed. You can mow the alfalfa periodically, leaving the mowings as sheet compost or putting them in the compost pile. Then you can till it under after a season or two, knowing that you have gotten rid of most of the weeds.

In the vegetable garden, corn is a fast-growing crop that will shade out the weeds once it gets a foot or two tall. Up to that point, you can hoe the emerging weeds a couple of times a week.

In the ornamental garden choose shrubs, perennials, and annual flowers for their vigorous, bushy growth that will shade out most of the weeds. For instance, you won't find many weeds in a healthy patch of zinnias or marigolds. Nor will you find weeds among sturdy plantings of perennial coneflowers. Shrubs such as forsythia, buddleia, and spirea will shade out the weeds, especially if they are planted closely. Until these plants get established, pull or hoe

Weeds are much easier to remove in loose organic soil. The entire root just pops out of the soil.

the weeds. A layer of mulch will help keep emerging weeds down.

Hand Weeding

Weeds are easy to pull in fertile, loose soil, especially when the soil is thoroughly moist after a rain. Then the entire root pops out of the compost-rich soil with ease. The weed tops break off in dry, hard-packed soil, leaving the root in the ground to resprout. Rich, porous organic soil will have weeds the first year. The second year there will be fewer weeds and by the third year, there will be hardly any weeds at all. The root systems of numerous grasses and weeds invade the soil rapidly. They compete for light and will rob other plants of precious nutrients and water. Dig and pull grasses and other pernicious weeds out by the roots regularly while they are still small and less deep-rooted.

Get in the habit of pulling a few weeds every time you are out in the garden. That is a key to efficient weed control.

Mechanical Weeding

Superficial soil cultivation with a hoe or other cultivator can stop weeds almost as soon as they germinate, before they get a good toehold in the soil. Most weed seeds that are buried more than two inches deep will not sprout. Those deeper weed seeds will not grow if you do not disturb the soil below that level. Small weeds are the easiest to control. A twice-weekly

Tilling the soil helps destroy weeds. Planting or transplanting soon after tilling gives new seeds and transplants a head start on weed seeds.

weed patrol with a hoe catches the weeds before they become a problem.

A weeding hoe slices like a knife. It is not for hacking and chopping. A slightly dull hoe can easily cut weeding efficiency in half. A sharp hoe slices weeds off at or just below soil level. The angle of a hoe blade can easily be changed to fit your body posture by placing it in a vice and bending the soft metal shank that attaches it to the handle.

It may take a little experimentation, but once you get a hoe adjusted, it is much easier and more efficient to use.

There are many different styles of weeding hoes. Check garden centers to find the one that suits you best. Some hoes have curved blades while others have straight ones.

Some have oscillating blades. There are gooseneck hoes and scuffle hoes. Those with smaller blades will, of course, be the better choice for heavily-planted or small gardens.

Whatever kind of hoe you choose, be sure that it is made of high-quality steel and has a handle that is comfortable for you to use.

High-wheel cultivators are miniature harrows or plows designed to be pushed by people rather than pulled by work animals. They come in several sizes with wheels that range from 8 to 22 inches in diame-

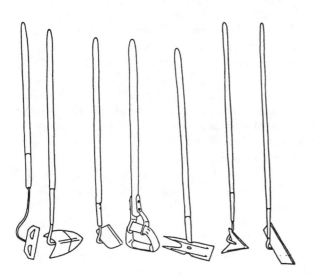

Choose a hoe that is right for the job.

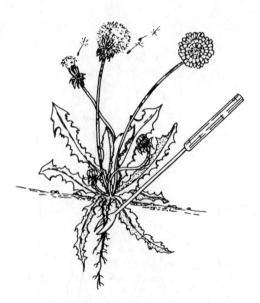

An asparagus fork (fork weeder) works very well to remove weeds that grow in rosette patterns with a strong central stem and root system.

ter. They can have cultivator tines, plow blades or weeding blades attached just behind the wheel. They are especially handy in vegetable gardens with long rows.

Several variations on this kind of cultivator are found in the comparatively new spiked-wheel cultivators. These handy gadgets have long straight handles and sets of revolving, tined wheels set together so that they can cultivate an area 6 to 10 inches wide. These are good for fairly small gardens with loose soil.

As with all garden tools, clean your hoe or cultivators and dry the blade or tines after you use it. And keep the blades sharp — it will make your work both easier and more efficient.

You can dig deep-rooted weeds with a fork weeder. Since it may cut tap roots well below the ground level, the weeds may return in four to six weeks. A similar result is achieved by using a shovel to chop weeds off below ground level. After 6 to 12 months of regular removal, nearly all weeds will disappear. They simply run out of energy to recover from the regular injury and removal of foliage and stems.

Another method for controlling dandelions and broadleaf weeds in lawns is to alter the pH of the soil. Dandelions in lawns are nearly eliminated by aerating and liming the soil to make it less acidic. Since this can take as long as three years to accomplish, it will work best in combination with the mechanical removal of weeds.

Regular hoeing of the soil surface before perennial weeds emerge will stop them before they start. Remove large perennial weed roots in long pieces if at all possible. If you do cut weed roots into small pieces,

A sharp hoe is one of the best weeding tools available.

some of them may return to haunt you by resprouting vigorously.

After hoeing the garden, leave annual weeds on the soil surface to dry out for a week or so. Then rake up the dehydrated residue and hot-compost it or leave it in place to cover with mulch. A regular program of mulching will usually smother most small weeds that were missed by the hoe. Weeds that do grow through mulch are amazingly easy to pull.

Mulching to Control Weeds

Many different mulches can be used to smother and exclude the sunlight from weeds.

* Although many gardeners do not like to use it, for both esthetic and organic reasons, black plastic can be very effective in eradicating both annual and perennial weeds. "Solarizing" is the technique of covering the ground to be cultivated with 2- to 4-mil blacks plastic for one to three months before cultivating. Lay out the plastic and anchor it down with soil, bricks or anything heavy. The opaque plastic deprives the foliage below of sunlight and during hot days it heats the surface layer of soil.

After one month of hot summer weather or three months of cool fall or spring weather, the majority of the vegetation below the plastic is dead, but soil life is still alive.

Remove the plastic and cover the soil with a six- to twelve-inch layer of compost and a couple of inches of manure and till under. Let the new garden bed settle for a about a week before planting.

Some gardeners cover the entire garden bed with black plastic and cut holes in which seedlings are

Weeds have a difficult time penetrating 6-10-page thick layers of newspaper. Wet the paper and cover with bark, or other similar kind of organic mulch, to keep it in place.

planted. A soaker hose can be laid underneath the plastic to irrigate.

Make sure to cut large enough holes so that plant stems do not touch the plastic. Black plastic gets very hot during the day but actually warms the soil very little. When a young, tender plant stem touches the hot, black plastic it will literally cook it at the soil line.

* Biodegradable plastic breaks down into frayed strips that flap in the wind after continued exposure to sunlight. It is not the most desirable to use. If you decide on biodegradable plastic, plan to use it only one year and then remove it completely before it shreds into unsightly pieces.

* Rock or rock dusts make an excellent mulch. Use rock mulches where they are readily available. Remember that although they become quite hot to touch on sunny days, they still protect the soil from evaporative moisture loss.

* Newspaper or brown paper shopping bags make an excellent weed barrier and mulch. If the paper is slightly wet it is easier to work with. Wet it thoroughly after application to keep it from blowing as you finish applying it. Inexpensive and readily available, newspaper layers should be at least six pages, preferably a dozen or more pages thick, before adding a soil or mulch covering to hold it in place. Cut an X through the newspaper with your garden knife to set a transplant or plant seed in the paper-mulched garden, covering with bark chips.

* Bark chips or compost alone can be used as weed barriers if laid down 4 inches or more thick. A covering that is a foot thick will stop all but the most persistent weed growth. A foot-thick layer of pine wood chips will even stop blackberries. For the best success, before applying the mulch, stamp down the weeds and blackberries so that they are on the ground. This solution is bulky, and heavy, but it is very effective. Acidic pine bark chips make an attractive ground cover that also smothers weeds.

* For shrubs that grow in more alkaline to neutral soils, use hardwood bark mulches, which are inclined

to raise the soil pH. Apply 2 to 4 inches thick over bare ground around shrubs. A layer 2 to 4 inches thick every year or so, whenever the previous layer has nearly decomposed, will keep tough weeds at bay. Occasional weeds that pop through mulch are easily hoed or pulled.

* If chips build up too thickly around the bud union on roses or any other grafted plant, suckers may result. Do not pile bark chips heavily around rhododendrons, azaleas, and other top feeders with shallow roots. The heavy bark chip mulch prevents feeding and will stunt growth. As a general rule, do not apply mulch more than 4 inches thick around plants; it may smother surface roots and change the ground level too much.

* Some bark chip suppliers have trucks with a long hose to blow the chips into the garden. This is a great option if chips must be moved uphill or over long distances.

* Do not lay down plastic and cover with bark chips! The first heavy rain will wash the chips away, exposing the plastic. And the plastic will not allow water to penetrate soil. The soil turns rock-hard and perennial grasses grow through cracks in the plastic.

* Woven weed barriers or strips of scrap carpet are sometimes used as weed barriers. Cover these barriers with rock or bark chips. The barrier lets water drain but will not let the weeds grow through. If you plan to till the ground in the future, do not use carpeting scraps as mulches — they become incorporated into the soil and top dressings to such a degree that it becomes difficult to remove them and impossible to till with them in place.

* Before applying mulches to weedy, grassy areas, mow or cut the area very short. Let the weeds lie where they were cut. This will return nutrients to the

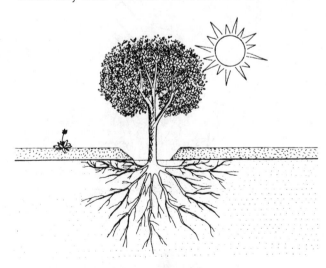

Woven weed barriers let moisture penetrate, but do not let weeds grow deep roots and get established..

soil. When cropped, short invasive broad-leafed and grassy weeds will find it more difficult to recover and grow through the mulch.

* Weeds are not all bad. Some weeds, like plantain, will improve the soil structure.

Although they can be unattractive and may attract undesirable insects, such as aphids, they can serve as a cost-free cover crop that can be tilled under whenever you wish to use the plot again.

Lawn Weeds

Lawn weeds with rosette-like growth such as dandelions and daisies are easy to kill with a pinch of table salt, which is sodium chloride, NaCL. Better yet, use the chemical ammonium sulfate, $(NH_4)2SO_4$, the inorganic fertilizer that contains 24 percent sulfur. The sulfur will kill the weeds.

Use just a pinch of ammonium sulfate on small weeds, slightly more for larger ones. Drop into the center of the rosette.

Apply this chemical salt after a rain or light overhead sprinkling so the dry salt will dissolve into the center of the weed. The salt kills the growing center of the weed down to the root. The excess is diluted and dispersed into the soil and there is not enough to be toxic to surrounding grass. Ammonium sulfate kills

Pouring ammonium sulfate, a common chemical lawn fertilizer, on the center of weeds that grow in a rosette is a good weed control.

weeds and leaches out of the soil quicker than table salt.

If you remove the top one-third of a weed's root, and cover it with soil, chances are good that it will not sprout again. If, in addition, a bit of salt, preferably ammonium sulfate, is applied to the top of the broken root in the ground, the weed is even more likely to die.

Where there are pernicious weeds in fairly small areas that are close to the kitchen, an even simpler solution exists; pour boiling water over the weeds. Repeat the treatment if necessary.

Moss Removal

Moss can be a hazard on paths and brick patios. It can be slick as ice in humid climates or when wet. Mosses often grow in areas of poor, compacted soil where there is little soil aeration. Loosening the soil and increasing its fertility can discourage the recurrence of moss once you've killed it.

Moss also can be a handsome ground cover in shady moist areas. Before mounting a no-exceptions extermination campaign on mosses, assess their positive and negative values.

The boiling water treatment is the easiest and most environmentally sound treatment for moss removal. Boiling water will effectively kill moss on bricks and soil.

Some experts recommend using gasoline, kerosene or similar petroleum products to kill mosses and weeds. Knowing that this treatment will sterilize the soil, a condition that may persist over several years, we caution against this treatment. If you must, use it only in places that you are sure you will never want to plant, such as driveways and sidewalks.

Fairy Rings and Other Mushrooms

Fairy rings are fungi, mushrooms that grow in a circle on lawns and gardens, often after a rainy spell. Mushrooms are the spore-containing fruiting bodies of the mycelium, the underground vegetative part of mushrooms.

Since mycelia can cover large areas, there is no effective way to get rid of the mushrooms permanently, but they will do gardens and lawns no harm. Their place in nature is to break down organic matter in the soil, so their very appearance is a positive sign of the existence of organic matter in the soil.

Rather than being frustrated by their existence, try to enjoy observing these curious evidences of one of the world's most unusual plant groups.

Herbicides

Safer's potassium-based, acid SharpShooter™ kills foliage on contact. It must be applied heavily on dry foliage for best results. Once the spray is applied, the foliage is dead in a few hours.

There is a great deal of concern in the gardening world about the chemicals that are manufactured solely to be used to kill undesirable weeds. The best-known and presumed safest herbicide today is glyphosate, known by the brand names, Kleenup and Roundup. It adsorbs or binds to the soil particles and so does not move around in the soil, according to the manufacturer.

Soil microorganisms break glyphosate down into carbon dioxide, nitrogen, water, and phosphate. The more microbial activity in the soil, the faster it breaks down. (Microbes are most active in warmer soils with plenty of moisture and a pH of 6.5 to 7.0.) Glyphosate is effective on both annual and perennial weeds when applied to growing foliage. Since it gets into the plants' systems, it kills the plant, including perennials.

Used as directed, in cases where other solutions are impractical or impossible, glyphosate is an effective alternative. As always, be sure to read the label and other information in the package before using.

Newer products that are acceptable to organic gardeners are fatty-acid-based herbicides, including Safer's SharpShooter™.

They provide good spot control, especially for annual weeds. They will kill the tops of perennial weeds, but the plants are likely to come back from the roots. To achieve the best results with herbicides, use them during hot, sunny weather when the plants are actively growing.

Herbicides vary greatly in both their effectiveness and their persistence in the environment. There are herbicides that are dangerous to apply near crops, especially food crops, but also near ornamental plants. In some cases, the slightest bit of overspray will stunt or kill plants that you want, and contaminate edibles. In other cases, some herbicides, even·in very small amounts, are dangerous, even life-threatening to animals and humans.

This is why it is so very important to read labels carefully and to use alternative, more conservative methods to control weeds whenever possible.

Common Weeds

It's important to know the enemy, and weeds are no exception. The following plants are common weeds throughout most of the country.

We have not included those plants which are also considered wildflowers, for example, evening primrose, goldenrod, yarrow, and coneflower. They are such handsome prospects for native and wildflower ornamental gardens that we can't really count them in with such plants as bindweed and ragweed.

Learn to recognize the following weeds from these descriptions and illustrations, especially when they are young seedlings, and you will be better able to keep your garden weed free. The weeds described are arranged botanically, by families, with the grasses first and the composites (daisy-like flowers) last.

BROOMSEDGE (*Andropogon virginicus*), a perennial, is a grassy plant 1 to 3 feet tall with a fibrous root system. The panicle (flower) has 2 to 4 finger-like clusters about an inch long with tufts of white hairs enclosed by reddish-brown leaves. Found mostly on poor land with low fertility, it disappears with fertilizer programs.

BROOMSEDGE

TRIPLE AWN grass

TRIPLE AWN grass (*Aristida oligantha*), an annual, is a grass 12 to 26 inches high with fibrous roots. The panicles are loose with narrow, one-flowered spikelets. Seeds bear three bristles (awns) 1 to 3 inches long. Found on open, dry, sterile soil, especially formerly cultivated, abandoned land.

DOWNY BROME GRASS

DOWNY BROME GRASS (*Bromus tectorum*), a winter annual or biennial, is a 6 to 24 inch high grass with fibrous roots. The light green leaves are covered with long, soft hairs. The often purplish panicles are quite dense, soft, and drooping, and appear in the spring. It is found in wastelands, meadows, and pastures.

LARGE CRABGRASS (*Digitaria sanguinalis*), an annual, has stout, mostly prostrate stems up to 3 feet long that root at the joints. The panicle has 3 to 10 segments in whorls at the top of the stems. It grows where the ground is warm and flowers in late summer to early fall. A serious weed in southern areas, it's found in lawns, gardens and fields.

LARGE CRABGRASS

BARNYARD GRASS

BARNYARD GRASS (*Echinochloa crusgalli*), an annual grass, grows 1 to 4 feet tall with thick coarse stems that branch at the base. Light green leaves are about ½ inch wide and panicles bearing compact side branches are green or purplish. Florets have short stiff bristles. Found in crop fields in late summer and fall.

STINKGRASS

STINKGRASS (*Eragrostis cilianensis*), an annual, grows 1 to 2 feet tall, has fibrous roots and flat, smooth leaves. The branched panicles have numerous spikelets about ½ inch long, each containing 20 to 40 florets or seeds that are dark gray-green to purple. The egg-shaped seeds are orange-red. This moderately serious weed has an un-unpleasant odor and is found in waste places and cultivated fields.

WILD BARLEY (*Hordeum jubatum*), a perennial also known as squirrel tail, grows 1 to 2 feet tall and has dense, fibrous roots. The alternate leaves are rough on upper surfaces. The flower spike is 2 to 5 inches long, nodding, with soft, yellowish-green or purple bristles about 2 inches long. Wild barley is found in pastures and other uncultivated areas.

WILD BARLEY

WITCHGRASS

WITCHGRASS (*Panicum capillare*), a spreading and branched annual with fibrous roots, grows 10 to 30 inches tall. Leaves and leaf sheaths are covered with soft hairs. The branched panicles spread as they open. Found in cultivated fields, meadows, gardens, and waste areas.

GREEN FOXTAIL

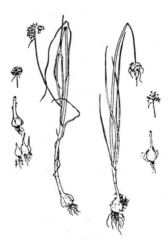

WILD GARLIC/ONION

GREEN FOXTAIL (*Setaria viridis*), an annual, grows 1 to 3 feet tall and has fibrous roots. Leaves are hairless and panicles are dense, 1 to 3 inches long and drooping near their ends. A serious widespread weed, it is commonly found throughout the country.

YELLOW FOXTAIL (*Setaria lutescens*), an annual, grows 1 to 2 feet tall and branches more than the other foxtails. The leaves are flat, often with a spiral twist and have long hairs on the upper surface near the base. The panicle is dense and erect. This serious weed is found everywhere except in woods.

SLENDER RUSH (*Juncus tenuis*), a perennial sedge, grows 6 inches to 2 feet tall and has fibrous roots. The round, hollow stems are not jointed. Narrow grass-like leaves are usually at the base of the stems. Flowers are in clusters of three at the tips of the stems. Rush is found along paths and roadsides, and in pastures and waste places.

YELLOW FOXTAIL

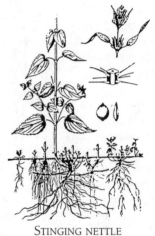

STINGING NETTLE

and bulblet roots, grows 1 to 3 feet high and has slender hollow, roundish leaves that are attached to a lower stem. Flowers are greenish-white on short stems above aerial bulblets. A serious weed, it is found in grain fields, pastures, and lawns.

WILD ONION (*Allium canadense*), a perennial, is similar to the above and is found in same places, but does not produce underground bulblets. Leaves rise from the base of the plant and are not hollow.

STINGING NETTLE (*Urtica procera*), a perennial, grows 2 to 7 feet high and has slightly branched stems that are covered with many stinging hairs. The coarse, dark green leaves are 3 to 6 inches long, pointed, with toothed margins, and are covered with stinging hairs. Separate male and female, are green, without petals, and grow in clusters in leaf axils. It is found in wastelands, roadsides, barnyards, fence rows, and thickets.

KNOTWEED

SLENDER RUSH

WILD GARLIC (*Allium vineale*), a perennial with bulb

KNOTWEED (*Polygonum aviculare*), an annual, has bluish-green, wiry, leafy stems that extend 4 inches to 2 feet in all directions and form a dense mat. Leaves are alternate and oblong. Flowers are small, yellow or white, and form in clusters at the junctions of leaves and

WILD BUCKWHEAT

stems. Found in hard, trampled areas of lawns, roadways, paths, and in yards and lawns.

WILD BUCK-WHEAT (*Polygonum convolvulus*), an annual, is a smooth slender vining weed that is branched at its base. Alternate heart-shaped leaves have smooth edges and small, greenish-white flowers grow in leaf axils. Seeds are triangular, black and quite shiny. A serious crop weed, it's found in both cultivated and uncultivated area, and is often mistaken for field bindweed but it is annual and has different seeds and flowers.

PENNSYLVANIA SMARTWEED (*Polygonum pennsylvanicum*), an annual, grows 1 to 4 feet tall and has stems that are smooth, swollen at their nodes, and branching. The alternate, smooth, pointed leaves are 2 to 6 inches long and the pink or rose flowers have five petals and grow along short spikes. It is found in wastelands, ditches and cultivated areas.

PENNSYLVANIA SMARTWEED

CURLED DOCK

CURLED DOCK (*Rumex crispus*), a perennial, grows 1 to 4 feet tall and has a large yellowish taproot. Stems are smooth and single or multiple. Leaves, mostly from the plant base, are smooth, 6 to 12 inches long and are lance-shaped with curly edges. Flower

LAMBSQUARTER

clusters are dense, grow at stem tips and are small and greenish, turning to red-brown when mature. It is found in pastures, roadsides, and waste areas.

LAMBSQUARTER (*Chenopodium album*), an annual, grows 3 to 4 feet tall, has a short taproot and alternate leaves that are 1 to 3 inches long and usually white mealy-coated, especially on the underside and when young. Small green flowers grow at the ends of branches and in leaf axils. It is often found in cultivated crops. Lambsquarter is easy to pull and is tops to eat as a steamed green — "collect your dinner vegetable as you weed the garden."

TUMBLEWEED (*Amaranthus albus*), an annual, grows 1 to 3 feet tall and has small leaves and small green flowers. The plant breaks off at the ground when mature and rolls over open fields with the wind. Plants often pile up against fences. It is found in both cultivated and fallow land.

TUMBLEWEED

PROSTRATE PIGWEED

PROSTRATE PIGWEED (*Amaranthus graecizans*), an annual, is a prostrate plant with 1 to 3 foot stems that are smooth, reddish, and erect at their ends. The small, alternate leaves are eggshaped, and inconspicuous flowers grow in the leaf

ROUGH PIGWEED

axils. This weed is found in gardens, fields and wastelands.

ROUGH PIGWEED (*Amaranthus retroflexus*), an annual, grows to 6 feet or more in height with a shallow red taproot and rough freely-branching stems. Leaves are dull green and small green flowers grow in dense panicles at branch ends and in leaf axils. Found in wastelands, cultivated fields, fence rows and yards.

PURSLANE (*Portulaca oleracea*), an annual, grows into a prostrate mat up to a foot or more in diameter. The leaves are alternate or in clusters, and are smooth, thick and juicy. Small yellow flowers appear in leaf and branch axils. It is often found in fields, wastelands, and gardens. This is another

PURSLANE

tasty edible weed that is regularly enjoyed in Mexico and France, usually as a steamed vegetable.

YELLOW WOOD SORREL

YELLOW WOOD SORREL (*Oxalis europaea*), a perennial or annual depending on the climate, grows 4 to 18 inches tall with weak, branched stems and sour leaves that have three heart-shaped leaflets. The five-petaled, yellow flowers grow in clusters. Rocket-shaped seed pods throw seeds, making this a serious

POISON IVY

weed in some areas. It is found in wastelands, pastures, lawns and nurseries.

POISON IVY (*Rhus radicans*) a woody perennial that grows as a low shrub or as a woody vine that climbs to the tops of trees. Leaves each have three shiny leaflets with smooth or irregular shallow notches. Small green flowers are five-petaled and in a head 1 to 3 inches long. Berries are white, round, and hard. All parts of the plants, fresh or dry, contain an oil that will cause skin irritation and blistering. The bright reds and yellows of fall foliage tempt the unwary. It is found in open woods, wasteland, old orchards, fence rows, and thickets.

Water hemlock

Water hemlock (*Cicuta maculata*), a perennial, grows 3 to 5 feet tall. The smooth stem branches near the top and may have purple streaks. Compound, alternate leaves are 8 to 12 inches long and smooth with toothed edges. Small white flower forms at the top of the plant in several small umbels. This is poison hemlock, and is found in low, wet lands and swamps, often in or at the edge of water.

WHORLED MILKWEED

WHORLED MILKWEED (*Asclepias verticillata*), a perennial, grows 1 to 2 feet tall, has milky sap and has a smooth slender stem that only branches at the top. The light green leaves are in groups of 3 to 7 in whorls around the stem. Greenish-white flowers have five petals and are in clusters at the top of the plant or in leaf axils. Seed pods are 2 to 4 inches long and contain numerous flat brown seeds, each with a tuft of hairs at its tip. The seeds fly away in the slightest breeze. It is found in fields, waste lands, and pastures.

FIELD BINDWEED

FIELD BINDWEED (*Convolvulus arvensis*), a perennial, has a large root system that may go as much as 25 to 30 feet deep. Slender, smooth stems grow 2 to 7 feet and more, and the plant will vine and spread up trees and fences as well as along the ground. Leaves are ovate with basal lobes. White or pink flowers are like morning glories and about an inch in diameter. It is found in all cultivated and noncultivated areas and is a serious weed that is difficult to get rid of.

STICKTIGHT (*Lappula echinata*), an annual, grows 1 to 2 feet tall and is covered with rough hairs. Leaves are narrow and oblong, 1 to 2 inches long and lower ones form a rosette at the ground line. Small flowers are blue with five petals and grow at bases of small leafy bracts along upper branches.

STICKTIGHT

Seed pods are rough with hooked spines. It is found in wooded areas, wasteland, and roadsides in dry soil.

COMMON RAGWEED (*Ambrosia artemisiifolia*), an annual, grows 1 to 4 feet tall and is shallow-rooted with nearly smooth leaves that are deeply cut into several lobes. Male flowers are in small clusters at branch ends and female flowers, fewer in number, are in leaf

COMMON RAGWEED

axils and forks of upper branches. Common ragweed is found in cultivated fields, old pastures, wasteland, and roadsides.

GIANT RAGWEED (*Ambrosia trifida*), an annual, grows 4 to 18 feet tall depending on soil fertility and moisture. Paired leaves are large, slightly hairy, and with three, or sometimes, five lobes. Male flowers are abundant on ends of branches and female flowers are sparse in upper leaf axils. It is found in bottom lands, mostly in moist, fertile soils.

GIANT RAGWEED

HORSEWEED (*Erigeron canadensis*), an annual, grows 1 to 6 feet tall on stout, unbranched stems with bristly hairs. The leaves are linear, dark green and either entire or toothed. The numerous flower heads are small and have greenish-white ray flowers around yellow disk flowers. Horseweed is found in wastelands, roadsides, and pastures.

HORSEWEED

PRICKLY LETTUCE (*Lactuca scariola*), an annual, grows 2 to 6 feet, has a large taproot and a stiff hollow stem that contains milky sap and is prickly on the lower part. The large coarse leaves have prickles along the margins and lower surfaces of midribs. The flower heads are open clusters of yellow ray flowers. It is found in wasteland and roadsides.

Prickly lettuce

DANDELION (*Taraxacum officinale*), a perennial, grows in rosettes with leaves 3 to 10 inches long that grow from a crown at or a little below the soil surface. It has milky sap and a thick taproot. The yellow flower heads of many ray florets are on a long, bare, hollow stem. Seeds are elongated and have a slender tip with a tuft of hairs. Found in lawns, waste places, gardens, and meadows. Early spring dandelion greens are edible, and often used in salads or as steamed greens. The flowers often are used to make wine.

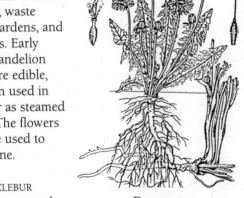

DANDELION

COCKLEBUR (*Xanthium pennsylvanicum*), an annual, grows 2 to 4 feet tall and is normally bushy. Stem is ridged, rough, and hairy, and alternate leaves are triangular, toothed or lobed and rough. Small male and female flowers are separate but grow together in clusters on upper leaf axils. The mature bur is hard and woody with hooked prickles. It is found in poor pastures, roadsides, cultivated and abandoned fields.

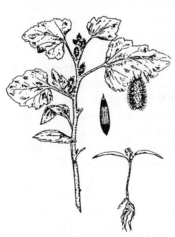

COCKLEBUR

Chapter Five

Pests & Diseases

About Pests & Diseases

Most plant pests are insects, small animals with segmented bodies, antennae, six legs, and, in the adult stage, usually with wings. Insects have four life stages — egg, larva, pupa and adult. Other invertebrate plant pests include mites with eight legs and no wings. Mites hatch from eggs into small forms of the adult stage and do not go through the extraordinary metamorphosis that transforms insects from larvae to adults. Nematodes, microscopic roundworms that live in the soil and feed in or on plant roots, make up yet another group of plant pests. Slugs and snails, serious plant pests in some areas, are animals from another invertebrate group.

Mammals, including rabbits, squirrels, gophers, woodchucks and deer can be aggravating plant pests that are hard to keep out of the garden. Under some circumstances, local dogs and cats can become unwelcome nuisances.

Plant diseases are categorized into three groups based on causes — fungus, bacterium or virus. The vast majority of plant diseases are caused by funguses. In addition, there are disease-like conditions caused by cultural conditions.

The kinds of pests and diseases that you may face will depend upon the plants you are growing, the weather, the geographical location, and the specific location of the garden (i.e. shade, sun, close to the house, near woods, etc.).

When plants show signs of pests or disease, analyze the symptoms. Identification of the specific cause is the first step toward treating the problem. Are there signs that something is eating the plants? Plant pests may chew plant parts (slugs and cutworms), suck the sap (scale and mites), or tunnel through the foliage (leaf miners).

Symptoms of disease include spots of various sizes and colors, abnormal localized swellings (galls), blights (sudden death of foliage, branches or flowers), rots (general decomposition of plant tissue), cankers (dead areas on bark or stems which are often discolored and may be raised or sunken), and general dwindling of plant health.

If large animals are the problem, you will see signs that they have been there. Animal droppings, broken plants, and eaten or missing foliage, fruit, or flowers will tell you that something besides you is enjoying your garden.

If you are unsure of the identification of a disease, pest, or other plant problem, get some help. Ask your county's Cooperative Extension Service agent, or nearby nursery or garden center expert. Wrap a fresh sample of the affected plant part in a bag and take it to the expert. If you see the insect or other pest, take it as well.

Make sure to take a large enough sample, such as a branch containing several leaves. Also take a sample of healthy growth if possible. Record some notes about the plant, such as the age, name, and location in the garden. Include care information, including any fertilizer or pesticide applications and watering frequency during the season.

Nursery people, Cooperative Extension Service agents, Master Gardener hotlines, and state nursery associations are often able to tell you what pests and diseases are likely to affect your area, and sometimes may know a few months before major infestations occur. They can help you learn how to spot the insects, fungus, or other diseases and conditions causing the infestation, and identify and an appropriate remedy. If a chemical pesticide is recommended, you can ask for an alternative, or organic, remedy and a list of preventive measures you can take.

Remember that pesticides are designed to kill organisms; they are all toxic. Just because a pesticide is botanically or naturally derived does not mean that it is safe. In fact, naturally derived pyrethrum is more toxic than malathion. However, the length of time that pyrethrum is toxic to insects and other organisms is shorter than that for most chemical pesticides. The main benefit of using botanical pesticides is that long-term toxicity is generally low.

Since home gardeners do not practice mono-culture, their gardens are usually not plagued with the massive insect infestations experienced on large farms, so they can use different tactics than large growers to combat problems.

Appropriate Philosophies for Managing Pests & Diseases

"One bug does not a problem make," says Robert Kourik in his book, *Your Edible Landscape-Naturally* (Santa Rosa, 1986.). The point is that you should not go crazy and spray toxic insecticides unless there is a massive infestation and no alternative solution. Toxic broad-spectrum sprays kill all insects, both good and bad! In many cases, there is a "good," or beneficial, insect that will attack and bring it under control.

One of the best ways to develop a habit of conservative pest control is to educate yourself in the ways of insects. Go outside and watch insects. You may find it fascinating. With careful observation, you will notice, for example, that snow peas usually do not get infested with aphids until after the peak harvest. You will discover that a few aphids on tomatoes or other plants create no problem, that ants gravitate to aphids in order to harvest the sweet honeydew given off by aphids, and that ladybird beetles and their larvae, which are aphid predators, usually are present where there are lots of aphids.

One estimate says that unchecked aphid growth would bury the earth a mile deep in aphids in one year! There are natural checks and balances at work to prevent that. In gardens, there also are checks and balances at work that make it possible to coexist with potential pests and still enjoy ample harvests.

Pesticides are a quick fix, but do not prevent pests from returning without constant re-application. The real solution to the pest problem is to eliminate the cause, not to treat the symptom with a quick fix approach.

Some insects are easier to control at a specific stage of their life – egg, larva, pupa, or adult. Note that we use the word "control," not the word "eliminate." Pests are never totally eradicated with any type of spraying. The pests always seem to reproduce faster than their beneficial counterparts. The best form of control is coexistence. Simply try to maintain a healthy balance between the good and bad insects. The better you understand insect and predator life cycles, the easier they are to control.

Organic gardens, unlike gardens treated with some pesticides, attract a large and diversified population of birds, insects, small mammals, amphibians, and microorganisms that together create a natural balance.

Integrated Pest Management (IPM) & Plant Health Care Programs (PHC)

Integrated pest management (IPM) was developed for commercial pest control, but the concept can be applied to even the smallest garden, and has gained popularity with home gardeners. IPM consists of the following:

* Identify the pest and use knowledge of its biology and natural enemies to control.
* Monitor pest populations using observation and traps.
* Discern the extent of injury to plants.
* Establish a tolerable threshold of injury.
* Use cultural, biological, and mechanical methods to control unacceptable pest populations with selected use of least toxic pesticides as a last resort.
* Keep records and evaluate the effects of each control strategy.

Pest controls include the following, simple techniques:

* Handpick or squash pests as soon as they are noticed.
* Spray insects with a jet of cold water.
* Use natural predators that consume pests.
* Use parasitic insects that kill particular pests by living on or in them.
* Use microbial organisms to make pests sick.
* Rotate crops.
* Use disease-resistant varieties.
* Keep a clean and tidy garden.
* Destroy diseased plants.
* Maintain healthy, fertile soil that has abundant microbial life.

Blasting insects, especially aphids and mites, off foliage with a jet of water is a marvelous deterrent and pest control. The blasted bugs and mites have a difficult time returning for a comfortable meal. Most of these pests are comparatively stationary sap suckers, the blast of water knocks them to the ground where they starve, die of exposure, or get eaten by beneficial insects.

Washing insects off foliage also cleans plants of the fine layer of dust that builds up in dry weather. This layer inhibits plant transpiration and provides places for pests, such as spider mites, to hide.

Insect larvae, cutworms, nematodes, root maggots, and wireworms are most common soilborne pests. Regular hoeing between garden plants brings some of these to the surface where they are exposed to fatal sunlight and air, or birds eat them.

Plants in organic gardens may suffer cosmetically from minor pest damage, but on the whole may be stronger than chemically grown plants, and better able to fend off these attackers.

A 6X magnifying glass or a 30 X light scope will help identify tiny eggs and pests.

All pesticides kill, and are toxic! Just because a pesticide is botanical, organic or natural in origin does not mean that it is not toxic. In fact, pyrethrum is more toxic than malathion, however the pyrethrum's toxic life is shorter than most chemical pesticides.

The main benefit of using botanical insecticides is that the long-term toxicity is generally low. They do not accumulate in the environment, animals, and wildlife the way many synthetic sprays do.

Plant Health Care Programs

The IPM philosophy promises to continue to be popular with all gardeners. Horticultural experts have been saying, "Why should we concentrate on 'managing pests' when what we want is healthy plants?"

That has resulted in a new, more encompassing horticultural philosophy that is fast gaining advocates. Called Plant Health Care (PHC), this program calls for addressing the entire garden and keeping this larger view as you plan and care for plants. The concept was articulated by Roger Funk of the Davey Tree Expert Company in the 1980s. In essence PHC is as follows.

First of all, identify and inventory all of your garden plants. Make regular health inspections. List your plant's needs. Finally, use only environmentally conscious pest management programs.

Funk stresses the fact that healthy plants get few diseases and are bothered by few pests. When plants are stressed by the wrong amounts of nutrients and water, by heat or cold, or by other environmental factors, they will be more susceptible to pests and diseases.

Try to incorporate the IPM methods into an overall PHC program. It sounds technical and overly structured, but in truth, it comes down to the application of a healthy dose of common sense.

Prevention of Pest & Disease Problems

Cleanliness and sanitation constitute the first step in preventing harmful insects and disease. Clean gardens have fewer problems with pests. Diseased plants, and rotting fruits and nuts should be hauled off, burned or buried deep in a "hot" compost pile. Leaves that are infected with scab, brown rot, powdery mildew, shot hole fungus, or peach leaf curl should not be used as mulch or cold compost.

Examine bulbs, corms and tubers closely before buying; a healthy one is evenly firm with a strong, fleshy skin. Shy away from those with bruises and loose skins; they may have suffered damage, and may grow poorly.

Plant disease and insect-resistant varieties. With an increasing number of new varieties available, it is much easier to find seeds and plants that conform to your special climate conditions.

F[1] hybrids grow more vigorously than most open-pollinated varieties. This condition is known as hybrid vigor. An F[1] hybrid is the first-generation product of two different parents. Plants grown from the seeds of F[1] hybrids will be open-pollinated and will include reversions to the parent types.

The more vigorous a plant is, the less susceptible it will be to pests and diseases. Plants that are over- or under-fertilized are more susceptible to pest attack. Pest and disease prevention tips include the following:

* Plant companion plants that repel or confuse pests with scents or tastes.
* Disinfect contaminated tools.

Blasting insects off foliage with a fine jet of water is a simple and safe way to discourage many pest insects.

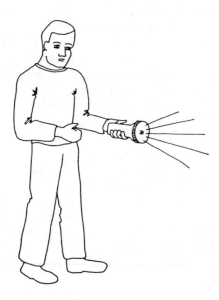

Patrol the garden on summer evenings with a flashlight when many garden pests feed. You may find snails and slugs on leaves and cutworms at the base of plants. Simply hand-pick these undesirables and drop them in a jar of kerosene, soapy water, or strong salt water. With luck, you will also find numerous desirable earthworms and maybe some frogs and toads.

* Keep foliage dry. Do not expose foliage to night moist.
* Select strong vigorous plants.
* Grow varieties suited to your area.
* Purchase disease- and pest-resistant seeds and plants.
* Do not crowd plants.
* Rotate crops.
* Identify pests and learn their life cycles.
* Remove dead and diseased plant parts from the garden.
* Never let the plants want for water or nutrients and keep an eye peeled for marauding pests.

Companion Plants

Everyone agrees that many plants affect one another. The question is the extent and significance of that influence. Intercropping different plants in order to control pests and disease is called companion planting. Only a few studies have been done that prove the effectiveness of various combinations, but many organic gardeners report good results with specific companion plantings. Companion planting is riddled with folklore so there is still a lot to learn in this area, but it seems worth considering.

The companion plant tradition holds that certain plants may produce substances that repel pests, and some plants when planted together will benefit each other's growth. Companion plants are also used as trap crops to attract pests, and keep them from dining on more desirable vegetable and flower crops.

Some marigold cultivars of the *Tagetes erecta* and *T. patula* species, according to Connecticut Agricultural Experiment Station studies, will repel nematodes, also known as eelworms, from the soil for two to three years if they are planted in an infested area and then tilled under. Planting them alone doesn't accomplish anything, and numerous tests indicate that they have no effect on insects above the ground.

When you plant cool-season lettuces in with tall, sun-loving tomatoes, the tomatoes provide shade for the lettuce. This is another practical form of companion planting.

Some years back, Peter Tomkins and Christopher Bird in *The Secret Life of Plants* (Harper & Row, 1973) described how plants can communicate with each other about everything from the weather to attacks by insects and humans. At the time, many scientists scoffed at their notions.

More recent scientific studies indicated that their observations have some validity. For instance, a study by a U.S. Forest Service experiment station in Lansing, Michigan indicated that drought-stressed trees emit ultrasonic sounds as a result of their water columns breaking in the sapwood. Their leaves change color and the salts, sugars, and amino acids become more concentrated in above-ground tissues. Trees and shrubs stressed by drought produce more volatile compounds, and thicker compounds, such as resins and latex, which some plants produce when wounded, flow more slowly.

All of this communicates to bark and wood-invading insects that these plants will be easy to invade. In this case, the trees' communications are to their detriment. In the garden, you may notice that insects are attracted to the odor of bruised stems — an observation similar to the Michigan study.

Plants can regulate pests in many ways. They can produce odors that deter and confuse pests. They can act as a "trap" plant by alluring pests away from the primary crop plant. Some gardeners plant Brussels sprouts to trap aphids and keep them away from the tomatoes and cucumbers.

Nasturtiums also work well to attract aphids. But be prepared to intervene with a soap solution or botanical spray if pests start to migrate to nearby food crops. Or just cut off the insect infected host plants and bury them in the compost pile.

Fall cleanup is one of the best ways to interrupt the life cycles of overwintering pests. Remove all plant residue from the garden and till the soil to dislodge eggs, larvae, and pupae from below the surface so that birds can eat them or they perish from exposure to the elements.

Nematodes and numerous flying insects are said to be repelled by chrysanthemums. The edible garland chrysanthemum is a favorite among many gardeners because it serves so many purposes — it's edible, repels nematodes and flying insects, and also is very pretty.

Members of the allium family — garlic, leeks, onions, and scallions — help repel many insects, and repel moles as well. These plants do not take up much space and can easily be interplanted among most all garden plants.

Companion plants can provide food, habitat, and breeding grounds for beneficial insects. Many adult beneficial insects are attracted to pollen and bright colors.

Two plant families that beneficial insects are especially attracted to are the parsley family (*Umbelliferae*) and the sunflower family (*Compositae*). Plants in the *Umbelliferae* family have flowers that resemble umbrellas — well-known examples include dill, carrot, parsnip, and Queen Anne's lace. Examples of the *Compositae* are daisies, yarrow, sunflowers, goldenrod, strawflower, zinnia, and santolina. Plants in this family have a central disc of tiny flowers surrounded by a multitude of ray flowers — together they make up

what we see as a single flower.

Little scientific research has been completed on attracting good, or beneficial, insects to the garden. Couple this with the fact that insect behavior can change rapidly and is different in different climates. However, there are a few facts that are agreed upon: blooming, pollen producing calendulas, marigolds, nasturtiums and poppies help repel aphids from tomatoes, roses, and other plants. These flowers themselves do not actually repel the aphids. They attract hover-flies, which lay eggs that hatch into larvae which eat thousands of aphids.

There are many different species of hover flies, also called syrphid flies, throughout the world. The female hover fly needs protein provided by pollen before she is able to lay eggs. Though not as well known as ladybugs, hover flies are one of the most valuable garden predators. Another example is the thread-waisted wasp which is attracted by daisies and dines on cabbage worms.

Anti-Companion Plants

Anti-companion plants exude chemicals that promote their own growth and discourage the growth of other plants. This is called allelopathy. Sunflowers, for example, produce natural chemicals that inhibit the growth of potatoes and other plants.

Black walnut trees produce substances that stunt and may kill tomatoes, blackberries, alfalfa, asparagus, chrysanthemums, potatoes, apple and pine trees. Some grasses, including the foxtails, are known to inhibit the growth of corn.

Leafy spurge, a weed, will reduce tomato growth when even small amounts of it are mixed into the soil. Nutsedge and quackgrass, also weeds, will inhibit corn growth.

Crop Rotation & Timing

Crop rotation is the practice of cultivating a different crop in the same area every year. These crops should be from different families for best results, because each family has its own nutrient needs and usually does not share diseases or attract the same insects as the others.

By rotating these family members from bed to bed, you will have less problems with pests that remain in the soil between crops and with soilborne diseases. For example, do not plant melons where you last grew cucumbers. Time plantings of annuals so that they are growing when populations of their particular pests are naturally low. Plant members of the cabbage family in early spring to mature early in the summer, or plant in mid-summer to mature late in the fall. If you do that, aphids will not be as aggravating a pest.

Delaying planting of corn and beans until after the soil has thoroughly warmed will reduce seed maggot damage. Make changes in planting or harvest times in order to avoid stages in insect pest life cycles that are damaging to your crops, such as when eggs hatch and larvae begin to feed.

Large Pest Predators

Encourage the following large predators to patrol your garden. They will consume large numbers of plant pests.

The number of insects that bats catch each night is close to their body weight. Among their targets are

numerous night-flying moths. Many of these moths are destructive caterpillars in their larval forms. Install bat houses and garden ponds to attract bats. Your local Audubon Society or conservation department can help you find patterns for building bat houses or sources for buying them ready-made. Garden ponds will attract insects which will in turn attract bats.

* Birds may eat blueberries and cherries but they make up for it by consuming many caterpillars, aphids, and other insects that go unnoticed. As you will learn, many wild birds are omnivores, eating both plants (usually fruit and seeds) and animals (usually insects) in season. Entice these predators by having birdhouses, birdseed, suet, bird baths, and plants for cover in the garden. Some insect-eating birds include: bluebirds, chickadees, titmice, mockingbirds, orioles, purple martins, robins, thrashers, warblers, and wrens.

Purple martins live in colonies and are adept at catching and eating insects in flight. You can buy or build martin houses for your yard. Check with the local Audubon Society or conservation department to obtain building plans.

You can attract wild birds by growing plants with edible fruits. Many birds prefer tart, wild berries to sweet cultivated berries. Include wild red and black chokecherry, barberry, hackberry, sumac, mountain ash, buckthorn, and viburnums in your ornamental plantings to defer their attention from the edible berries you prefer. Birds also like to eat the fruits and seeds of arborvitae, cedar, hemlock, and many pines.

Some insect-eating birds are attracted to suet. For larger birds, bind a lump of suet to a tree branch. To attract small birds, hang a lump of suet or a pinecone soaked in suet from a string. Peanut butter is a good substitute for suet.

Birds like to seek the protection of a tree or bush when they are startled, so the more trees and dense shrubs you have for cover, the better.

Owls deserve special mention as predators. Barn

owls can clean out a population of gophers in just a few nights. Owls also eat many nocturnal mice and voles. If you are fortunate enough to have an owls as neighbors, encourage them to stay by leaving them alone.

Moles and shrews are insectivores and so should be welcome in any garden. They eat insects, larvae and slugs. Unfortunately, many gardeners associate them with rodents which can be garden pests. Attempting to poison moles and shrews should be considered blasphemy to gardeners. Shrews will eat their own weight or more in insects and insect larvae every day — such an ally should be encouraged in both vegetable and ornamental gardens.

* Frogs and toads are relentless insect and slug predators. A pond or body of water is necessary for frogs and toads for breeding. Most frogs prefer to live in or near water. Toads require a relatively natural setting with cool hiding places. create conditions to attract frogs and toads because, once they are mature, they will try to return home if moved. When toads make your garden their home, they seldom leave! In recent years, frog and toad populations have been drastically diminishing. No one is quite sure what is causing this although many experts believe that the losses are due to things that we have done to the environment — water and air pollution, destruction of habitat and so forth.

* Snakes, lizards and salamanders are assets to the garden. Large snakes eat gophers, moles, squirrels and mice. Smaller snakes eat slugs and insects. Lizards and salamanders also eat insects and other pests. Attract snakes, lizards, and salamanders with cool, covered areas for habitat. Always check the tall grass, especially along fence rows, for snakes before mowing or using the power string trimmer.

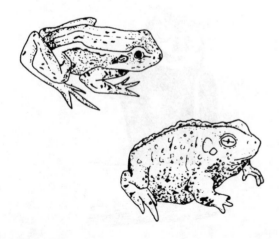

Frogs and toads are excellent predators.

Beneficial Insects

Names like aphid wolf, assassin bug, dragonfly, mealybug destroyer and tiger beetle describe predatory insects, the tenacious flesh eaters of the garden. They are usually equipped with crushing or piercing jaws and are larger, stronger, and more agile than their prey. Predatory larvae must search out and devour insects for existence and many are more ferocious predators than their parents.

Parasites eat pest insects from the inside: Adults lay eggs in or on the host, the eggs hatch, the larva emerge and once inside the host, begin to feed. Some host insects die within 48 hours while others take several weeks. Most hosts get sick and quit eating within 24 hours of the parasite entering the body. Some parasites release a bacteria that kills the host.

Beneficial insects are attracted by the blooms (which supply pollen and nectar) of a wide variety of plants, such as alfalfa, candytuft, carrot, coriander, fennel, ox-eye daisy, goldenrod, Queen Anne's lace, white and sweet clover, and yarrow.

Remember that indiscriminate use of broad spectrum insecticides (even botanical ones such as pyrethrum and rotenone) kill all insects including predators that are beneficial. Therefore, limit spraying of any pesticides — herbicides, insecticides, or fungicides — to spot applications when more conservative measures do not work.

When purchasing beneficial insects for release in the garden, the following rules-of-thumb are helpful:

* Beneficial insects need to be released as soon as pests are seen. Most require several releases at 1-3-week intervals in the spring when flowers start to bloom.
* Insect pests are generally slow-moving and beneficial insects that prey on those pests are usually fast and agile.
* During very hot or very cool weather, beneficial insect predators will be comparatively inactive and do little, if any, feeding.
* Beneficial insects must have an ample supply of food in the garden or they will leave.
* Trichogramma wasps, green lacewings, praying mantises, and lady beetles are the best known and most available predatory insects for bio-control in the garden.

Other beneficial insect predators to welcome to your garden are described below. Those in the list with a "star" by their name are available commercially; the rest are not.

Assassin Bugs

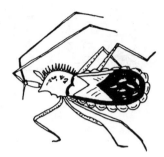

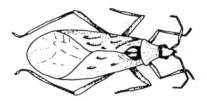

Assassin bugs, of the family Reduviidae, have slender, tan black-winged bodies ½-inch long. These fierce predators eat aphids, caterpillars, fly larvae, bees, and beetles. They use their strong front legs to snatch insects which they bite and inject with a toxin. Handle assassin bugs with respect. They may give a stinging bite that is unpleasant but causes nothing more than itchy flesh except in a few people who have an allergic reaction to the bite.

Attract these beneficial insects by planting alfalfa, goldenrod, Mexican tea, or oleander.

Centipedes

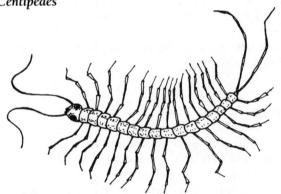

Centipedes (Class Chilopoda) are many-legged, fast-moving predators of many insects, slugs, and snails. They provide good insect control both indoors and out. They hide in mulch and low-growing ground covers, and stalk their prey at night.

Damsel Bugs

Damsel bugs, of the Nabidae family, are so green that they blend into surrounding foliage with ease.

Only one quarter-inch-long, these thin, tiny winged insects stalk aphids, caterpillars, leafhoppers, thrips, and mites, using their powerful front legs to capture their prey. They feel most at home in the foliage of low-growing plants. Alfalfa will attract damsel bugs.

Predatory Flies

Syrphid flies (Order Diptera) are members of the large Syrphidae family. Some gardeners may know them as robber flies, flower flies, or hover flies. They are a little larger than common houseflies. The adult fly's brightly colored body glistens in the sunlight as they hover over flowers to feed on nectar and pollen. The predatory fly can pluck butterflies, beetles, grasshoppers, and wasps from mid-air.

The green or tan larvae (maggots) of the hover fly can consume an aphid a minute for hours on end, but their diet also includes leafhoppers, mealybugs and

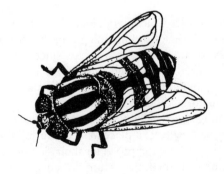

The larvae of the hover fly can consume an aphid a minute for hours on end.

scale. Hover flies are attracted to gardens with many blooming flowers, especially calendulas, marigolds, and nasturtiums. Adults lay their eggs among aphid colonies. The eggs hatch into larvae with voracious appetites for aphids.

Tachinid flies (*Bigonicheta spinipennis*) are difficult to distinguish from houseflies. Tanchinids, unlike houseflies, frequent gardens that provide honeydew and nectar for food.

Some of these drab-looking flies deposit eggs directly in caterpillars and others lay their eggs on foliage. When the larvae hatch, they devour the host.

Beetles

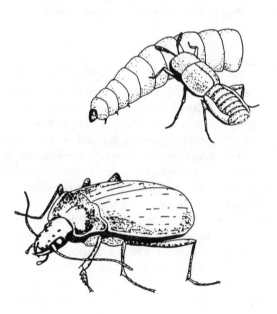

Beetles (Order Coleoptera), including ground, rove, tiger, whirligig, and lightning bug (firefly), are dark colored and can be from a ⅛ to 1-inch-long. These reclusive beetles catch and devour a wide variety of prey, including caterpillars, cutworms, larvae, grubs, numerous other insects, and eggs.

Encourage beetles by planting ground covers and mulching so they have a place to sleep during the day. At night they are on the prowl for their slow-moving prey. When disturbed, they scurry for cover.

Firefly larvae or glowworms are not as "bright" as the adult firefly (lightning bug). fireflies are most common in the southern states. They feed on slugs and snails. This violent little larvae predator paralyzes its prey before eating it. They live in the ground and hunt slugs and snails when they come out at night. Low-growing vegetation attracts adult fireflies.

Lacewings

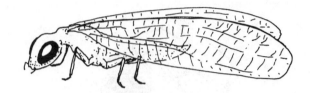

Lacewings (*Order Neuroptera*) have beautiful, frail, lacy wings of green or brown that carry them in erratic flight patterns. Adults are from ¼ to ¾ inch long and feed on honeydew, nectar, and pollen.

Larvae look like tiny alligators that grow up to ½ inch long. This predator consumes aphids, caterpillar eggs, corn earworms, mealybugs, mites, scale, and thrips so unmercifully that they are affectionately called aphid wolves or aphid lions.

The green lacewing is an important commercial pest control. Encourage egg-laying lacewing adults by interplanting blooming flowers among vegetables or set out a slurry of honey and water in the garden. The lacewings do not overwinter well in cool climates and the commercially available eggs may have to be reintroduced each spring.

Ladybugs

Ladybird beetles (Order Coleoptera, family Coccinellidae), are one of the best-known garden predators. There are numerous species. The most common one in this country is the convergent lady beetle (*Hippodamia convergens*), which is orange with dark spots. Both the adult and their dark gray-colored larvae eat scores of aphids, scale, and insect eggs a day. The larvae dine on a greater assortment of insects than the adults, including beetles, bugs, and weevils. They can wolf down over 30 aphids an hour.

Ladybugs are coaxed into the garden by planting a wide selection of plants. A large bag of 5,000 ladybugs will usually cost just a few dollars more than a container of 1,000. After aphids show an increase in population, there will be enough food to sustain them.

Release several handfuls in the evening by gently setting them among garden plants in several locations.

Beneficial Nematodes

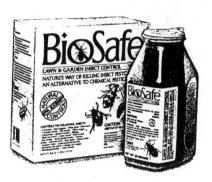

Store the remainder in the refrigerator where they will continue to hibernate for several weeks.

Ladybugs tend to migrate, so release them at dusk into a garden which has damp soil and a good cover of mulch for them to feel at home and find new hiding places. Releases are more effective in the spring, since they prefer cool weather to the hot temperatures of summer, when they will often migrate to a cooler shady spot in your neighbor's yard.

Most ladybugs that are sold commercially are collected in the Sierra mountains of California when they are fat and dormant. Upon purchase, they have little desire to hunt until their supply of fat is used up, which may take several weeks of flying. For this reason they may not be the best predator value to home gardeners, although they can have good value in a greenhouse or other confined garden situation.

If you have plenty of aphids, you can attract ladybird beetles easily. Adults also eat honeydew from aphids. Commercial insectaries feed the beetles with a mixture of yeast and sugar that is a byproduct of the cheese industry. Setting Wheast (a commercial protein food to provide for predatory insects when other food supplies are low) out in the garden early in the spring will entice the beetles that in your yard to stay.

Mealybug Destroyer

Mealybug Destroyer (*Crytolaemus montrouzeri*) is a small black and orange member of the ladybird beetle family. The adults are called crypts. Both adults and larva attack mealybugs in all stages of life. They also feed on some stages of scale and aphids. The adult is ⅛-inch long and looks like a small dark-colored ladybug. The larvae resembles the mealybug. Like the ladybirds, these will be more effective in enclosed places. Outdoors they are more inclined to rove.

Not all nematodes are plant pests, in fact, several species of microscopic, beneficial, parasitic nematodes are on the market. The most popular is *Steinernema* (formerly *Nemoplactana*) *carpocapsae*, often referred to as Nc nematodes and *Heterorhabditis bacteriophora*, also known *as H. heliothidis.* The most popular nematodes are produced by BioSafe in Palo Alto, California. Nc nematodes attack numerous adult, larvae and eggs of many ants, caterpillars, beetles, bugs, flies, and borers. Over 200 pests that attack plant roots are prey to these helpful parasitic nematodes.

Nc nematodes are harmless to people, pets, wildlife, honey bees, earthworms and beneficial insects. They can live in the soil for over a year without feeding. Release nematodes in water using a sprayer on or near infestations. They can also be released at the opening of bore holes or into corn cobs using a syringe. Follow supplier's directions or nematodes may perish.

When ordering these beneficial parasites, take care to keep the nematodes and their bedding moist. If the bedding dries out, or if the temperature reaches extremes of hot or cold, they may perish.

Praying Mantis

The European praying mantises (*Mantis religiosa*) and the native American mantises (*Stag momantis carolina*) grow up to 4 inches long. They are relentless predators that devour almost anything that cross their path, including beneficial insects. For that reason, they are currently somewhat out of favor as biological controls.

These four-inch long predators kill their victims with a crushing chomp to the back of the neck with their powerful jaws. A mass of their eggs can be purchased on cards and set out in the garden in the spring to hatch. Occasionally, a trained eye will spot a

Spiders

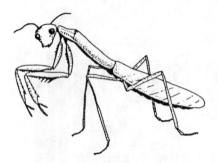

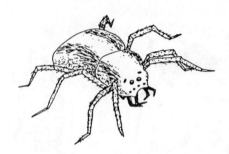

mass of their eggs on a plant leaf in the autumn. To keep the eggs, prune off the entire twig and leaf containing the cluster. Store the twig and the eggs in the refrigerator, or in a sheltered spot outdoors in the garden, so they will hatch out the following spring. The eggs will live through a hard freeze, but do not leave them in a warm house for the winter or they will hatch out too soon. Large populations of insects will attract praying mantises. If they do not find enough food in your garden, they search for gardens that do.

Spiders consume many garden pests, including flying insects, and sometimes grasshoppers that are three times their size. When you see one of the many species of spiders in your garden, leave it alone. It will continue hunting day and night for garden insects.

Spiders may be frightening to some people but, despite their appearance, they are an asset in any garden. Many spiders build webs to snare their pray. Other spiders catch their prey on the run. They paralyze the prey with a bite, then dissolve and eat the innards of their victims.

Predatory Snails

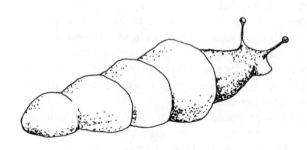

The predatory decollate snail (*Ruminia decollata*) is proving effective against brown garden snails and other garden snails that are pests, reducing undesirable snail populations considerably where they are present. This beneficial snail comes from the Mediterranean region and is being used commercially in California citrus orchards.

Although it may feed on some tender young seedlings, it ignores them when they are past this stage. If you introduce the decollate snail into your garden, watch it carefully and be prepared to destroy it if it becomes destructive to harmless snails or other non-pest insects.

Only two spiders present a threat to humans — the black widow and the brown recluse; both are more often found in homes rather than gardens. A bite from the female black widow spider is painful but rarely fatal. The venom affects the nerves. The female is jet black, with a domed abdomen and has a red hourglass-shaped spot on her underside. The body is about ¾-inch long. Black widows are seldom found in the garden. They favor dark quiet locations with enough room to move around such as tool sheds, basements, water meter boxes, and garages.

Brown recluse spiders are shy and unaggressive. They hunt in large areas around their webs, which are often in corners, and are occasionally found in bedding or clothing. They will bite when pushed or pinched.

These spiders have longer legs in relation to their ⅓-inch bodies than the black widows. There is a clear, distinctive violin-shaped mark on the top of the body just behind the head. The bite, if neglected, can cause an ulcerous wound and bad scar. In rare cases, the bite can cause kidney failure. If you are bitten, seek medical attention.

Parasitic Wasps

Parasitic wasps (Hymenoptera order) are attracted primarily by the presence of their prey. You also will attract parasitic wasps by planting fennel and yarrow.

* Many members of the Chalcidoidea family are parasitic. In general, chalcid wasps are very tiny, dark or light brown, and fly-like in appearance with large eyes. They prey on aphids, numerous caterpillars, and the eggs of many insects. These wasps prefer warm, humid weather and gardens with lots of prey. They do not do well in dry, dusty climates.
* *Edovu puttleri* is a chalcid wasp that parasitizes the eggs of several species of beetles, most notably, the Colorado potato beetle.
* *Encarsia formosa*, a chalcid, is only ⅛ inch long, much smaller than its prey, which is primarily the whitefly larvae. The adult feeds on larvae, and lays eggs in and around them. The wasps are shipped as eggs in parasitized whitefly eggs.
* *Pediobius foveolatus* are tiny parasitic wasps that kill Mexican bean beetles.
* Trichogramma wasps are about one quarter the size of a pinhead. They lay their eggs inside the eggs of over 200 different pest host eggs including cabbage worms, corn earworms, and tomato hornworms. Several species of trichogramma inject eggs into host eggs. The larvae emerge with a gluttonous appetite, consuming host eggs before the embryos can mature. Trichogramma eggs arrive on cards of 300 to 500 parasitized eggs that are full of adults ready to emerge. For best results, set new eggs out weekly during the spring before pests reach epidemic proportions. The wasps die off in droves during cold winters and will need to be released each spring for continued assistance.
* The two most important groups are brachonids and ichneumons. Brachonid wasps are very tiny, blood red with dark wings. They lay eggs in aphids, many different caterpillars, and the larvae of numerous beetles. The eggs produce wasp larvae that consume their host from the inside. Brachonid larvae are responsible for the control of many devastating pest larva, including tomato hornworms.
* The family Ichneumonidae comprises about 20 percent of all parasitic insects. Ichneumons, in the same family as brachonids, have tiny, slender, dark bodies with transparent lacy wings. Adults feed on nectar, pollen, and the larvae of butterflies and moths. Ichneumon wasps lay their eggs in or near host caterpillar pupa. The wasp larvae feed on caterpillars and eggs.

Large Pests

In recent years, the natural balance between predator and prey among the large animal populations has been upset. The classic example is the whitetail deer in the Northeast which homeowners, especially in the exurban areas around New York City, describe as a nuisance. Its natural predators were killed off or driven away by loss of habitat years ago.

Birds

Although most birds are welcome guests in any garden, there are some that can make quick work of a berry or fruit crop, especially cherries. Others will go after freshly planted seeds, especially large-seeded ones like corn, and young lettuce or pea plants. But you can use spun fiber and netting to protect your crops.

The most effective way to keep birds from berries, tender flowers and freshly planted seed is to cover the plants or garden bed with plastic or wire netting. When installing the netting, make sure it is securely fastened around the perimeter of the protected fruit. Hungry birds may get under the netting and be hurt when trying to escape.

Scarecrows, garden mobiles, plastic snakes, and blasting cannons may be useful as temporary controls. Birds may cause the most damage during winter or early spring months when they have very little to eat. Winter vegetables, budding flower bulbs, emerging fruit tree and berry buds make a tempting cold season meal for feathered marauders. You can try putting out bird food to feed them as a way to deter them from your garden plants.

New grass seed must be covered so that birds do not see it. It is difficult to rake all the grass seed into the soil, so cover it with a lightweight mulch of grass clippings, peat moss, straw, plastic, or spun fiber.

Garden pools with fish can be cleaned out in an afternoon by predatory birds such as kingfishers, herons, and cranes. Deter them by providing plenty of plants that the fish can use as shelter.

Cats &Dogs

Cats always seem to seek out freshly tilled soil to bury their feces. Discourage the furry felines by chasing them out, or apply anise oil or another strong-smelling repellent.

Dogs leave messes on the lawn and also urinate on foliage. A fence is the most secure way to keep dogs out of the garden. Even though there may be leash laws in your area, that is no guarantee that dog owners will respect the requirement and keep their pets off your property. Having your own dog also keeps intruders at bay while your dog is around. When one dog "marks" in your yard, all the dogs that pass by will "mark" in your yard!

Prickly hedge clippings, like those from barberry bushes, will keep most animals out of a garden. Strong odors such as garlic, basil, sage, and peppermint will repel some animals.

Strong solutions of hot pepper sauce such as Tabasco will keep most animals from eating plants. Blend and mix solutions of red hot peppers with some water and a drop of detergent to make the solution stick. Strain the liquid so you can use it in a sprayer.

Deer and Elk

Deer and elk love newly formed growth on rose bushes and young fruit trees of all sorts, but they will eat most all vegetation including the bark from trees in the winter when food is scarce. In addition, they may destroy crops by trampling them.

When deer and elk are unable to forage food in the winter, do not try feeding them hay and grain to keep them from damaging trees and gardens — this will

only get them into the habit of relying on you and your property. If you must feed these wild animals, feed them well away from the house and garden area.

For added protection, trees and other plants can be individually caged with wire or netting. Deer may be repelled by the smell of blood and human hair. Place handfuls of dried bloodmeal in cloth sacks and dip them in water to activate the smell. Hang the sacks from a tree to discourage dogs and other predators from eating it.

Put handfuls of human hair in small cloth sacks and hang them from a garden fence. Scented soaps have repelled deer from some gardens when hung along a fence. Remember though, if deer are very hungry, the smell of bloodmeal, human hair, scented soap or anything else will not deter them.

Deer can easily bound over 8-foot fences. The best deer fence is 6 to 8 feet tall with the top foot sloping outward, away from the garden at a 45 degree angle. Electric fences and large dogs are also excellent deterrents to these four-legged intruders.

In some parts of the country, including the Northeast, deer have become such a problem that they are referred to as rats with antlers. Some farmers and gardeners have elected a permanent way of managing deer — they shoot and kill them, but this is unsafe, impractical and unlawful in suburban and urban locations.

Gophers

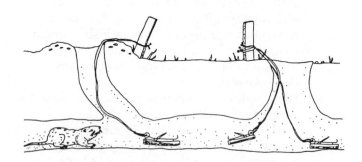

Pocket gophers are small burrowing rodents that eat plant roots and foliage. They are herbivorous and find fleshy roots, such as asparagus, carrots, and dahlias, a real treat. Should a family of gophers move into your garden, get rid of them as soon as possible! Females can bear up to five litters of four to eight offspring a year. A family of gophers can clean out a large garden or ruin a lawn in a matter of weeks.

Encourage the presence of cats, dogs, gopher and king snakes, barn owls and even skunks, all of which are natural gopher predators. Nocturnal barn owls and skunks can get rid of large groups of night-feeding gophers in just a few weeks.

Trying to flood gophers out by filling their holes with water is virtually useless, according to most experts. Feeding them chewing gum to clog their intestines does not work, it will just make them come back for more.

Smoke bombs and highway flares will chase them a few feet away. Small windmills that look like sunflowers are supposed to agitate the ground and drive the gophers away, but once gophers move in, it will take more than a few vibrations to drive them out.

The only sure way to get rid of gophers if no natural predators exist is by trapping. There are several gopher traps available, including some that capture them alive. It will take some skill before you are able to catch gophers with traps regularly. You must avoid getting human scent on any part of the traps. If gophers sense human odor they will simply push soil over the trap to spring it or render it otherwise ineffective. Traps are put in gopher runways and so don't need to be baited.

Follow instructions exactly for trapping gophers. Set traps in main runs. Find a main run with a probe — a ½-inch wide steel spike or the equivalent — that you push down in the areas around piles of dirt. Secure the trap to a stake outside the run to prevent the gopher from disappearing.

A fence of poultry wire or ½-inch hardware cloth buried 1-foot deep and standing 3 feet above the ground will keep gophers out of the garden. Line raised beds with chicken wire before filling them with soil, to keep gophers out. Driving metal sheets around the perimeter of the garden beds will also prevent gophers from getting into the garden.

Some gardeners claim that the euphorbia plant nicknamed the "gopher plant" or the "mole plant" (*Euphorbia lathyris*) tends to deter both gophers and moles. This European plant has naturalized in America and is an annual or biennial up to three feet tall with stout, unbranched stems. The leaves grow 2 to 6 inches long and the flowers grow in umbels.

Thompson & Morgan (P.O. Box 1308, Jackson NJ 08527) carries seeds, and Taylor's Herb Gardens (1535 Lone Oak Road, Vista CA 92084) carries both seeds and plants.

Mice and Voles

Normally, mice and voles are not much of a problem in the garden. But they may become a problem if they chew bark from around the base of shrubs and trees (girdling), eat root crops, or go after melons.

Keep mulch a foot away from tree trunks and woody plants and install a wire mesh around the trunks of these plants in the winter if these rodents become a problem.

The best mouse deterrent is a cat that is serious about hunting. Mouse traps also work well on smaller populations, but removing a large number of mice with traps can be tedious.

Moles

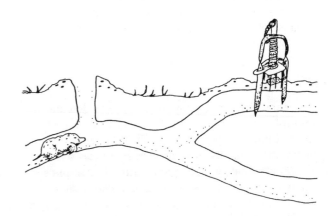

Moles are not really pests. They are primarily insectivores that eat cutworms and other soil grubs. They perform a valuable service in this regard and they also condition the soil by digging through it.

However, they are little appreciated by gardeners. Tunneling may dislodge plant roots and bulbs. Tunneling and the ejection of earth from the tunnels causes hazards for lawn mowers which often scalp the turf from the top of the tunnel ridges. In addition, many people find the sight of raised mole tunnels, scalped ridges, and out-of-kilter plants more than they can bear.

Those who wish to repel moles can try either castor plants or gopher (mole) plants (*Euphorbia lathyris*). Plant a border of either around the area you wish to protect from moles. Many gardeners swear by these plants. Castor bean leaves and castor oil, as well as applications of tobacco and red pepper will repel moles if put into the main runs.

Here's how you can use castor oil to repel moles: blend 2 tablespoons of caster oil with 3 tablespons of dish soap concentrate and 10 tablespoons of water. Mix in a blender. Use this as a concentrate at the rate of 2 tablespoons per gallon of water. Apply as a soil drench directly over mole holes.

Smoke devices such as highway flares and mole bombs are half-baked solutions. The smoke soon dissipates and the rodents return.

Stomping their tunnels down is a minor deterrent but does help you learn their main routes. The tunnels that are reopened are main runs where traps should be set or repellents applied.

Barrel traps, scissor traps, and guillotine traps are effective and kill moles instantly. The majority of experts endorse traps as the best way to get rid of moles. Other traps are available that will catch them live. Set several traps, cover them to block out light, and mark them with a stake. Poisons are out of the question because they will also kill people, pets, and birds if they should happen to eat them.

Owls, snakes, dogs, and cats often kill moles but, because of their odor, usually don't eat them.

Rabbits

Rabbits eat almost anything in the garden and they multiply — well, like rabbits! Cute little cottontails are most common in urban areas. Their larger cousin, the jackrabbit, inhabits rural areas from Kansas west.

Repel rabbits with a light dusting of rock phosphate on young leaves or dried blood sprinkled around the base of plants. A cow manure tea sprayed on leaves and the soil also may keep them from dining on crops. Rabbits find plants dusted with hot pepper or a spray of dilute fish emulsion and bonemeal repulsive. Remember to wash the manure-treated vegetables before eating. There also are a number of commercial rabbit repellents, but be wary of using these on edibles.

A dog will help keep rabbits in check, but the only surefire way to keep them out of the garden is to fence them out with one-inch poultry wire. The poultry wire should be buried at least six inches in the ground to prevent burrowing and rise two or three feet above ground. Wrap fruit tree trunks with a wire mesh or aluminum foil to keep rabbets from chewing bark in the winter or early spring.

Raccoons

Raccoons feed at night and prefer garbage to garden produce, but they love fresh ears of corn most of all. Keep your garbage lid secure and keep a vigil on ripening corn. A barking dog is probably the best raccoon deterrent. However, a raccoon can kill or maim a dog that attacks it, and can easily drown a large dog in deep water. Bring pets in at night if you live around deep creeks, ditches, or ponds.

Raccoons will also clean all of the fish out of your garden pond. The best deterrent is to cover the pond with protective wire.

Electric fencing can be effective in keeping raccoons from your corn and other vegetables. Regular fencing, unless it is in the form of a cage, will not keep these clever animals from your crops; they will easily climb over the top of most fences. Trapping or shooting are the only sure means for getting rid of raccoons. Even when you remove them, others are likely to move into the vacated area.

Squirrels & Chipmunks

Squirrels and chipmunks are extremely destructive in some regions of the country, especially in suburban neighborhoods. They will eat corn and fruit, often nibbling a few bites from each piece — just enough to spoil it.

Hot pepper solutions may discourage them from feeding. Trapping or shooting are the only sure means of getting rid of them. In the case of squirrels, there may be so many that others will quickly move into an area where you have gotten rid of the original squirrels.

Woodchucks

Woodchucks are common garden pests in exurban and rural areas of the Northeast and Midwest. They most often feed in early morning or late in the day. They can make a meal of your salad garden in no time.

A sturdy rabbit-proof fence of strong chicken wire, set six inches into the ground and rising three feet above it, will also keep woodchucks out of the garden. The other alternatives are to trap them or shoot them.

Insects & Other Small Pests

The following are among gardeners' worst insect and other small pests in many parts of the country.

Ants come in a a wide variety of shapes and sizes. They seldom harm plants, but some ant species farm aphids and mealybugs, carrying them from plant to plant and protecting them from predators. Ants and their young feed on the sweet, sticky honeydew exuded by the aphids and mealybugs.

Controlling the aphids or mealybugs usually controls the ants. If the ants become an overwhelming problem, mix some sugar and borax soap in equal parts and deposit it in a covered coffee can with a window cut in it (see Slug and Snail Hotel). The ants are attracted to the sweet mix and carry it back to the nest along with the borax. The borax will kill those ants it contacts. Diatomaceous earth or boric acid crystals sprinkled lightly along baseboards and in corners of cupboards and pantry closets are environmentally sound ways to get rid of most ants and other crawling insects.

Ants will not cross a line of bonemeal or pulverized charcoal. To keep ants from entering the house, sprinkle a little powdered cinnamon or squeeze some lemon juice around their points of entry.

A quick application of pyrethrum will kill ants most effectively. Pyrethrum is the best choice when ants have invaded the kitchen. Remember to cover or remove all food and eating utensils from the counter before spraying.

Discourage ants from climbing trees or other plants by smearing a three-inch ring of Tanglefoot™ or other sticky material around the trunk or stems.

Aphids

Aphids, also called plant lice, include many species. They are in the same animal group as scale, mealybugs and whiteflies. They are some of the worst insect pests in the garden as they attack almost all plants. These insects are about the size of a pin head and can be a menagerie of colors including green, yellow and red. Some have wings, but most do not. Aphids puncture foliage and suck out plant fluids.

They are most common on flower buds, leaf undersides and soft plant parts. They are attracted to both sickly plants and plants that have been over-fertilized with nitrogen. Aphids excrete excess sap and sugars in a sticky honeydew that transmits viral diseases and fosters the growth of sooty molds.

Aphids give birth to live young. In a few short weeks, one aphid can spawn a colony of over one hundred thousand! Interplanting with anise, chives, coriander, garlic, nasturtiums and petunias tends to repel aphids.

Control aphids on plants by rubbing the foliage gently between your fingers to squish them. Blasting them off the plants with a jet of water is one of the easiest and surest ways to control aphids. Ladybugs or lacewings purchased at the nursery or from mail order catalogs can be released. Work to attract hoverflies, whose larvae consume thousands of aphids.

If all this fails to arrest aphids, homemade lime-juice sprays, hot pepper sprays or tobacco sprays work well. Safer's Insecticidal Soap, ryania, sabadilla, or pyrethrum sprays will certainly do the trick as a last resort. Remember to only spot spray the infested areas of plants.

Armyworms

Armyworms are usually about ½ inch long and greenish with dark stripes. They travel in large groups, hence the name, and are a serious pest to both lawns and crops.

Like the sod webworm and cutworms, they are the larval forms of butterflies or moths that often live in the thatch area of lawns. Examine the sod carefully all the way to its roots to diagnose the kind of insect that is eating the foliage.

The most conservative approach to control is to pick them and put them in a container with some kerosene or saturated salt solution to die. Since much of the feeding is done at night, this may be difficult.

Another form of control is to plant only endophytic grasses, those that have endophytic fungi in their tissues that repel or kill insects. These include some perennial ryegrasses (Citation II, Commander, Pennant, Regal Repel and Sunrise) and some of the turf-type tall fescues (Apache and Kentucky 31).

Bacillus thuringiensis (BT) is a good control when applied correctly. This biological control that affects only larval forms of insects prevents the larvae from maturing.

If all else fails, spot-treat the affected areas with pyrethrum.

Bumblebees, Hornets & Yellow Jackets

When bumblebees, hornets, yellow jackets or other ground- or tree-dwelling stinging insects choose your garden or compost pile as their home, they become unwelcome pests.

Honeybees, on the other hand, are necessary for the pollination and thus the fruit of many plants. They should be welcome in every garden. They will not bother you if you don't bother them.

When you disturb the hives or underground dwelling of bumblebees, hornets or yellow jackets, they may resent it highly enough to sting you. Unlike the honeybee, they can sting again and again.

Diatomaceous earth, the abrasive dust made from deposits of fossilized diatoms, will kill the insects when it is drizzled into tunnels.

Hornet nests in trees are harder to deal with. You can knock them down after dark when they are inactive, but we believe even this may be hazardous. If you try it, wear a complete covering of thick clothing, including a bee veil. The only surely safe way to bring down a hornet nest is to wait for a hard freeze, which kills the hornets.

For underground tunnels, many people recommend the old-fashioned boiling water treatment following by covering up the entrance. This, too, is better done at night when the bees or wasps are less active and in their nest.

Pyrethrum insecticides are comparatively safe biological controls for these insects. Application will be difficult since they are so easily aggravated. Apply the insecticide generously to the entrances of their hive or tunnel.

Beetles

Beetle plant pests come in many forms. Japanese beetles are probably the best known and worst garden pests in some parts of the country in some years. They are most common in the Northeast but have been slowly making their way across the country. They have crossed the Mississippi River now and show no signs of quitting.

Other beetle pests include Colorado potato beetles, bean beetles, elmleaf beetles, flea beetles, blister beetles and wood-boring beetles, all of which can be serious pests under certain circumstances.

In this section we are dealing with those beetles that are garden pests as adults. Other sections will deal with the beetle larvae or grubs that are garden pests.

There are a number of ways to control plant-eating beetles in the garden. The first is to regularly pick the beetles from the plants. You can put them in a container of salty or soapy water, or collect them in a plastic bag which you then put in the sun for a few hours or submerge in soapy water. Either method will kill the beetles.

You can vacuum them from the plants, then put the collection bag inside a plastic bag and leave it in the sun for a few hours.

Some beetles can be successfully trapped and then destroyed. Colors such as yellow or pheromones (hormone-like materials with odors that attract the beetle) are used to bring beetles to the traps.

There are parasitic nematodes that will kill some beetles. Two bacteria that are effective controls are *Bacillus thuringiensis* (BT) and milky spore disease (*Bacillus popilliae* and *B. lentimorbus*). Read labels thoroughly — different forms are fatal to different insects.

Pyrethrum insecticides can be used effectively against adult beetles. Be sure to use them conservatively and wisely, because they will kill beneficial insects as well as pests.

Extracts of the neem tree have proven effective against all stages of Japanese beetles as both a killing insecticide and a beetle repellent.

Borers

Borers are the larvae of numerous insects that tunnel or bore through canes, stems, or trunks. Examples include the squash vine, European corn, peach tree, round- and flat-headed, stock, and strawberry crown borers. They cause the foliage on the branch or stem to wilt. Look for a small entry hole and moist sawdust castings on canes or stems.

Electric traps are very effective against night flying moths that spawn hordes of borers — remember that these traps indiscriminately kill all flying insects, good as well as bad, that are attracted to night lights. A dusting of black pepper or camphor around the base of plants repels egg-laying moths. Control most borers by pruning branches below the damaged area and destroying the branches.

Sometimes tree borers that enter larger tree trunks can be killed or fished out of their tunnels with a small wire or pocket knife. Or spray infested tree borer holes with oil spray, ryania, or insecticidal soap. Make sure to get the spray deep down into the hole.

The European corn borer is an inch-long caterpillar that is tan with dark body spots and head. The adult is a night-flying, yellowish brown moth that appears in the garden from May to June. The preferred food is corn, but they will attack numerous other plants as well.

Handpick these caterpillars from corn stalks and cobs with a knife or fingernail as soon as you notice their moist castings and the damage they cause. Adult moths are attracted to light traps.

Several birds, including swallows, are natural European corn borer predators. Ladybugs can consume over 50 corn borer eggs daily and lacewings also eat many eggs.

Tachinid flies and trichogramma wasp larvae are responsible for disposing of over one third of the corn borers in the Corn Belt. Both BT and ryania are effective in controlling European corn borers.

Cabbage Loopers

Cabbage loopers are worms that measure up to an inch and a half long. They are pastel green with vertical stripes. They loop or double up as they crawl around chewing holes in leaves. Cabbage loopers overwinter in a dark, protective cocoon attached to a leaf. The brown adult moth is nocturnal.

The commercially available trichogramma wasp that lays eggs on and in the looper is a natural enemy as are birds, frogs, and toads. Control cabbage loopers by hand-picking or spray with insecticidal soap, lime spray, or BT. As a last resort, use rotenone or a pyrethrum insecticide.

Cabbage Root Maggots

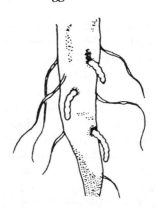

Cabbage root maggots cut dingy channels and burrows into the stems and roots of cabbage family vegetables just below the soil's surface. They also infest root crops, including radishes and turnips.

These pests winter over as brown puparia in the soil. In the spring, they emerge as adult flies, somewhat smaller than houseflies, and soon lay eggs at the bases of young plants.

The squirmy larvae which hatch several days later are ⅓ inch long, white and have no legs. The adult fly lays her eggs around the base of the stem in the soil. Infested broccoli, cabbage, or root crops wilt and produce heads that are deformed or none at all. Wounds made by the root maggots also foster soft rot and fungal diseases.

Control cabbage maggots by removing and destroying heavily infested plants. Protect remaining plants with a sprinkling of diatomaceous earth or a lime and wood ash mix around the bases of plants.

Avoid cabbage root maggot attacks by growing short-season radishes that mature in only 25 to 30 days. Long-season and winter radishes may be riddled with root maggot channels by the time they are harvested. Beneficial nematodes also do a good job of controlling maggots.

Cabbage Worms

The pale green imported cabbage worm, distinguished by a yellowish-green stripe running down its back, grows to an inch or more in length and has closely-cropped hairs. The adult imported cabbage worm is a pale white butterfly with three or four black spots on its wings and dark tips on the top wing tips.

If you are growing any member of the cabbage family — and even if you aren't — chances are you will see the adult butterflies fluttering from plant to plant depositing eggs in the spring. The green worms hatch out in about a week and chew huge holes that may skeletonize leaves. Discourage these pests by inter-planting garlic, nasturtiums, onions, rosemary, and sage.

Unfortunately, most birds do not like the bad tasting, toxic internal fluids of cabbage worms. The prolific parasitic brachonid and trichogramma wasps are very effective cabbage worm predators.

A finely-textured crop cover, such as Agronet™ or Reemay™, is a good protective covering that prevents entry of the adult butterflies intent on laying eggs. Tilling the soil in the fall is another good control because it will expose young pupae to desiccating air.

Control with a spray of insecticidal soap, a lime mix (½ pound of agricultural lime soaked in 5 quarts of water for 24 hours — use the liquid above the settled lime as a spray or soil drench) or both. BT is very effective on large infestations of both types of cabbage worms. As a last resort, use rotenone or pyrethrum insecticides.

Carrot Rust Flies

Carrot rust fly adults, only ⅛ inch long, are black and shiny. They lay their eggs at the base of carrots. The maggots feed underground on carrots and their relatives. Wild carrot relatives such as cow parsnip and fools parsley are common hosts of this fly.

Companion or interplanting with onions, garlic, or French marigolds is said to be effective in repelling carrot rust flies.

Protect plants by mixing a sprinkling of diatomaceous earth or a lime and wood ash mix into the soil surface when you plant carrots.

Chinch Bugs

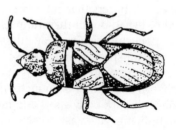

Chinch bugs have a quarter-inch long reddish black body with white wings and they smell bad if squashed. They attack corn, ornamental and turf grasses by puncturing foliage and sucking plant fluids. Chinch bug infestations stunt, wilt, or kill corn and cause large, dry dead spots in lawns. This pest is worst during hot, dry summer weather.

Prevent chinch bugs by removing grassy weeds around the garden and by tilling in the fall to prevent overwintering. Remove and reseed damaged lawn areas. Dethatch lawn and dust with diatomaceous earth or if infested, drench with insecticidal soap as soon as damage is noticed. Cutting the lawn as low as possible (scalp) during active growth will physically kill many cinch bugs and expose eggs. Cover the closely cropped lawn with a quarter- to half-inch layer of well-aged chicken manure. The short blades of grass will be revitalized.

Codling Moth

In spring, this grayish brown adult moth with a small ¾ inch wingspan produces a very destructive inch-long caterpillar (larva) that is pink and white with a brown head. The larvae will eat pears, quinces, and walnuts but prefer apples.

Trichogramma wasps will parasitize numerous eggs if released as soon as codling moths start to lay eggs. Use a dormant oil spray in early spring to smother eggs. Soap and fish oil sprays will dislodge caterpillars from leaves. A dusting of ryania is most effective for infestations. Once larvae have entered the fruit, usually apples, it is destroyed. Remove affected fruit. In the fall, clean up and destroy litter beneath the tree where the cocooned pests winter over.

Corn Earworms

Corn earworms, also known as the tomato fruit-worm or cotton bollworm, are the worst corn pest. They can be found anywhere corn is grown. The gray adult moth has dark blotches on its wings. It lays eggs that hatch and grow to be two-inch long, brown, green or yellow caterpillars with both light and dark stripes running the length of their bodies. After 3 to 4 weeks, they leave the ear and enter the soil where they pupate.

You may find this caterpillar on young corn plants or within the ears leaving a trail of telltale castings. They also attack many flowers, fruits, and vegetables including beans, peppers, lettuce, and tomatoes. They like tomatoes best, and tunnel through one fruit after another.

Beetle larvae and moles are two natural predators of the pupae in the soil. Birds such as the English sparrows and redwing blackbirds feed on the caterpillars but may damage garden crops while doing so.

Hand-picking these large, easy-to-spot caterpillars is most effective in small gardens. Use homemade garlic and onion sprays in larger gardens. *Trichogramma minutum* and chalcid wasps parasitize corn earworms. Apply dustings of BT when silks first start to form and re-apply every 5 to 6 days or after a rain.

Crickets

Mole crickets, 1 ½ inch long, live underground during the day and come out at night to forage. Their tunnels may cut seedling roots.

Black field crickets, also mostly nocturnal, eat many things, including grains and other plants. They usually don't present much of a problem in the garden.

A protozoan pathogen (*Nosema locustae*) will kill both grasshoppers and crickets by infecting their fat tissue. Boric acid crystals also will kill these insects, in this case as a stomach poison.

Cucumber Beetles

Cucumber beetles are serious pests, both as larvae and as adults. There are a half dozen species of cucumber beetles in the genus *Diabrotica* that are serious pests. The adults are yellow or green and often marked with black spots or stripes. The adults feed on leaves, pollen and flower parts of many plants, especially corn and members of the squash family. The larvae, white ⅓-inch grubs with brown heads, feed heavily on plant roots and are known as corn rootworms.

Adults overwinter in crop debris and, in the spring, lay eggs in the soil near plants.

Both adults and larvae carry and can transmit bacterial wilt and cucumber mosaic virus.

Control these pests by removing and destroying crop residues in the fall, especially around favorite plants, cucumbers and other cucurbits, beans, corn, and sweet potatoes. Sticky traps can help control cucumber beetle adults. Parasitic nematodes will control larvae when applied to the soil weekly. Use pyrethrin or rotenone to control adults.

Cutworms

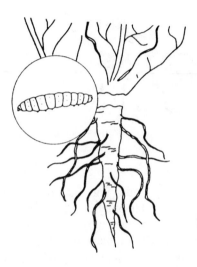

Cutworms are plump, brown to light green ½ to 1 ½-inch-long worms (caterpillars or larvae) that coil up when disturbed. Many types of cutworms live just below the surface of the soil. These troublesome pests feed on the bases of the plants, cutting them off at soil level. They feed on one plant at a time, then move to the next. Other species climb up plants to attack foliage and fruit. Both types turn into adult night-flying moths.

If you find a plant that has mysteriously been cut off at the base, search just under the surface of the soil around the dead plant. If you are prompt in your search, the cutworm will be lingering at the scene of the crime. If you wait several days, the cutworm could be several feet away and very difficult to find. Simply squash the culprit or drop in a container of salty or soapy water. Or you can go on night patrol with a flashlight and hand-pick them.

Encircle other plants in the area with a stiff three-inch-wide barrier of cardboard anchored an inch deep in the soil. A light sprinkling of cornmeal, which cutworms are unable to digest, around problem areas will kill them.

Prevent damage by sprinkling chicken manure, crushed eggshells, or moist wood ashes around the bases of plants. Blackbirds, firefly larvae, meadowlarks, moles, and toads find cutworms a real treat. Brachonid wasps, parasitic nematodes, and tachinid flies all parasitize cutworms. Numerous bacteria, fungi and viruses also keep cutworm infestations in check.

Control cutworms with a dusting of diatomaceous earth or BT. Adult moths are attracted to electronic light traps.

Earwigs

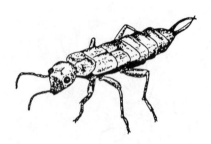

European earwigs, young and old, are reddish-brown with unmistakable pinchers on the tail end of their body. They like to crawl into budding flowers to eat the succulent growth or gnaw away at leaves. They do relatively little damage to most vegetables, but European earwigs can distort and spoil enough prize flower buds to warrant attention.

Earwigs actually can be a benefit to gardens since they also eat pests such as aphids. When earwigs eat small holes in the leaf margins of young plants, they are often blamed for the plant damage done by other garden pests. These are nocturnal animals so if you see a lot of plant damage, check carefully at night to see exactly what is doing it. Put down mulch or compost and the earwigs may be attracted to the organisms there and leave your plants alone.

European earwigs like to sneak into the house and eat food stored in cupboards or the pantry. Earwigs like to hide out in dark, moist places. Trap these pests in a rolled up newspaper, with lengths of bamboo, old pieces of hose, or rhubarb stalks tied into a bundle. Set the trap among the plants and check each morning. Dump the night's catch out in the garden pond for the fish or into a glass of salty or soapy water.

The tachinid fly is the European earwig's natural enemy. A direct spray of insecticidal soap will dehydrate and kill all earwigs.

Don't confuse earwigs with the rove beetle which preys on many small garden pests. The clearest differ-

ence is that the beetle lacks the earwig's clearly defined pincers on its rear.

Flea Beetles

Flea beetles are small, dark insects about $\frac{1}{16}$ inch long that bound like fleas when approached and make hundreds of tiny "shot holes" in the leaves of brassica (cabbage family) seedlings and tomato (nightshade family) crops. If the seedlings are strong and healthy, they are able to outgrow the damage. But in adverse weather that slows seedling growth, flea beetles may stunt or kill the plants. Discourage flea beetles by planting a shady living mulch.

Nc nematodes parasitize the beetles. Apply a few drops of water or bedding containing the nematodes around the base of plants. Control flea beetles with garlic or hot pepper sprays or a dusting of lime. A dusting of talcum powder may discourage flea beetles. Also use ryania or sabadilla to control flea beetles. As a last resort, apply rotenone or pyrethrum insecticides on serious infestations.

Fruit Fly

Fruit flies are small (roughly $\frac{1}{8}$ inch long) flies that, depending on the species, eat fruit of different kinds and lay eggs in that fruit. Anyone who has let bananas get overripe in the house knows what fruit flies look like.

In some areas, including the citrus groves of California, certain fruit flies can be serious pests. Controlling them can be a challenge. Some of the BTs are good controls for these persistent insects. Citrus oils, insecticidal soaps, neem, and some of the specific pheromones also have proven effective in controlling fruit flies.

Grasshoppers & Locusts

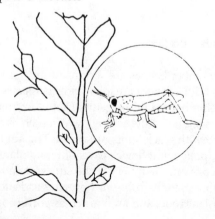

Many species of grasshoppers eat and gnaw through leaves and stems, destroying entire plants without necessarily eating the whole thing. Up to two inches long, grasshoppers propel themselves with long, strong back legs.

When conditions are right — or should we say wrong — short-horned grasshoppers gather in large numbers and eat voraciously. These are the locusts which periodically occur in hordes and eat their way across miles of cropland. Great swarms may interfere with traffic and may shut out much of the sun's light. No one knows what causes these creatures to swarm or to stop swarming.

Tilling the soil right after harvest prevents many grasshoppers from depositing eggs and exposes eggs that have already been laid. A thick fall mulch will keep many of the egg deposits in the soil from hatching.

Protect tender seedlings from grasshopper damage with Agronet™ or cheese cloth. Numerous birds, insects, snakes, and toads prey on grasshoppers. Spiders also snare large numbers of grasshoppers in their webs. Rodents, squirrels, mice, and voles eat grasshoppers and their eggs.

Grasshopper controls also include hot pepper and soap sprays, and sabadilla. To control grasshoppers and locusts, apply the commercially available protozoan parasite *Nosema locustae*. The protozoan insecticide will kill half of the targeted grasshopper population with a month of application.

Prevent damage to specific crops by covering with spun fiber or cheese cloth. Trap grasshoppers with a half-full jar of 1 part molasses to 10 parts of water.

Gypsy Moth Larvae

The two-inch long hairy brown Gypsy moth caterpillar (larva) feeds on a multitude of fruit, ornamental, and shade trees during spring and early summer. The adult moths are light brown or yellowish brown. The gypsy moth is most prevalent in the Northeast where periodically the infestation is so bad that most trees are defoliated to some degree.

They can be trapped with a piece of burlap wrapped loosely around the trunk of the target tree. The larvae are trapped in the burlap as they crawl down the trunk at night. Simply crush the caterpillars in the burlap, put them in a sealed plastic bag in the sun or shake them out into strong saltwater.

A direct spray of lime or insecticidal soap will stop larvae. BT is a good control for acute infestations. Neem is another biological insecticide with very low toxicity to mammals to control gypsy moth caterpillars. Pyrethrum sprays are good choices as well.

Some experts recommend a policy of "grin and bear it" where these pests are concerned. They believe that this hands-off technique will maximize the infestation and thus shorten the period of the pest outbreak as well as lengthening the periods between severe outbreaks. It will take strong-minded gardeners to follow this regime when caterpillars are climbing all over everything, including themselves!

Hornworms

Appropriately named, these green-striped four- to five-inch-long caterpillars sport a red horn (tobacco hornworm) or a black horn (tomato hornworm). More common in the Midwest and eastern states than in the west, hornworms have ravenous appetites for foliage and fruit of tomatoes, peppers, potatoes, and eggplant.

They winterover several inches underground in a hard protective cocoon. Adult moths with a wingspan up to five inches first appear about dusk during late spring. The moth's unique quality of hovering in mid air while feeding on nectar earned them the name "hummingbird moth."

Careful examination of plants and hand picking is the best control of all — nothing is more environmentally sound! Encourage brachonid wasps which are natural parasitic predators. If you must, use BT or ryania to control infestations. The night-flying moth is also attracted to lighted electronic traps.

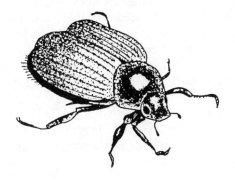

Japanese Beetles

Japanese beetles are shiny greenish-blue oval insects about ½ inch long that feed on just about any kind of plant. Accidentally imported to America before World War I, Japanese beetle populations exploded in the absence of natural enemies to check their growth.

In Japan, a bacteria that causes a fatal blood disease kept the beetles' growth in check. Bacteria, which causes infected beetles to turn a milky white and die, was isolated in 1933 by U.S. government entomologists. The bacteria (*Bacillus popilliae*) was given the name milky spore disease. The bacteria is a commercially available powder that is applied to the soil where it lives for years. Each year, the bacteria grows and spreads over a larger area. It is completely harmless to other soil life, insects, plants, and animals.

The larvae of the Japanese beetle live in the soil and often in turf-grass sod until they mature into adult beetles and fly away. Both larvae and adults are plant eaters.

Birds, mostly flickers and starlings, love to dine on Japanese beetles and their grubs. In fact, they will abandon grain at bird feeders to stalk juicy grubs in the lawn and garden. Skunks and moles eat the grubs. Spiders are also active Japanese beetle predators.

Apply milky spore disease powder by the spoonful (according to directions) on lawns or grassy areas on three- or four-foot centers. The bacteria takes several years to spread before it keeps most Japanese beetles under control. In the meantime, plant garlic and geraniums to repel beetles. Handpick for quick control of a few beetles. Sabadilla and rotenone are also effective controls.

June Bugs

These brown, fat, oval beetles cause the most damage as larvae. The grubs are often found in the soil of lawns and gardens along with Japanese beetle larvae. They eat plant roots. If they are numerous, you may be able to easily peel sod back where they have severed the roots. The adults eat leaves of deciduous and coniferous trees and may damage potato and strawberry foliage in gardens. They fly against screens in late spring, clattering about as they head for light, especially in the early evening.

Use milky spore disease to destroy the larvae. In cool climates, it may take two or more years for milky spore disease to effectively reduce the grub population.

Leafhoppers

Leafhoppers include many small, eighth-inch-long, wedge-shaped insects that are green, white, or yellow. The aster leafhopper, beet leafhopper (also called whiteflies in the West), and potato leafhopper are a few examples of the different species. All leafhopper species have wings shaped like a peaked roof when they are at rest. These sap-sucking insects attack many different plants causing loss of vigor and leaves that turn yellow or brown.

Prevent and control leafhopper attacks by removing dense weeds and keep plant residues cleaned up. Lacewings will eat leafhopper eggs.

Control leafhoppers by covering vegetables with Agronet™ or spray with sabadilla. Use spot treatments of pyrethrum spray for serious infestations. Some species are attracted to black light traps.

Watch for commercial adaptations of fungal diseases recommended for control of leafhoppers. These naturally occurring insecticides will be more and more common in the future.

Leafminers

The adult leafminer fly lays eggs that hatch into eighth-inch-long green or black maggots. These tiny maggots burrow between leaf surfaces, leaving a telltale white tunnel outline. The damage is seldom fatal or causes much of as problem, but it is unsightly. If populations are very large, leafminers can restrict plant growth.

Some crops that they like are bean, blackberry, cabbage, lettuce, beets, Swiss chard, pepper, potato, and spinach. If you have problems one year, then the next time you plant that crop, cover with a spun fiber and seal the edges at the soil level. Make sure to plant in a different location from the previous year because the pupae overwinter in the soil.

Ladybugs and lacewings eat eggs. Unless the infestation is severe, you can remove and destroy infested foliage and the plants will recover.

Mealybugs

Mealybugs are common on house plants, fruit trees, and vegetables. These relatives of scale look like

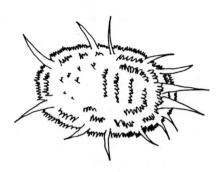

small bits of cotton one eighth- to one quarter-inch long on stems, leaf undersides, and especially in the axillae between leaves and stems. Mealybugs and aphids both attract ants which farm them, and they both foster sooty mold growth by exuding honeydew.

These sucking insects can stunt plants or even kill them. Their waxy covering and the way they hide in small places between plant parts make them hard to kill.

Lacewings, Australian ladybird beetles, and a small beetle known as the mealybug destroyer (*Cryptolaemus montrouzeri*) are natural predators that are available commercially. Parasitic chalcid wasps are another natural enemy of several species of mealybugs.

Control mealybugs by flushing them from foliage with a jet of cold water. A fine-bristled toothbrush or cotton swab dipped in mineral oil or rubbing alcohol makes a marvelous weapon to wield against mealy bugs. Just apply the oil or alcohol to the stationary insects where they are clinging to the plants. Insecticidal soap is also a good control for mealybugs.

Mexican Bean Beetle

The destructive Mexican bean beetle is often confused with the ladybug which is in the same family. The yellowish-colored adults have 16 black spots on their dome-shaped back, distinguishing them from ladybugs has 12 or fewer spots and are more orange in color.

Adult Mexican bean beetles live through the winter and emerge from their hiding places in the late spring to start their path of destruction through bean crops and produce one or two more generations before the weather turns cold.

Early planting could get beans through the summer unscathed. Floating row covers can help keep Mexican bean beetles from your bush beans. Destroy any orange-yellow beetle eggs found on the undersides of bean leaves and orange, spined larvae feeding on the leaves. After harvesting, remove and hot compost all debris to discourage overwintering.

Planting a row of potatoes next to a row of beans repels Mexican bean beetles well in all beans except limas. This intercropping scheme also repels Colorado potato beetles. Hand pick beetles, but take care to count the spots! Don't destroy our garden friends, the ladybugs.

Some species of ladybugs prey on Mexican bean beetle eggs and larvae. The anchor bug and the spined soldier beetle are other predators. The parasitic wasp *Pediobius foveolatus* is commercially available. Use ryania or neem for acute infestations and rotenone or pyrethrum only as a last resort.

Nematodes or Eelworms

There are hundreds of thousands of species of microscopic nematodes, also known as eelworms or round worms. Some are destructive to plants; others are beneficial garden-pest parasites.

Nematodes that are plant pests are common in some parts of the country where they feed on plant roots or leaves, causing severe injury to many garden crops. Carrots are often targets of root-feeding nematodes. Harmful nematodes also go after potatoes, beans, turnips, squash and cucumbers.

Symptoms of nematode damage include dwarfed plants with sickly growth, poorly formed leaves, flowers, roots and stems, dieback and chlorotic (yellowing between leaf veins) foliage. Some nematodes cause swellings, root knots or galls to form that block the flow of fluids through plants. Be careful not to confuse nematode root knots with nitrogen-fixing-nodes found on legume (bean, pea, and clover) roots. Wounds inflicted by nematodes provide entrances for disease organisms.

Root-knot nematodes are very tiny worms that live in and around roots, especially under moist conditions. They are very difficult to see and detect. To inspect for nematodes, uproot a sickly plant or soil next to a suspect plant and examine the roots very carefully with a magnifying glass. Nematodes appear as very tiny translucent worms wiggling around the roots. Carefully inspect the roots for damage and check against other symptoms listed above before taking action.

Prevent infestations by planting the variety of French marigolds (*Tagetes patula*). If they are thickly planted and then plowed under, they will repel nematodes for up to three years. Their roots exude "root diffusant" chemical that kills or repels soil nematodes. Simply planting these marigolds in the same garden plot is not going to repel nematodes. They must be tilled under.

Black mustard and white mustard plants produce oils that drive destructive nematodes away. Crop rotations also slow proliferation of destructive nematodes. It's never a good idea to continually plant crops from the same families in the same places year after year.

Many predacious fungi will trap nematodes and other soil fungi. The beneficial fungi also produce unpleasant substances that repel nematodes.

The best control for nematodes is BT. The most effective strains of BT BT/H-14 to control nematodes is sold under the brand name Vectobac™. A couple of soil drenchings at 7-day intervals should eliminate them in about ten days to two weeks. Neem, the extract from the tropical neem tree, is effective in controlling root-knot nematodes.

Scale Insects

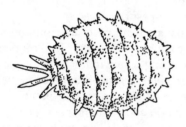

Many species of scale insects feed on the juices of numerous flowers, shrubs, trees, and vegetables. Scale are found in clusters on plant leaves, stems or fruit. They appear as tiny, raised, immobile spots. Scale ranges in color from white through brown to black. Some are hard, others soft and cotton-like. The two general groupings are armored scales and soft scales. Young scale insects wander on plants looking for a likely spot to settle down. The adults are sedentary.

These pest suck plant juices. When they exist in large numbers, the infested plants become stunted and pale green or chlorotic. The scale may be difficult to notice when they blend in with foliage and hide under leaves.

Reduce infestations by scraping as many scale insects as possible from woody growth without damaging the plant. Use a fine-bristled toothbrush or cotton swab dipped in mineral oil or rubbing alcohol to remove small infestations. Apply the poison to the insects where they are clinging to branches. Just touch the scale with the moist swab. The alcohol dries the scale out quickly.

Control scale by suffocation with dormant-oil and soapy sprays. Insecticidal soap is an excellent control for spot treatments.

Ladybugs and lacewings are good biological scale controls. When other food sources are low, feed these predatory insects the commercial protein food called Wheast. There also are scale parasitoids, a tiny yellow wasp (*Aphytis melinus*) for armored scales and a tiny yellow and black wasp (*Metaphycus helvolus*) for soft scales.

Slugs and Snails

Slugs and snails are soft, slimy mollusks that hide by day and feed at night. Slugs look like snails without shells. They will eat almost any vegetation, roots included, leaving a slimy trail of silvery mucus in their wake. These creatures winter over in warm, damp locations in most climates. They reproduce prolifically and the young mollusks often eat relatively more than adults. Slugs and snails especially like tender seedlings. They will migrate to adjacent gardens in quest of food. A clean, dry perimeter around the garden will make it difficult for them to pass.

To control these mollusks, take the kids on a nighttime slug and snail patrols with flashlights. Hand pick all the slugs you spotlight. Or, arm the kids with a spray bottle containing a 50 percent ammonia/water solution. When sprayed sparingly, the solution dissolves mollusks without harming the plants.

Night time trips through the lawn will catch many slugs and snails grazing. Step on them. Come back in 15-30 minutes to crush more pests feeding on the crushed slugs and snails.

A thin layer of lime, diatomaceous earth or salty beach sand 2 to 6 inches wide around individual plants, beds or the entire garden will present an impassable barrier to slugs and snails. The lime is not thick enough to alter the pH and will repel or dissolve pests. The razor-sharp edges of the diatomaceous earth or beach sand will slice their soft bodies, causing internal fluids to leak out.

To trap slugs and snails, attach short one-inch feet on a wide board and leave it in the garden. The pests will seek refuge under the board. Just pick up the board every day or two and shake the slugs off. Step on them, feed them to the chickens, or cut them in two and add to the compost pile as a source of nitrogen.

A slug and snail hotel is easy to make. Several snail and slug hotels are also available at nurseries and garden centers. In this kind of hotel the snails and slugs check in, but they never leave! Use a hack saw to cut a window (slot) about an inch high and three inches long near the base of a coffee can. Pour in a little beer or yeast dissolved in water into the hotel. Better yet, a jam and water mix. Put the plastic lid on the hotel/coffee can to prevent the rain from entering and stop evaporation. The lid will also discourage birds and animals from eating the mix. Set the slot or door of the hotel near the soil line. The slugs and snails enter at night for a food orgy only to drown. Remove the lid and pour the dead slugs into the compost pile.

Poisonous baits are available for slugs and snails. These baits will usually have metaldahyde as a base. Simply confine the bait to a slug hotel. The hotel must keep the bait off the soil and dry. By following this method, none of the poison bait touches the soil and the bait is inaccessible to children, pets and birds. Place baited slug and snail hotels in out-of-the-way places.

The predatory snail (*Ruminia decollata*), available commercially, is yet another way to combat plant-eating slugs and snails.

Dolomitic lime, when spread lightly throughout the garden, will kill slugs and snails. It will not harm foliage in light concentrations and does not wash away with a light rain.

Small slugs and snails actually eat more than the adults. The chemical measurol, found in many commercial slug and snail bait will not attract young slugs or snails, therefore you should choose other controls to catch the young ones.

Sod Webworm

Sod webworms are the gray-brown to green to dirty white larvae of several moths in the *Crambus* genus that are pests of grains, grasses and lawns. They can be a serious lawn pest. The treatment for sod webworms is the same as for cutworms and armyworms. The sod webworm, ½ to 1 inch in length, feeds on grass blades at night. They can cause large brown patches in the lawn. To diagnose, look for them at or slightly above the soil level in the layer of dead grass below the green grass blades.

Another way to diagnose webworms is to apply a soapy solution (1 tablespoon of liquid detergent or soap per 2 quarts of water) to the suspected area. Watch closely for several minutes to see if soap-irritated caterpillars appear.

BT offers good control to the larvae. Parasitic nematodes are another excellent biological control for sod webworms.

If the infestation is severe, you can use pyrethrum.

Sow Bugs & Pillbugs

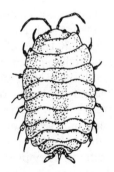

These interesting creatures are members of the Crustacea class, and so are more closely related to lobsters than to thrips or beetles. They are the only crustaceans that live entirely out of water. The way to tell pillbugs from sowbugs is that sowbugs have two small appendages at the end of their bodies and pillbugs are the ones that can roll up into a ball when disturbed. These creatures are about ½ inch or slightly more in length.

Sowbugs and pillbugs rely on damp conditions and so will never become pests under dry conditions. They normally are beneficial organisms that feed on dead and decaying foliage rather than attack healthy plants. But sowbugs will eat tender seedlings, particularly those of beans and peas. They will also chew on squashes or strawberries that touch the ground.

Prevent this pest by keeping the garden free of too much decaying debris. Control with a conservative spot dose of pyrethrum spray or a dusting of wood ashes. A weak lime spray will also deter them. If sowbugs are a problem in the compost pile, dust with lime and keep the pile cooking so it is too hot for them to inhabit.

Diatomaceous earth scattered over the area where beans and peas have been sown will discourage sowbugs and pillbugs. You will have to experiment with the amount needed to discourage these crustaceans — too little will not repel them and too much can cause the soil surface to harden into a comparatively impenetrable layer.

Spider Mites

Spider mites are smaller than the period at the end of this sentence and range in color from green and yellow to red. Relatives of spiders and ticks, spider mites have eight legs which distinguishes them from six-legged insects. Most are so small that you will need a 30X magnifying light scope to identify them.

There are many species of spider mites. They are most commonly found on house plants but also affect many different garden plants. They thrive in warm, dry conditions. They pierce leaves and suck out plant juices, leaving small yellowish-white spots on leaves (stippling). These spots are the telltale signs that spider mites are hiding on leaf undersides.

Spider mites may spin tiny webs between leaves and stems that require careful scrutiny to detect. Warm weather hastens mite development and helps multiply their numbers. Cool damp weather keeps mites under control naturally.

Several different predatory mites are available commercially. The most commonly used species is *Phytoseiulus persimilis*, which is used on commercial crops both in greenhouses and outdoors to control pest mites and thrips.

Control pest mites on house plants and outdoor plants by blasting them off the foliage with a jet of cold water. Pay particular attention to the undersides of leaves. When treating house plants during the growing season, leave the plants outdoors in a warm, shady location for a few days and then respray with a jet of water. If infestation is severe, use insecticidal soap, or a mild lime or pyrethrum spray.

Stink Bugs (Squash Bugs)

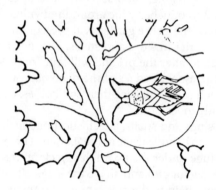

Dark-brown adult stink bugs, also called squash bugs, are just over a half-inch long and stink when squashed. Young stink bugs are half the size of adults with green bodies and a head with a red tint. They feed on plant sap and release a toxin into plants that causes wilting. Seedling cucumbers, melons and squash may fall victim to stink bugs. First the leaf fringes turn crisp and dark. Later the entire vine dies. Older plants may loose parts or runners in the same manner.

Repel stink bugs by interplanting radishes, marigolds or nasturtiums. A garden free of debris and plant residues eliminates hiding places. Stink bugs often overwinter under garden debris. Crop rotation and fall tilling help keep overwintering bugs in check. Trellised vines are less susceptible to attack.

Handpick stink bugs before they reach infestation levels. Tachinid flies are natural enemies that deposit parasites in this pest. Sabadilla is an effective insecticide for stink bug infestations.

Tent Caterpillars

Several butterfly larvae, mostly of the *Malacosoma* genus, are categorized as tent caterpillars. The most common is the eastern tent caterpillar. All tent caterpillars hatch in large numbers and can completely

food. They attack many different flowers and vegetables. When they infest a crop, thrips scar and distort leaves and flower buds causing foliage to turn pale before dying. In ornamental gardens, their damage is especially noticeable on such things as white rosebuds. Heavily infested plants may have leaves that appear brown or silver rather than wilted — the spots of fecal matter may well be more noticeable than the thrips themselves. Thrips often occur in the same places as aphids and whiteflies.

Crop rotation will confuse thrips and does a good job of keeping them in check. Many weeds serve as hosts and should be removed. A reflective aluminum foil mulch on the ground under plants will turn the thrips' world upside down, confusing and repelling them.

Lacewings prey on thrips. Mites that prey on thrips also are becoming available. For acute infestations, use insecticidal soap. As a last resort, use dilute oil sprays or rotenone. Thrips are susceptible to dustings of diatomaceous earth or sulfur when applied directly to infested areas.

Weevils

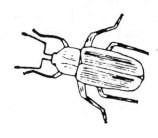

strip deciduous shrubs and trees of foliage. When conditions are right for these larvae, large areas may be defoliated. Wild varieties of apple and cherry trees are favorite plants of tent caterpillars, but many fruit and shade trees can also be attacked. Trees seldom die from these attacks but they are unsightly and unnerving to gardeners.

Easy-to-spot tents of webbing occur mostly in the areas between branches and trunks of infested trees. The nests are small when the caterpillars first hatch, then grow to be a three-dimensional tents a foot or more long and wide as the hordes of caterpillars grow larger. Feeding takes place mostly at night which protects them from birds. During the day they are usually gathered together inside the tough webbing. They stop feeding in early summer, when the caterpillars mature and enter the pupal stage.

Control tent caterpillars by torching the tents or cutting out infested growth whenever you see signs of the eggs or webbing and burn it or simply crush caterpillars and eggs.

BT is an excellent control for tent caterpillars. Horticultural oils also are good controls for these larvae. Natural enemies of tent caterpillars are parasitic flies and wasps that deposit eggs or live maggots into their prey. Baltimore orioles find tent caterpillars a delicacy. Look for this bird's nest dangling like a sack from tree branches.

Thrips

Tiny winged thrips are weak fliers that rasp on leaves and flower buds, sucking the plant juices for

There are numerous species of weevils including those that attack grain, beans, and nut. The adults are beetles with curved snouts which gives rise to their other names —snout beetles or curculios. Weevil larvae do most of the damage to plants. The black vine weevil is a plant pest that attacks the roots of many shrubs, evergreens, and berry species. It crawls from plant to plant since it can't fly. The larva is fat white grub that curls up when disturbed.

When weevil larvae attack a plant, they tunnel into the roots. Eventually, the plant wilts, even when well watered. You may be able to easily pick the plant from the soil — the root system may be destroyed and the plant looks as if it had been cut off at soil level. If you look closely at the soil, you will see the weevil larvae.

The nut weevil has a snout up to three-quarters-inch long, as long as its entire main body. The female weevil uses this snout to bite holes in nuts in which she lays eggs. These adult weevils can fly. The eggs hatch into small grub worms about the time the nut matures and falls to the ground. These grubs eat the nutmeat and burrow into the ground to overwinter. Control nut weevils by cleaning up and freezing or burning infested nuts and foliage so the larvae cannot enter the soil, pupate, and emerge as adults the next season.

Other weevils that feed on foliage at night, hide in the soil or debris at the base of the plant by day. Adults lay eggs in the soil that hatch into rootworms (larvae). The larvae feed on roots and are a creamy white, often with spots and a dark head.

Fortunately, there now are biological controls that work well in controlling weevils. Commercially available parasitic nematodes prey on larvae. Two beneficial nematodes are *Steinernema carpocapsae* and *Heterorhabditis heliothidis*. Since these parasitic nematodes prey only on certain stages of the weevil grub, they will have to be applied several times a year where there are infestations of the weevils. They can be mixed with water and sprayed on the soil beneath the foliage.

Use Tanglefoot™ or some other sticky substance to trap weevils before they climb on to foliage. A dusting of rotenone around roots controls acute infestations of weevils.

Whiteflies

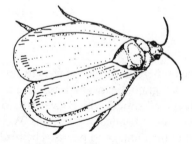

White flies are common indoors, in greenhouses and in gardens. They overwinter well in warm climates but die off during cold northern winters. Identification is easy. If you flick the foliage of infested plants with your hand, you will see what many call "flying dandruff" that quickly settles back on the foliage.

The tiny parasitic wasp, *Encarsia formosa*, attacks adult whiteflies. Both ladybugs and lacewings eat whitefly eggs. All three are commercially available or can be attracted to the garden.

Control with sticky yellow traps (white flies are attracted to the color yellow) hung or placed near infested areas. Ryania, oil, and insecticidal soap are also effective against white flies. (See also leafhoppers)

Wireworms

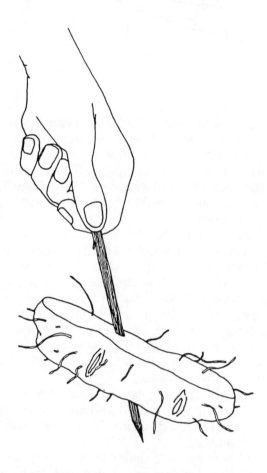

Wireworms are the thin, shiny dark yellowish skinned larvae of click beetles. They remain in the larval form for two to six years. Click beetles have the interesting habit of "clicking" when laid on their backs to upright themselves. The larvae are soil pests that chew small holes in root crops such as potatoes and carrots. They also will attack planted seeds and underground parts of just about any plant.

Prevent wireworms by heavy spring and fall tilling to grind up and expose eggs and larvae. If your soil is infested with wireworms, grow a catch crop of wheat or potatoes among the crops in the garden. Another method is to secure potatoes with the eyes cut out to prevent sprouting, on sticks and bury them around the garden. Lift the wireworm infested potatoes and dispose of them.

The parasitic nematodes mentioned as a control for weevils also are effective in controlling wireworms and other plant pests that live in the soil.

Plant Diseases in General

Plant diseases are caused by bacteria, fungus, virus, other parasites or growth-inhibiting environmental conditions. Prevent diseases by avoiding conditions that cause them.

Many plant diseases are caused or encouraged by poor drainage, poor or imbalanced soil fertility, inadequate air circulation, insect damage and unsanitary conditions. For example, aphids that pierce and suck plant juices transmit viruses when they move from one plant to the next. The wounds aphids make begin to decay and become infected with airborne diseases.

Soil infertility and poor drainage are normally indicated by sickly plants that are prone to disease and insect attack. Throwing more fertilizers at the soil and trying to control pests on sickly plants may be more trouble than it is worth. In the case of poor soil, it is generally better to remove the sickly plants, build the soil and start over with new, healthy plants.

Living soil is full of natural substances that work around the clock to keep plants and soils free of disease. Rich, healthy organic soil is one of the best forms of insurance you can have against plant diseases.

You, the gardener, may be responsible for spreading diseases by handling wet diseased plants and then touching uninfected plants. Smokers may unwittingly spread tobacco mosaic virus to their tomatoes.

Whenever possible, work in the garden when foliage is dry. Most bacteria and fungi need moisture to travel from one plant to another. Removing and destroying any diseased foliage and washing your hands afterward will go a long way to retain overall garden health. Cut and compost heavy weed growth around the garden.

Plant disease-resistant varieties. Look for new varieties that not only grow better in your climate but are much more resistant to disease. Years of careful breeding have given us all kinds of surprising plants.

Most disease organisms can overwinter on infected garden foliage. Composting or tilling fallen leaves, stems and refuse will help keep diseases from resur-

facing. Some diseases, such as potato blight and crown gall live in the soil. Destroying infected plants and not tossing them in the compost pile will keep these disease occurrences to a minimum. The heat generated from the compost pile will kill many diseases. But if you are not diligent about careful composting to get the high temperatures, it is better to destroy diseased plants.

Crop rotation prevents soil-borne diseases from accumulating and infecting subsequent crops. Rotating crops keeps the diseases isolated. When the infecting organisms do not have the right plant families to attack, most will perish. Fusarium and Verticillium are two persistent funguses that can remain viable for 10 to 15 years.

Allow enough space between plants for air to circulate freely. Good air circulation prevents ever-present air-borne fungal spores from settling on foliage.

Plant diseases are more difficult to identify than insect attacks. They may start inside the plant or attack the roots and give little or no notice before killing plants. Many times by the time you notice a disease, it is too late to do anything about it. Other diseases such as gray mold or rust do show externally on foliage. They are much easier to identify and control.

Molds, yeasts, and mushrooms are all funguses. They reproduce by means of tiny spores which spread on the air. The best organic way to cope with fungal diseases in the garden is prevention by keeping the garden clean and using good cultural practices. If the disease is so severe that you decide to use a fungicide, identify the disease, choose the least toxic fungicide and use all appropriate safety precautions.

Bacterial diseases are caused by primitive one-celled plants called bacteria. A disease caused by a bacterium will be more difficult to diagnose than one caused by a fungus.

Viruses, too small to be seen with a microscope, also cause plant diseases. They often are carried from plant to plant by other organisms, or by vectors such as insects, mites, or nematodes.

Bacterial and viral diseases are more difficult to control than those caused by fungi. Often the only solution is to destroy the infected plants and choose another species or a disease-resistant cultivar.

Some conditions that look like diseases are caused not by a fungus, bacterium, or virus but by the culture, the care you are providing. The classic example of a disease-mimicking condition is blossom end rot in tomatoes.

The following are some of the more common diseases.

Anthracnose

The first signs of this fungal disease appear in spring as small, reddish or dark textured spots on foliage. The spots get bigger and more plentiful, and the center becomes sunken, taking on a gray color as the plants grow. As the disease progresses, the spotted leaves deform or dry out and drop or cling to stems.

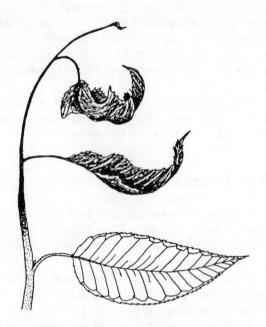

The sign of fire blight, caused by a bacterium, is sudden wilting. New shoots turn dark and die. Pythium blight, also called cottony blight or greasy spot causes dark blotches on grass or other foliage and is most common in hot humid weather. Southern blight, a fungal disease that causes sudden leaf drop, also is most active in hot humid weather.

Potato and tomato blight occur when drainage is poor and weather conditions are cool and damp. Since raised beds heat up faster and drain well, these blights have a difficult time getting started if you grow in raised beds.

Use a Bordeaux mix (lime/copper sulfate) to control fungal blights. However, the only solution to stopping many blights in their advanced stages, especially those caused by bacteria, is to remove the plants and start over by tilling the soil deeply and amending it with compost to improve drainage. Choose disease-resistant plants whenever possible.

The fungal spores are spread by wind, rain, insects, and gardeners. Spores develop quickly under the cool, moist conditions of spring.

Careful sanitation prevents the disease from spreading once it starts. Affected foliage should be removed and burned, or composted in a very active hot pile.

This disease overwinters on infected leaf refuse. It can also stay in living tissue on perennial plants.

A Bordeaux (lime/copper sulfate) spray is effective to control anthracnose on trees and woody perennials.

Blight

The general term blight describes many plant diseases. Signs of blight include dark blotches on foliage, slow growth, sudden wilting and plant death. Most blights spread quickly through large areas of plants. Avoid blights by maintaining the proper nutrient balance in the soil and supply good drainage.

Blossom-End Rot

Blossom-end rot of tomatoes is characterized by a dark, watery spot at the blossom end of the forming tomato. Usually occurring when the tomato is less than halfway mature, the spot spreads and turns darker as the end of the fruit looks more and more rotted.

This is not a disease caused by fungus as most people think; It is a cultural condition usually caused by inconsistent watering, which results in a calcium deficiency.

Avoid blossom-end rot by mulching the garden and watering when needed. A soil that is rich in trees. Instead, you should disinfect the wound — nurseries and garden centers can help you find an appropriate disinfectant. One of the simplest is liquid laundry bleach (sodium hypochlorite) used in a solution of 1 part bleach to 9 parts water. Studies have shown that if you apply pruning paint, you are likely to confine fungus spores under the paint next to the wood. You will avoid fungal reinfections more by letting the scarred wood remain open to light and allowing the tree to heal the wound naturally.

Crown Gall

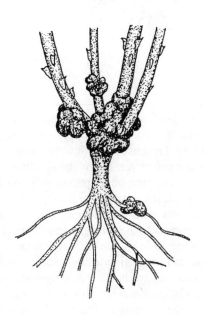

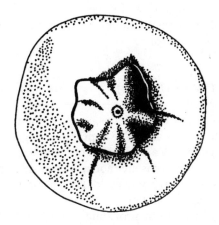

humus will hold water more evenly. You can add dolomitic limestone which is high in calcium at the end of the season to help solve the problem the following year.

Canker

Cankers on soft or woody trunks and branches dwell below the cracked external bark. This dark fungus causes rot and discoloration of affected growth.

Many times, canker begins on trees after their trunks have been hit with a lawn mower. The trunk is bruised. The disease enters this bruised area and starts to spread. Citrus and dogwood trees are especially susceptible to canker.

Control canker by cutting out all of the infected area with a saw, knife or chisel. Experts no longer recommend applying a pruning paint to scarred areas of

Crown gall, a bacterial disease, attacks many plants, especially those of the rose family. The ugly galls are often an inch or more in diameter. The disease causes retarded growth, leaf yellowing and drop, but seldom death.

Control crown gall by removing and destroying affected portions. Badly infected plants should be removed and destroyed. Avoid making new wounds on stems or trunks, since this disease enters through cut and bruised areas. Once the entire gall is removed, disinfect the wound and your tools.

Look for plant varieties that are resistant to crown gall.

Crown gall is no relation to the various sorts of galls caused by gall-causing insects or microbes. These do little harm to the plant and are quite fascinating in showing how plants and other organisms can live together. You commonly see insect galls on certain goldenrods, oaks and maples; they are small plant tumors that form to wall off the organism from the host plant's active tissues.

Damping-off

Damping-off is a soil-born fungal disease that attacks young seedlings, cuttings, and transplants at the soil line. The base of the infected stem rots where it meets the soil or just below the soil line.

Prevent damping-off by providing good air circulation for seedlings, cuttings, or transplants. Make sure the soil drains freely and is damp but not soggy. Many seed companies treat seeds susceptible to damping-off with a chemical fungicide such as Captan.

Avoid damping-off by using a sterile, well-draining mix for growing seeds. After sowing your seeds, sprinkle a light layer of milled sphagnum peatmoss over the top of the planting medium. Sphagnum moss has fungicidal properties.

Downy and Powdery Mildew

Downy, or false, mildew shows up on leaves, creating pale patches. Powdery mildew is a fine pale gray powdery coating on buds, growing shoots and leaves. Both downy and powdery mildews are fungi that attack a wide variety of plants. Both mildews cause foliage to yellow and an overall slowing in growth. Powdery mildew is limited to the surface of foliage. Downy mildew enters the plant's system, growing outward, and is fatal. Powdery mildew is at its worst when roots dry out and foliage is moist. It can be fatal.

Prevent both mildews by avoiding the conditions that they thrive in – cool, damp and humid locations. Mulch the soil and keep foliage dry when watering to keep disease-causing conditions in check. If watering with sprinklers or hoses, be sure to allow time for the foliage to dry before night falls. Fungi like dark, moist places.

The best control is to look for disease-resistant plant varieties. Control downy and powdery mildew by spraying with Bordeaux mixture. If the condition is severe, remove the infected foliage and compost or destroy it. Many times a combination of both methods is necessary for control.

Gray Mold Disease (Botrytis)

Gray mold, a form of botrytis, is one of the most common garden diseases. The appearance of gray mold signifies the advanced stages of many blights. The first signs of botrytis are motley brown splotches that progress to a furry gray mold. Botrytis prospers under cool, damp conditions.

Prevent gray mold by providing plants, especially seedlings, plenty of air circulation. Avoid over-watering and over-fertilizing with nitrogen. Mulch that stays soggy and damp in shady areas promotes gray mold and should be avoided. Control by pruning and destroying infected growth.

Leaf Curl

Leaf curl is most common on peaches, raspberries, and rhododendrons. Leaves and buds discolor, curl and crinkle soon after unfolding. Usually only portions of the plant are affected, but in severe cases all of the leaves buckle. In advanced stages, a powdery gray mold forms on affected leaves. These fungal spores overwinter on woody bark. Growth is sickly, flowers and fruit are deformed and drop prematurely.

This serious fungal disease is transported by overhead irrigation or rain. Avoid sprinkle irrigation, and plant peach trees in dry spots, such as under roof eves.

Remove affected leaves as soon as they show signs of curl. Destroy diseased foliage or place in a "hot" compost pile. Raspberries seriously affected by leaf curl should be removed, destroyed, and replaced with disease-free stock.

Control leaf curl on deciduous plants with an application of Bordeaux mixture during dormancy. Spray is ineffective after buds swell and open. Reapply the fungicide if rainfall washes off the first application soon after spraying.

Leaf Spot

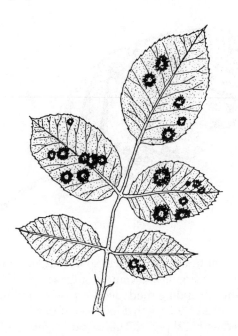

Leaf spot is the symptomatic name given to many diseases. The diseases, which can be caused by bacteria, fungi, or nematodes, cause black spots to form on foliage. Affected fruits are misshapen and unevenly ripe. It is the most common and can be fatal in moist, humid garden climates. Excessive watering and lack of air circulation in cold frames promotes fungal leaf spots. Leaf spot is a common affliction of roses and is a serious, fatal disease in cherry trees. Motley leaf spots grow so large on cherry leaves that they merge with one another. Affected leaves wither and drop.

Prevent fungal leaf spots with crop rotations and adequate air circulation. Control infected foliage by removing and destroying it. Usually hard pruning of rose bushes in winter destroys any leaf spot fungus that tries to overwinter. Take care to destroy all pruned branches as soon as possible.

If the infection is severe, spot-treat with a fungicide. Sulfur-based fungicides are the least toxic.

Red thread

Red thread is a fungal disease that can affect most grasses. It appears as dead patches in lawns combined with red fungus growth on leaf blades. Spot treatments with a low-toxicity fungicide such as sulfur can control this disease if it becomes severe.

Rot

Rots are caused by various fungi and bacteria and can infect the fruit, flowers, roots, stems, and trunks of many plants.

Root rot and dry rot (common in bulbs) are soil-borne diseases that are usually promoted by poor drainage and heavy, frequent watering, especially in the late afternoon and evening. The roots or bulbs turn brown and slimy. The foliage may discolor, wilt and even die. Aphids, nematodes, and other insects are the vectors for these diseases.

Prevent root and bulb rots by supplying adequate drainage and water infrequently during the morning. Crop rotation helps prevent root rot because the specific disease that attacks one family of plants may not affect another.

Many rots can be avoided by planting resistant plant varieties, cutting out infected areas, keeping soil well drained, pruning to increase air circulation, starting cuttings in a sterilized planting medium, and destroying affected plant parts.

Tomatoes may suffer from blossom-end rot. This is not a rot in the same sense as the others described in this section.

Rust

Rust are reddish rust-colored fungi that affect a wide variety of plants. In some cases they may be fatal. Among the most common plants affected are turf grasses. Many lawns get rust during damp, humid weather. Heavy morning dews promote rust. The blades or leaves and stems of foliage turn brown, black, red or yellow when covered with the fungus. The blades or leaves wither and drop. In severe infections, entire plants wither and die.

Prevent the spread of rust by keeping foliage as dry as possible and watering as infrequently as possible. Water only at soil level in areas of severe rust infections.

Control rust by removing and destroying affected foliage. Crop lawns short, picking up the residue with a bagger. Destroy or hot-compost the clippings. In severe cases, after you have tried everything else, spray the rest of the affected plant or lawn with a mild sulfur mix. Asparagus rust appears as brown-red infestations on the plants' branches and foliage. Since it can overwinter, destroy infected foliage. Plant resistant varieties and space the plants so that there is good air circulation.

Some rusts, such as cedar-apple rust, have alternate hosts, in this case, an apple relative and a juniper. White pine blister rust needs susceptible relatives of currants. You can reduce these rusts by eliminating one of the alternate hosts.

Spraying with sulfur is a conservative treatment for these fungal diseases.

Scab

Scab is a fungal disease that appears on a variety of plants. It can look like dark, pus-like spots, yellow spots that turn black or raised spots, some with a warty or corky appearance. Scab may attack foliage, branches or fruit.

This disease is not a problem in dry, arid climates. Scab grows best in damp, cool weather. The fungi overwinters in infected fallen foliage.

Control scab by removing and destroying infected branches, foliage, and fruit soon as they appear. Rotate crops to circumvent this disease that lingers in the soil. Plant scab-resistant varieties. If infection is severe, use a conservative fungicide such as sulfur.

Shotgun or Shothole Fungus

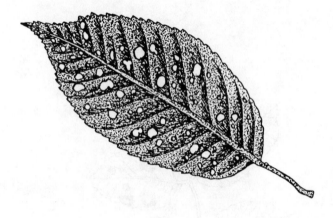

Similar to anthracnose and leaf spot, shotgun fungus attacks the margins and centers of the leaves of several plants, including rhododendron. Shotgun fungus makes holes in foliage that look like they have been blasted with a shotgun. This disease favors cool damp weather.

Keeping foliage dry is the most conservative, if often impossible, control. Remove and destroy infected foliage. In severe cases, spray plants with a sulfur or Bordeaux mix.

Sooty Mold

Sooty mold is a black surface fungus that grows on sticky honeydew excreted by aphids, mealy bugs, some scale and young whiteflies. This unsightly mold is not a big problem, but restricts flower bud and vegetable production.

The dark mold attacks many plants and is most common on citrus, elm, magnolias, maples and some popular trees.

Control sooty mold by first controlling the insects that excrete honeydew. The mold will disappear once the honeydew is eliminated. In severe cases, use a horticultural oil spray to smother aphids and their eggs.

Wilt or Yellows

Wilts or yellows may be fungal or bacterial diseases. They are best controlled by planting resistant plant varieties.

Fusarium wilt, also called yellows, is a soil-borne fungus that is most common in warm, humid weather. Wilt spreads quickly in temperatures above 90° and is kept in check when the soil temperature is below 60°. This fungus gets into plant circulation systems. Diagnose fusarium by cutting into a branch or stem — if it is blackish-brown inside, it is fusarium wilt.

Vercillium wilt may cause several branches or the entire plant or tree to wilt suddenly. The foliage turns yellow before dropping. Some plants and trees wilt suddenly while others may take much longer.

Control vercillium wilt by removing and destroying all dead branches and foliage. Fertilize affected plants heavily to promote new, strong growth. If an entire plant or tree is affected, remove it and do not plant a similar wilt-prone specimen in the same ground.

Replace bulbs, corms or tuberous roots that have been affected by fusarium wilt.

A common bacterial wilt is transmitted by the striped cucumber beetle and its larva as they feed on cucumber, melon, or squash plants. Control for the wilt by controlling cucumber beetles.

Viruses

Viruses are still a mystery. They act like living organisms in some instances and nonliving chemicals in other cases. We do know that viruses are spread by insect, mite, plant, animal and human vectors. Infected tools often carry viruses from one plant to another.

Typical symptoms of viral infection are sickly growth and low yields of flowers and fruits. In some cases, viral diseases can cause sudden wilt and death. Once a plant gets a virus, there's little you can do.

Mosaic is one of the most common forms of virus. It causes mottled yellow and green spots on blossoms and leaves. Leaf curl is another form that viral diseases take. Leaf curl causes leaves to curl up and stimulates excessive branching which inhibits the flow of fluids within the plant. Once affected with some viruses, virtually nothing can be done to save the plant. Remove and destroy affected plants. Replace with new, healthy stock that is resistant to viruses. Tobacco mosaic is a common viral disease. This virus disease gets into the system of tomatoes and other members of the nightshade family (eggplants, peppers, potatoes, and tobacco). The disease stops the flow of fluids within the stems. The tomatoes may appear healthy, but the leaves gradually grow smaller, and if you break open a stem, it will be black and mushy inside. The only solution to this condition is to pull the plant and burn it to prevent the disease from spreading.

Tobacco mosaic virus is spread by insect vectors and by people. If you use tobacco, wash your hands before handling eggplants, peppers, and tomatoes to prevent the possible spread of tobacco mosaic virus.

One of the most common viral diseases is cucumber mosaic virus which is transmitted by the striped cucumber beetle as it chews on the leaves of cucumber, melon, squash, and pumpkin plants. The larvae also can transmit the disease as it feeds on plant roots. Control the virus by controlling the beetle.

Organic Pesticides

Botanical sprays are made from plants and other naturally occurring substances. Some botanical sprays are toxic to insects; others are just offensive and act as repellents.

Always follow the directions on the package of all products. The application rate and frequency printed on the containers is extremely important, and must be followed for effective control.

Bacillus thuringiensis, commonly referred to as BT, is the best known of several bacteria that have been

BT can be applied directly into the stems with a syringe.

discovered to attack the larval forms of insects. Milky spore disease (*Bacillus popilliae*) turns the grubs white as it kills them, thus the name. Other related microbial insecticides are *B. lentimorbus* and *B. sphaericus*.

In 1948, *B. lentimorbus* and *B. popilliae* were combined in a product called Doom, the first of many commercial bacterial insecticides. Aimed at controlling Japanese beetles and some of the other lawn grubs, this milky spore disease compound proved very successful when used exactly as directed.

Caterpillars and worms eat the bacteria that is applied to the surface of the foliage and within a short time their digestive systems are poisoned. Cabbage loopers, cabbage worms, corn earworms, cutworms, gypsy moth larvae, hornworms and some nematodes are controlled. Bacterial insecticides containing one or more of the above-listed pathogens are sold as dormant spore dusts or liquids under many commercial names.

BT was first made into a commercial product in 1958. Since then, more than a half dozen different strains of BT have been discovered and purified into marketable bacterial insecticides. *B. thuringiensis* var. *kurstaki* (BTK) is toxic to many moth and caterpillar larvae, including many of the species that feed on vegetable, ornamentals and lawn grasses. *B. thuringiensis* var. *israelensis* (BTI) is effective against the larvae of mosquitoes, black flies and fungus gnats. *B. thuringiensis* var. *san diego* (BTSD) targets the larvae of Colorado potato beetles and elm beetle adults. *B. thuringiensis* var. *tenebrionis* (BT) is lethal to Colorado potato beetle larvae. Other varieties are currently under development.

Since BT usually does not produce spores within insect bodies, several applications may have to be made to control an insect pest infestation.

All of these microbial bacteria are nontoxic to humans, animals and plants. Because these microbial insecticides are living creatures, they are extremely perishable. They must be kept within prescribed temperature ranges and applied according to directions. They are more effective when applied at certain stages of the target pests' lives. Be sure to read and follow instructions or get expert advice.

Diatomaceous Earth

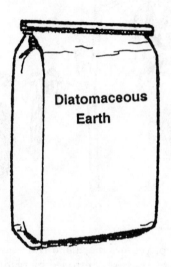

Diatomaceous earth (DE) is the naturally occurring mined material that includes fossilized silica shell remains of the tiny one-celled or colonial creatures called diatoms. DE is fatal to most soft-bodied insects including aphids, slugs, and spider mites. DE also contains 14 trace minerals in a chelated (available) form.

DE is not registered as a pesticide or fungicide, so we can only make recommendations based on the research and observations of expert gardeners. DE is not active itself — it has its effect on insects and other soft-bodied pests when they walk on it or it is dusted on them.

DE also will kill beneficial insects. It first abrades the waxy coating on pest shells or skin, allowing body fluids to leak out. If the pest ingests the razor-sharp diatomaceous earth, it acts similarly on the creature's gut.

Earthworms, animals, humans and birds however, can digest diatomaceous earth with no ill effects. Use a protective mask and goggles when handling this fine powder to guard against respiratory and eye irritations.

Spread DE in a 2- to 6-inch wide band to prevent slugs and snails from crossing over to eat plants. A dusting of DE is most effective as it must be dry to control pests. Use a plastic bottle or commercial duster to apply DE dust to the undersides of foliage. The dust sticks to the leaves where it stays until washed off by rain or irrigation. For best results, do not water for 48 hours after application.

Mix 1 part DE with 3 to 5 parts water and a few drops of biodegradable dish soap to use as a spray. Apply this spray to infestations of pest insects.

Caution! Do not use swimming pool diatomaceous earth. Chemically treated and heated, it contains crystalline silica that is very hazardous if inhaled. The body is unable to dissolve the crystalline form of silica which causes chronic irritation.

Homemade Garden Pest Repellent Sprays

Many homemade spray preparations are outstanding pest repellents. A strong hot taste or smelly odor are the main principles behind most home-brewed pest-repellent potions. Note that many of the strong hot mixes will repel more than insects. They can protect plants from being eaten by rabbits, squirrels, and other large pests. The sprays are normally made by mixing repellent plants with a little water in a blender. The resulting slurry concentrate should be strained through a nylon stocking or fine cheesecloth before being diluted with water for application, to keep it from clogging a sprayer.

Cooking or heating preparations generally destroys active ingredients. To draw out ingredients, mince plant and soak in mineral oil for a couple of days. Add this oil to the water including a little detergent or soap to emulsify (suspend) the oil droplets in water.

Detergents and soaps are good wetting and sticking agents for these preparations. The soap dissolves best if a teaspoon of alcohol is also added to each quart of water.

Chrysanthemum, marigold, and nasturtium blossoms; pennyroyal, garlic, chive, onion, hot pepper, insect juice (target insects mixed in a blender), horseradish, mints, oregano, tomato, and tobacco residues all will repel many insects including aphids, caterpillars, mites, and whiteflies. Mixes that include tobacco may kill these pests if it is strong enough. These mixes can vary in proportions, but always filter the blended slurry before mixing with water for the final spray. One good recipe is 1 teaspoon of hot pepper or Tabasco sauce and 4 cloves of garlic blended with a quart of water.

A mix of one-eighth to one-quarter cup of hydrated lime mixed with a quart of water makes an effective

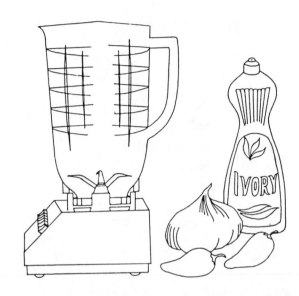

Mix homemade sprays in a blender and filter with cheesecloth before diluting in water for a spray.

insect spray, especially on tiny pests such as spider mites. Mix a non-detergent soap with the lime; the soap acts as both a sticking agent and insecticide. Lime can be caustic in large doses. Always try the spray on a test plant and wait a few days to check for adverse effects to the plant before applying to similar plants. Sprays that include camomile plant parts are used to prevent damping-off and mildew.

Liquid laundry bleach usually is a compound called sodium hypochlorite that is a good fungicide. Usually sold as a five percent solution, it is an eye and skin irritant so wear gloves and goggles when using it. Mix 1 part bleach to 9 parts water and use this solution as a general disinfectant for greenhouse equipment, tools, and plant wounds. The bleach solution breaks down rapidly and therefore has little if any residual effect.

Another natural spray is made from chopped tomato leaves soaked in water. The water is used as a spray against white cabbage butterflies.

A spray made from pests ground up in a blender and emulsified in water will reputedly repel related pests.

Insecticidal Soaps

Insecticidal soaps are mild contact insecticides made from fatty acids of animals and plants. These

Safer's™
Insecticidal
Soap

soaps are safe for bees, animals, and humans. The soap controls soft-bodied insects such as aphids, mealybugs, spider mites, thrips, and whiteflies by penetrating and clogging body membranes.

Safer's Insecticidal Soap is a well-known commercial product. It is a potassium-salt based liquid concentrate that is toxic to insects but not to animals or humans. It is most effective when applied at the first appearance of insects pests.

Soft soaps such as Ivory liquid dish soap, Castille soap, and Murphy's Oil soap, are biodegradable and kill insects in a similar manner as insecticidal soap, but they are not as potent. Do not use detergent soaps as they may be caustic. Mix a few capfuls of one of these soaps to a quart of water to make a spray.

These soaps can also be used as a wetting agent when watering down peat moss, dry potting soil, or seedlings. Both soap and detergent reduce the surface tension of the water to give better penetration. Ivory or Castille soap can also be used as a spreader-sticker to mix with sprays. The soaps help the spray stick to the foliage better, which is important when using contact sprays. The soft soaps will only last for about one day before dissipating.

You will have to reapply these sprays after rain or above ground watering.

Nicotine (sulfate) and Tobacco Sprays

Nicotine is a non-persistent pesticide derived from tobacco. Although naturally derived, it is not usually recommended in organic programs because of its toxicity. It is toxic to most insects and humans if a concentrate is swallowed. This very poisonous compound affects the neuromuscular system, causing insects to go into convulsions and die. Many times nicotine is mixed with sulfur. One well-known brand on the market is Black Flag's Nicotine Sulfate.

Nicotine sulfate (tobacco juice mixed with sulfur) is an excellent insecticide on all plants except members of the nightshade family (eggplant, tomatoes, peppers and potatoes). You can purchase bottled nicotine sulfate or simply use tobacco diluted in water. Apply the nicotine as a spray to kill aphids.

There are far less toxic ways of coping with aphids such as knocking them down with a hard spray of water. It is wise to choose the most conservative means of pest control.

Horticultural Oil

Horticultural oil sprays are safe, non-poisonous and non-polluting insecticides. Similar to medicinal mineral oil, they kill slow moving and immobile sucking insects by smothering and suffocating them. The thin oily film is invisible to humans. Oil spray control is useful in dealing with aphids, scale, spider mites, whiteflies, mealybugs, and thrips.

Modern horticultural oil sprays are petroleum products but are far lighter than the old forms and easier on the plants. They usually can be applied at any temperature without harming plants. To insure the least possibility of leaf scorch from oil sprays, plants should be watered before applying oil sprays. Also, oil sprays are best applied on cloudy days or in the early morning.

Fish oil is an old product, but has recently been used as a dormant spray as well as a spreader sticker for fungicides and pesticides (do not use with copper sprays). When dry, fish oil constitutes a durable coating that is difficult to wash off. Make sure to clean your equipment after applying fish oil, to prevent clogging.

Cruder oil, including petroleum distillates and diesel fuels, contain sulfur compounds that are poisonous to plants. For that reason, these heavy oils are called "weed oils" and used only for weed control on roadways and railroad rights of way.

Sulfur

Sulfur, one of the oldest insecticides, remains useful today even though there are countless more sophisticated pest controls. One reason for its continuing popularity is its low toxicity to humans. Sulfur dust, wettable sulfur, and sulfur in large particles are the three main forms of sulfur.

Sulfur is also a good control for fungal diseases. Commercial products that add copper and oils to the sulfur are more potent than sulfur alone against plant diseases. For that reason, don't use the commercial combination if you plan to apply oil sprays within a month. Avoid scorching foliage by never applying sulfur when temperatures are above 85 to 90° F.

Sulfur is a useful insecticide as well as a fungicide. It is toxic to insects and even more toxic to mites.

Wood Ash

Wood ashes work as a pest repellent for some gardeners. According to some experts, they will repel rabbits and flea beetles. Repel squash bugs by sprinkling plants with water that has soaked with a handful of wood ashes and a handful of horticultural lime for a day or more. A mix of equal parts of wood ashes and dehydrated lime with water can be used to repel beetles. Wood ashes will discourage and repel root maggots when scattered around the base of plants.

Botanical Pesticides

A number of naturally occurring substances derived from plants are popular pesticides among organic gardeners. Among them are the following.

Citrus Oils

Citrus oils, the byproducts of the fruit and juice industries, derived from citrus peels, have insecticidal properties. They appear to be contact poisons and are recommended for use against fleas, aphids, and mites. They also will kill fruit flies, fire ants, flies, paper wasps, and crickets. They are comparatively new to the marketplace and show promise in controlling a wide range of garden and agricultural pests.

Citrus oils, including limonene and linalool, are nontoxic to humans, although in high doses they could irritate skin, eyes, and mucous membranes. Some cats may be sensitive to applications of citrus oils for flea control.

Although very effective, citrus oils break down rapidly.

Garlic Oil

Garlic oil, long used as an insect repellent, is an effective control for some nematodes, larval mosquitoes, aphids, cabbage butterfly larvae, and Colorado

potato beetle larvae. Unfortunately, it also will kill some of the natural controls for aphids, which is why it should be used only when natural controls appear to be absent.

Neem

Neem oil, while relatively new to this country, has been used for many years as a botanical insecticide in Africa and southeast Asia where the neem tree (*Azadirachta indica*) is native. The neem tree, also a handsome ornamental shade tree, is grown in the southern part of our country.

Neem oil is extracted from the foliage and seeds of the tree and is an effective control for dozens of insect pests, including Japanese beetles, leafminers, Colorado potato beetles, mealybugs, whiteflies, caterpillars, crickets, and grasshoppers.

Neem oil acts as both a contact pesticide and a systemic. When bitter, strong-smelling neem oil is added to the soil, the essential ingredients become systemic, entering the plant's stems and foliage. Pests then either pass up the bitter, strong smelling plant parts, or eat them and die before maturing.

Neem oil has very low toxicity to mammals. The active ingredients break down rapidly in sunlight and within a few weeks in the soil.

Pyrethrum

Pyrethrum is an extremely powerful insecticide extracted from the flowers of the pyrethrum chrysanthemum (*Chrysanthemum coccineum* and *C. cinergrii folium*). A broad spectrum pesticide, pyrethrum is very toxic to most insects, including those that are beneficial. If applied as a spray, pyrethrum is a very effective control of flying insects. But if insects do not receive killing doses, they may revive. Pyrethrum is often combined with rotenone or ryania to insure effectiveness. Use this non-selective insecticide to spot spray only heavily infested plants.

Pyrethrum refers to the plant and pyrethrin is the name of the active compound that is toxic to insects. Pyrethroids are synthetic materials that resemble the natural pyrethrin but are more toxic and more persistent.

Although pyrethrum is comparatively safe to use, repeated contact may cause allergic reactions or skin irritation in humans. It can be toxic to cats in formulations that include more than .04 percent pyrethrum. Purchase as a dust or liquid.

Although this and other insecticides often are sold in aerosol formulations, aerosols do not target the pests as tightly as other forms of application; too much is generally released into the air. Aerosol spray is very convenient, but can burn foliage if can is held closer than one foot from the plant. Some aerosols also contain piperonyl butoxide which is toxic to people. All forms of pyrethrum dissipate within a few hours in the presence of air and sunlight.

Quassia

Quassia, made from a South American tree (*Quassia amara*), offers one of the safest botanical pest controls. The tree can be grown in subtropical parts of our country.

Quassia usually is sold in the form of bark and wood chips or shavings. To prepare the spray, soak the material in water for 2 to 3 days, then simmer on low heat for a couple of hours. Strain and mix with soft soap.

Studies are showing that the tree-of-heaven (*Ailanthus altissima*) may have similar properties.

Quassia is harmless to bees and ladybugs, but kills other beneficial insects in the early stages of their lives. This spray is effective on most soft-bodied insects, including aphids, leaf miners, and some caterpillars. Most other insects are not affected.

Ryania

Ryania is made from the stems and roots of the tropical shrub Ryania speciosa. Sold and applied as a dust, ryania is a contact stomach poison that is toxic to aphids, thrips, European corn borers, flea beetles, Mexican bean beetles, hornworms, leaf rollers, coddling moths and several other caterpillars.

Once the pests consume the dust, they stop feeding immediately. Ryania is slow acting and takes up to 24 hours or so to kill target insects. It is less harmful to beneficial insects and is considered harmless to humans and other warm-blooded animals. This insecticide is often mixed with rotenone and pyrethrum.

Rotenone

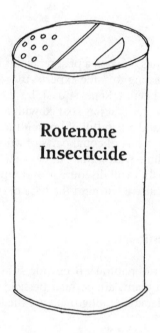

Rotenone is an extract of the roots of several plants including derris species, Lonchocarpus species and Tephrosia species. The latter two also are used as fish poisons in South America and Africa. Applied as a spray (wettable powder) or dust, this non-selective contact insecticide is a stomach poison and slow-acting nerve poison to beetles, caterpillars, flies, mosquitoes, imported cabbageworms, thrips, weevils and beneficial insects.

Popular since the mid 1800's, rotenone does not harm plants, and won't linger in the soil. The spray or dust residues break down in three to seven days in the presence of light and air. Use this spray only as a last resort, and be careful not to let it wash into garden pools or streams, as it is extremely toxic to fish. It is also toxic to birds and pigs.

Sabadilla

Sabadilla is an alkaloid pesticide made from the seeds of a tropical lily, Schoenocaulon officinale, a native of Central and South America. A contact and stomach poison, sabadilla has been used for over four centuries to control aphids, beetles, cabbage loopers, imported cabbage worm, chinch bugs, grasshoppers, and squash bugs. It also is toxic to honey bees, and moderately toxic to mammals.

Sabadilla breaks down rapidly in sunlight. Although safer than rotenone, the dust may irritate eyes and nasal membranes if inhaled. Make sure to wear a mask and goggles when applying. It should be used conservatively, and only when all else fails.

Pest Traps & Barriers

Black lights can be used to catch some egg-laying moths. Light and fan traps attract many insects, including beneficial insects, and their use may do more harm than good.

Pheromones, substances that attract insects by resembling their species' sex hormones, are available for some insect pests and can be good controls when used in combination with traps. When using sex-lure traps, place them away from sensitive plants so insects will be drawn away from them.

Sticky Traps

Sticky traps such as flypaper or Tanglefoot™ are very effective. Sticky resins or other sticky materials can be smeared on attractive yellow or red objects to simulate ripe fruit. When the pests land on the "fruit" they are stuck forever! Tanglefoot™ can also be used as a barrier on plant stems and trunks.

These are particularly effective against white flies which can be tough pests in greenhouses and outdoor gardens.

Because gypsy moth caterpillars go up and down tree trunks, it's possible to make a caterpillar trap of sticky material on paper or cloth wrapped around tree trunks.

You can make your own sticky trap cards by cutting them from bright yellow poster board or painting small boards with bright yellow enamel. Paint the yellow areas with a heavy grade automotive oil and place among or near infested plants. When the yellow areas are covered with bugs, just wash them off and repaint with oil.

Home Made Traps

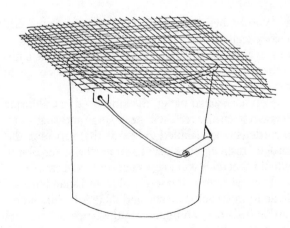

A simple screen placed over a bucket or jar of sweetened water makes an excellent insect trap. Pour some water into a bucket and sweeten it with molasses or sugar and include some protein-like powdered egg or yeast. Pests such as corn borers, cucumber beetles, cutworms, tomato horn worms, and more are attracted to this sweet trap, fall in and drown.

Make a cucumber beetle trap by putting sliced pieces of cucumber or melon in a cardboard milk carton.

A successful yellow jacket trap can be made of a bucket of soapy water over which you tie a slice of juicy fruit such as melon. The yellow jackets will eat the bait and fall in the soapy water. The soap or detergent breaks the surface tension and so the insects sink and drown.

A board in the garden can act as a trap for stink (squash) bugs. They will hide under the board. Then all you have to do is turn the board over and stomp on them.

Earwigs which are nocturnal like to hide in cool dark places during the day. Trap them in short sections of old hose, pipe or bamboo. Empty the traps each morning and dump the earwigs into a salty or soapy solution to kill them.

A cut potato is a simple slug trap. Place the sliced potato under infested plants to attract slugs. Then collect them and dispose of them. Bury a sliced piece of potato to attract wireworms.

An old-fashioned trap for cutworms is to spread a mix of molasses, wheat bran and hardwood sawdust near affected plants. They will crawl in the mixture and then can't get out.

Traps to hold hand-picked pests are easy to make. Drop pest insects in a container of paint thinner, kerosene-topped water, soapy or salt water.

Barriers

Wood ashes, fine sawdust and diatomaceous earth make excellent barriers against slugs and snails as long as they are dry. Spread a 2- to 6-inch wide path of these substances around individual plants or plant areas.

Copper-backed paper, the kind used in California to encircle citrus trees, will keep slugs and snails out of gardens when stapled to boards that surround the garden area. Copper sleeves around the stems of individual vegetables will keep slugs and snails at bay.

There also are commercial slug and snail fences made from recycled plastic and table salt. Surround garden beds or each plant with the fence, according to directions. Slugs and snails will not cross it. The salt bleeds into the soil at a very slow rate and does not affect fertility.

If slugs and snails already are in the area you wish to guard, make extra efforts to remove them by hand picking at night or using any of a number of home-

made or commercial traps.

Sticky substances such as Tanglefoot™ or Stickum™ make good barriers against ants, gypsy moth caterpillars and other garden pests that craw up and down plant stems and trunks. Paint the substance in a ring around the trunk or stem to catch the unwelcome pests.

Simple cardboard collars set about an inch into the soil will keep cutworms and other grubs from chewing on tomato seedlings.

Spun fiber and floating row covers are installed to exclude pests as well as to provide warmth and protection from the elements. Sold under many names, including Reemay™ and Agronet™, these products are outstanding. They are porous enough to pass air and moisture, but the weave is too fine for insects to penetrate. These products are highly recommended for insect control and for extending growing seasons. Covering plants with spun fiber works exceptionally well to exclude cabbage flies, beetles, slugs, and many large insects.

Organic Fungicides

The fungicides listed here have low environmental impact and are recommended, if needed, in organic gardens. Many other commercially available fungicides are highly toxic and should be used with great care if at all in the home garden.

The less toxic pesticides often act more slowly on the target pests. This is one of the compromises you must be willing to make if you want to garden more organically.

As with any garden chemical or compound, you should read instructions carefully and follow the recommendations for mixing, application, and conditions under which the substance should be applied. Some of the naturally occurring fungicides, including copper and sulfur, have important temperature range restrictions when applying.

If it is too hot when you apply copper- and sulfur-based sprays, these pesticides may burn the foliage, creating more damage than benefit. It's better to apply these fungicides during a period of cool weather. Copper- and sulfur-based pesticides are used as both insecticides and fungicides.

Bordeaux Mixture & Copper as Fungicides

Bordeaux mix combines copper, sulfur, and lime in an effective fungicide. It was first used in French vineyards during the last half of the nineteenth century to discourage theft. Vintners soon discovered that the material, when painted on grape vines, eliminated powdery mildew, an introduced scourge of French vineyards at that time.

Variations of this fungicide use other materials in combination with copper sulfate. Wettable powders combine with water to make a sprayable solution. This fungicide coats foliage with a fine layer that remains active for several weeks.

Copper sulfate alone, also called bluestone, is available for use as a fungicide. Bluestone is available is several forms — solid, wettable powder, dust or concentrated liquid.

Never apply Bordeaux mixture or any other pesticide, including copper sulfate, when the temperature is above 85° F. Cool weather application will produce the greatest effect from these fungicides.

Copper compounds are poisonous to fish and aquatic invertebrates. Copper compounds are moderately toxic to humans and irritating to skin and eyes. Therefore, these compounds should be treated with respect. Use mask, goggles, and protective clothing to apply.

Diatomaceous Earth & Sphagnum Moss

Diatomaceous earth, a valuable multi-purpose substance is not just a good insecticide and barrier to soft-bodied pests, it also is a good control for damping-off. It's often applied as an alternative to the popular commercial product, Captan.

Milled sphagnum moss is another good deterrent to for avoiding damp-off. Use a sprinkling of milled sphagnumee peatmoss on top of seed flats after you have planted the seeds. This should greatly reduce damp-off problems.

Fish Oil

Fish oil is a traditional substance that has long been used as both an insecticide and fungicide. More recently, it's being used as a dormant spray as well as a spreader sticker for fungicides and pesticides. Fish oil makes a hard coating that is difficult to wash off after it's dry. Clean equipment carefully and thoroughly after applying fish oil to prevent clogging.

Never use fish oils with copper products.

Sulfur Based Fungicides

Sulfur is useful as a fungicide, insecticide, and miticide. By itself it has low toxicity for humans, but the dust should not be inhaled. Sulfur compounds are highly irritating to skin, eyes, and mucous membranes. Use mask, goggles, and protective clothing when applying. In considering its use, you should remember that it is toxic to beneficial insects and microorganisms as well as the undesirable ones.

It can be used as a dust or wettable powder to mix with water and a wetting agent to make a spray. It is effective against rust and will prevent mildew, scabs and several other fungal diseases. When heated, sulfur is very strong smelling and, in this form, has been used as a fumigant for centuries.

When sulfur is in a pesticide with copper and oils, the combination is very strong and should be used sparingly only in cool weather to avoid burning seedlings and succulent foliage.

Applying Sprays and Powders

* Treat all pesticides with caution and respect. Remember they are poisons.

* Keep pesticides out of the reach of children.

* Always take protective measures when spraying any kind of pesticide. Wear a long-sleeved shirt, pants, hat, gloves, goggles, and a respirator. Shower thoroughly after applying any toxic spray. Wash your "spraying clothing" separately from your regular clothes.

* Only apply spray or dust to the target plant or ground around the plant that is infested with insect pests. Fungicides must be applied to the entire plant and adjacent plants.

* Spot spray whenever possible. Many pesticides kill beneficial insects.

* More expensive pressure sprayers costing over $10 are available that hold up to two quarts of spray.

* Use a small hand sprayer.

Some of the best sprayers are inexpensive pump-and-squirt models that hold only one quart of solution.

* Buy a sprayer that has a nozzle that is easy to take apart and clean. Rebuilding kits are available for more expensive sprayers.

* More expensive pressure sprayers costing over $10 are available that hold up to two quarts of spray.

* Follow directions on the label regarding dilutions and rates of application as well as frequency. Do not concentrate or arbitrarily mix different materials.

* Dusters are very convenient. They are great to apply diatomaceous earth, lime, sulfur, or any other powder.

* Keep organic controls in their own containers that are well labeled.

* Always pour out excess spray and dispose of safely.

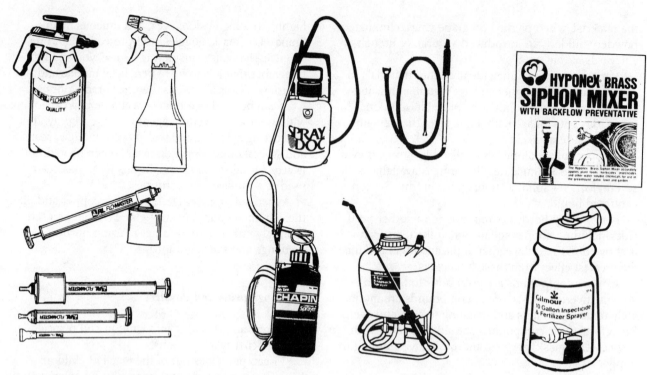

The sprayers are grouped in categories of size. The small sprayers on the left are made for small jobs when the spray needs to be very direct. These sprayers are excellent for most needs. The larger sprayers will hold from 1 ½ gallons to 3 gallons of spray. The sprayers in this group are also very accurate. The siphon mixer and the hose-end sprayers are to spread fertilizers. They would apply too much pesticide.

   * Spray on calm, windless days in the morning or evening. Do not spray when the sun is shining on foliage.
   * Do not spray open flowers, it could kill bees.
   * Spray plants that have been watered. Spraying dry plants may stress them severely.
   * If you must use aerosols, remember not to apply them too closely. The spray is close to freezing when it exits the nozzle. By the time the spray is a foot away from the nozzle, it has warmed to ambient temperature.

Chapter Six

Vegetable & Herb Gardens

About Vegetable & Herb Gardens

Is there anything better than salads made of vegetables from your own garden warm from the sun and harvested at their flavorful peak? Vegetable and herb gardens come in all forms, from large, traditionally rectangular plots to small collections of salad vegetables and herbs beautifully tucked into ornamental beds. A small kitchen garden might grow on sunny windowsills or in planters or window boxes.

Whatever kind of vegetable and herb garden you choose, it will help to know about seed selection, plant care, and ways to keep the garden productive throughout and even beyond the growing season.

For the best results in vegetable gardening, plan on paper. Depending on your climate, you may wish to have two to four seasonal plans that can merge from one to another as the plants mature and the seasons change. Group plants by the length of their growing periods. For instance, if you plant early spring crops in one section, later crops can be planted in the same area. Plan to place the tallest and the climbing plants on the north side of garden bed so that they don't shade the shorter vegetables.

Vegetable gardens are most productive if they are on level ground in loose, fertile, well-draining soil, with at least six hours of sunlight each day. Avoid windy sites, and low spots that are slow to warm and fast to cool. If possible, have the vegetable garden near a water source, and convenient for you.

Vegetable gardens planted near shrubs and trees will have to compete for nutrients and water. In addition, they may receive too much shade. Change the location of related vegetables so that they are not in the same place more often than once in every three years. This will help avoid insect and disease buildup.

Seeds

Careful seed selection can make the difference between a successful garden and complete failure. Knowing a bit about vegetable and flower seeds, including the difference between hybrids and open-pollinated varieties, will help you in a number of ways. For instance, open-pollinated seeds usually grow true to type, whereas only about 50 percent of hybrid seeds will be true to the hybrid type in the second generation.

"In the last hundred years there have been three revolutionary developments in plant breeding methods. These are the general acceptance of the Medelian Laws, the use of hybrids, and the development of disease-resistant strains," said Lyman N. White in his 1981 book, *Heirlooms and Genetics*.

The plant-breeding discoveries of the Austrian monk, Gregor Mendel, were published way back in 1866. Although his work proved to be the basis for the scientific study of heredity, it wasn't until the next century that the knowledge was applied to plant breeding. In fact, the greatest advances in plant breeding have come only since World War II.

Sweet corn was the first home garden vegetable to be hybridized. The Connecticut Agricultural Experiment Station hybridized sweet corn 'Redgreen' in 1924. The first hybrid sweet corn to capture a large part of the home garden market was Purdue's 'Golden Cross Bantam' introduced in 1932.

The second vegetable to be hybridized was squash. 'Yankee Hybrid' was introduced and received an All-America Selection award in 1941. In the 1940s, David Burpee of the Burpee Seed Company, hired Dr. Oved Shifriss and urged him to create vegetable hybrids by crossing inbred lines. Inbred lines are the results of breeding closely related individuals. The first hybrid cucumber 'Burpee Hybrid' in 1945 and the first hybrid tomato 'Burpee Big Boy' in 1949 were among the results of Dr. Shrifriss's work.

Many seed packets carry the phrases "All-America Selection" or "AAS Winner." Since 1933, major seed companies have supported the annual competitions to test and promote the best new cultivars of vegetables and flowers. Seed varieties chosen as All-America Selections winners have demonstrated superior growth and flavor in a wide variety of climates across America.

Unless you are familiar with local or regional plant varieties that have superior qualities, buying AAS varieties is recommended. When you grow from seed, you soon will have to deal with seedlings. To get healthy seedlings and bountiful harvests, choose vegetable varieties that grow well in your area. If possible, purchase seed from a local seed company. Ask a knowledgeable expert at your local nursery or garden center which varieties to grow and how to grow them in your climate. When in doubt, choose seeds that are All-America Selections.

Hybrids Versus Open-Pollinated Varieties

The important thing to know about hybrids is that plant breeders make these crosses both to create improved cultivars and to incorporate disease tolerance. Hybridization often improves plant vigor, increases yield and results in a stronger root system. These results are collectively referred to as hybrid vigor. Hybrids often are more adaptable to diverse growing conditions.

In turn, the greater disease and pest tolerance plus the greater yield of the top hybrid vegetables has meant that both home gardeners and commercial growers can greatly reduce or even eliminate their use of pesticides.

The drawback to hybrids is that gardeners cannot save seed to replant the next year and the seed often costs more. In addition, the shift to hybrid varieties by major seed companies means that fewer of the old standard varieties are kept in stock.

Although the strong demand for hybrid vegetables remains, there are still many open-pollinated varieties in the market. First of all, some vegetables do not lend themselves to hybridization. Peas, beans, and lettuce, for instance, all are open-pollinated varieties. In the case of beets and carrots, while some hybrids now are available, the great majority of varieties are open pollinated. Clearly, both hybrids and open-pollinated seeds will continue to share the home gardening and commercial marketplaces.

Gardeners soon discover that certain seed varieties are better adapted to growing under certain conditions than others. For example, the early-maturing, cold-tolerant, 'Oregon Spring' tomato grows in cool weather, setting flowers and fruit well before the larger beefsteak varieties. If you live in a cool region, with a short growing season, selecting 'Oregon Spring' rather than a late-maturing beefsteak tomato will make a fruitful harvest almost certain. If you love broccoli but live in a warm climate, planting heat-tolerant 'Premium Crop' rather than 'Green Valiant' will prolong the harvest.

Some of the seed varieties developed for modern agriculture are bred for qualities such as long shelf life, uniformity, disease resistance, and the ability to withstand mechanical harvesting with little damage. Taste is often not a high-priority quality and, in addition, commercial crops usually are picked before they are ripe.

Eating carefully selected varieties with superior taste, rather than tough vegetables that were developed for mechanized handling and picked green is one of gardening's great rewards.

Heirloom Seeds

Some old-fashioned, open-pollinated seeds continue to be very popular today, such as 'Kentucky Wonder' pole bean. But since the number of new and open-pollinated vegetable cultivars has grown so large, many varieties have become difficult to find and some are extinct. The reason for this is primarily that seed companies, because of space limitations in fields, warehouses and catalogs, have had to drop older varieties in order to introduce promising new cultivars. Another reason that some of the old vegetable varieties have lost favor in today's market is that they have short shelf lives and so are unsuited to commercial production.

Some gardeners have begun collecting heirloom plant varieties in the same way that others collect antique furniture. Others grow certain plant varieties because of their superior flavor, high productivity or disease and pest resistance. Yet others grow old plant varieties that have been handed down from generation to generation.

The old plant varieties represent gene pools that should be saved. Their characteristics could prove valuable to today's plant breeders and might prove to be the source of valuable medicinal or otherwise useful substances in the future. If nothing else, they have value because they represent another era and are a part of our cultural history.

Fortunately, several groups have been organized to preserve the heirloom varieties. The Seed Savers Exchange (RR 3, Box 239, Decorah, IA 52101), founded and headed by Kent Whealy, is the largest. With the help of a large network of interested gardeners, Whealy and his Seed Savers Exchange have gathered and grown more than 5,000 open-pollinated and heirloom vegetable seeds. Annual dues are only $10 and the Garden Seed Inventory which lists many of the heirloom varieties is available for $12 postpaid.

Some gardening and regional magazines carry swap columns or letters to the editor that provide an arena for those seeking heirloom seeds.

Even when the seeds seem very expensive, they are an excellent value if you grow them well. Whether you are looking for old-fashioned heirloom seeds or modern hybrids, look for such qualities as taste, disease and pest resistance, cold and heat tolerance. Look for plant seeds that are noted for thriving under conditions that prevail in your region. The right seeds will help make your garden a success.

Diversity, that is, growing more than one variety of a particular vegetable, has definite advantages. Plant the old reliable varieties, but also take a chance on a few new varieties each year. As added insurance, and to learn more about the vegetable varieties that grow well in your area, always plant more than one variety of the same type of plant. When you grow only one variety, you might lose it if weather conditions are poor or the plants are attacked by a pest or disease.

Some seed is treated with a fungicide to prevent such diseases as damping-off, a disease that causes seedlings to rot at the soil line. Typically, the fungicide is colored and some seed companies state in their catalog or on the seed packet that it is treated. Some seed is only available with a coating of fungicide. At least one major seed producer is using naturally occurring diatomaceous earth to protect seed.

If you have a large garden or can store the seed for several years under conditions that keep it viable, purchasing in larger portions is economical. Most of the cost of retail seed is in the packaging. You can buy one gram of tomato seed for $1.05, for example, rather than ¼ gram at $.90. You decide which is best for you.

Starting Seeds

For the largest selection and lowest cost, grow plants from seed. You can start seed indoors in shallow nursery flats, egg cartons, peat pellets, cell blocks or any small, clean containers. Use bagged seed-starting mix or make your own.

If you have started seeds in a flat, they will need to be transplanted to individual larger size containers with a mix that has some soil in it. The best addition is compost you have made yourself and sifted. Or, if you have built the quality of your soil for several years, you can sift and use that. You may have to rely on the bagged compost and potting soil available commercially.

When a seed germinates, the first "leaves" you will see are the cotyledons. When two sets of true leaves have appeared, you can move the seedling to a larger pot. Seeds and seedlings must be watered regularly, especially in a heated environment. The soil should not be soggy, but must be kept constantly moist.

Look in catalogs or garden centers for the device generally called a soil block. It will form 1.5- to 4-inch

blocks or cubes from soil. Fine, fertile, absorbent, slightly moist potting soil is packed into the soil block, then the formed blocks of soil are pushed out.

Easy Potting Mixes

Soil-Based Mix for Outdoor Containers

1 cubic foot topsoil
1 cubic foot vermiculite
1 cubic foot peat moss or compost
1 quart dried cow manure
¾ cup ground limestone
1 cup blood meal
2 cups super phosphate

Soil-Less Mix for Outdoor Containers

5 cubic feet ground bark
5 cubic feet sand
5 cubic feet peat moss
1 pound, 10 ounces 5-10-10
2 pounds ground limestone
½ pound iron sulfate

Cornell Soil-Less Mix for Seedlings and House Plants

4 quarts horticultural vermiculite
4 quarts shredded peat moss
1 tablespoon superphosphate
2 tablespoons dolomitic limestone
4 tablespoons dried cow manure

A good blocking mix can be made of 2 parts each of black peat moss, coarse sand, and brown peat moss; 10 parts each of compost and soil; and ⅙ part lime and ¾ part base fertilizer—an organic fertilizer made of equal parts blood meal, colloidal phosphate, and greensand.

One or several seeds are planted in the soil-block. They are the most natural form of "pot" to use for transplanting, and unlike plastic cell packs, will not disturb the root ball. Transplanting is virtually shock-free.

If starting seeds in your home, sow the seeds, then place the container in a sunny, south-facing window. If there is not enough light, the seedlings may become lanky and spindly. Set them under a fluorescent gro-light so they have enough light for good balanced growth. A combination of fluorescent and incandescent light can provide the balance and light spectrum needed for healthy plant growth.

All-America Selection (AAS) Vegetable Winners

The following award-winning vegetables have earned AAS medals since 1945. This means that these vegetables will perform well under a variety of environmental conditions throughout the United States and Canada.

Variety	Year
BEAN, LIMA	
Bush Fordhook 242	1945
Bush Early Market	1945
Peerless	1948
Triumph	1949
BEAN, SNAP	
Improved Commodore	1945
Florida Belle	1945
Longreen	1946
Ranger Snapbean	1947
Cherokee Wax	1948
Puregold Wax	1948
Supergreen	1948
Topcrop	1950
Stringless Hort Snapbean	1952
Wade	1952
Seminole	1955
Greencrop	1957
Choctaw Wax	1958
Pearlgreen	1958
Gardengreen Snapbean	1959
Executive	1963
Goldcrop	1974
Derby	1990
Kentucky Blue (pole)	1991
BEET	
Ruby Queen	1957
BROCCOLI	
Cleopatra	1964
Zenith	1964
Green Comet	1969
Premium Crop	1975
BRUSSELS SPROUTS	
Jade Cross	1959
CABBAGE	
O. S. Cross	1951
Emerald Cross	1963
Savoy King	1965
Stonehead	1969
Harvester Queen	1969
Redhead	1971
Ruby Ball	1972
Savoy Ace	1977
CANTALOUPE	
Granite State	1951
Golden Delight	1952
Pennsweet	1955
Samson	1965
CARROT	
Gold Pak	1956
Thumbelina	1992
CAULIFLOWER	
Ideal Snowball	1949
Snow King	1969
Snow Crown	1975

CORN, SWEET	
Goldengrain Hybrid	1945
Erie	1947
Flagship	1949
Lochlef	1951
Big Mo	1951
Golden State	1951
Golden Beauty Hybrid	1955
Early Xtra Sweet	1971
How Sweet It Is	1986
Honey 'N Pearl	1988
CUCUMBER	
Surecrop	1951
Smoothie	1957
Triumph	1965
Spartan Valor	1968
Victory	1972
Liberty	1978
Saladin	1979
Sweet Success	1983
Salad Bush	1988
DILL	
Fernleaf	1992
EGGPLANT	
New Hampshire Hybrid	1939
KOHLRABI	
Grand Duke	1979
Bronze Beauty	1947
Penlake	1949
Premier Great Lakes	1949
Salad Bowl	1952
Ruby	1958
Buttercrunch (Bibb)	1963
Butter King	1966
Red Sails	1985
MUSTARD	
Prizewinner, C.L.S.	1951
Greenwave	1957
OKRA	
Blondy	1986
Burgundy	1988
ONION	
Excel Bermuda	1948
PEA	
Freezonian	1948
Victory Freezer	1948
Sugar Snap	1979
Sugar Ann	1984
PEPPER	
Vinedale	1952
Bell Boy	1967

LETTUCE	
Dutch Treat	1979
Gypsy	1981
Super Chili	1988
MexiBell	1988
Super Cayenne	1990
PUMPKIN	
Allneck Cushaw	1952
Spirit	1977
Autumn Gold	1987
RADISH	
Cherry Belle	1949
Champion	1957
SPINACH	
America	1952
Melody	1977
SQUASH	
Caserta	1949
Unconn	1950
Black Beauty	1957
Greayzini Zucchini	1963
Hercules Butternut	1963
Chefini	1965
Gold Nugget	1966
Kindred	1969
St. Pat Scallop	1969
Waltham Butternut	1970
Aristocrat Zucchini	1973
Bush Acorn Table King	1974
Scallopini	1977
Sweet Mama	1979
Early Butternut	1979
Gold Rush	1980
Peter Pan	1982
Jersey Golden Acorn	1982
Sunburst	1985
Cream of the Crop	1990
Sun Drops	1990
Tivoli	1991
TOMATO	
Urbana	1951
Spring Giant	1967
Small Fry	1970
Florimerica	1978
Celebrity	1984
TURNIP	
Just Right	1960
Tokyo Cross	1969
WATERMELON	
Congo	1950
New Hampshire Midget	1951
Yellow Baby	1975
Sweet Favorite	1978
Golden Crown	1991

Fluorescent growlights are available at prices that vary from $3 to $18 or more, depending on the fixture. They are good heat sources. Leave growlight lamps on for 16 to 20 hours per day and keep them within 2-4 inches of the seedlings for maximum growth, following directions that came with the growlight.

Increasingly, both expert and amateur gardeners are growing their own seedlings. However, many choose to purchase at least some of their vegetables as started seedlings from a local nursery or plant center. The price of seeds and seedlings is low compared to the harvest you, friends and family will enjoy.

Transplanted seedlings get a head-start on directly-seeded crops, and they mature earlier. A healthy seedling is predictable and virtually guarantees uniformity in plantings, while direct-seeding can result in gaps in rows if conditions are not favorable.

The key factors for successful germination of seeds are consistent moisture and proper temperature. When at or near the optimum temperature, germination is more certain and rapid. If above or below this range, or if moisture is not consistent, seeds will germinate irregularly.

It is easy to overwater seeds before they germinate. Remember, seeds have no roots and need little water, just enough to keep the seed coat moist to enable the roots and shoots to break out of the sheath, or seed coat. Compacted soil with a crusty surface is almost impossible for most tender shoots to penetrate.

Placing a piece of newspaper, burlap, a thin layer of fine mulch over the seed bed helps retain moisture evenly and keeps soil from forming a crust. Remove the paper or burlap as soon as the seed germinates. If possible, arrange your seed flats and pots so you can water from below, and let the water rise up through the soil from the bottom of the container.

If you plan to grow more than just a few seeds, purchase commercial sterilized seed-starting medium or make your own. Horticultural vermiculite by itself or mixed half and half with perlite is a good seed mix. Place it in large flat pans or commercial seed flats with good drainage and soak. When it has drained well, sow the seeds, then sprinkle some milled sphagnum moss over the top to discourage damping off.

To maintain bottom heat as required for the seeds, invest in a horticultural heating pad or cable with a thermostat. More seeds fail to germinate because of lack of the required soil temperature than just about anything else.

Take the time to read the seed packet thoroughly. It contains much of the information you will need to grow the seeds. You will find the information includes the seeds' temperature and light requirements as well as how deep the seeds should be planted.

Other important factors usually found on seed packets are when to plant, time required to maturity, description of the plant, transplanting or thinning suggestions, ultimate size and gardening hints.

Other alternatives are a home greenhouse, cold frames or hot frames and, of course, directly in the garden. Cold frames are unheated enclosed beds warmed only by the sun. Hot frames are heated by decomposing animal manure placed deep below the seed bed, electricity, or a fossil fuel.

A cold frame is a perfect place to transfer one- to two-week-old brassica seedlings in cold weather and less hardy transplants when the weather warms. Cold frames generally stay 10 to 15° warmer than the daytime temperature and 5 to 10° warmer at night. Seedlings also can be grown in a hot frame where temperatures can be regulated.

Fertilize small seedlings with fish emulsion or any soluble, complete fertilizer. Be sparing with the fertilizer; apply it at one-quarter the recommended strength. Some "organic" gardeners use the chemical fertilizers Peter's Root 'N Bloom, "Schultz-Instant" Liquid Plant Food or Ra-Pid-Gro.

When transplanting from seed flats, note that egg cartons, peat pots and paper bands do not always decompose rapidly enough for fragile seedling roots. These containers may inhibit their growth. When planting these types of containers in the soil, plan to remove the seedling from the container or, in the case of peat pots, to tear off the top rim of the pot so that it is below the soil line or it will dry out and not decompose.

Soak soil-blocks, peat pellets, or soil just before transplanting seedlings. Gently set the soil block in a pre-dug hole, tamp soil firmly around the roots. Water thoroughly to seat the transplant and ensure good soil contact. Keep them evenly moist for one to two weeks after transplanting.

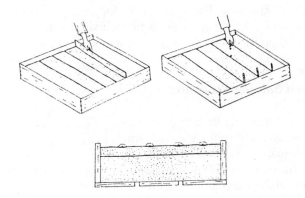

Mark straight lines in the flat with string. Space seeds closely together. Then use a board to press the seeds firmly into the soil before watering.

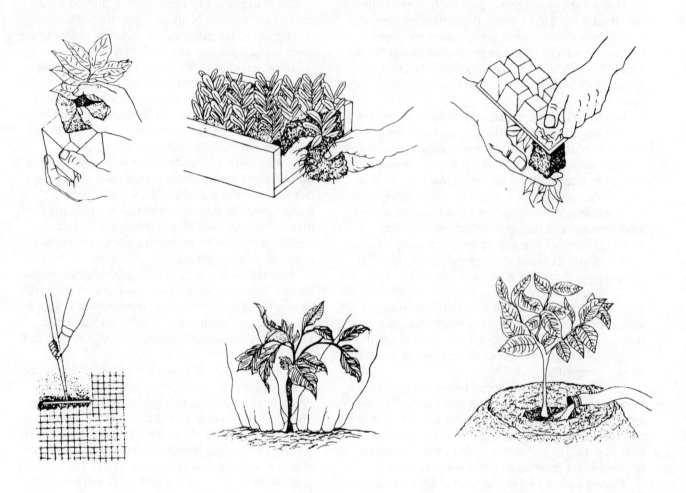

Remove the plants from their containers, taking care to disturb the root ball as little as possible. Use a bow rake to mark a grid on the soil so that spacing the seedlings equally apart will be easier. Dig a hole for each seedling in the prepared bed. Carefully set seedlings in holes and pack soil firmly around the transplant before watering in.

Most seed has a shelf life of two to four years if it is stored in a stable environment of about 70° F. and 70 percent humidity. The seed will last longer if a packet or two of silica gel or a layer of powdered milk is placed on the bottom of a glass jar with the seeds.

Seed Sowing Outdoors

Soil temperature is important to seed germination. If the soil is too cold, the seeds will rot rather than germinate.

Inexpensive soil thermometers are available that will help you monitor the garden soil.

Plant cool weather vegetables such as onions, spinach, parsnips, carrots, radishes, beets, cabbage and peas when the soil temperature reaches 40° F. When the soil temperature reaches 50° F., plant corn,

asparagus and tomatoes. Wait until the soil temperature reaches 60° F. or more to plant squash, cucumbers, beans, peppers and melons.

Seed sizes vary widely, with some as small as a pinhead, some shaped like short pieces of string, and others as large as your thumbnail. A rule of thumb in planting seeds is to set them into the soil at about three times the depth of the seed's largest dimension.

Seeders space seeds at regular intervals in the soil and cover them. There are several kinds of seeders from which to choose including fluid, vacuum, belt, and cup seeders. If you have a large garden, and plant in long straight rows, a seeder is a good investment. A string, stretched between two stakes, serves as a guide to keep a row straight.

Dry seeds take a longer time to germinate than premoistened seeds. You can speed the germination of bean, corn and pea seeds putting the seeds in a glass of water for several days until they swell and germinate. Each day, give the seeds fresh water until they sprout.

Most seeds will sprout at between 60 and 100° F. The best sprouting temperature for warm-weather vegetable seeds such as tomatoes and melons, is between 75 and 85°. On either side of this temperature range, sprouting may be slow or inhibited.

You can figure that for every 10° the temperature drops below the ideal germination level, germination time will double. Many seeds will not sprout at all if the temperature is too low.

Cool-weather plants will germinate and grow in cooler temperatures. Most spinach, peas, radishes and lettuce varieties, for example, will sprout at 50° F., with 55° being an ideal temperature.

Outdoor soil temperature should be 60° or warmer for most summer vegetables to sprout and grow well. The soil can be warmed by building a raised bed or by growing plants in a cold frame. The cold frame or a cloche not only helps the sun warm the soil, it protects the soil at night so that it does not cool too fast.

If you have the space, sow a lot of extra seeds and thin several times for a month or two after they have sprouted. The small culls of greens or beets are tender and tasty.

You can carefully remove thinnings and then replant the them, or you can thin tiny seedlings with a small, sharp pair of scissors. Snip them off at the soil line, taking the thin, weak plants first. The final thinning should be to space the seedlings according to your experience or the suggestions on the seed packet.

Do not plant seedlings or any other edible plants within 200 to 300 feet of busy roads. They tend to absorb excessive amounts of lead from exhaust fumes. Locations near heavy traffic also may expose them to heavy metals such as cadmium. A 6- to 10-foot wall or hedge will block most of the pollutants before they can foul vegetables.

Take care not to cultivate vegetables over sites where old buildings stood. The earth in such a site may include toxic lead-based paint and plaster fragments. These materials may contain lead and other heavy metals that can sometimes de taken up by edible plants, then passed on to animals and humans that eat them. Young children are most susceptible to these poisons.

The reason that heavy metals are not more of a problem in garden vegetables is that most of the heavy metals are likely to be in insoluble forms when soil pH is above 6. Since the ideal soil pH for vegetable gardens is 6.5 to 7.0, heavy metals should not pose a problem. Yet we do recommend that you not plant edibles where there is any likelihood of heavy metals. For the same reason, we recommend not using sludge-based fertilizers on edible plants. They may contain heavy metals.

Tomato, pepper and cabbage seedlings are among the most commonly purchased vegetables. You can usually purchase seedlings of several different varieties. The reason many gardeners purchase seedlings is that they do not need numerous plants, so it is economical in time, money, and space to buy seedlings.

The term "hardening-off" means to gradually introduce seedlings to a new environment. Seedlings grown in a nursery or indoors have not been exposed to the elements and must be gradually introduced to their new outdoor environment.

To harden-off seedlings, place them outdoors in a shady location for a day or two and bring them indoors at night. Next place them in the sunshine for a couple of hours and leave them in the shade the rest of the day. Increase the amount of sunshine they get gradually over the course of a week.

A good rule of thumb is to harden-off seedlings for a week before transplanting them into the outdoor garden.

Buying Seedlings

Purchasing vegetable seedlings at a tip-top retail nursery takes little skill. If you have limited gardening experience, purchasing from some large outlets can be somewhat risky if staff people are not familiar with the seedlings or their care.

Buy seedlings that are kept in good growing conditions. Do not buy seedlings that have been constantly in sunny locations. The small amount of soil around the roots in small plastic pots/packs can heat up and "cook" the roots. The temperature is more constant in a shade house, which protects the tender plants from the sun, and from climate extremes. The root system is the most important part of the seedling. Select seedlings that have good color and are of uniform size.

The best seedlings to transplant have a root system that holds the soil together and have just begun to reach the outside of the soil in the small container. If only rootbound plants are available, soak the soil with water before planting. Remove any matted roots that have grown out of the container, then gently separate the remaining roots just before planting so that they will penetrate the soil better, and be less inclined to bunch-up.

You may prefer to buy very young seedlings with small root systems and hold them at home in a partially shady location to harden off for a week or two before transplanting. You can watch their progress as they gradually get used to their new environment.

Pull plants apart gently when transplanting from flats. Take care not to squeeze roots and crush tender root hairs. The key to successful transplanting is to not let the roots dry out. Plants that are exposed to the air for only a few seconds between seedling flat and pot or garden bed will have the least shock from transplanting.

Keep fertilizer mixes out of direct contact with seedlings. Dig planting holes twice as deep as needed. Mix about a half-cup of complete organic fertilizer per gallon of soil and set it directly below the seedling.

It is a harsh shock for some seedlings when they are moved from a warm shade house or greenhouse to cool soil and cooler nighttime temperatures. Help them survive by carefully and gradually introducing them to their new environment or only purchasing them when temperatures are conducive to good growth.

Preparing Vegetable Beds

The following are two excellent methods for preparing, maintaining and planting vegetable beds.

First, in late September or October, spread a layer of shredded (run over them with the lawn mower) leaves two or three inches thick, covered by a layer of aged horse or steer manure ½-inch thick.

In areas of naturally acidic soils, spread 50 pounds of dolomite lime per 100 square feet of bed on clay soils, 25 pounds on sandy soils. Spread ½ to 2 pounds of clover seed, depending on the species, per 1,000 square feet for a cover crop. Choose a clover that is suited to your climate. Till it all in to a shallow depth of two to three inches. Remember the seed must be shallow enough for it to sprout.

In March, April or whenever the soil can be easily worked, apply about one gallon of a complete organic fertilizer mix per 100 square feet of soil. Till the fertilizer and the clover cover crop into the soil, wait a week or two and till it again. Rake the surface to an even texture and seed the soil with early peas, radishes, turnips, lettuce and spinach. Harvest the crops as they become ripe. These first crops will mature quickly and should all be harvested in plenty of time to plant a summer crop.

Spread another layer of Solomon's fertilizer mix on the soil. Till it in along with the remains from the spring garden, and plant the fall/winter garden in June or July.

Another method for preparing and maintaining vegetable beds is as follows. In early April as soon as the soil can be worked, spread six inches of last fall's compost, covered by a ½-inch layer of aged horse, chicken, rabbit, or steer manure, 20 pounds of rock phosphate, and, in areas of acidic soil, 50 pounds of dolomitic lime over 100 square feet bed for clay soils. In acid-soil regions, use 10 pounds of rock phosphate and 25 pounds of dolomite lime for sandy soils per 100 square feet. Till it all in to a depth of about 6 inches. Wait two weeks and till again. Rake surface to an even texture and plant intensively radishes, peas, turnips, lettuce, carrots, and spinach. Leave one half of the garden open to plant tomatoes, squash, peppers, and green beans when the weather warms. Intensive gardening spaces plants as closely as possible, creating a leafy canopy that, like a living mulch, cuts down on weeds while it conserves moisture and buffers soil temperature.

When the early, first half of the garden is harvested, plant peppers, cucumbers, eggplant, tomatoes and other warm weather edibles.

Cool Weather Vegetables

Planting dates for vegetables depend upon the general climate, the average first and last dates of killing frosts, and the specific vegetables. Cool-weather vegetables, such as cabbage and its relatives, are very hardy and can stand temperatures down to 28° F. without damage. Tender warm-weather vegetables, including green beans and melons, are injured or killed by temperatures that fall below 40°.

Check with your local Cooperative Extension Service or garden center to find the average first and last dates of killing frost in your area.

In warmer parts of the country, it may be possible to get three, four or even more garden crops per year. In the northern reaches, you may still be able to get three crops per year if you plan carefully and extend the growing season by covering crops with with spun fiber or plastic.

In the maritime Northwest, Northern California, and much of the South, fall crops started in July will grow to full size by the end of September. If started too soon, they mature early, and if started too late, the harvest will be small.

The latest time to plant a fall crop or winter garden should be the middle of August. In warmer climates with long periods of frost-free weather, winter gardens can be started in late August.

The winter crops of warm climates will be harvested by April or May the following year. This same plot will be the next year's summer garden. Europeans have been winter gardening for centuries and finally, in the early 1970's, Americans got the winter garden bug.

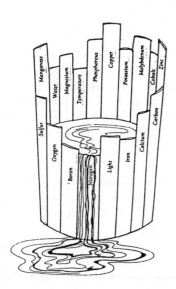

If one of the elements (nutrients, sunlight, water, air or soil) that a plant needs to grow is lacking, it will only grow as fast and as big as the limiting element will allow.

If your climate allows, you may find that winter gardens are actually less work and more rewarding than producing heavy fall crops and preserving them.

Winter vegetables protect themselves from freezing temperatures by increasing the amount of sugars and starches in their cells which acts like antifreeze. This makes many vegetables, such as Brussels sprouts and parsnips, taste sweeter after a good freeze. Climates without freezing weather may produce bland or bitter Brussels sprouts. These winter vegetables pump water out of the leaf cells as the temperature gets colder so that the cell walls do not rupture.

Plants will winter over better if the temperature slowly declines rather than drops quickly to below freezing. This way they can gradually build up sugars and pump fluids out of their leaves. If there is a cold snap, vegetables that would normally survive may be stunted or killed.

This means that winter gardening is next to impossible in the Midwest and Plains States which have a continental climate that may range from warm to frigid in a matter of hours.

Protecting winter gardens from the wind will decrease the potential for cold injury to the vegetables considerably. Crop covers will extend the growing season and buffer sudden temperature changes to some degree.

Very hardy vegetables that can be planted a month to six weeks before the average frost-free date in the spring are broccoli, cabbage, kale, lettuce, onions, potatoes, peas, spinach, and turnips. You can plant beets, carrots, cauliflower, chard, leeks, mustard, parsnips, and radishes about two to four weeks before the spring frost-free date.

Warm Weather Vegetables

Warm-weather vegetables need night temperatures of 60 to 65° F. and day temperatures of 75 to 85° if they are to grow vigorously. Soil temperatures must be 50° or more for corn, tomatoes and asparagus seeds to germinate. Soil temperatures must be 60° or more for the seeds of squash, cucumber, green beans, peppers and melons to germinate.

Snap beans, celery, okra, sweet corn, squash, soybeans, and tomatoes usually can be safely planted on the average frost-free date in the spring. Wait one to two weeks after the frost-free date to plant all other beans, eggplant, peppers, cucumbers, melons, and sweet potatoes.

Many of the warm-weather vegetables are poor choices for gardens in northern New England and the Pacific Northwest. These regions simply do not have enough hot sunny days for vegetables such as okra and melons.

Kitchen Gardens

The average area of a household vegetable garden is between 500 and 600 square feet and includes the 10 most popular vegetables which are tomatoes, peppers, beans, cucumbers, onions, lettuce, squash carrots, radishes, and corn.

Many of these average gardens are tilled and planted on the first sunny weekend in the spring. If tomatoes, peppers, beans, cucumbers, onions, lettuce, squash, carrots, radishes and corn are all planted the same day, they will all be ripe the same day. A little of this produce is eaten, some is given away, but the majority may bolt or rot.

With just a little management and imagination, this average garden can turn into a proper kitchen garden, one in which all of the produce is eaten as it becomes ripe. A true kitchen garden will yield hundreds of fresh, tasty, nutritious meals. When the planting dates are staggered over six to eight months, you will have fresh produce for most of the year depending on your climate and the seed varieties you plant.

Plant vegetables and herbs as close to the kitchen or back door. They taste best garden fresh. If garden produce is easy to pick, it will be eaten more often.

Place herbs and ornamental perennials close to the house but not in vegetable beds. Having these garden beds near the house makes them easier to care for. Maintenance is much easier when you have to take just a few steps to do a few minutes of weeding or other gardening chores.

You can plant Jerusalem artichokes, corn, and potatoes—which all need more room—far from the house. They need less care and can be irrigated with a drip system if rainfall is undependable in your area.

Fast growing winter squash needs little care and should be planted on the outward boundaries of the garden. But they also make excellent shade when trellised near the house.

Many ornamentals have edible flowers and leaves and so would be good prospects for the kitchen garden. The chayote squash (*Sechium edule*) ranges from smooth skinned to spiny, light to dark green. A three-year-old chayote squash vine grown in a warm southern state can produce up to 300 fruits a year. Both the squash and the seeds are edible. The tips of the vine are also edible. That's enough chayote for the entire neighborhood. Other squash blossoms are edible as well.

Daylilies, a favorite perennial, have delicious flowers and buds, especially in the tetraploid forms. The tender leaves and buds of hostas have long been an Oriental culinary treat. Nasturtium flowers brighten a green salad as they add a peppery tang. The kitchen garden might include some of these traditional perennial ornamentals that are increasingly known for their edible qualities.

Herbs

An herb garden can be as simple as a few pots of chives, mints and basils at the edge of a sunny patio or as complex as a traditional knot garden with intricate patterns and many different herbs.

The important thing to know about herbs is that they are not very demanding and will do well in ordinary soil as long as they have good drainage and at least a half day of sun. The majority will thrive in soil that is neutral to slightly basic and not very fertile. In fact, herbs will be more aromatic and flavorful if the soil is somewhat poor in nutrients. But well-drained soil is important if your soil is compacted or heavy clay. Improve drainage by adding compost, perlite, or vermiculite. Better yet, add some of each and work them into the soil to the depth of about a foot.

The True Mints

The true mints are zesty perennials of several characteristic flavors and scents that are notorious for their usually rampant growth. They often will climb out of their appointed beds and appear in other garden areas where they may be less than welcome. They spread by roots and runners and also are able to start rootlets wherever the stems touch the ground.

Label them well and plant them in containers or beds that have barriers. Regular stem and root pruning will help keep mints from spreading. Don't let this invasive habit keep you from growing the mints. They are among the most flavorful herbs. Lemonade, iced teas, and the famous mint julep would be sad potions, indeed, without mint.

* SPEARMINT (*Mentha spicata*) is probably the best known true mint. It has rich green leaves, grows two to three feet in height, and has spikes of pink flowers. It comes in both curly and plain-leaved types. Some spearmints are stronger in flavor than others so you may wish to sample several before choosing one for your garden. In addition to being a flavorful garnish for cold drinks and hot teas, spearmint is the key to the mint sauce that so beautifully accompanies lamb.

* PEPPERMINT (*Mentha x piperata*) has a sharp taste that is familiar to all. Its glossy leaves are darker than spearmint and have a ruddy cast. Peppermint grows to a height of about a foot and a half.

* APPLE MINT (*Mentha suaveolens*) has rounded, woolly leaves with an apple scent. This mint has white flowers and reaches three feet in height. Apple mint makes delightful teas and is especially good for making candied mint leaves.

* PINEAPPLE MINT (*Mentha suaveolens* cv. 'Variegata') is a pineapple-flavored cultivar of apple mint and has similar uses. It has attractive cream and green variegated leaves.

* CURLY MINT (*Mentha* aquatica var. crispa) has a milder mint flavor and is noted for its small, curled, light green leaves.

* ORANGE MINT (*Mentha X piperata* var. *citrata*), also called bergamot mint, is known for its large, dark green leaves with wavy edges and distinct citrus scent and flavor. This is a different plant from the bergamot that is also known as bee balm (*Monarda didyma*) which also has a citrus flavor and fragrance. The origin of the common name, bergamot, for both plants is their similarity to bergamot oil which comes from a tropical tree, orange bergamot tree (*Citrus aurantium*).

Other Mint Family Herbs

No other plant family has contributed more useful herbs than the mint family. More than 60 genera and species of this plant group are commonly cultivated. These square-stemmed plants have equal and opposite leaves, clues to their kinship.

* BASIL (*Ocimum basilicum*) comes in many attractive annual varieties and cultivars. Most are bright green but there also are purple varieties.

The plants may be rangy and tall or small and bushy, depending on the cultivar. In recent years, some interesting new variations in taste and fragrance have been developed.

Basil, the so-called tomato herb, is spicy and excellent with tomato dishes, salads, fish, meat, eggs, and cheese.

* THE PERENNIAL WHITE HOREHOUND (*Marrubium vulgare*) has a rather weedy appearance and reaches about two feet in height. Its gray-green foliage makes it attractive for edging or as part of a silver-white-gray garden.

* LAVENDER (*Lavendula* species), one of the more traditional herbs is used in sachets, potpourris, perfumes, and bath oils but not in cooking. The varieties range from foot-tall dwarfs to long-stemmed three footers. The silvery foliage is handsome in ornamental gardens. This tender shrubby perennial is a beautiful addition to flower arrangements.

* SWEET MARJORAM (*Origanum Majorana*) is a tender perennial that is closely related to oregano and grows one to two feet tall. Its flavor blends well with meats, salads, vinegars, teas, and tomatoes.

* OREGANO (*Oreganum vulgare*) is the plant usually thought of as the pizza herb. The current wisdom is that, much like curry, oregano is more of a flavor than a specific plant. If you want a strong oregano flavor, you will be better off to choose marjoram. The bushy oregano plants, with pink or white flowers, will survive winter weather in sheltered sites.

* ROSEMARY (*Rosmarinus officinalis*), known as the herb of remembrance, grows two to six feet high, depending on the variety and climate. A tender perennial shrub, it comes in several forms, including a prostrate creeping variety and others with interesting leaf and color variations. This strongly aromatic herb is especially good with soups, stews, poultry and meats.

* SAGE (*Salvia* species) is one of the familiar smells and tastes of Thanksgiving. The most common species if perennial garden sage (*S. officinalis*), a two-to three-foot shrubby perennial with oval grayish leaves with a pebbly texture like a lizard's skin. There also are dwarf and variegated varieties as well as annual and biennial forms. Sages are especially good with poultry, stuffings, lamb and sausage.

* PINEAPPLE SAGE (*Salvia elegans*) is a tender perennial with a delightful fragrance. It grows easily from cuttings and has beautiful red flowers that attract humming birds.

* SAVORY (*Satureja* species), both the hardy perennial winter savory (*S. montana*) and the annual summer savory (*S. hortensis*) easily grown from seed,

grows to a height of about a foot and a half. Savory leaves are great additions to soups, meats, fish, eggs and, most especially, green beans.

* THE THYMES (*Thymus* species) are among the most attractive perennial herbs. There are numerous thyme varieties with wide-ranging flavors, colors, textures, and growing patterns. There are both prostrate and upright forms. Use thyme sparingly in soups, stews and sauces.

Parsley Family Herbs

Next to the mint family, the parsley, or carrot, family has more representatives that are grown in herb gardens and used in the kitchen than any other group. The family name, Umbelliferae, is from the diminutive of the Latin word for umbrella and refers to the flat-topped or rounded flower clusters.

* THE TRUE PARSLEYS of the genus *Petroselinum* are biennials usually grown as annuals. There are a half dozen different species but the most popular are the curly French parsley (*P. crispum*) and the Italian or plain-leafed parsley (*P. crispum* var. *tuberosum*). Curly parsley makes a handsome edging for any garden bed. Many cooks and herb gardeners favor the Italian parsley because of its superior flavor.

* DILL (*Anethum graveolens*) is known as the pickle herb. This graceful umbellifer has loose feathery foliage and grows up to three feet in height. Recently, dwarf cultivars have come into the marketplace that grow only 18 inches tall and so are good choices for small gardens and containers. The leaves are used as both garnish and flavoring with meats, soups, sauces, salads, and especially with beets. Dill is an annual that is easy to grow from seed. Sow it directly in the garden each spring.

* ANISE (*Pimpinella Anisum*) is an annual that grows a couple of feet tall and should be sown directly in the garden as it does not transplant well. Famous for its licorice flavor, its leaves and seeds have been used for many years as a spicy flavoring for garnishes and salads. The seeds are used in breads, stews, soups and as a flavoring for wines, liquors, soaps, and perfumes.

* CARAWAY (*Carum Carvi*) is another feathery-leafed member of the parsley family that has long been used as a flavoring. About two feet tall, it self sows but, being a true biennial, it will not produce flowers and seeds the first season. The same is true of parsley. The leaves are used in soups and salads while the seeds are used in breads and cheeses.

* CHERVIL (*Anthriscus Cerefolium*), and several other closely related small herbs, have deeply toothed, flattish leaves and are used in the same way as the pars-

leys. Chervil is a hardy annual, that you can sow the seeds in the garden in the fall. Plant them where they will grow and cover the seeds lightly with soil.

* LOVAGE (*Levisticum officinale*), long used as a treatment for sore throats, is a six-foot perennial. Its aromatic leaves are good in soups and stews either fresh or dried and taste much like celery leaves. The young stems may be eaten as a steamed vegetable.

* CORIANDER (*Coriandrum sativum*), also known as cilantro or Chinese parsley. Its leaves are widely used as a culinary herb in Mexico and southeast Asia. The seeds are also used as a flavoring. Coriander is an annual herb that is easy to grow. Those who like this herb really adore it while others can't bear even a whiff of it. This is an herb that elicits strong reactions. It is the ingredient that distinguishes a true Mexican salsa.

* ANGELICA (*Angelica Archangelica*) is a biennial that grows up to six feet tall with yellow-green leaves and greenish-white flowers. The roots and stems may be boiled and eaten like celery. The seeds and stem-derived oil are used as a flavoring in many liqueurs, including chartreuse, Benedictine and vermouth.

Amaryllis Family Herbs

The third major plant family represented in the herb garden is the amaryllis family which includes daffodils, amaryllis, snowflakes, snowdrops and stargrass as well as onions, chives, and garlic.

* CHIVES (*Allium Schoenoprasum*) is a must for every herb garden. These perennial onion cousins that are grown from seed or plant divisions grow compactly to a height of about one foot. The round hollow dark green leaves have a mild onion flavor. Chives make excellent borders and edgings and have attractive pink flowers in the spring. When harvesting, cut some of the outer leaves to the ground, but never cut them all. Use chive leaves as a garnish or mild flavoring in cottage cheese, salads, soups, stews and anything else that would be improved by a light oniony taste. Use the flowers to color and flavor white vinegars.

* GARLIC CHIVES (*Allium tuberosum*), also perennials, have flatter leaves than the plain chives. Use the leaves as you would plain chives when you want a mild garlicky flavor in sauces, soups, and stews.

Daisy Family Herbs

Many members of the daisy or composite family are grown in herb gardens, especially some of the plants in the genera, *Artemisia* and *Chrysanthemum*.

Most noteworthy is French tarragon (*Artemisia Dracunculus* var. *sativa*), an odd plant in that it never flowers or sets seeds and so must be propagated by cuttings or root divisions. Do not get this herb mixed up with the one called Russian tarragon which does set seed but is worthless as a culinary herb. Tarragon is a major kitchen herb used to flavor vinegars, meats, fish, and poultry.

The wormwoods and southernwoods are members of the *Artemisia* genus often used in herb gardens for both ornamentation and for their aromatic qualities. Most of these are traditionally used for fragrance and for their reputed insect-repelling qualities. Herbs of the *Chrysanthemum* genus include costmary, pyrethrum, and feverfew, all used for both their aromas and their insect repellent traits.

Santolinas, of the genus *Santolina*, are composites used for borders and edgings in herb gardens because of their attractive bright green and gray-green foliages and compact growth habits. Their handsome foliages are excellent in small arrangements.

Tansy (*Tanacetum vulgare*) is another composite often grown in the herb garden. It may grow up to four feet in height and has pungent ferny foliage and small yellow button-type flowers. The flowers are a particular favorite of many beneficial insects. Tansy will spread quickly and so should be grown where this will not create problems.

Vegetable Varieties

Choose vegetables for their eating quality, disease resistance and early maturing qualities. Since the 1950s, plants have increasingly been bred to resist diseases. There now are over four dozen viruses and other diseases that specific vegetable cultivars can tolerate or resist due to breeding.

Select ones that fit into your gardening plans and your garden beds. Compact vegetable varieties are wonderful. They bear heavily, take up less space, and often require less maintenance.

Some edibles can be chosen for their beauty to mix into ornamental plantings. For instance, ruby chard, 'Romanesco' broccoli, nasturtiums, and radiccio are edible and ornamental. Red-stemmed chards, leaf lettuces, chives and edible violas go great with alyssum and other annual flowering plants.

In regions with hot summers, leaf lettuces will grow well as shade crops. In shady sites, lettuce is less likely to bolt (go to seed) and get bitter. Okra and many varieties of melons do not grow well in the cool maritime Northwest climate. These are the kinds of things you will learn as you garden over the years.

As you grow vegetables, you will begin to learn more about the requirements of the plants in combination with the limits of your regional climate. The Cooperative Extension Service, nurseries, garden centers, gardening friends, and botanical gardens all can serve as sources of information when you need answers. Also, remember that lots of valuable information about a plant's seeds, seedlings, habits, and requirements are on the back of the seed packet.

Artichoke, Globe

Globe artichoke (*Cynara scolymus*) is a large herbaceous perennial thistle, native to the Western Mediterranean region (North Africa). It grows three to five feet tall with equal spread. The dramatic, arching, silvery leaves contrast well against green foliage. The massive flowers are a showy lavender and quite fragrant. Dried flowers are beautiful in arrangements. Use in flower beds or vegetable gardens. Do not allow the flowers to open if you plan to eat them.

Harvest the buds when they are about four inches in diameter, before they start to open. Globe artichokes, somewhat demanding in care, require loose, well-drained soil and regular feeding to produce the rapid growth which yields the most tender artichokes. A heavy mulch in mild winter climates will protect them down to 20° F. In cold climates with less than 100 frost-free days, production is not as high. Artichokes may be grown as annuals or over wintered indoors.

Asparagus

Modern asparagus (*Asparagus officinalis*) cultivars are improved forms of an ancient herbaceous perennial native to Europe, Asia, and North Africa. You can enjoy its spring spears in all but the very coldest of climates. The fleshy, octopus-like roots produce shoots that grow into delicate fern-like foliage if uncut. Both male and female plants produce foliage. The females yield insignificant, small flowers that set pea-sized red berries by midsummer. The newer varieties with pre-

dominantly male plants are more productive.

Commercial asparagus crops are grown in very well-drained soil. Fast-growing shoots or "spears" pop through the soil after winter dormancy for a delightful early spring harvest that lasts 6-8 weeks. If plants are at least 4 years old, a second, smaller harvest in the fall is also possible by cutting all the foliage back to the ground about midsummer. Large-diameter, fast-growing shoots are the most tender. 'Mary Washington' is a rust-free, long-time asparagus favorite. The newer varieties, such as 'SYN4-56' and 'UC 157', are much more productive. 'SYN4-56' is resistant to rust and fusarium.

Beans

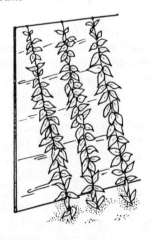

The most difficult aspect of beans is deciding which ones to grow. The classification of beans often is according to their use rather than their biological relationships. A number of species of the genus *Phaseolus*, known as green or snap beans, have resulted in many cultivars. Today, numerous varieties of this native of the Americas offers almost limitless choices. Bush or pole varieties can be green, blue, purple, or yellow. The pods taste best when eaten young and garden-fresh. Pinto, fava and lima beans are normally shelled and eaten fresh, or they can be dried and stored for over a year. The edible seeds and pods are only part of the benefit that beans can offer the garden. Beans are legumes that add nitrogen to the soil. Nitrogen from the air is "fixed" on root nodules with the help of beneficial rhizobia bacteria. The bacteria usually exists in the soil, but may not be plentiful in earth where chemical fertilizers have been used to the exclusion of compost and other organic matter. For highest yields and nitrogen fixing, inoculate beans with the bacteria

before sowing. A fraction of this nitrogen is stored in the roots that are left in the soil after the beans have been harvested.

* Bush and pole beans (*Phaseolus vulgaris* var. *humilis*) are names that describe two different growing habits. Bush (snap) beans are 1- to 2- foot bushes that mature quickly. Some varieties yield up to five pickings over a six-week period. Small white, purple or red flowers bloom shortly before small succulent pods are set. Plant both types of beans and you will have fast-growing bush beans early and the later maturing pole beans in the fall. Bush bean varieties include varieties with green, yellow, and purple pods. The flavorful yellow wax varieties are easy to spot when harvesting. Purple varieties are also easy to see and turn a vibrant green when cooked.

Pole (snap) beans have the richest flavor. They can climb to over 8 feet. They yield heavily if picked clean regularly from midsummer until the weather cools in the fall. Pole beans are a good choice for containers, or where space is limited. The long vines yield twice as much as bush beans, but start producing about two weeks later. They are easy to harvest, remain clean, and are less prone to insect attacks. The white, purple or red flowers bloom continuously and set pods soon after the flowers fold.

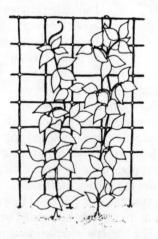

* Scarlet runner beans (*P. coccineus*) are tender perennials grown as annuals. A close cousin of snap beans, they grow swiftly and form dense vines on trellises or other frames. The bright red flowers make it an unusual ornamental that may be grown on string trellises on the west side of porches or patios. These runner beans belong to a separate species suited for cooler climates. They produce fuzzy, long (6 to 12 inches), flat pods during cool summer weather. The

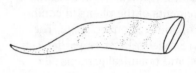

Flat bean pod

Round bean pod

flavor is too strong and beany for many people to eat fresh, but they are delicious when cooked. Runner beans thrive in cooler temperatures than many beans and bear heavy crops, which makes them a good choice for early harvests in cool climates. They stop setting flowers if just a few pods are left to mature or if the temperature rises above. The flowers are spectacular and many gardeners plant them solely for their captivating scarlet blossoms. High productivity is achieved in warmer climates by planting in partial shade, such as that provided by interplanting with corn. Runner beans form such a dense screen of foliage that they make an excellent wigwam for children to play in when grown on a teepee of poles.

* The so-called shell beans are lima beans (*P. lunatus*) which also come in both bush and pole forms. Limas are called butter beans in the South. They need a long growing season to mature and so may not produce well in northern states during cool years. They should be grown in soils comparatively poor in nitrogen so that they do not go to foliage more than crop.

The flowers range in color from black on white to scarlet. The pod or shell is normally shucked and the large beans are eaten fresh. Most varieties prefer warm, well-drained soil, but others thrive in somewhat cooler ground. Hot summers and autumn weather with little dew or rain is necessary for seeds to mature and dry. Flowers range in color from black on white to scarlet. Dried beans can be stored and used later in soups, chili, or stew.

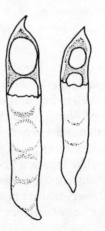

* Broad or fava beans (*Vicia faba*) are also included in this category of shell beans because they are normally shelled and eaten fresh or dried. The only bean native to the Mediterranean region, favas have large seeds and grow in broad, flat

pods up to 18 inches long. They are either eaten with pods when immature or fresh shelled, or dried and stored. Some varieties are cold tolerant to 15° F of frost or less. They prefer a long cool winter and spring to mature pods. Hot weather causes blossom drop. A few people, usually of Mediterranean origin, have a genetic enzyme deficiency that causes a severe or fatal reaction to Fava beans and pollen.

* Soybeans (*Glycine max*), a rich source of protein, are usually thought of as an agricultural crop but there are some cultivars that are suitable for the home garden. Soybeans need a long season to mature. Grow soybeans just as you would snap beans. Keep them watered during dry periods. You can harvest them for use as fresh shell green beans as soon as the seeds appear plump in the pods, but hulling them requires steaming them for ten minutes first. They are better harvested for dry beans when the pods are dry but the stems are still green.

Beet

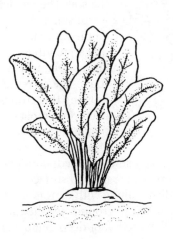

Beets (*Beta vulgaris*) are native to the Mediterranean region, and are a good winter crop in mild climates. This biennial, grown as an annual, is a good spring, summer, and fall crop in most other climates. Beet greens make a wonderful steamed vegetable. Many people enjoy the tops even more than the beets themselves. They develop best during warm sunny days and cool nights. Plant bolt-resistant varieties for summer harvests in hot climates. Broadcast seeds in thick patches every two to four weeks for a continued supply. Four or five plants grow from each seed, and the seedlings require thinning. However, the globe variety, 'Monopoly,' is a monogerm, only producing one plant per seed. Thin young beets, and eat the succulent tops or transplant when one to two inches tall. Harvest beet roots when they are the most tender, about half the size found in supermarkets. White or golden globe varieties do not bleed when sliced, and roots and greens together taste milder than red beets. The key to a sweet-tasting beet is even soil moisture and rapid growth.

Broccoli

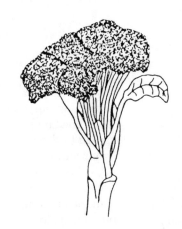

Broccoli (*Brassica oleracea*, Botrytis group), a native to coastal Europe, is extremely nutritious, and if harvested regularly, may continue to bear for over a month. This brassica produces best in cool climates. In hot weather, broccoli can bolt suddenly and be plagued with insect attacks. If seedlings are subjected to a sudden cold snap, the florets may "button"—form tiny, premature heads. The unopened flower shoots and stems (spears) are eaten in most varieties. If the buds pass their prime, somewhat bitter tasting yellow flowers sprout. Chinese broccoli (broccoli raab) produces short, edible leafy tops with a mustard-like flavor. Broccoli grows well in containers. The silvery gray foliage is beautiful, but difficult to keep looking nice.

Brussels Sprouts

Brussels sprouts (*Brassica oleracea*, Gemmifera group), native to Belgium, have an excellent flavor when grown, harvested, and cooked properly. The fresh, firm, tightly packed sprouts are sweeter and more tender after being nipped by frost which turns starch into sugar. Enjoy a long harvest from first frost through late spring by planting early maturing and late maturing varieties. This brassica requires regular feeding and watering for strong growth through the summer. Use a low-nitrogen complete fertilizer mix. Too much nitrogen causes loose sprouts and lanky stems, which are less cold tolerant. The tips of stems are pinched off by commercial growers three to five weeks before harvesting so sprouts will fill the stem. Some gardeners remove healthy lower leaves as they harvest sprouts so more light will help to develop remaining sprouts, while others retain leaves to help shed rain from sprouts.

Cabbage

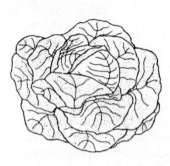

Cabbage (*Brassica oleracea*, Capitata group) tastes great both garden fresh or lightly steamed. The days of eating limp, over-boiled cabbage with the life cooked out of it are long past. The cabbage harvest can last nearly all year round by selecting the proper varieties and planting at the correct time. Late-season varieties take up quite a bit of space, while early-maturing types require less room and can be closer spaced. Small-headed early varieties are normally best when eaten fresh. Larger types make good sauerkraut or cole slaw. Chinese cabbage (*B. rapa*, var. *chinensis*), including bok choi and pak choi, is rapidly gaining popularity because it is very quick to mature, and has an exotic flavor. Like most other cole crops, cabbage is a heavy feeder, with a shallow root system. It requires plenty of fertilizer and regular watering to form robust, tender heads. Mulch soil to retain moisture during dry weather.

Cauliflower

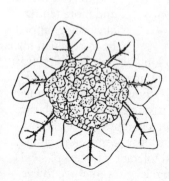

Cauliflower (*Brassica oleracea*, Botrytis group) is the fussiest member of the cabbage family, but the added attention is more than repaid with sweet, tender, white, green, or purple curd-like flower heads. Blue-green leaves surround the heads. For good results, the soil must be deep and fertile, growth must be rapid and this brassica must never suffer drought. Blanching, the practice of covering the head to shield sunshine to ensure tender head development, is customary. But self-blanching varieties (some taste similar to broccoli) are easier to grow. Heads of self-blanching varieties can turn slightly pink or purple from stress and still taste good. In cool coastal climates, with proper variety selection, the harvest of cauliflower can last up to nine months, except during very cold winters or long, hot summers.

Carrot

Carrots (*Daucus carota* var. *sativus*) take a long time to germinate, up to 3 weeks in cool weather before tiny fern-like carrot greens pop through the soil. They prefer warm soil and ample water for quick growth to yield sweet, tender roots. The secret to growing this crop is deep soil preparation and rapid growth. The seed bed should be fine, and raked smooth. Seeds won't be able to push through a crusty, compacted surface. Some gardeners sow radishes along with carrots. The radishes germinate first to "break ground" for the carrots. Prepare the soil well, up to a foot deep, removing any stones or debris that will cause roots to fork. Carrots also grow well in a container full of loose potting soil. In deeply cultivated, fertile soil, carrots can grow so closely together that weeds have a hard time getting started. Thin rows and eat thinnings. Removing young, sweet carrots makes more room for their neighbors. The short varieties are the earliest, sweetest, and easiest to grow. Intermediate sizes are good all-round varieties. When immature, they are sweetest. When mature, they are still very tasty and store well. Long-rooted varieties store well in the ground during winter.

Celery & Celeriac

Celery (*Apium graveolens* var. *dulce*) is probably the most demanding of all garden vegetables. Celeriac

(also named *Apium graveolens* var. *repaceum*), is a close relative of celery, requiring similar conditions for growth, except that it is less sensitive to temperature. Years ago, celery was blanched by mounding up soil or placing a dark cover around stems to tenderize and whiten the stalks. It is not necessary to do this. Celery and celeriac are heavy feeders and need fertile organic soil. The small diameter, deep root system is adapted to grow in wet, bog soil, drawing in a lot of water. Regular deep watering is a must if you want to harvest tender, succulent crops. Space plants 6 inches apart, fertilize with manure tea or fish emulsion every three weeks and keep plants mulched.

Sweet Corn

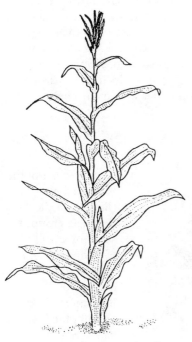

Corn (*Zea mays* var. *rugosa*), a type of maize, is a major American contribution to the vegetable world. Sweet corn is bred for a low-starch, high-sugar content. When picked, the sugar stored in kernels converts to starch at a very rapid rate. This is why corn is sweetest when eaten within minutes of picking. However, the newer strains of super-sweet corn contain twice the sugar, and the sugar-to-starch conversion is much slower.

Cobs are six to ten inches long. One to three cobs grow on four to 15-foot-tall stalks. The tassels on the top of the stalk contain male flowers that fertilize the female flower silks which grow out of the cob. Tassels form only after corn has received enough days of heat. In fact, breeders classify corn by "heat units" (HU); that is, the number of hours over 50° F. that each variety needs to mature. This explains why corn sown early may mature at the same time as seed sown later, during warmer weather.

Do not plant sweet and super-sweet types close to one another or the male flowers from one type may fertilize the female flowers of the other, which reduces quality. Since corn is pollinated by the wind, always plant the same variety of corn in a block containing several rows rather than one long row, to ensure pollination. If the weather is calm and windless, shaking the stalks after the silk has set will cause male pollen to rain downward and pollinate the female silk. Complete pollination ensures that a cob full of kernels will develop. Short cobs are common to fast-maturing varieties. Long ears on both short and tall stalks are the norm in later varieties.

Cucumber

Cucumbers (*Cucumis sativus*) are warm-weather vine or bush crops that are favorites in salads fresh from the vine, or when preserved as pickles. A native to southern Asia, cucumbers come in all shapes and sizes. Pickling cukes are short and stubby; slicers are long and slender. Apple or lemon cucumbers are spherical and yellow. Armenian cucumbers are really a long, slender melon that grows up to three feet in length. Each type of cucumber has its own distinctive flavor. The short pickling varieties are bitter when eaten fresh. When used to make pickles, they should be picked when only a few inches long. Some slicing varieties possess a tough, bitter skin that needs to be peeled before eating the sweet creamy flesh within. Since cucumbers are mostly water, many commercial growers cover them with a thin layer of wax after harvesting to retain moisture. To enjoy the peak flavor of cucumbers, they should be eaten within a few hours of harvest.

Eggplant or Aubergine

Eggplant, also known as aubergine, is native to Asia and Africa. It needs daytime temperatures of 60 to 95° F. and minimum nighttime temperatures of 65 to yield fruit. If the temperature dips below this point, eggplants will not grow or produce fruit. For earliest production in northern climates, grow seedlings indoors and transplant them into a coldframe, or under plastic tunnels until the temperature has warmed both ground and air.

The oblong (egg-shaped) purple fruit is most common, but varieties are available in green, yellow, white, and striped that can be oblong, round, or cylindrical in form.

Endive

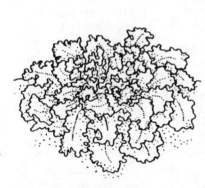

Endive (*Chicorium endiva*), a native of India, has curled, cut or lobed leaves that form a heavy rosette up to 18 inches across. Endive varieties with broad, flat leaves are known as escarole or broad-leaved endive.

Endive is an excellent crop for cool climates. It will overwinter in temperatures down to 10° F! Endive loses bitterness when gradually exposed to freezing temperatures. Warm weather increases bitterness. A great addition to salads, and one of the few greens available in the winter.

Garlic and Shallots

Garlic (*Allium sativum*) should be grown by all gardeners! The compound bulb consists of six to 12 individual segments (cloves), and a leaf stalk, which produces seeds and bulblets. Grow either the common

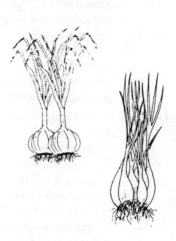

type found in grocery stores or the elephant garlic which is several times larger. Plant garlic cloves in the fall for harvest the following year. In very cold areas, plant garlic cloves in the spring. When garlic is ready to harvest, its tops turn yellow and fall over. After pulling garlic, let it dry in the sun for a couple of days, then store it in a cool, dry place.

This native of the Mediterranean region boasts insecticidal and antibiotic qualities. Many people claim it also has numerous health benefits when regularly eaten. Gourmet cooks would be lost without this essential culinary ingredient. Garlic is an excellent insecticide and fungicide when minced or juiced and mixed with water and applied as a spray. As a fungicide, garlic helps control downy mildew, various rusts, bean anthracnose, some leaf spots, and blights.

Shallots (*Allium cepa*, Aggregatum group) grow in clumps like garlic but are smaller and brown. Plant the individual cloves just as you would garlic. Like garlic, shallots are ready to harvest when their tops yellow and begin to die. You can use the immature bulbs just as you would green onions. Shallots are grown primarily for their bulbs which have a distinctive flavor that is very popular with many chefs.

Kale

A member of the brassica family, kale (*Brassica oleracea*, Acephala group) is so hardy it will overwinter even when temperatures dip to -10° F. Benjamin Franklin brought the first kale seeds to America from Scotland over two centuries ago. It will grow all year round in most climates, but grows best in cool weather. Warm temperatures induce mild dormancy and make leaves quite bitter and leathery. As with many brassicas, kale tastes best after being nipped by frost. There are several edible ornamental varieties that are popular in flower beds and containers to provide winter color. The ruffled leaves add to the circular bands of color in these ornamental types. One of the few salad greens available in winter, kale is packed with vitamins, and very low in calories.

Kohlrabi

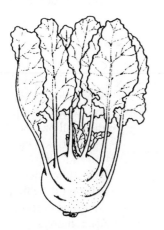

Kohlrabi (*Brassica oleracea*, Gongylodes group) is another member of the brassica family. It has a turnip-like swollen stem that grows just above the ground with leaves sprouting from its top and sides. Kohlrabi's bulbous stem has the taste of the most delicate cabbage, with the consistency of a turnip. It tastes good either raw or cooked. A biennial grown as an annual, kohlrabi is very easy to care for and has few problems with diseases or insects. Like most cabbage family plants, kohlrabi grows best when planted early in the spring and harvested before warm weather makes it spicy and woody. Mid to late-summer plantings can be harvested after frost has killed most other vegetables.

Leek

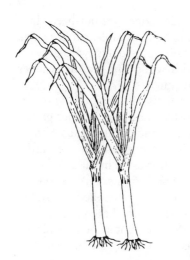

Leeks (*Allium ampeloprasum*, Porrum group), like garlic, have flat leaves. The flat leaves help distinguish leeks from other members of the onion family. Leeks do not have a round bulb like onions but rather a thick succulent stem. To get long white stems, you must cover the stems with hilled-up soil when the plants are about half grown. Harvest leeks any time after the stalks are about an inch in diameter. They will be even sweeter if allowed to grow bigger. Leeks need a long growing season. Autumn leeks are tender and sweet. Overwintering varieties are very frost-hardy, which may keep you in garden fresh "onions" year round. Most bulb onions are harvested in the fall and stored for the winter. Leeks, on the other hand, will hold in the garden and can be used throughout the winter when needed, even when there is snow on the ground. This is a notable quality especially in damp climates where bulb onions do not store well.

Lettuce

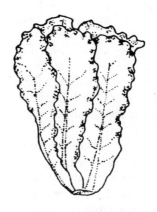

Lettuce (*Lactuca sativa*) is a crop that all gardeners can grow with very little effort. Lettuce comes in several types: Head lettuce, loose-leaf, butterhead, and Romaine (or cos) lettuce (*L. sativa longifolia*). The leaf lettuces are available in several colors and leaf types, many pretty enough to use as borders in ornamental gardens. The onset of hot weather turns cool-weather lettuce varieties bitter and induces bolting, but there are several heat-tolerant varieties. The aim in growing lettuce is to maintain a constant supply all summer long. This requires successive sowing. Since lettuce is a light feeder, requires little direct sunlight, and is fast-growing, it is perfect to interplant between crops that take longer to mature. There are varieties for all tastes and climates. Growing the proper variety for your climate and season will keep you in lettuce as long as weather allows. Many varieties tolerate frost to 20° F if hardened-off gradually. When it's too cold to grow outdoors, lettuce can be grown easily in a greenhouse, in an insulated cold frame or in a plastic tunnel. In regions with hot summers, grow lettuce in a shady site to lessen the likelihood of bolting and for a more successful crop.

Melons

True cantaloupes (*Cucumis melo* var. *cantaloupensis*) are more common in Europe than

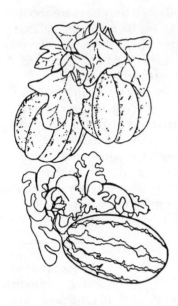

America. muskmelons (*C. melo* var. *reticulatus*), often referred to as cantaloupes, differ from muskmelons in several ways. Muskmelons have an exterior netting with superficial veins. The edible flesh ranges in color from salmon to various shades of green and has a musky fragrance. When ripe, the fruit pulls from the vine easily. The skin of most true cantaloupes has a rough, scaly texture, with well pronounced, dark vein tracks. The flesh is orange and aromatic. When ripe, the fruit must be cut from the vine. Nichols Garden Nursery (1190 North Pacific Hwy., Albany, OR 97321) is one seed company that carries true cantaloupe seed varieties.

Honeydew melons (*C. melo* var. *inodorus*) are winter melons, so called because they are late to ripen and can be stored up to a month. These melons are larger, round to oblong, with a waxy skin that can be wrinkled or smooth. They do not have a robust, musky aroma. Low disease tolerance and the long season make these melons more difficult to grow.

Watermelons (*Citrullus lanatus*) are included in this section with the above melons because their growth is similar. Watermelons come in two basic shapes, round and oblong. The smooth skin is green and sometimes with stripes, and the flesh is red yellow or white.

Even though some melons now have bush forms, they still need a lot of space in the garden. Their vines may grow six to ten feet long. Plant melons in hills of soil about 13 to 14 inches in diameter and 2 to 3 inches high. Plant 8 to 10 seeds and thin to the strongest four plants after the true leaves appear.

Okra

The seed pods of okra (*Abelmoschus esculentus*), an ancient, warm-weather plant, add a distinctive flavor to many recipes of the deep South. Okra is a main ingredient in gumbo and southern stews.

Okra is easy to grow in warm climates, yielding numerous pods over a long season. Warm weather is the key to growing this crop. Okra produces numer-

ous pods soon after the very ornamental red and yellow flowers appear. Pods should be picked daily because the plant will stop producing if pods are allowed to ripen. Standard plants grow four to seven feet tall. Space-saving dwarf types grow only two to four feet tall.

Onions and Scallions

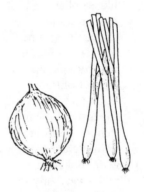

Growing good bulb onions (*Allium cepa*, Cepa group) and scallions can be a little tricky. First, you must know the basic differences between the different types of these Asian natives.

Sweet Spanish onions, commercially grown in Utah, northern New Mexico and central California, are big, sweet, soft, long-season types. They bulb from July through August. In latitudes above 45°, bulbing is restricted by decreasing sunlight and the bulbs tend to be small and pungent.

Storage onions were developed for northern climates, rapidly producing hard, durable, narrow rings with heavy skins. Short-season storage types grow well in northern latitudes, while long-season varieties are choice for southern climates.

Overwintered bulb onions can also be long or short season. The large, flat, long-season types grow best in southern California, and east to Texas. Short-season types, developed for temperate climates, are sown in late summer and harvested in June.

Scallions (*Allium cepa* or *A. fistulosum*) are sweet, savory gourmet onions that can be cooked or used in salads and as garnishes. The bulb of the plant is tiny and the entire plant is used. They may be juvenile forms of regular onions or bunching onions. They may be grown from seeds, onion sets, or onion seedlings.

Bunching onions (*A. fistulosum*), are of three different types. Those derived from sweet Spanish types are harvested before longer nights of autumn signal bulbs to develop. They are sweet and tender, with a thin skin. They are sown from spring through mid-summer. The long harvest starts about two months after planting. The other two bunching onion types are overwintering types and do not bulb when the nights become longer. A single planting of these can be harvested for months.

The various onions can be grown either from seeds or from onion sets which are small, immature onion bulbs. Since onions require a long season to mature, it is usually far more convenient to grow them from sets. In frost-free regions, plant onions in the fall for spring harvest. In regions with cold winters, plant onions in the spring for fall harvest or, in the case of bunching onions, for harvest during the winter and following spring. You can also start your own seeds and plant out the onion seedlings when they are ready.

Parsnip, Rutabaga & Salsify

These three root crops are not commonly grown, and their popularity seems to continue waning. They deserve renewed consideration by home gardeners. They all have similar growth habits, even though they are not from the same families. This collection of root crops is very easy to grow, requiring little attention. They are long-season crops that store well, either in the garden or in a root cellar, and they make excellent garden-fresh meals during the winter.

Parsnip (*Pastinaca sativa*), native to Eurasia, was a staple in Europe prior to potatoes being introduced. A biennial grown as an annual, it has a rich, nutty taste that is superb in soups, stews, or when steamed and eaten with a pat of butter. The flavor is improved by light frost. The roots store very well in the ground, even in the coldest of climates.

Rutabagas (*Brassica napus*, Napobrassica group) or yellow turnips are also called Canadian or Swedish turnips. They are prone to a few plant ills common to the brassica family, especially cabbage fly root maggot attack. Protect the young crop with floating row covers. A close relative of turnips, rutabagas taste similar, but have yellow flesh and a sweeter flavor. They store well in the ground all winter long if mulched heavily to prevent freezing.

Salsify (*Tragopogon porrifolius*), also known as the oyster plant, has a delicate flavor when cooked, that is similar to oysters. The two to three-foot plant with its eight-inch taproot is a biennial grown as an annual. It will grow best in loose, rich soil. You can harvest in the fall or through the winter and spring. Seldom seen in gardens, this Mediterranean native looks like a large, white carrot, but is easier to grow. Many salsify aficionados prefer the even more delicate taste of the black oyster plant (*Scorzonera hispanica*), a close cousin of salsify.

Pea

Plant garden or English peas (*Pisum sativum*), a Eurasian native, very early in the spring for the best crop. Garden peas thrive in cool weather. Southern gardeners plant peas in fall through midwinter, while northern gardeners plant from February through April. In raised beds, peas can be planted 2-3 weeks earlier than in flat beds. If planted too late, peas get heat stress during hot weather, growth is stunted, leaves wilt, blossoms drop, and pod growth terminates. Peas often are the season's first vegetable. Ripe, succulent peas also inspire countless gardeners to get out and plant the rest of the garden. Peas also make a good fall crop when planted in mid to late summer.

Sugar peas or snow peas, and 'Sugar Snap' type peas (*P. sativum* var. *macrocarpon*) have small peas and edible pods. These should be picked very young and eaten raw or steamed. The 'Sugar Snap' series of peas are a development of the 1980s and have larger sweeter peas and thicker pods. Grow them just as you would English peas.

Peas are legumes, and produce their own nitrogen by capturing it from the air in the soil. Nitrogen-fixing nodules, located on the roots, concentrate this nitrogen. Plants need only an initial fertilization with a good source of potassium and phosphorus.

Peppers

Peppers, both sweet (*Capsicum annuam*) and hot (*Capsicum frutescens*), are Mediterranean natives and members of the *Solanaceae* or nightshade family along with tomatoes, eggplants, and potatoes. Peppers require ample heat to grow and set fruit. Nighttime temperatures below 50° F. will stunt seedling peppers so badly that they may never recover. A Wall-O-Water™, cold frame or spun fiber covering will provide young plants with cold protection in the spring and early summer. This added warmth allows peppers to develop and bear much earlier and heavier. Choose smaller sweet peppers for growing in cool, short-season climates.

Potato

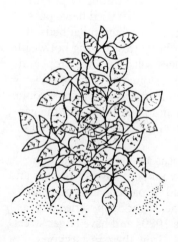

Common white potatoes (*Solanum tuberosum*), native to Peru but known as Irish potatoes, are a major food staple in many parts of the world. The average American eats over 130 pounds annually. Yet, most people think that just the two or three types of potatoes sold in supermarkets are available. There are over 200 different varieties with different shapes, sizes, colors, textures, and tastes. A very diverse selection can be found by exploring seed catalogs. The most notable is Ronnigers Seed Potatoes (Star Route, Moyie Springs, ID, 83845) which lists more than 100 varieties. True, potatoes require ample garden space and can be purchased inexpensively at the supermarket. But unlike commercially grown crops, home-grown tubers are free of sprout-inhibiting chemicals. Once you try garden-fresh varieties, commercial crops will seem like little more than a ball of bland starch.

Use seed potatoes grown especially for that purpose. Don't try to grow garden potatoes from those you buy in a grocery store. They may carry potato diseases and also may have been treated to prevent sprouting. Cut the seed potato into egg sized pieces. Each one should have three eyes, the dents from which sprouts will grow. Let the pieces dry for several days to avoid the risk of rot. Plant pieces about a foot apart and about four inches deep in hilled rows two to three feet apart.

Dig a few new potatoes as soon as the plants flower, but wait until the plant foliage begins to turn yellow to harvest full-sized tubers. Sweet potatoes (*Ipomoea batatas*) are considered by most gardeners as an exclusive warm-weather Southern crop. Not even cousins of the true potato, sweet potatoes are related to morning glories and are originally from tropical America. With a little care, sweet potatoes will grow in climates with a minimum of four frost-free months. Careful variety selection, and planting rooted slips (sprouted pieces of older potatoes), when the ground has warmed to 55° F. will overcome most climatic obstacles.

Yams (*Dioscorea* species) are often confused with sweet potatoes. True yams are longer, slender, and a different genus entirely. Yams are tropical vines with edible tuberous roots that grow only in tropical and subtropical climates where the temperatures stay above freezing year round.

Radish

Children love to grow radishes (*Raphanus sativus*), a Eurasian native, because they grow so swiftly. Many varieties are ready to eat within a month and require frequent watering, which is one of children's favorite chores. Radishes, members of the brassica family, are nearly trouble-free when cultured rapidly and grown during cool weather. Here's a vegetable that will fill temporary bare areas of the garden or will mark rows of slow-maturing crops. There are also long-season radishes such as the giant Japanese (Daikon) varieties or the black Spanish types. Since radishes are a member of the brassica family, the infamous cabbage fly root maggots have time to launch an attack on the long-season radishes. Prevent root maggot attacks by applying diatomaceous earth, wood ashes or beneficial Nc nematodes when planting. You can also cover the area with spun fiber when the seeds are planted and keep the crop covered until it is all harvested. By planting different types, you can enjoy fresh radishes most of the year.

Rhubarb

Rhubarb is a perennial plant that makes an outstanding addition to larger gardens, but takes up too much space in smaller gardens, unless you happen to love it's succulent stems and deep green decorative foliage. The tart, pink to red stalks (leaf stems) are ready to harvest in the early spring, before much of the other garden bounty is ready. Do not eat the green leaves and roots which contain oxalic acid and are very toxic to people.

Rhubarb can be grown in any climate, under just about any conditions. Buy the roots in early spring and set the crowns about two inches below the soil surface. The soil should be well-prepared, and rich organic matter added for best results. Do not pick until the second year after planting and then, pick for only one to two weeks. After that, you should be able to have as much as two months of harvest, but never pick more than half of the rhubarb stalks at any one harvest. You should divide rhubarb if the stalks begin to grow thin. Rhubarb prefers a hard freeze during winter, but this is not necessary for good production. Rhubarb benefits most from a healthy addition of manure, once very early in the year and again in mid-summer.

Spinach and Chard

You can enjoy nutritious spinach (*Spinacia oleracea*), a southwest Asian native, for most of the year with the proper variety selection. Unlike the canned spinach that fortified Popeye, garden-fresh spinach is sweet, tender, and succulent. There are two basic classifications of spinach, summer and winter, plus the pseudo variety, New Zealand spinach (*Tetragonia tetragonioides*), which is actually a member of the beet family.

Spinach is packed with iron, but the high concentration of oxalic acid renders it a poor choice in large quantities in children's diets.

Chard or Swiss chard (*Beta vulgaris* var. *cicla*), a native of Southern Europe, is also a member of the beet family. The spectacular edible red, white, or green foliage makes it a very ornamental addition to any garden. Chard culture is virtually the same as spinach culture.

Both should be planted from seed in the fall to early spring in mild frost-free regions and in the spring to mid-summer in regions with cold winters. In areas with hot summers, look for spinach cultivars that are resistant to bolting, going to seed. Chard does not transplant well so you should sow it directly in the garden. To speed the germination of spinach seeds, put them in the refrigerator for a week before planting if the soil temperature is warm. Spinach planted late in the summer makes a good fall crop.

New Zealand spinach, though no relative of true spinach, is prepared in the same way, steamed lightly. This is a good plant for regions with hot summers because it won't bolt. You can start the seeds indoors and set them out when the soil warms in the spring.

Squash

Squashes, which were originally cultivated by American Indians, come in two basic types, summer and winter squashes. Summer squashes (*Cucurbita pepo*) ripen from July through October and have relatively soft skins. Winter squash (which may be *C.*

maxima, C. mixta, C. moschata, or *C., pepo*) needs a longer growing season and is ready to harvest in October or November. The hard skin of winter squash makes it easier to store without refrigeration for several months. Both summer and winter squash are very easy to grow, but must be protected against the squash vine borer.

If space is limited, grow bush varieties. Sprawling winter squash vines will take over large areas of the garden. You can grow some of the squashes on trellises if they are small-fruiting varieties. For large fruiting varieties, you need a stout frame to support the weight of the mature squashes. Grow squash from seeds sown directly in the garden, following the spacing directions on the seed packet. They all are warm-season vegetables and so can't be planted until the soil has warmed to 60° F. If your growing season is too short for squashes, you can start the seeds indoors and then transplant them.

Tomato

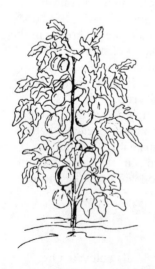

A vegetable garden, whether far to the north or deep in the south, must include tomatoes (*Lycopersicon lycopersicum*) to be complete. Entire books have been devoted to garden tomatoes so, obviously, we can only give you a few highlights on these rewarding garden plants. A special satisfaction comes from picking that first vine-ripened fruit, slicing it open, and enjoying the zesty-sweet taste and refined fleshy texture. Home-grown tomatoes are allowed to ripen on the vine, developing sweet, rich pulp, and a tender skin. Variety selection is important if you are to achieve the best flavor and the best production in your climate. You can choose from numerous tomato types, including colors that are yellow, orange, striped, and the usual red; and sizes that range from the huge beefsteak types to the tiny cherry and container varieties. Paste tomatoes such as 'Roma' are also becoming very popular in home gardens. You can choose varieties that mature early, mid-season, and late. Choose tomato cultivars that are disease resistant. This is indicated on the seed packet by the initials "V" for verticillium wilt, "F" for fusarium wilt, "N" for nematodes and "A" for alternaria—all prominent tomato diseases.

As a member of the *Solanaceae* (or nightshade) family, this South American native needs warm weather to grow and produce fruit; tomato blossoms fall off below 50° F. When temperatures are above 90°, you also will get blossom drop. For the Pacific Northwest, the cultivar 'Oregon Spring' is an absolute cool-season standout. It can be set out just after last frost with no damage and produce large flavorful beefsteak fruit even before cherry tomatoes are ripe! In the Midwest, 'Mosupreme' and others bred in this demanding climate, are topnotch performers in the home garden.

Tomatoes come in two general forms. Determinate plants are bush types that have a limited size and tend to ripen all their fruit at once. Indeterminate types are vines that will continue to grow and bear fruit until killed by cold weather. They need to be staked or caged. There also are compact bush tomatoes that are ideal for container growing.

You can start tomatoes from seed indoors about six weeks before outside planting is possible or grow them as purchased seedlings. When planting seedlings, strip the leaves from the lower half of the main stem and plant the seedling on a slant deep in the ground, with just its topknot of leaves above the soil level. Roots will develop all along the stem that is below ground. Mulch the tomato bed as soon as the soil has warmed to about 60° F. and keep the soil evenly moist. This will prevent blossom end rot which is caused by uneven soil moisture and a lack of calcium. Tomatoes will thrive in very rich soil. Some gardeners have had sensational luck by planting tomatoes directly into a pile of compost.

Turnip

Turnips (*Brassica rapa,* Roman group) are native to Eurasia and probably one of the most underrated vegetables in America. The swollen root, usually two to three inches in diameter, yields white or yellow flesh with a mild to zesty taste. Many varieties mature flavorful roots quickly and are and resistant to diseases

and pests. The trick to harvesting a good turnip is to grow it fast in cool weather. The sugars concentrate in the root during cool weather, making them much sweeter than when grown in hot weather.

Turnips mature in only five to seven weeks, so can be planted every couple of weeks until just a few weeks before the average first frost date. Sow turnip seeds about one-half inch deep in rows a foot and a half or less apart. When the seedlings come up, thin them so they are three to five inches apart. Keep turnips well watered to keep them growing fast.

Chapter Seven

Flower Gardens

About Flower Gardens

One of the best ways to choose annual, biennial, and perennial flower varieties is to take a stroll through your neighborhood, visit plant nurseries , botanical, and other public gardens (especially in the spring) to find out what grows well in your local climate. Make notes on which plants you like best so that you can ask for them when you shop. In addition, the county office of your state university's Cooperative Extension Service will have information available on what will grow well in your area.

For choosing flower varieties, preparing the soil and planting follow the same general guidelines as for vegetables.

To choose plants, order the mail order seed catalogs that carry the kinds of plants you want, especially those from your local area. These catalogs often have excellent color photos and good descriptions of plants and their growing conditions, but beware of descriptions that are too flowery.

A basic plan or sketch of border plantings will help you add structure to your landscape and is helpful when picking plants. Take your plan to the nursery and ask one of the plant experts for suggestions. If you go to the nursery at an off time when they are not likely to be busy, such as a Monday or Tuesday morning, they will be happy to help you. But if you go on a weekend day in the spring, they will probably be too busy to give you much time.

The climate, hours of sun per day, soil, and orientation toward the sun of an ornamental border will dictate the types of flowering plants that will grow vigorously and productively. Many flowering plants bloom so prolifically that they need only occasional deadheading—cutting of flowers that have passed their peak. Examples of these are marigolds, snapdragons, petunias and zinnias. To deadhead, simply snap off old, spent flower heads. You can use pruners to snip off several spent flowers at once.

Biennials perform well in flower beds and borders. They are planted in mid to late summer of one year and bloom the following year.

Trees, shrubs, and roses can form the framework of ornamental beds and borders. Annuals that provide just one growing season of color; perennials, which live for several years can be added later. Shrubs need extra time to get established. An attractive and easy-to-maintain ornamental border usually contains a mixture of shrubs, trees and herbaceous perennials. Herbaceous perennials are those that die back to the ground in the fall and produce new growth each spring. Spring-blooming and summer bulbs are also good choices for ornamental beds. Many will come up early in the year to give late winter and early spring color and inspire you to get out in the garden and plant annuals to continue the color throughout the summer and fall.

Instant color is very satisfying in a new bed or border. Plant fast-flowering annuals for this effect. Annuals are good choices for filling in the gaps between larger shrubs and in between young plants in newly planted beds.

Avoid planting annuals so close to developing shrubs or perennials that they compete for sunlight and nutrients. Borders with a wide array of bulbs and early-flowering perennials provide color before shrubs break their dormancy. Plant early spring bulbs near the perennials. The new growth on the perennials will cover up and hide the withering bulb leaves later in the spring, making the garden more attractive. The bulbs will also be protected from accidental digging since you will avoid digging near the base of perennials.

Climbing plants add a dimension of height to the garden. They can cover unsightly walls or objects, or be trained no a trellis.

Give the entire perennial garden a complete dressing of well-rotted manure and compost every spring. Lightly cultivate the compost, manure and a complete fertilizer into the soil around the drip lines of perennials. Wait to lay down a two- to four-inch layer of organic mulch until the soil has warmed up later in the spring.

Be sure to read the seed packet information so that you can discover any special conditions needed for the seeds you plan to grow. For instance, aster, carnation, delphinium, phlox, primula, and snapdragon seeds will germinate better if placed in the freezer to simulate winter dormancy for 48 hours before planting. Seeds from these plants require freezing weather for the highest germination.

Flowering plants are most effective when planted so that their foliage touches at maturity, which usually is early summer for annuals and at the end of the first growing season for perennials. This helps keep the soil cool during summer heat, helps cut down soil moisture evaporation, and reduces weed growth.

A good guide for estimating the number of plants you will need per square foot is as follows:

Spacing Plants	Sq. Ft.
4"	9.1
6"	4.0
8"	2.3
10"	1.4
12"	1.0
15"	.65
18"	.45
24"	.25

If you have a garden bed that is 10 feet long and 3 feet wide (30 square feet) and you want to plant on 8" centers, multiply 30 x 2.3 = 69 plants.

Tender, Half Hardy, Hardy & Heat Resistant Annuals

Annual flowers are those which complete their entire life cycle within a single growing season. They are noted for their prolific, long blooming periods. Annuals are classified according to their hardiness and the time of year they should be planted. Those classifications are tender, half-hardy, hardy, and heat resistant. These are guidelines only. In warm humid areas, some of the annuals may prove perennial. The regional specifics of rain, humidity, day and night temperatures, soil and other environmental factors all have a bearing on the success or failure of garden plants.

Tender annuals, also called warm-weather annuals, are those which can not tolerate even a light frost. They should be planted only after all chance of frost is past. Cosmos, petunias, and zinnias are good examples of tender annuals. Many of these are truly tender perennials and biennials but are included with annuals since they must be grown as such in most of the United States.

Half-hardy annuals include those that will tolerate a light frost. They can be planted earlier than the tender annuals. Calceolaria and schizanthus are half-hardy annuals.

Hardy annuals can stand colder weather. Their seeds may be sown either in early spring or the fall. Larkspur, pansies, snapdragons and stock fall into this category.

Hardy annuals are the easiest to grow from seed and can be sown directly in the garden soil, or in a cold frame to get an extra month to six-week jump on the season.

Half-hardy annuals are more difficult to grow than hardy ones, especially in cooler northern climates. Most of these annuals require a minimum temperature

Left to right: Petunia 'Polo Salmon', Impatiens 'Tango' and the Zinnia 'Scarlet Splendor'. All three varieties are AAS winners. Note that the Impatiens is a perennial, but grown as an annual in most climates.

All-America Selection (AAS) Flower Winners

The following are some of the AAS annual flower winners that have been chosen over the years for their excellent performance in test locations throughout the United States and Canada. If you choose AAS winners, you know you are likely to have a productive flower garden. Watch for the AAS symbol on the seed packet. Although the awards began in 1933, we are only giving those that must be treated as annuals throughout most of the country and those award winners from 1960 through the early 1990s since there are so many. This abbreviated list should give you an idea of the extent of the AAS flowers.

Variety	Year		Variety	Year		Variety	Year
ACHILLEA			MORNING GLORY			SWEET WILLIAM	
Summer Pastels	1990		Early Call	1970		Red Monarch	1966
ALYSSUM			NIEREMBERGIA			TORENIA	
Rosie O'Day	1961		Mont Blanc	1993		Clown Mixture	1989
CARNATION			NICOTIANA			VERBENA	
Juliet	1975		Nicki-Red	1979		Imagination	1993
Scarlet Luminette	1982						
			PANSY			VINCA	
CELOSIA			Giant Majestic Mixed	1966		Polka Dot	1969
Fireglow	1964		Majestic White Blotch	1966		Pretty In Rose	1991
Golden Triumph	1968		Imperial Blue	1975		Parasol	1991
Red Fox	1974		Orange Prince	1979		Pretty In White	1992
Apricot Brandy	1981		Jolly Joker	1990			
Century Mixed	1985		Maxim Marina	1991		ZINNIA	
New Look	1988		Padparadja	1991		Old Mexico	1962
Castle Pink	1990					Red Man	1962
			PETUNIA			Firecracker	1963
CORNFLOWER			Coral Satin	1961		Thumbelina	1963
Snow Ball	1969		Appleblossom	1965		Tom Thumb Pink Buttons	1964
			Circus	1972		Bonanza	1964
COSMOS			Blushing Maid	1977		Yellow Zenith	1965
Sunset	1966		Red Picotee	1983		Wild Cherry	1968
Diablo	1974		Purple Pirouette	1987		Torch	1969
Sunny Red	1986		Ultra Crimson Star	1988		Cherry Buttons	1969
			Orchid Daddy	1989		Rosy Future	1969
IMPATIENS			Polo Burgundy Star	1990		Peter Pan Pink	1971
Blitz	1981		Polo Salmon	1990		Peter Pan Plum	1971
Tango	1989					Carved Ivory	1972
			SNAPDRAGON			Peter Pan Scarlet	1973
MARIGOLD			Rocket Rose	1960		Scarlett Ruffles	1974
Toreador	1960		Rocket Bronze	1960		Peter Pan Orange	1974
Spun Gold	1960		Rocket Golden	1960		Red Sun	1978
Spun Yellow	1966		Rocket Orchid	1960		Peter Pan Cream	1978
Golden Jubilee	1967		Rocket White	1960		Cherry Ruffles	1978
First Lady	1968		Rocket Red	1960		Yellow Ruffles	1978
Orange Jubilee	1968		Floral Carpet Rose	1965		Gold Sun	1979
Bolero	1970		Bright Butterflies	1966		Peter Pan Gold	1979
Gold Galore	1972		Madam Butterfly	1970		Peter Pan Flame	1980
Happy Face	1973		Little Darling	1971		Small World Cherry	1982
Showboat	1974		Princess White Purple Eye	1987		Fantastic Light Pink	1982
Primrose Lady	1977					Border Beauty Rose	1984
Yellow Galore	1977		SWEET PEA			Yellow Marvel	1985
Queen Sophia	1979		San Francisco	1967		Scarlet Splendor	1990
Janie	1980						
Golden Gate	1989						

of 65° to germinate. Start this type of annual indoors under fluorescent lamps or set them in a warm sunny window. A bottom-heat cable will ensure good germination and growth of plants that require warmer temperatures. Transplant them into garden beds when warm weather arrives.

Heat-resistant annuals are those flowering plants that thrive in extremes of summer heat. Zinnias, marigolds, and petunias fill this bill nicely as long as they have enough soil moisture.

A final category that should be mentioned is the so-called winter annual group. These are plants that, in the warmer regions of our country, such as lower California and Florida, can be planted in the fall and will bloom throughout the winter. Calendula is a good example of this group.

Annual flowers come in such a multitude of colors, shapes and sizes that it is difficult to choose which ones to grow. Some annuals, such as the small 'Magic Carpet' snapdragons, reseed themselves, which makes replanting unnecessary inmost years.

Some annuals grow low and sprawl to form a living carpet on the ground while others grow tall and thin. Some have delicate foliage and flowers while others are robust with big leaves and flowers. Each type has its own particular space and use in garden design.

Remember, annuals should be hardened off, gradually exposed to outdoor conditions for about a week, before they can be transplanted. Give annual flowers fertilizers rich in phosphorus, the middle number of fertilizer formulations, such as bone meal or bat guano to promote bud set and blooming.

Check with local nursery experts, botanical gardens and area gardeners for advice on specific annual cultivars. The Professional Plant Growers Association recently reported that sweet alyssum, fibrous begonias, geraniums, impatiens, New Guinea impatiens, French marigolds, pansies, petunias, salvia, and vinca are the most popular annual flowers.

Biennials

Both foxglove (left) and delphinium are biennials.

Biennials are flowering plants with two-year life cycles. Most biennials spend their first season making green growth, developing strong foliage and root systems in order to store up food and nutrients for flowers and seeds. The following spring, biennials push their growth into those flowers and seeds. Because they often self-seed so well, biennials can fool you into thinking that they are perennials. The distinction between annuals, biennials, and perennials is not always clear cut. A lot depends on the climate and region where they are growing. Like most flowering plants, biennials grow in just about any soil, but the richer and better structured the soil, the better they will grow.

Biennials are available in seed, and may also be available as started plants in cell packs at nurseries and garden centers. These plants are easy to grow from seed because they are usually planted during the middle to late part of the summer, and can be easily maintained with the rest of the garden.

Biennials require much the same care and growing conditions as annuals. They can be sown in a bare spot or shady corner of the garden and transplanted later in the fall after summer annuals are finished blooming. In warmer climes, biennials can add bright shades of grays and greens to drab winter landscapes. Then, next spring and summer the biennials will flower.

Dame's rocket (*Hesperis matronnalis*), feverfew (*Chrysanthemum parthenium*), foxglove (*Digitalis purpurea cultivars*), hollyhock (*Althea rosea*), Iceland poppy (*Papaver nudicaule*), money plant (*Lunaria annua*), and mullein (*Verbascum* species) are among the better known biennials.

Perennials

Herbaceous perennials have longer life cycles than either annuals or biennials. Some, including herbaceous peonies and daylilies, will live for many decades. Most perennials die back to the ground when cold weather arrives and renew their growth in the spring. Some are nearly evergreen in warmer climates. Some perennials may become quite woody over the years. Some shrubs such as bluebeard (*Caryopteris*) are definitely shrubs, but treated as perennials in colder parts of the country.

Some flowering plants such as the bright geraniums (*Pelargonium* species) of pots and window boxes are perennial in warmer climates. Don't be confused by the various terms used to refer to perennials—terms such as tender or hardy. These words, if used by local experts, simply refer to the perennials' chances of thriving in that region.

A good garden center or nursery expert can help you identify sheltered sites for those plants more sensitive to wind, cold, and heat. Buildings, walls, berms, and other plants all provide shelter from prevailing weather. In general, plants that are tender should be sheltered from prevailing winds and low sites that hold cold air during the winter. Plants such as pansies, that are susceptible to heat damage and may crash during hot spells, should be sheltered from afternoon sun.

Perennials can be propagated from seed, clump division or by root or shoot cuttings. Unless you have great patience, you may wish to shorten the time until perennials mature by choosing to buy young plants rather than starting them from seed. When you buy young plants, it will take two to three years for most of them to mature.

You can plant containerized perennials in either spring or fall. You can even plant them in the heat of summer if you water every day in consistent amounts. If planted in the fall, avoid cold damage by mulching around the bases of plants as soon as the first frost arrives.

As with all plants, water or "puddle in" perennial plants when transplanting and continue to check their water needs for the next year or two, especially during hot, dry weather. Don't water by the calendar. Water by the need. Feel of the soil or use a moisture meter to check on soil moisture around plant roots.

Clumping perennials such as coral bells, daylilies, and hostas can be divided every two to five years if you wish to multiply your plant collections. Some plants, such as daylilies and irises, may become too crowded and stop flowering if they are allowed to grow undivided for many years.

Dividing the root clumps will rejuvenate the growth of perennials such as these. To divide, dig the clump and split into several pieces with a sharp spade, then replant the divisions. In some cases, as with daylilies, two spading forks can be shoved into a thick root clump, then pried apart to make the divisions.

They need dividing when they produce spindly and scanty growth and blossoms. Other perennials like the herbaceous peonies prefer to be left alone and will continue flowering vigorously for many years.

Ornamental Grasses

Ornamental grasses deserve attention as handsome choices for flower and/or shrub gardens. They come in many colors and sizes and, in every case, the graceful foliage adds special qualities to garden beds. Ornamental grasses bring year-round beauty to the garden. Even in winter, the leaves and flower heads of some of the grasses are beautiful. While there are both annual and perennial ornamental grasses, it is the perennial varieties that have captured the eye of garden designers and gardeners from coast to coast.

The sedges (*Carex* species) are grass family members that come in several colors, variegate, and sizes. They will thrive in sun to shade, yet are suitable for wet areas. Blue sheep's fescue (*Festuca ovina* var. *glauca*) is a small silvery-blue grass for the full sun that makes a good border plant with its six to eight-inch pincushion clumps.

Left to right: Canna 'Tropical Rose', *Dianthus* 'Ideal Violet", *and the geranium* 'Freckles'. *All three of these perennials are AAS winners..*

The maidenhair grasses (*Miscanthus* species) with their graceful flower plumes offer all sorts of cultivars from the 10-foot giant miscanthus to 'Morning Light' which has variegated foliage and grows four or five feet in height. They prefer fertile, moist garden soil but can tolerate extreme drought once established. They also can tolerate soils that are wet.

The fountain grasses (*Pennisetum* species) with bristled flower spikelets are somewhat smaller, only two to four feet tall, with flat narrow leaves. They grow best in fertile soil and are good choices for borders and sites near water.

Mix a few ornamental grasses in with flowering plants for lovely contrasts of texture and color.

Wildflowers

What is a wildflower? The definitions are almost as varied as the wildflowers themselves. Some consider wildflowers to be any that are not in cultivation. At the other end of the spectrum, wildflower can mean a plant that has always, since before Columbus, grown in a given area. That would mean that oxeye daisies which were brought to this country by early settlers are not wildflowers. It would also mean that some of the wildflowers of the New England woods are not considered wildflowers if grown where they are not native.

Many of North America's native plants were collected and taken to Europe where they were grown and bred for improved qualities, then exported back to North America where they are cherished garden plants. Sunflowers, asters, and columbines are examples.

John Shopland, superintendent of the University of Missouri Horticulture Research Center, has been doing field studies of native prairie plants vs. flowering plants of English gardens. Shopland reports that the English garden took lots of spraying to control caterpillars, irrigation to keep growing, and weeding to maintain order.

The native plants in Shopland's test gardens just kept growing without much attention. They grew so vigorously that they forced out weeds. In the spring, this second-year garden was burned off and, other than that, nothing was done to or for the native plants. The natives include black-eyed Susan, ashy sunflower, goldenrod, wild bergamot, butterfly weed and others. The prairie flowers are backed up by big bluestem, a native prairie grass.

Digging native wildflowers from national forests is illegal without special permits. This recognizes the fact that the pressures of civilization have started to destroy natural stands of wildflowers in some areas. Never pick or dig endangered plants. The best policy is to never dig or pick wildflowers unless they are threatened by development.

Only buy wildflowers that have been commercially propagated. Collecting a few seeds is okay, but do not dig any plants! Collect seeds, only with permission, of course, from the woodland and prairie gardens of friends and acquaintances. Many seed catalogs offer wild flowers, and some specialize in native plants and

Columbine and Trillium are two native wilidflowers.

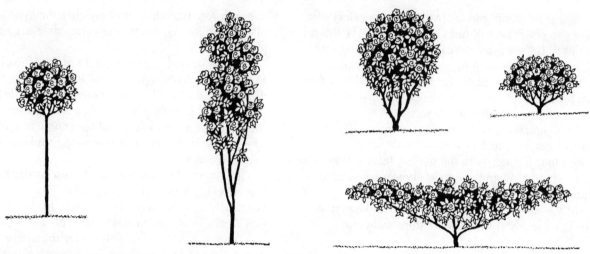

Different pruning styles for roses.

wildflowers. When cultured, many wildflowers grow much larger and bloom prolifically.

When growing native plants, the trick is to match the environment from which it came. If it's a high-prairie plant, than it will grow best in a sunny location with good drainage. If it came from low-lying woodlands, it will do best in a shady, moist location with soil that is loaded with compost.

Here are a few suggestions for wildflower gardens, along with the best growing conditions for the flowers named. Some annual and biennial wildflowers for sunny beds and good garden soil are black-eyed Susan (*Rudbeckia hirta*), California poppy (*Eschscholtzia*), spiked lobelia (*Lobelia spicata*), and yellow goatsbeard (*Tragopogon pratensis*).

Spring-blooming perennial wildflowers for dry, open woodlands with filtered light are New England aster (*Aster novae-angliae*), bloodroot (*Sanguinaria canadensis*), bunchberry (*Cornus canadensis*), cranesbill (*Geranium maculatum*), pink bleeding heart (*Dicentra eximia*), Solomon's seal (*Polygonatum biflorum*), and white trillium (*Trillium grandiflorum*). These are plants for the shade, since it is only in early spring before trees leaf out that they get sunlight.

Perennial wildflowers for full sun include smooth aster (*Aster laevis*), Kansas gayfeather (*Liatris pycnostachya*), Oswego tea (*Monarda didyma*), prairie phlox (*Phlox pilosa*), shooting star (*Dodecatheon Meadia*), and red turtlehead (*Chelone obliqua*).

Wildflowers for desert areas include desert delphinium (*Delphinium parishii*), beavertail cactus (*Opuntia basilaris*), desert four-o'clock (*Mirabilis multiflora*), sky lupine (*Lupinus nanus*), and coral bells (*Heuchera sanguinea*).

There are many native plant, prairie, woodland, and wildflower societies in the country where you can learn more about the plants of your region.

Roses

Although roses are shrubs, we have included them with flowers since they are primarily grown for their blossoms.

Roses are native to the North Temperate Zone around the world. Fossils prove that the rose existed long before mankind. Modern roses probably owe more to the Chinese than any other people. When Westerners first entered China in the eighteenth century, they saw spectacular roses growing in Chinese gardens. The Chinese had been breeding roses for many centuries. In the Western world, roses were known to the ancient Romans and appear to have become important first in the Middle East, from where they spread westward.

The beauty of rose flowers have earned this plant group the title of Queen of the Garden. Today's roses come in many types, each with its own special place in the garden. The classifications can sometimes become quite confusing.

First of all, there are species roses which are original native ancestors of the present-day roses. A typical species rose is the prairie rose (*Rosa setigera*), a three to six-foot climbing rose found throughout much of the middle United States.

Hybrid tea roses, which are grafted onto sturdier rose roots, are probably the best known and most popular of modern roses. They bloom fairly constantly throughout the season and bear large double flowers of many colors singly on long sturdy stems. 'Peace' is the best known variety of the hundreds of hybrid teas.

Floribunda roses are hardier than the hybrid teas, bloom throughout the growing season, are tolerant of a wide range of growing conditions, and bear clusters of double flowers.

Modern shrub roses are increasingly popular as hedges for small gardens and as specimen plants in larger gardens. Some bloom but once a season while others have reliably recurrent flowers. The shrub roses are grown on their own roots. Nearly 300 different cultivars of shrub roses are available and they have quite a variety of flowers and growing habits. Generally speaking, shrub roses should be allowed to reach their own natural mature shape. When shaping is needed, you should trim rather than prune hard.

Climbing and rambling roses are top choices for growing on fences, trellises and pergolas. Ramblers have more relaxed growth than the climbers which are more upright in habit and usually produce larger flowers. Modern climbers with recurrent blooms are vigorous, tough, and tolerant. Outside of training them to go where you want, about the only care they need is deadheading to encourage more flowers.

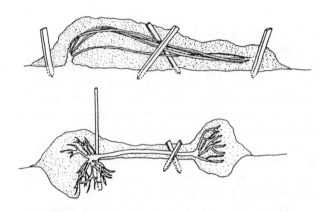

Protect standard and climbing roses from winter weather with a layer of mulch.

Miniature roses are enjoying increasing popularity because of the strength and vigor in their small packages. They grow on their own roots and come in many colors and flower forms. They must not be treated as house plants in spite of the fact that they will grow very well in containers. All roses need a cold season for their good health.

Standard roses are an aberration; bushy roses grafted onto a tall stem. They are not a true rose type as are the ones described above. In cold climates, standard roses must be dug up and placed on their sides during winter, and well mulched.

Ask your local nursery expert, rosarian, Cooperative Extension Service agent, or botanical garden specialist which rose varieties will do best in your region. There are roses for every climate. Look for All-America Rose Selection winners that have proven themselves in a wide range of test gardens throughout the country.

Planting

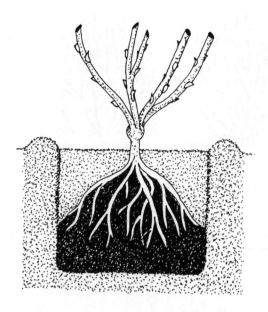

Planting depth of a rose. Note the mound of soil that spreads the roots.

The most economical way to buy roses is bare-root in the early spring while the plants are still dormant. Container-grown roses can be planted any time of the year but will be more expensive. Many hybrid and selected roses, except the miniatures and shrub roses, are grafted to a wild rootstock to increase their hardiness.

Plant grafted roses with the bud union (the bulge at the base of the stem where the graft was made) just above or just below the soil line. The bud union should be just above the soil line in warm climates so that the sun can reach it and cause it to send out new canes, and just below the soil line in cold climates to protect it from the cold.

Roses are greedy feeders that require sunny sites and well draining soil that is rich and friable. They should not be planted where they are exposed to strong prevailing winds.

Prepare rose beds by digging to twice the depth of the shovel blade and working in generous amounts of compost, well-rotted cow or horse manure, and topsoil if necessary. Prepare the soil a month or more before you plant the roses. Rose beds are the place for the tedious labor known as double digging. Double-digging is a worthwhile investment if you plan to grow a number of roses.

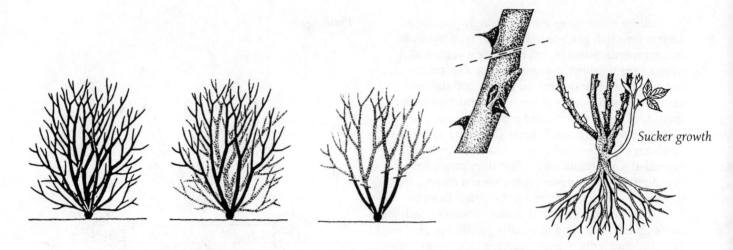

Sucker growth

To prune a rose bush in the winter/spring, first remove larger branches to open up the center of the bush, then cut the remaining branches to a height of 12 to 18 inches. Make cuts at a 45 degree angle so that water will not set on the pruned area. Remove any sucker growth that grows below the bud union.

Care

Roses are heavy feeders. For strong and prolific flowering, side dress roses monthly in summer with a complete fertilizer or biweekly with a dilute liquid fertilizer formulated for flowering plants. Do not feed in the fall when plants are about to go dormant.

Roses need lots of water and good drainage. Water roses deeply two or three times each week during hot summer months and less often during cool weather. Keep the water off the leaves to help prevent fungal diseases and insect damage. A soaker hose or hand watering at soil level are the preferred methods of irrigation. Deadheading the faded blooms will help keep roses flowering.

Overwintering floribunda and tea roses in extremely harsh climates takes a little bit of time in the fall. Cut the stems back to about 18 inches to avoid having them buffeted by winter winds, then hill up loamy soil to a depth of about a foot around the bases of the plants. The preferred method of overwintering standard roses in climates with freezing weather and snows is to uproot the plants, lay them on their sides and cover them with mulch. This seems to be tough treatment for roses, but they tolerate it very well.

Pruning

As described above, it's best to prune hybrid tea and floribunda rose growth back to about 18 inches after the first hard freeze and hill soil around the plant bases. When roses start to grow in the spring, prune back to live wood if cold weather killed some branches. Pruning roses hard forces vigorous growth.

Always prune the stems to at least a 45-degree angle so that rainwater will not set on the cuts. Prune roses to an outside bud to keep rose growth toward the outside of the bush. This will promote more air circulation inside the bush, slowing insect attack, and decreasing chances of fungal diseases.

Remove spindly weak shoots and those that are growing crossways against other growth. For larger blooms, prune smaller flower buds, allowing the plant strength to go to the remaining flower buds.

Suckers sometimes grow from the wild rootstock below the graft. If you see growth that is unlike the rest of the rose, chances are it is a root sucker, growth that is from the rootstock below the graft union. Remove the sucker before it grows unwieldy branches and poor flowers.

Problems

First of all, choose rose cultivars known for their resistance to pests and diseases. Give roses well-prepared soils, plenty of nutrients, and the best possible growing conditions and you will have few disease problems.

'Mister Lincoln', 'Pink Peace', 'Pristine', 'Tiffany', and ''Tropicana' are hybrid tea roses that show superior resistance to black spot. Grandiflora roses with good resistance to black spot are 'Prominent' and 'Queen Elizabeth'. Floribundas with high resistance to black spot include 'Europeana', 'First Edition', 'Razzle Dazzle', and 'Rose Parade'. These roses also are highly resistant to powdery mildew.

Aphids and thrips are among the most common and destructive rose pests. They can be easily controlled with a fine hard spray of water two or three times a week. Fungal diseases such as powdery mildew and black spot are common to roses. The first control measure is to be sure that rose foliage is dry at night. Again, choose resistant varieties. Rose dusts, which include fungicides, will drastically cut down fungal occurrences. If you prefer organic methods, a light dusting of sulfur or a spray of wettable sulfur is an old-fashioned remedy for fungal diseases. Do not apply sulfur in hot dry weather as it may burn the foliage. Prune off fungus-affected foliage and destroy it. Rinse pruners in a diluted bleach solution before using them elsewhere in the garden.

Propagation of Perennials &Roses

We have already discussed multiplying some perennials by divisions. Many perennials and roses also are easily propagated by stem cuttings. Geraniums, coreopsis, monarda, daisies, and dianthus are among the many perennials that will grow from cuttings. Miniature and shrub roses that grow on their own roots are better choices for rose cuttings.

The best time to take stem cuttings of most plants is when they are vigorously growing, after early spring growth, and usually during late spring to mid- or even late-summer.

Choose cuttings that are vigorous and representative of the plants. Each cutting should be just a few inches long and should have at least three leaf nodes. Cut the bottom of the stem on a slant so as to expose the maximum amount of undifferentiated tissue in the stem. That is where the new roots will come from. Then strip leaves from the lower one-half of the stem and stick it in a rooting medium such as moist vermiculite or sand mixed half and half with organic loam.

Be sure that the planting medium is moist but not soggy and that drainage is good. Tent plastic film over the flat or container to conserve moisture and place it in indirect light. Every few days, check for new roots by gently pulling on a cutting. Resistance indicates new root growth. Once the plant has new roots and is showing signs of foliage growth as well, you can transplant the cuttings into pots or a garden bed.

Ground layering is another choice for plants with long, low stems that can be bent to the ground without breaking. Shrub roses are good prospects for ground layering as are many of the low-growing herbaceous perennials that are often grown as ground covers. Iris, daylilies and other plants with parallel-veined leaves are not good choices for propagation by cuttings or ground layering.

Bend the stem to be ground-layered down along the ground, strip a few leaves from the middle of the stem and bury that area with a handful or two of soil. If the stem is springy, pin it down with a bent wire, two twigs, or some other means of containment. In a couple of weeks or so, depending upon weather and the plant, a new root system will form on the buried stem section. Cut the stem on the parent side and lift the new plant to put in its new location. Ground layering is easy because the new plant has the benefit of the parent plant's circulation, water, and nutrients until it is able to grow on its own.

Bulbs

Garden bulbs are generally divided into those that bloom in the spring and those that bloom or have attractive foliage in the summer garden.

Spring-blooming bulbs which are planted in the fall include daffodils, tulips, hyacinths, crocus, Dutch iris and lily-of-the-valley. Summer-blooming bulbs and tubers include the true lilies, dahlias, cannas, caladiums, tuberous begonias, iris, and gladioli. Many of the summer-blooming bulbs are tender in colder climates and have to be dug up each fall for replanting in the spring.

When purchasing spring-blooming bulbs, be sure that they are nursery-propagated and not dug from the wild. In recent years, environmentally concerned gardeners were distressed by the discovery that some of the small minor spring-blooming bulbs were collected in the wild, primarily in Turkey, rather than being products of cultivation. Suppliers, including the Dutch bulb companies which provide a large percentage of our bulbs, do label the origins of their bulbs. Most retailers and mail-order houses in this country also label bulb origins and, if they don't label, they can tell you. So just ask about bulbs if the information on the package is not clear.

Bulbs, corms, rhizomes, and tubers all store food and are loosely referred to as bulbs even though technically the latter three are not. After flowering, the foliage of the spring-blooming bulbs withers and dies after storing nutrients for the next season within the bulb. The vigor of the following year's flowers depend on strong, healthy growth the previous year.

Corms are rounded underground thickenings of plant stems that are typical of crocus, gladiolus, and cyclamen.

Rhizomes, such as found in German iris roots, are horizontal and are either underground or partially underground thickened stems from which plants grow. Tubers, typified by dahlias and potatoes are thick underground stems that have buds or eyes.

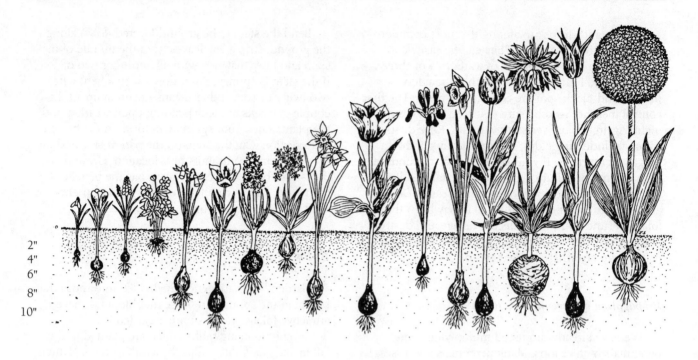

2"
4"
6"
8"
10"

This drawing shows the planting depth of many different bulbs. Scale = 4:1

Planting

Good drainage is a requirement for healthy bulb growth. Soft, fleshy bulbs particularly require good drainage to prevent rot. They will tolerate any type of soil as long as it is well drained. Raised beds offer excellent drainage and will warm spring-flowering bulbs for earlier blooming. In heavy clay soils, add plenty of compost before planting bulbs or prepare a raised bed for them.

When buying bulbs, make sure they are firm and without soft places or injury. Bulbs are most spectacular when planted in blocks or groups. Plant the same varieties of bulbs in each group so they will all flower at the same time.

When buying bulbs, look for the handy instruction sheets that come with many of them. This will give you a number of planting and care tips. A good rule of thumb is to plant bulbs twice as deep as the largest dimension of the bulb in good soil and the same depth of the bulb in heavy clay soils. In colder climates, plant the spring-blooming bulbs deeper, more like about three times the height of the bulb.

Some bulbs will not flower if planted too near the surface. Summer-flowering bulbs like cool roots and warm foliage. Ideally, to achieve these conditions, bulbs such as lilies should be planted in the shade of a shrub or ground cover. Plant spring-flowering bulbs in late summer for the following year. Plant summer- and fall-blooming bulbs in early spring and summer. Plant early spring-flowering bulbs like crocus, daffodils, and tulips around the base of deciduous shrubs for early color and to protect them from accidental digging.

To create a natural meadow affect, plant bulbs in tall grass that is cut only two or three times a year. Or scatter clumps of small, very early-flowering bulbs such as crocus or Spanish bells in the lawn and postpone cutting the grass until the bulb foliage has ripened and wilted.

The foliage of spring-flowering bulbs must be allowed to turn yellow and die back naturally. If mowed or cut before they have ripened and died, the flowers of next year will be jeopardized. The foliage makes the nutrients that fire next year's blooms.

For that reason, naturalize only the early-blooming narcissus, crocus and other early bulbs in lawn areas so that their foliage will die back before the mowing begins. You can plant the spring-blooming bulbs within the perimeters of herbaceous perennials that will grow up after the bulbs have bloomed and hide the wilted foliage.

When planning bulb purchases, look for early, mid-season and late spring-blooming bulbs. Narcissus of all sorts, crocuses and other small bulbs will reliably multiply and return year after year. Some of the tulips, especially species tulips, will do the same but, in general, tulips do not return as vigorously as those listed above.

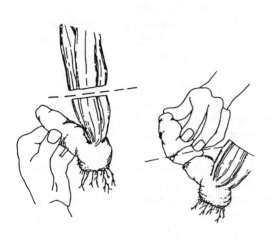

To divide an iris, cut the foliage an inch above the tuberous root and cut or break off the root into 2-inch or longer sections.

Divide gladiolus corms by removing the foliage, and peel off the cormels around the larger corm.

Divide daylilies and similar plants by prying the thick root mass apart, and separate into clumps or single plants.

Divide tuberous begonia tubers so each section has a growing bud.

Divide lilies by pulling off a few of the scales to plant.

Divide dahlia tubers by cutting the individual tubers apart. Make sure to leave an active "eye" on each piece.

Plan to plant bulbs in odd-numbered groupings of no less than three or five. A handsome combination is to plant two layers of bulbs. For instance, plant white *Anemone blanda* beneath early narcissus or tulips of contrasting colors. Spring-blooming bulbs for the Deep South must be pre-cooled since winter weather is needed for them to bloom. Since there are so many summer bulbs from which to choose that don't need to be dug up, most gardeners don't bother with those that require cold treatment.

The true lilies are good choices for gardens nationwide. Select varieties that will bloom at different times of the summer in order to have these magnificent flowers in your garden all season long.

Dahlias are sun-loving plants grown from tubers. They come in a multitude of sizes, shapes, colors and flower forms. A marvelous addition to the sunny garden, dahlias will flower from late spring through frost. Whether you grow the small container-type dahlias or the monstrous dinner-plate exhibition varieties, you will be pleased with dahlia flower production.

The irises also offer varieties that bloom from spring through early summer. There are the early-blooming Dutch iris that grow 18 to 24 inches tall from bulbs. There also are the very short, early-blooming Danfordii and crested irises. German bearded irises of many colors are familiar to all as they grow so well in garden beds over much of the country. The Siberian irises and Japanese irises offer further variety for garden sites of all sorts. Look into the iris group if the *fleur de lis* shape of their flowers appeals to you as much as it does to us.

For shady gardens in hot weather, it's hard to beat the bright colored foliage of caladium bulbs for decorative borders. The combinations of green, white, pink, and red will brighten shady spots with humusy soil.

These are but a few of the summer bulbs. Don't forget the newer dwarf varieties of canna lilies that are more delicate in size and color than the old-fashioned, six-foot red cannas that still can be seen in many town squares in America. Look for crocosmia, a flowering corm that is gaining popularity and can be left in the ground in Zones 5-8.

Dividing Bulbs

Bulbs and corms will multiply if they are in good soil with ample nutrients. If they have increased appreciably, as you can tell by the many flowers in the spring clumps, you can lift the bulbs after the blooming period has gone by and the foliage has ripened. True bulbs and corms create small offshoots which can be cut off and planted to multiply the plants. Split them and replant them or hold them for fall planting.

The rhizomes of German bearded irises are best divided during the heat of summer after they have bloomed. Dividing them and replanting will increase the flowers and invigorate the plants if they have become too crowded. Lift the rhizomes, trim the foliage to short fans and cut out any soft areas. Cut the rhizomes into generous "Y" shapes with a healthy fan of foliage on each of the two short arms of the "Y." Allow these to callous and dry in the sun for a few days. Replant them horizontally as they were before and about halfway underground. Aim the foliage fans in the direction you want the iris growth to go.

Tuberous plants, such as dahlias, can be multiplied just as potatoes are. Cut up the healthy tubers before planting in the spring so that each section has at least one healthy eye or bud. Allow the sections to dry or callous in the sun for several days.

Care

As a general rule, bulb beds should be heavily amended with organic matter and a complete fertilizer prior to planting. An application of a balanced fertilizer in the spring when bulbs are up, but prior to flowering, will encourage good growth and healthy flowers both this season and next. Organic fertilizers such as fish emulsion and composted manure are good choices for the bulbs as well.

Be sure to mark where spring-blooming bulbs are growing so they will not be dug up accidentally after the foliage disappears. Remember not to remove foliage from the bulbs until it is very yellow. This foliage must remain attached to the bulb to build energy for next year's flower. Tying foliage in knots retards its curing and may stunt blooming the following year.

Lift tender cold-sensitive bulbs like cannas, caladiums, gladioli and dahlias to prevent frost damage. Use a spading fork to dig them up in the fall before the first heavy frost. These plants will have grown several new bulbs. Rinse the soil off, label them, let them dry out, and store them in a cool, frost-free basement or tool shed for replanting in the spring.

Chapter Eight
Fruit Trees, Berries & Grapes

About Fruit Trees, Berries & Grapes

Picking vine-ripened fresh fruit, berries and grapes from your own garden is a pleasure matched by few other garden achievements. When you begin to grow some or the new varieties of fruit trees, berries, and grapes and find out how easy it is, you will wonder why you waited so long.

Exactly what you plant for fruit production will depend upon your climate, space, and soil. With the dwarf trees available today, you can have apples, peaches, and cherries even in a comparatively small yard. Raspberries, strawberries, and grapes are easy to fit into small sunny locations. Strawberries make a handsome border. Raspberries and grapes can be grown vertically in limited spaces.

One key to growing your own fruit is to let the trees, bushes, plants, and vines serve dual purposes. Use apple and peach trees as features of the front, back, or side yards. Use a cherry tree to shade the patio. Let strawberries serve as a groundcover. Grape vines can cover a trellis or pergola to provide shady spots for contemplation on hot summer days. Once you start thinking this way, you will develop your own innovative ideas.

Don't try to plant everything at once. Far better to add one or two fruiting plants each year. This gives you a chance to know both the plants and the garden. The first year's planting should be easy to maintain. Most plants will take several years to mature and begin producing an abundance of fruit; the exact timing will depend upon the species and the cultivar.

Unless you are planting trees in rows according to orchard traditions, place them aesthetically as well as for ease of maintenance. The flowers and fruit of many trees make them attractive choices as ornamental features for your landscape.

Plant fruit tree varieties that bloom and ripen sequentially. This will hedge your bet against inclement or erratic weather. It also prolongs the harvest season.

Some fruit tree nurseries graft two, three, or even more varieties onto a single trunk or root and trunk.

Those who have severely restricted spaces in which to grow might consider these as space-saving trees.

Local retail nurseries may not offer all the varieties you want. If you do not see a specific variety, ask them to order it. You can also check local wholesale and mail order nurseries.

Purchasing stock from a local nursery lets you pick out your own trees and ensures they should grow well in the local area. The nursery owner should be able to give you excellent hands-on advice in growing specific varieties in your climate.

Hardiness

Fruit trees, berries and grapes are all rated by their tolerance to cold. This "hardiness" rating is referenced against the USDA gardening zones. Figure out which Zone your garden is in, then check with local experts and Cooperative Extension Service for help in choosing fruiting plants that will thrive in your region. For example, Portland, Oregon is in USDA Zone 8, Denver, Colorado is in Zones 5 to 6, New York City is in Zones 7 to 8 and Atlanta, Georgia is also Zones 7 to 8. Each of these areas have other limiting factors in their climates, but the USDA Zone tells you the average minimum temperature for your location.

In discussing fruit trees, the hardiness rating refers to the tree wood, not necessarily the foliage or flower buds. Flower buds are less tolerant of cold when they are about to open.

Most plants are hardier in dry areas than in moist climates as long as they have adequate soil moisture. Cold feels colder and heat feels hotter in areas of high humidity. Numerous fruit trees and ornamentals thrive in arid Salt Lake City that might die during cold, humid, windy winters of the northern mid continental region.

Snow cover also makes a difference since it insulates plant roots from temperature extremes. In northern regions, gardeners are always pleased to have snow cover on their gardens and orchards.

Freshly planted trees are less hardy (5 to 10°)

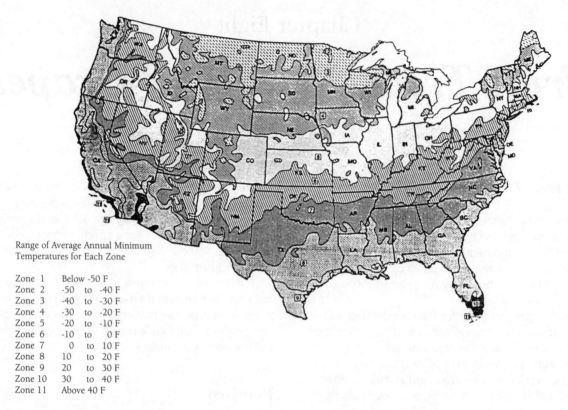

Range of Average Annual Minimum
Temperatures for Each Zone

Zone 1	Below -50 F
Zone 2	-50 to -40 F
Zone 3	-40 to -30 F
Zone 4	-30 to -20 F
Zone 5	-20 to -10 F
Zone 6	-10 to 0 F
Zone 7	0 to 10 F
Zone 8	10 to 20 F
Zone 9	20 to 30 F
Zone 10	30 to 40 F
Zone 11	Above 40 F

US Department of Agriculture Hardiness Zone Map.

than trees which have been planted for one to two years. These are in turn less hardy (5 to 10°) than trees which are well established.

Hardiness is increased by slow transitions from fall coolness to winter cold. If the temperature drops rapidly, many so-called hardy trees and shrubs may not be prepared for the extremes, or may not be sufficiently hardened off. They may lose branches or even die.

Be careful to plant varieties that are marginally hardy only in the most protected micro-climates, next to walls or other sites where they are protected from icy winds and where the ambient temperature is buffered by stored heat in nearby walls or buildings. This kind of a microclimate may be just enough to ripen less hardy fruit in a cold climate.

When trees, shrubs, and even smaller plants are freshly planted, they may "heave" (pop up a few inches from the ground) during the winter if there are spells of wildly fluctuating temperatures or sudden spells of very cold weather. Heaving is caused by the freshly turned soil expanding as it freezes. If this happens, be sure to stamp them back in place as soon as you can. You can reduce the danger of heaving by applying a two to four-inch layer of organic mulch right after the first hard freeze.

Shallow-rooted trees can actually dry up and die in frozen ground if there is not enough soil moisture. Check soil moisture during the winter as well as during the growing season. You can water any time the temperature is above freezing. Deeply rooted trees get through winter cold spells more easily. Mulching new trees too heavily will encourage the growth of shallow root systems, and can actually make roots more vulnerable to freezing weather.

Heat-sensitive fruit trees can be planted along the east side of buildings or next to trees that shade them in the afternoon. In hot climates avoid planting varieties that are borderline cool-weather trees. Fruit trees that thrive in hot summer weather include almond, apricot, avocado, butternut, citrus, fig, hickory, nectarine, olive, peach, pecan, pineapple guava, pomegranate, and black walnut. If you see any of these trees in cooler climates, they are either trees that also tolerate cold, such as the hickory and black walnut, or they are new and hardy varieties being given the right care.

Fertilizers applied too late in the summer create succulent growth that is less hardy than new growth from earlier in the year. Low branches create cold pockets around the bases of trees. For every foot of growth that is pruned from the bottom of a tree, about one degree of warmth is gained.

Chill Factor

The chill factor or chilling requirement is the actual number of hours of exposure to the cold that a fruit tree needs each winter if it is to produce fruit. In the warmer regions of Zone 7 and above, be sure to select fruits that have low chilling requirements. Apples, peaches nectarines, pears and cherries are among the fruits that have chilling requirements. Good spring blossom and leaf growth depends on this vital need. In warm winter areas, the number of hours above 60° will offset the total chilling effect.

Knowing the hours of winter chill is vital to choosing fruit and nut trees in areas where warm winters are common.

When you buy fruit trees, be sure to tell the seller where you plan on planting them and what kind of conditions the trees will face. If you have questions about what kind of trees to grow, the time to ask is before you buy not after you plant. Be careful not confuse chill requirements with winter hardiness.

More and more nurseries are carrying top-quality selections of both relatively exotic trees and improved varieties of old favorites for both northern and southern climates.

Pollination

Some fruiting plants have flowers that will pollinate themselves and so are self-fruitful. Other trees have flowers that are self-sterile. These trees need another tree of the same species but a different variety to pollinate its flowers and thus produce fruit.

There are several ways to solve this problem. The first is to be sure that the appropriate pollinator trees are nearby so that bees will visit both trees and pollinate the flowers. The second is to use trees that have a second variety top-grafted on them to provide pollination.

Stark Bro's Nurseries catalog not only describes the many fine fruit trees they sell, it also includes information that will serve as an education in fruit growing. This family company is best known for having found and propagated the apple called 'Delicious.' They note that most peaches are self-pollinating so you can plant a single tree with confidence. Those that do need pollinators have notations in their catalog descriptions.

Nectarines are generally self-pollinating. Most apples need pollinators and even those that don't will bear more heavily if cross-pollinated by another variety. Self-pollinating varieties and recommended pollinators are noted in the descriptions of the cultivars. Crabapple can pollinate apple trees. If you include both an early and a late-blooming crab apple, they should pollinate just about all of the apples adequately.

European plums generally are self-pollinating, but Japanese plums require another Japanese plum variety as a pollinator. Pears need pollinators and must be planted within one-quarter mile of another pear cultivar if they are to bear well.

Some cherries are self-pollinating while others require a pollinator of another variety. Persimmons, both native and the Orientals, are self-pollinating. Almonds and apricots also are self-pollinating species. Although pecans are generally self-pollinating trees, they will bear heavier crops if cross-pollinated by other varieties.

Grapes, strawberries, gooseberries, blackberries, raspberries, elderberries and currants are all self-pollinators. Blueberries, on the other hand, require cross-pollinators for big yields. The hardy kiwi has separate male and female plants; both must be planted together if you want to have the tasty fruits.

The most important aspect of pollination is that you should know enough about the requirements of fruiting plants to know that you must ask when you buy the plants. Read the catalog and label information and, if that is not sufficient, ask an expert to help you.

Basic Fruit Tree Types

Standard fruit trees grow to 30 feet or more and can live to be over 100 years old. Standard trees produce one to three years later than dwarf trees but produce much more fruit over a longer lifespan.

Standard trees also have some physical drawbacks for home gardeners. Upper branches are difficult to pick, prune, or spray, if necessary. A hose sprayer can only spray 20 to 30 feet. Very tall ladders are needed to pick the uppermost branches. If you have standard fruit trees, you will want some kind of fruit picker on a pole to reach upper branches.

To make your own fruit picker for high branches, fasten a one-pound coffee can to a two- by two-inch board eight feet long. Cut a "V" in the top edge of the coffee can with tin snips. Place a piece of foam

Homemade fruit picker.

Fruit trees range in size from genetic dwarf, dwarf, semi-dwarf, and standard.

rubber in the bottom of the can to keep fruit from bruising. Use the "V" in the can to cut fruit off at the stem and let the fruit fall into the coffee can.

Semi-dwarf trees are 15 to 45 percent smaller than standard trees. They produce fruit after three or four years and live from 50 to 60 years. Semi-dwarf trees make excellent small home orchards. They spread up to 30 feet wide. They grow to a size that is in between the standard and dwarf.

Dwarf trees, which are 50 to 60 percent smaller than standard trees, live up to 50 years and bear fruit after the second or third year. For their size, dwarf trees are excellent producers. Dwarf trees are perfect

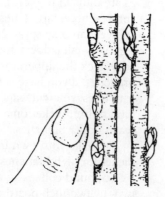

Internodal length between standard and genetic dwarf fruit trees. Nodes on genetic dwarf are closer together.

for the home garden. They are easy to pick and maintain. Up to four dwarf trees can be planted in the area where only one standard tree would fit. This makes way for a larger selection of trees.

Very dwarf or miniature trees, which are up to 65 percent smaller than their standard relatives, are very popular and new varieties are being bred every year. They produce fruit for about 30 years. There are genetic miniatures as well as those dwarfed by root stock. They seldom grow taller than eight feet and include tasty species such as peach, nectarine, cherry, apple, and almond.

Modern apple trees usually are made up of two or three grafts, including root stock, trunk, and the fruit-bearing top graft. The root and trunk stocks are what make the tree standard, dwarf, or very dwarf. That is how you can have the same kind of apple on several sizes of trees. The interactions of grafts greatly influence the characteristics of the tree.

Other modern fruit trees also may be grafted to enhance certain qualities. Look for information on mature size and environmental requirements when buying fruit trees.

Dwarf fruit trees are generally the best choices for the home gardener. These trees have slow growth and are bred to maintain their compact growth. They are heavy producers for their size.

Dwarfs lend themselves to special planting considerations in order to stretch out their temperature requirements. They grow well next to a house where they stay warmer and can be sheltered from winds. They also will grow well in containers on a deck or patio.

Many gardeners plant them in a half whisky barrel. These trees have comparatively little soil and must be fertilized every two to three weeks during the active growing season. The soil must be changed every two years. Use rich loamy silt or organic potting soil for best results. If the tree is frost-sensitive, move the container indoors for the winter. For containers with apples and other fruit trees that require cold weather in order to fruit, sink the containers entirely in the ground or insulate them from fast, hard freezes by surrounding the containers with hay or straw bales.

Planting Bare-Rooted Trees

Purchase bare-rooted trees in late fall, winter, or early spring. Exactly when they will be available for shipping or selling may be different in different regions. The key to bare-rooted plants is that they will transplant far better if they are dormant during the process.

Bare-rooted trees cost less than containerized or balled-and-burlapped trees. Choose bare-rooted trees with sturdy trunks and even branching. The grower or retail nursery will have already pruned the roots so you will not need to. Soak bare-rooted trees in a bucket of water containing a very diluted fertilizer solution overnight before planting, especially if purchased mail-order.

Place fruit trees four times their mature height away from flower and vegetable beds so they do not rob the crops of nutrients.

Dig a hole four times as big as the estimated root volume of the plant or tree to be planted. The hole should have a wide top and be tapered down to the bottom. A large hole loosens the soil for future root growth. Remember most roots grow in the top six to eight inches of the soil. Create a low mound in the center of the hole. Spread the tree roots out over this mound.

Studies show that trees planted without soil amendments often grow better than trees that are planted with amended soil in the planting hole, especially in regions with heavy clay soils. When the planting hole is backfilled with amended soil, the roots have a difficult time branching out of the planting hole to denser, less fertile soil beyond.

The roots become potbound in the planting hole so that it functions like a container. This phenomena, logically called the "clay pot effect," is common in clay or hard-packed soil. Often the roots circle the planting hole just as they would in a container. When backfilled with the same soil, roots quickly grow beyond the planting hole in search of more nutrients. If you use soil amendments, spade them into a large hole

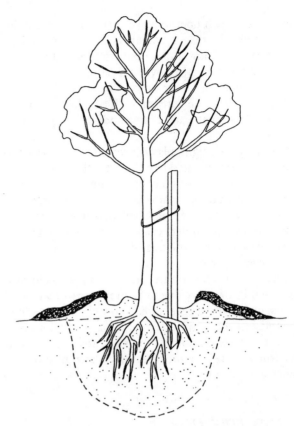

This bare root tree is staked to provide added stability in a windy location. Note the way the soil is mounded to to provide a basin that holds water.

and mix well with native soil.

Plants should be installed at a slightly higher level than they were before if planted into heavy clay soils or very moist soils. Raised beds may be needed in extreme cases of soggy or clayey soils.

Organic soil amendments are necessary to improve drainage and fertility in all soils. In sandy soils, adding organic matter will improve water and nutrient retention qualities. Always use more organic amendments, like compost, well-rotted manure, or peat moss than inert amendments like perlite and vermiculite. Organic amendments will add nutrients to the soil as well as provide better drainage and texture. Good drainage in the top 12 inches of soil is particularly essential to help prevent fungal diseases in moist climates.

Water the tree heavily right after planting, then tamp the soil down around the roots with your feet. Tamping the soil will eliminate air pockets and seat the soil firmly around the roots. For the first two years after planting, be sure that the root zones never dry out completely. Keep root-zone soil moist but not soggy.

Staking transplanted trees is only necessary in very windy and high traffic areas. Young trees are usually better off if not staked. Stress caused by winds help trees develop stiff fiber to make them stronger. Staking prevents healthy reaction to stress. If you must stake, secure the trunk low and do not bind too tightly.

When planting a tree over a layer of hardpan, which is sometimes three or four feet deep, make sure to break holes in the hardpan with a pickax or long digging bar so that water drains and deep roots can penetrate it.

Firm, but not tight, plastic protective covers for the trunks of newly planted tree (look for those that look like curly white ribbons a couple of inches wide) will prevent sunscald that may occur on warm winter days. Planting fruit trees in lawns that are watered with overhead sprinklers can encourage fungal tree diseases especially if the trees go into the night with wet foliage.

Plastic protectors on tree trunks also will help protect them from injury due to lawn mowers or weed eaters, two of the biggest threats to a young tree's life. Wounds on young trunks provide easy entry for diseases and pests. Establish a mulched area around fruit tree trunks to reduce the threat from lawn maintenance equipment.

Pruning Fruit Trees

It's important to understand a bit of tree physiology in order to learn how to prune wisely. The central or terminal leader is the top or main growing tip of a tree. Terminal buds grow at the ends of branches. When you cut the central leader or terminal buds, then the dormant, lateral buds that grow off the sides of branches will begin to sprout. This reaction is due to increased growth hormones reaching the lateral buds rather than the top or outermost buds.

Pruning alters the structural growth of a fruit tree. Prune at least one half inch above buds. Prune branches above buds that grow outward. Trimming or shearing shapes plants and directs their future growth.

When pruning old established trees, remove all dead and diseased wood. If the dead wood appears diseased, clean pruners by dipping them into rubbing alcohol or a 10-percent solution of laundry bleach before cutting healthy growth. Next, remove all wood that grows contrary to the general lines of the tree. This is called crossing wood. These branches rub against desired growth, steal sunlight, and prevent air circulation in the central part of the tree.

Remove weak, spindly wood. Weak branches will not grow healthy fruit. However, a weak branch may be left and trained to be a strong main branch. The spindly shoots that grow straight up are called suckers or water sprouts. Remove these suckers in mid to late summer to avoid stimulating more sucker growth.

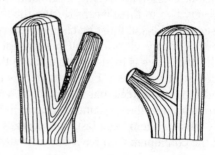

This cut away shows that the branch on the right, with an angle of 45 degrees is stronger than the branch on the left with a growth angle of less than 45 degrees.

Summer pruning removes leaves that shade fruit, opens up the canopy of the tree, and lets air circulate better which inhibits many pests and diseases. Be careful not to prune too much in the summer, because it could stimulate more new sucker growth.

In cool climates, be careful not to pinch or prune too late in the growing season. Late pruning stimulates new growth that will not be hardened-off for winter. Winter or dormant-season pruning stimulates new branches, and more branch and leafy growth. Prune trees so that the remaining branches are left at a 45-to 60-degree angle. These branches are strongest and produce the most fruit. A small stick or other brace can be placed between young branches to train them in developing the desired 45- to 60-degree angle. Branch angles less than 45 degrees are weak. (see drawing above)

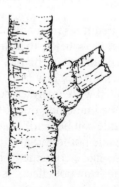

Leave the tree collar on the branch when pruning. The collar contains natural chemicals that speed the healing of the pruned wound.

When pruning branches, leave the branch collar on the tree. The branch collar is vital to have a healthy, fast healing, branch wound. The branch collar contains a natural protective chemical. Cuts that are flush with the trunk remove the source of this chemical and promote rot below the branch and deep within the tree.

Don't use paint or any other material on pruning wounds. Experts believe that painting tree wounds does more harm than good, sealing in disease organisms against the wound where they can't wash away. The self-healing chemical produced around the tree collar is the best medicine for healing.

Four Main Pruning Styles for Fruit Trees

* *No pruning.* This non-method is easy and works well, but has one major drawback in that unpruned trees are not as well formed as pruned trees.

The best shrubs and trees to grow without pruning are citrus, chestnut, fig, loquat, olive, quince, walnut, persimmon, pomegranate, and many subtropical fruits.

Unpruned spur-type apples, those that bear fruit on many short spur-type branches, and other fruits often outbear pruned trees, but the fruits are generally smaller.

* *Open center pruning.* This style calls for the central leader or whip to be removed after three to five branches have developed. This popular style, also called the vase style, opens up the center of the tree to air circulation and sunshine. The major drawback to this type of pruning is that branches may split when heavily ladened with fruit. In mild climates, the open center pruning is the most useful. Both apple and peach trees are easy to prune in this fashion.

* *Delayed open center pruning.* This is a popular alternative to the open center style. Let the central leader grow for a few years before pruning it back to just above the first three to five sturdy lateral branches. For impressive form, a long life and strong lateral branches, this delayed open center form of pruning is hard to beat.

* *Christmas tree shape.* Pruning dwarf trees to a Christmas tree-like shape is probably the most productive for edible landscapes. The trees provide higher yields for less work. The cone shape lets the sunlight reach the lower branches. With this method of pruning, only a small percent of the central leader is shaded during peak fruiting. Purchase dwarf trees that are evenly branched to get the best results when pruning in this style. Spread branches with clothes pins or small sticks that are notched on both ends to achieve the ideal 45- to 60-degree angled branches.

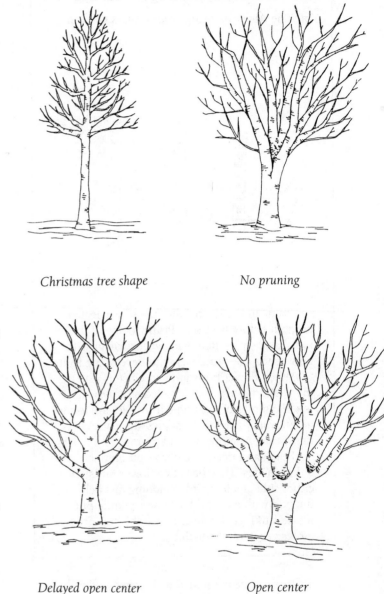

Christmas tree shape   *No pruning*

Delayed open center   *Open center*

Pruning & Training for More Fruit

Pruning in summer promotes more fruit. After the tree sets fruit, prune long branches to lower the profile of the tree. This will promote more fruit and less green growth.

"Spacers" made of 1" x 4" boards can be placed between the branches in mid to late spring when the branches are most flexible. This practice helps shape growth and support fruit. Check the flexibility of the branches for several weeks in the spring and use your judgment to choose the best time to insert spacers.

Rule of Finger: Insert your finger in the fork of a branch, if you can see light below your finger, the branch needs to be spread. If there is no light below your finger, the branch is at the proper angle.

Notching Above or Below Nodes Alters Growth

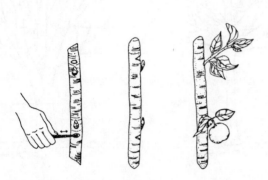

Prune in the spring after trees have leafed out, but before fruit sets. Prune to any of the four basic styles. Removing vegetative growth now sends the extra energy to developing fruit.

When flower buds grow in clusters on many short twigs, that is called spur-type fruiting. Examples of spur-type fruit trees are found in cultivars of almonds, apples, apricots, cherries, pears, Asian pears, and plums.

Peach and nectarine trees fruit on one-year-old branches. They have two flower buds on either side of a leaf bud. Notching just below the bud with a round file or sharp knife promotes fruiting. Notching above the bud promotes vegetative growth.

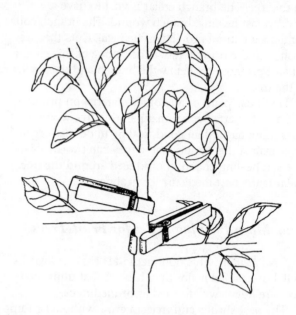

Larger branches can be spaced with small sticks and clothes pins work well to space young tender branches.

An alternative to using spacers and props is to thin the fruit by one third when it is marble-sized. This will encourage the remaining fruit to grow larger.

Spacers can be combined with props under the bottom branches to help support heavy fruit crops. If a branch should crack or split, either prune the branch off or mend the wound with duct tape. The tape will fall apart by the time the wound heals and starts to grow.

In general, a more or less pyramidal shape is desirable for fruit trees since it guarantees that the branches all will get sunlight.

Once the fruit forms, extra weight is placed on the branches and they begin to stretch out horizontally under the weight of the new fruit. Stakes may need to be set under branches to prop them up. To prop up a fruit tree branch, measure the distance between the branch and the ground. Add a few inches then cut a 2" x 4" or 1" x 4" board to length. Cut a notch in one end and prop the branch up inserting the notch under the branch. Tacking a piece of carpet or rubber over the notch will keep the branch from being scarred.

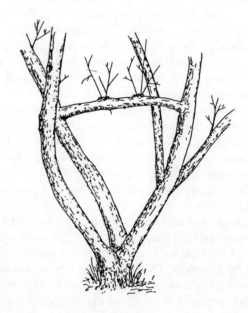

"Pleaching" weaving crossing branches together, strengthen and brace lateral branches. Over time the branches graft together, into one.

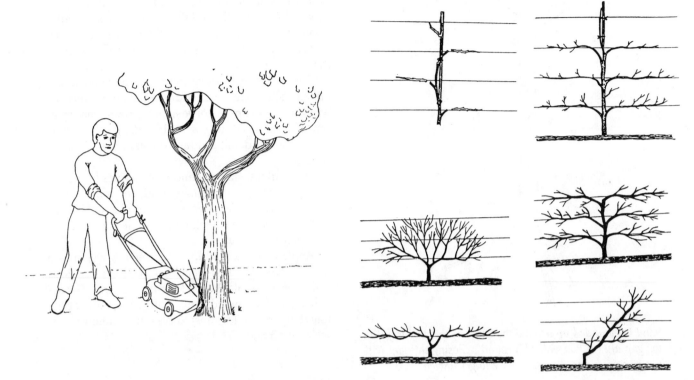

Hitting trees with a lawn mower causes wounds that become an easy place for pests and disease to take hold.

Espalier

An espalier is a plant trained to grow flat against a fence, trellis, or wall. This method is a productive and ornamental form of fruit tree cultivation.

The tree branches may be trained into many shapes. Espaliers can be fan-shaped, diagonal, interlacing diagonal, angular or just about any shape you want them to be. The more they follow the natural growth of the plant, the easier they will be to train and maintain.

A combination of pruning and tying the branches is used to develop espaliers. A trellis of wire, wood, or piping will serve as a good training shape, or you can pin branches directly to a brick or stone wall. We don't recommend espaliers against wooden buildings because of the need for painting the wood. If that is the only possible site, then place and train the espalier on a trellis two feet out from the wooden wall to allow maintenance to go on behind it.

The spur-type fruit trees are the most productive espaliers because they fruit on new spurs of growth each year and tolerate heavy pruning. Pears, apples, peaches, cherries, and apricots all offer good opportunities for an espalier.

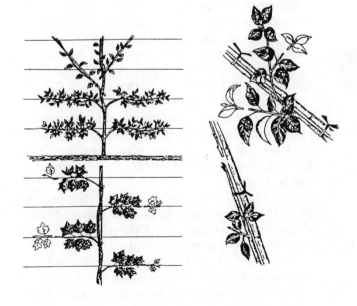

Espaliered fruit trees are more productive than conventionally pruned trees. It takes several years of training to train an espalier tree, but the result is worth it.

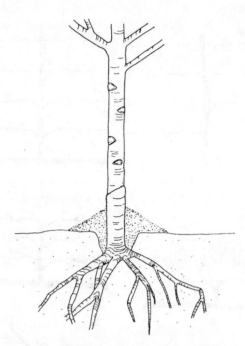

Sand is mounded up around the trunk of this tree to fill in the gap after it has walked "around". Closing this gap will not give pests and disease a place to get started.

Fruit Tree Varieties

Closely related trees can be grafted together or sometimes bred together. For instance, apricots, almonds, and nectarines all can be grafted onto the same plum tree. This four-way tree will provide months of edible fruit. Sometimes one of the fruits becomes dominant if the graft takes better or if the climate favors the variety over another type.

Similarly grafted three-way and four-way apple trees are sometimes offered through nursery centers or mail order houses. Our feeling about these is that single-cultivar fruit trees are generally more satisfying, but multiple-grafted trees certainly do save space if that is critical.

You might want to consider some of the fruit trees for hedges. For instance, the hollyleaf cherry (*Prunus ilicifolia*) will grow into a dense hedge, has edible fruit, and attracts beneficial insects and birds.

Note that different fruit trees will act differently in some areas than others. For instance, in San Jose, California, cherries are not supposed to bear, but in slightly elevated cooler micro-climates in that area, they bear very well.

Fruit eating in San Jose starts in mid-May with loquats and strawberries, followed by citrus, figs, raspberries, walnuts, chestnuts, kiwis, Asian pears, plums, and apples all the way through October.

If you live in an arid climate, you should know that unirrigated apple orchards yield two-thirds less than irrigated gardens. If you live in some parts of central California, it is possible to eat fresh apples off your trees for six to nine months of the year if you choose the right varieties.

Some fruit trees are notoriously adaptable to an unbelievable range of environmental conditions. The 'Whitney' crab apple, for instance, grows well from central Canada all the way to Florida. It can grow in a muddy bog and still produce outstanding edible apples.

Washington state is famous for apples for good reason. Its temperate climate produces some of the world's finest apples. Apples do not like high temperatures, especially in dry climates. Apple skins are scorched by hot sun.

Apple varieties that do comparatively well in warm areas are 'Akane', 'Red Delicious', 'Golden Delicious', 'Fuji', 'Gala', 'Apple Babe', 'Mutsu', 'Empire', 'Garden Delicious', 'Summered', and 'Anna'. The most desirable temperature for most apples in summertime is between 65 and 75° F.

Aprium & Pluot

Floyd Zaiger of Modesto, California, a master plant hybridzer, developed these two new fruits. The aprium is 75 percent apricot and 25 percent plum while the pluot is the opposite, more plum than apricot. These apricot-plum crosses combine the finest qualities of both parent trees.

Grow apriums and pluots just like plums. They grow well anywhere plums flourish, generally from Zones 5 or 6 to Zones 7 or 8. These fruits are comparatively new and so have not been time-tested in all parts of the country. For general descriptions and care, see descriptions of apricots and plums.

Apple

Apples (*Malus* species) grow and produce well in more climates than any other deciduous fruit tree. Most do best in Zones 4 to 7. More than 1,000 varieties of apples offer everything from the elegant old-fashioned fruits to modern delectable disease-resistant, low-care varieties. They are delicious fresh, or in pies, sauces, baked, and dried. They also make excellent juice and cider.

Some varieties need pollination by another variety while others are serf-fertile. Planting a combination tree that has a recommended pollinator grafted to the same trunk or rootstock will ensure good fruit production. Crabapples bloom profusely and are excellent pollinators for apple cultivars.

Apple trees were first dwarfed over two millennia ago. Dwarfing is achieved by grafting varietal apples onto rootstocks that control size. Most famous of these rootstocks are those known as Mallings, which originated in 1912 and are propagated at the East Malling Research Station in Kent, England.

Dwarf and semi-dwarf apples must have the bud unions between rooting stocks and the scion tops placed at the soil surface or one inch above the soil surface to avoid having the scion send out non-dwarfed shoots.

Apples thrive on well-draining soil with moderate fertility and full sun. Top production requires good irrigation during dry weather. Apple varieties with smaller spur-type fruit grafted to dwarf rootstock are the best choices for espaliering.

For the least problems with pests and diseases, choose earliest-fruiting apples such as 'Stark Lodi' or 'Stark Adina'. Their fruits are already ripe by mid-July in Missouri when most other apples are just beginning to form fruit.

Size: Mini-dwarf 4'-8', dwarf 8'-14', semi-dwarf 12'-20', standard 20'-40'. Various sizes of apples are available because of grafts with dwarfing root stocks. Genetic dwarfs and spur types also are available.

Bearing age: 3-4 years for dwarfs, 4-8 years with standards.

Life Expectancy: Approximately 60 years or more.

Hardiness: To Zone 3

Chilling hours required: 900-1,000 for most varieties.

Pollination: Although some apples will set good crops without cross-pollination, all apples will produce better crops if there are appropriate pollinators nearby. Suggested pollinators are listed in catalog or plant label descriptions.

Recommended varieties: Two Israeli apples, 'Ein Shemer' and 'Anna', make it possible for gardeners to grow apples in warm climates. 'Anna' requires only 300-350 chilling hours and so can be grown as far south as Gainesville, Florida. 'Ein Shemer' requires only 400-450 chilling hours. These two subtropical apples will cross-pollinate. Early apples include 'Gravenstein', 'Jerseymac', 'Lodi', 'Niagara','Red Astrachan', 'Tydeman's Red', 'Vista Bella', and 'Yellow Transparent.' Midseason apples include 'Akane', 'Hazen', 'Jonamac', 'Jonathan', 'McIntosh', 'Mitsu', 'Prima', 'Priscilla', 'Red Delicious', 'State Fair' and 'Summerland McIntosh.' Midseason to late apples include 'Burgundy' and 'Cortland.' Late apples include 'Gloster', 'Golden Delicious', 'Granny Smith', 'Honeygold', 'Idared', 'Jonagold', 'Keepsake', 'Melrose', 'Nittany', 'Red Baron', 'Rome Beauty', 'Spigold', 'Stark Blushing Golden', 'Stayman', 'Sweet Sixteen', 'Winesap', and 'Winter Banana.'

Diseases: Codling moth, apple maggots, fall webworms, tent caterpillars, green fruit worms, leafhoppers, mites, and leaf rollers all are common apple pests. Apples also are susceptible to a number of fungal diseases, including apple scab, fire blight, cedar apple rust, and powdery mildew.

Organic gardeners recommend getting used to having a few flaws in fruit rather than constantly spraying with broad spectrum pesticides. Hand-pick pests where possible and keep foliage dry to help prevent fungal disease. A planned schedule of low toxicity botanical sprays, using disease-resistant varieties and pest traps, and dormant oil sprays in spring, will control most problems.

Apricot

Apricots (*Prunus*) grow best in climates with little rainfall during the growing season, because they are very susceptible to several diseases. They are plants for Zones 5 through 7. Flowers set early in the spring and are sensitive to late frosts. Cross breeding with Manchurian apricots provides some that are more hardy to late spring cold. Plant on the north side of a building to delay flowering triggered by intense early spring sun but make sure they get full sun during summer months. These trees need well-drained, fertile, sandy soil. Water well during dry spells.

Size: Dwarf, 6-10', standard, 15-30'.

Bearing age: 3-4 years

Hardiness: When established, Zones 5-7

Pollination: Apricots are self-pollinating. In colder areas, encourage heavier crops by planting a second variety.

Pruning: Spurs bear fruit for about 3 years. Annual pruning encourages trees to develop new spurs. Remove old branches and inside branches that keep sunlight from center of tree.

Varieties: 'Manchu', 'Moongold' and 'Sungold' are hardiest and can be grown even in Zone 4. 'Stark Earli-Orange' is an early apricot, ripening in June in Missouri. Mid-season apricots that ripen in July include 'Alfred', 'Goldcot', 'Hardy Iowa', 'Henderson', 'Moorpark', 'Sundrop' and 'Wilson Delicious.'

Diseases: Although insect pests normally are not a problem, apricots are susceptible to diseases including verticillium wilt, rots and bacterial gumming. Avoid planting in sites where other crops such as fruits, melons, tomatoes and peppers may have had these diseases. Apricots are susceptible to the same pests and diseases as peaches.

Avocado

Avocado trees (*Persea americana*), Central American natives, are lush, rapid-growing evergreens. Grafted seedlings will do better than those grown from seeds. Flower bloom lasts from December through early April, thus the harvest also is long. Varieties differ greatly in habit of growth and vigor. Trunks must be protected during their first year or so.

Size: 30' or more.
Bearing age: 2-3 years.
Hardiness: Zones 9-10
Pollination: Several cultivars should be planted together to assure good pollination.
Pruning: Little required except to restrict tree to its site as necessary.
Varieties: Most avocados are hybrids of the Mexican, Guatemalan, and West Indian races. Mexican types are the hardiest to cold weather but their thin skins are injured by Florida heat and humidity. California gardeners will have greatest success with cultivars such as 'Mexicola', 'Puebla' and 'Zutano.' Florida gardeners will find more success with cultivars such as 'Taylor', 'Lula', and 'Booth."
Diseases: Essentially trouble free when disease-resistant varieties are chosen and planted where there's good drainage.

Cherry

Cherry trees (*Prunus* species) grow well in many climates because they bloom later than most fruit trees, although the fruit is the first to ripen. Because birds love cherries, we advise planting dwarf trees so that you can cover them with netting.

This stone fruit tree thrives on well-draining soil and routine deep watering in summer, but climate is the most important factor in growing cherries. Sour cherries are far more hardy than sweet cherries. In the right climate, sweet cherries are more vigorous.

Size: Sweet semi-dwarf to 15', sour pie cherries can be pruned to 8' - 12' in height.
Bearing age: 2-3 years
Pollination: Most sweet varieties except Stella and Lapins need another cherry tree within 120 feet to pollinate. Sour pie cherries are all self-fertile and often make good pollinators for sweet cherries.
Hardiness: Sweet, minus 20° F when established

Zone 5), sour pie cherries, minus 30° F when established (Zone 4). Chilling hours required: 1,100-1,300.
Pruning: Spread branches with sticks or tie them down to spread and lower the profile of the tree. Remove central leader and spread branches. Prune in early spring during dormancy.
Varieties: 'Montmorency' and 'Suda Hardy' are good sour or tart cherries. 'Sam', 'Bing', 'Emperor Francis', 'Windsor' and 'Schmidt are good sweet cherries.
Diseases: Aphids and leaf spot are two main cherry problems. Knock aphids off with a hard spray of water. Avoid leaf spot and other fungi by not allowing the trees to go into the night with wet foliage. Sour cherries have fewer disease and insect problems than the sweet varieties.

Citrus

Frost-sensitive citrus, orange, lemon, lime, grapefruit, kumquat, tangerine, and tangelos (*Citrus* species) are good evergreen landscape and fruit-bearing trees in Zones 9-10. In colder Zones, dwarf varieties make excellent container plants for the patio and can be brought indoors during the winter or overwintered in a heated greenhouse. They will experience leaf drop when you move them indoors from outdoors.

Citrus trees need very good drainage and are sensitive to soggy soil. Fertilize monthly during active growth. The ideal temperature range for citrus plants is from 70-75° F. during the daytime and 50-55° F. at night. Humidity would be from 35-40 percent. Watch closely for insects if you move trees indoors. Repot container plants every four to five years, pruning roots and replacing as much soil as possible.

Size: 2-20' depending on variety.
Bearing age: 2 years after planting Hardiness: To 18° F, depending on variety (Zones 9-10)
Pruning: Comparatively little pruning is needed. Remove crossing or dead wood, prune to compact size if grown in container. Never remove more than 20percent of growth in one year.
Pollination: All citrus are self-fertile. Shake trees during flowering or use a small artist's paintbrush to distribute pollen.
Varieties: Grafted varieties of various descriptions are available in grapefruit, lemon, lime, kumquat, Mandarin orange, sour orange and sweet orange.
Diseases: Virus-free stock and good rootstocks have eliminated much disease but, in Florida, citrus trees get pests and fungal diseases that may not be problems in dry, desert areas.

Fig

Figs (*Ficus carica*) grow best in warm-winter climates. Although sensitive to frost, they will grow in colder areas with some protection. The large tropical foliage makes some figs majestic landscaping plants.

Most fig varieties bear two crops; the first in midsummer on last year's wood and the second crop on the current season's growth in fall. Fruit is ready to harvest just before it drops from the tree.

Figs grow well in full sun, but will tolerate partial shade. While they grow best in soils amended with plenty of compost, they will tolerate most soils with good drainage. Keep figs well watered during dry periods. Figs can be grown in tubs outdoors in summer and indoors in winter in colder climates.

Size: Prune to 10', unpruned, a fig can reach 20-30' or more and spread to 90' or more.
Bearing age: 2-4 years after planting.
Hardiness: Some varieties to 5° F. when established (Zones 7-8).
Pollination: Most varieties do not need pollination. Special insects pollinate some figs.
Pruning: Growing edible figs as bushes with three to four trunks probably is the easiest pattern of growth to maintain.
Varieties: 'Brown Turkey', 'Celeste', 'Kadota' and 'Mission'.
Diseases: Major diseases are fig rusts and root knot nematodes (in areas where they are endemic). The best treatment is to keep trees growing vigorously.

Peach & Nectarine

Nectarines grow smooth-skinned fruit and peaches are fuzzy. Both have the same scientific name, *Prunus Persica*. These stone fruits are among the great treats of early summer. Both trees are vigorous growers and require regular pruning and thinning of fruit. Both have the same cultural requirements. They need well-drained soil, full sun, and regular fertilizing. Thin fruits when they are 1-1 /2" in diameter so those remaining are 6 - 10" apart.

Size: 12 - 15' tall, Genetic dwarfs grow 4 - 6' tall.
Bearing age: 2-3 years after planting
Hardiness: Minus 15 F. when established (Zone 6). Chilling hours required: 700-1,000.
Pruning: Nectarines and peaches flower and bear fruit on new wood. Prune annually to maintain vigor and best fruit production. Prune to a vase shape to minimize disease problems and allow good air circulation.

Pollination: Most are self-fertile, but check with the nursery where you buy the tree to ensure that the variety you choose will pollinate its own flowers. 'J.H. Hale', 'June Elberta', and 'Halberta' are the exceptions and must be pollinated by another variety of peach or nectarine.
Varieties: 'Stark Gulf Pride' is a nectarine to grow in southern areas with less than 200 chilling hours. Other good nectarines are 'Babcock', 'Mericrest', 'Stark Delicious', 'Stark Redgold', and 'Sunred.' 'Stark Gulf Queen' is a peach that requires only 300 chilling hours. Other good peaches that require more chilling hours (750-950) are 'Harken', 'Newhaven', 'Reliance', ' Stark Early White Giant', 'Summercrest', 'Topaz' and 'Yakima Hale'.
Diseases: Peaches and nectarines are susceptible to peach tree borers, root knot nematodes, mites, aphids, green fruit worms, Japanese beetles, tent caterpillars, and moth larvae as well as other common fruit tree pests and diseases.

Bacterial leaf spot, powdery mildew, peach leaf curl, and brown rot are peach and nectarine diseases. Canker and peach tree borers are the most serious problems. Dig borers out of bark in early spring and clean wounds. Prune and destroy any soft gummy cankers. Remove and destroy infected foliage and fruit. Handpick moth larvae as much as possible. Knock mites and moth larvae out with a hard spray of water or insecticidal soap. The best way to avoid peach and nectarine diseases is to select resistant varieties.

Pear (European)

Pears (*Pyrus* species) bear later than most other fruit trees, extending the fresh fruit season of the garden. They are hardier than peaches but less hardy than apples and so grow in a more limited territory. Pears come in three types, European, Asian, and hybrids of the first two. European pears must be harvested when hard and left for a week or two to finish ripening before eating. Once harvested, let the fruit ripen at 60 - 75° F. Lower temperatures prolong shelf life. Winter varieties need about 6 weeks of cold storage (32 - 40° F.) before ripening at room temperature.

European pears grow best in New England, the Great Lakes region and the Northwest. Asian pears and the hybrids will grow in somewhat colder regions. Pears need full sun. They tolerate heavy damp soil better than most other fruit trees.

Size: 12 - 25', Bearing age: 2-4 years after planting.
Hardiness: Minus 20° F. when established (Zone 5).
Pollination: All pears need cross-pollination. Almost

any variety that blooms at the same time will serve as a pollinator tree if it's within one-quarter mile.

Pruning: Prune to central leader or espalier

Varieties: 'Anjou', 'Bartlett', 'Comice', 'Gorham', 'Harrow Delight' and 'Seckel' are good European pear selections.

Diseases: Pears attract a number of insect fruit pests, including green fruit worms, apple maggots, aphids, scale, mites, and codling moths. In some areas, the pear psylla, a very small sucking insect, is a major pest—like aphids, they exude honeydew which often gets sooty mold on it, a good way to diagnose pear psylla infestations high in the trees. Knock insects off with insecticidal soaps or hard water sprays. Dormant oil spray early in the spring will smother eggs and adults. Fire blight, a bacterial disease, can be severe in pears. They also can get cedar apple rust. Pears also are susceptible to many viral diseases. Control insects which may carry viruses. Choose varieties that are resistant to common pear diseases.

Pear (Asian, Japanese & Korean)

Also known as apple pears, Asian pears are round and more tender and juicy than European pears. An excellent choice for small gardens, they bloom profusely and the dark-green summer foliage turns a striking reddish hue in fall.

They are grown more in the West but are hardy enough to grow also in the East and Midwest.

Two types are available: Light-skinned early ripening ones and dark-skinned late ripening ones. The dark-skinned varieties store better.

Size: Left unpruned they can grow to 20', but can be pruned to keep them 12 - 15'.

Bearing age: Generally the year after planting.

Hardiness: Minus 10° F. when established (Zone 6).

Pruning: Not much needed unless to control size.

Pollination: Plant two varieties for best pollination. Early-blooming European varieties can be used as pollinators.

Varieties: 'Hosui', Shinseiki', and '20th Century' are good Asian pears.

Diseases: Asian pears are more resistant than European pears to fire blight and the pear psylla, an insect pest.

Persimmon

Persimmons (*Diospyros* species) are not cultivated to any great degree except as prospects for home gar-

dens. Native American persimmons, with 1 $\frac{1}{2}$-inch fruit, grow widely from Connecticut to Florida and Texas. A number of cultivars are available. The Oriental persimmon, which has much larger pulpy fruit, grows best in the cotton belt, around Zone 8.

Persimmons will grow in any decent soil as long as it is well-draining and irrigated in dry weather.

Size: 40' tall.

Bearing age: 4-6 years after planting.

Hardiness: When established, Zones 5-6 for American species, Zone 8 for Oriental species.

Pollination: American persimmons are self-fertile but a pollinator such as 'Gailey' is required for good fruiting of the Oriental persimmon 'Fuyu.'

Pruning: Prune while dormant in early spring if you want to keep the size of the tree small. Cut out old branches periodically to encourage new ones. Persimmons bear flowers and fruit on new wood.

Fertilize: Need little fertilizer.

Varieties: 'Tanenashi' and 'Fuyu' are best for the Southeast; "Hachiya' and 'Fuyu' are best for the West.

Diseases: Persimmons are mostly pest and disease free but occasionally can have scale and borer.

Plums & Prunes

Plums (*Prunus* species) are from two main groups known as European and Japanese because of their origins. They are available in a wide range of tastes, sizes, colors and shapes.

Japanese plums, introduced to America by Luther Burbank, are normally larger and bloom earlier than European plums. European plums are hardier (Zones 4-9), later to ripen, and are generally self-fertile.

The high sugar content of European plums makes them excellent for sun drying as prunes. Japanese plums are less hardy (Zones 6-10) and have larger fruits with a sweet-sour flavor. There are also hybrids of the two types.

Plums require moderately fertile, well-drained soil and full sun. When established, plums are somewhat drought tolerant, but produce best if watered deeply. Japanese plums should be thinned to 4 - 6 inches apart.

Size: Up to 20' tall.

Bearing age: 2-3 years after planting.

Hardiness: Minus 15- 20° F when established (Zone 5). Early blooming Japanese plums will drop blossoms if nipped by frost.

Pruning: In general, many recommend pruning European plums to a central leader and Japanese plums to a vase shape with an open center. Japanese plums need regular hard pruning to control fast bushy growth.

Pollination: Most European varieties are self-fertile. Japanese plums need another Japanese variety for cross-pollination.

Varieties: 'Stanley' and 'Early Italian' are good prune type plums. 'Blufire' and 'Stark Blue Ribbon' are topnotch European plums. Good Japanese plum cultivars are 'Pearl Premier', 'Burbank Red Ace', 'Santa Rosa' and 'Redheart.'

Diseases: Choose disease resistant varieties. Plums are prone to many of the same diseases that the other fruit trees are, especially those of their close relatives, peaches and apricots.

Nut Trees

Most popular nut trees not only offer tasty harvests of their husked seeds each year, but also are likely prospects as shade and specimen trees in home landscapes. Among the favorites, depending on the climate, are Chinese chestnuts, pecans, and walnuts.

When choosing any of these trees for the home garden, learn enough about them to know both pluses and minuses. Chinese chestnuts, for instance, have prickly nut husks that make them poor choices near patios and other areas where there is foot traffic.

A few of the more common nut trees are described in the following paragraphs.

* ALMONDS (*Prunus dulcis*), a close relative of apricots, peaches, and plums, are grown as ornamentals and for the nut in the pit of the dryish fruit. There are bitter and sweet almonds, the first grown for its oils, the latter grown primarily for its edible kernel. Almonds, which are self-sterile, are grown similarly to apricots, peaches or plums. They grow in Zones 5-9 in well-draining soil.

* CHINESE CHESTNUTS (*Castanea mollissima*) are small relatives of the American chestnut that are more resistant to the blight that killed the American chestnut in the 1930s. Chestnut hybridizations promise to bring us new resistant chestnut cultivars. This fast-growing tree will reach 50 feet in height and produces prickly seed husks in the fall, each containing two or three brown one-inch nuts. Chinese chestnuts grow best in Zones 4-8 with acid soils (5.5-6.5 pH).

* HAZELNUTS OR FILBERTS (*Corylus* species) are small trees only 5-20 feet tall that bear sweet nuts in the fall. A number of varieties are available for different regions in Zones 4-8. More than one variety must be planted within 25 feet of each other for them to cross pollinate. If unpruned, they will become thickets. Most gardeners prefer to prune and train hazelnuts as single

trunk trees, but you can also plant them along a border to form a bushy hedge. They like well-draining soil with a pH of 6.0-6.5.

* PECANS (*Carya illinoinensis*) are the largest of the hickories, growing to 100 feet or more. There are southern pecans for Zones 7-10 and northern pecans that will grow in Zones 5-7. A soil pH of 5.8-7.0 plus well-draining soil in the growing season is required. The vigor of pecans will increase with the depth and quality of fertile friable soil. Pecans have high nutrient requirements. Large trees should receive five to six pounds of 10-10-10 fertilizer per inch of trunk diameter each year. Pecans tend to bear in alternate years with that tendency increasing as the trees mature. Nuts of this variety, as well as others, should be collected as soon as they fall.

* WALNUTS (*Juglans* species) come in several types. The Persian, or English, walnut is the best known. It will grow in Zones 5-9. The Carpathian variety of this species is one of the hardiest. Hardier yet is the black walnut which is native to this country and is unqualifiedly hardy throughout Zones 5-9. The butternut, another walnut, is the hardiest of all the walnuts, growing well in Zones 4-8. While English and black walnuts will tolerate a pH range from 6.0-8.0, butternuts do better on slightly acid soil with a pH of 6.0-7.0. Walnuts grow fast when young, reaching 20 feet in only five to eight years. They will thrive in fertile, deep and well-draining soils. Look for named cultivars that are recommended for your region.

Berries

The promises of sweet ripe berries on cereal, in preserves and pies, and also served alone in all their glory make berry picking in the hot summer sun more a pleasure than a chore. These are the jewels of the home garden. Not only do they gleam in many colors, they also cost nearly a king's ransom in the local marketplace during most times of the year.

We hate to be repetitious but, once you see how easy some of these fruits are to grow, you will truly wonder why you waited so long to grow them.

Cane fruits like blackberries, raspberries, and loganberries love lots of water and are heavy feeders. They are prone to rust and mildew when their foliage stays moist too long. Wide spaces between rows will promote air circulation and, when combined with drip irrigation, will keep those maladies in check. You also can grow them along a fence line for good circulation.

Most cane berries only fruit on second-year wood. Everbearing raspberries are the exception since they bear in the fall on first-year wood and then again on the same canes the following summer. After canes have fruited, they should be removed. The everbearing raspberries should be pruned after the second round of fruit.

Many berry patches are left to overgrow because it is a prickly chore to remove the canes that have fruited. A simple solution to cutting single canes out is to plant an even number of rows of canes. Each year after the harvest, cut down every other row with hedge clippers or a lawnmower. Then the next year cut down the alternate rows.

Strawberries loose their vigor after two or three years. These berries are subject to disease and slow growth could mean they have contracted one. Weeds, especially perennial grasses, are difficult to remove from between strawberry plants. Sometimes digging them up, and pulling out the grass roots is the only way to ensure a healthy crop. Many commercial growers replace plants for each crop to retain high production.

Blackberry

Blackberries (*Rubus* species), including the cultivars known as 'Boysenberry', 'Dewberry', 'Loganberry' and 'Youngberry', that are good choices for Zone 7 southern gardens, bear fruit on second-year canes. Some have thorns, others do not; some are erect while others have a more trailing growth habit. The bearing

canes should be pruned back to ground level after all the fruit has been picked.

Blackberries will produce best when grown in well-draining, fertile, loamy soil that is moist but not soggy. Choose disease-resistant varieties.

Size: 5-6 feet, less if pruned.
Bearing age: Two years.
Hardiness: Depends on variety, up to -20 F. when established (Zones 5-6), but often have winter die-back from sudden cold snaps.
Pruning: Most varieties are best grown on fence, trellis or other support. They can be tied up or just draped on supports. Plants can be pruned and trained as with new growth tied to top of support. Prune weak and broken canes as well as those that have borne fruit. Prune lateral branches of second-year canes in the spring to 8-12 buds each. In late June, pinch the tips of first-year canes to encourage branching.
Pollination: Self-fruitful.
Varieties: Early blackberries include 'Bailey' and 'Brazos.' Midseason blackberries include 'Jerseyblack', 'Lawton' and 'Young.' Late-season varieties include 'Boysen', 'Smoothstem' and 'Thornless Evergreen.' Check with nursery experts or the Cooperative Extension Service for varieties that thrive in your region.

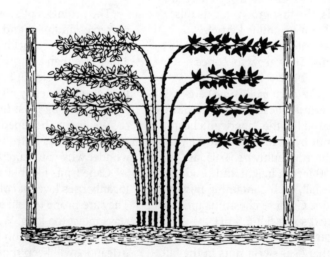

The canes that bore berries last year will not bear again and should be pruned to make room for new canes.

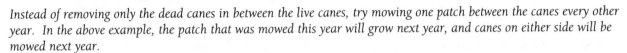

Instead of removing only the dead canes in between the live canes, try mowing one patch between the canes every other year. In the above example, the patch that was mowed this year will grow next year, and canes on either side will be mowed next year.

Blueberry

Blueberries (*Vaccinium* species) not only produce fruit but are attractive landscape plants that come in sizes from 10 inches to 7 feet tall. The attractive glossy green leaves change to orange, yellow, and red in the autumn.

These native fruits require well-drained, acidic, fertile, loamy soil with a pH of 4.5-5 for best results. In cool climates they will take full sun. In hot climates they grow best in partial shade. Lowbush blueberries also grow in partial shade under pines and other evergreen trees in the Adirondack Mountains and similar areas. Incorporate plenty of acidic composted wood mulch and compost into planting sites. In alkaline soils, you may have to resort to growing blueberries in containers.

Because the root system is shallow, a thick mulch is needed and frequent watering is necessary during hot weather. Keep the mulch 1-2 inches away from the main stem. Fertilize with composted manure in early spring.

Size: Standard (highbush) 5-7', dwarf (lowbush) 10"-3'

Bearing age: 6-8 years. Remove flowers the year after planting so roots can get established. Larger plants may begin to bear fruit the following year.

Hardiness: Standard varieties are hardy to -25 F. when fully dormant (Zone 4), dwarf varieties to -30° F when dormant (Zone 3). Rabbiteye blueberry, more appropriate for gardens in the South, are for Zones 7-9 but do need a few weeks of cool weather in order to set fruit the following season.

Pruning: Fruit develops on second-year wood. Prune lowbush blueberries only to remove dead and broken wood. Prune highbush blueberries and rab-

biteyes each year after they are three to four years old by removing one to four of the old-wood branches to the ground each year to encourage new growth.

Pollination: Cross pollination needed. For best fruit production, plant at least two different varieties.

Varieties: Lowbush cultivars for northern gardens include 'Tophat' and 'Wells Delight.' Highbush blueberries for the North include 'Elliot', 'Northblue' and 'Patriot.' Highbush blueberries for the South include 'Challenger' and 'Sunshine.' Rabbiteye blueberries for southern gardens include 'Choice', 'Climax', and 'Woodard.' Your area Cooperative Extension Service can give regional recommendations.

Currant & Gooseberry

Currants and gooseberries (both *Ribes* species) are in the same genus and have the same general requirements for healthy growth. Both are easy to grow and quite maintenance free. Both can be container grown, and are good prospects for espaliers.

These are shallow-rooted plants that thrive in moist, well-draining soil with neutral pH, around 7.0. Space plants on four-foot centers, water well during dry spells, and mulch with compost or well-rotted manure.

Size: Currants are 4-6 feet tall if unpruned and 3-4 feet tall if pruned. Gooseberries are 6-8 feet tall if unpruned and 5-7 feet if pruned.

Bearing age: 3 years after planting.

Hardiness: -30 F. when established (Zones 3-5).

Pruning: Prune currants and gooseberries by removing weak and damaged canes to ground level. Pinch the growing tips of new canes to encourage branching. Remove canes 4 years old and older as soon as the amount of their fruit dwindles. A healthy bush should include a mix of young and older canes and be fairly open in the center for better air circulation.

Pollination: Generally self-fertile but will bear larger crops if several cultivars are planted.

Varieties: Plant only disease-resistant cultivars. Black currants are prohibited by law in some states because they are alternate hosts to the white pine blister rust.

Raspberries

Raspberries (*Rubus* species) are extremely perishable, which helps make them rare in the marketplace except for a short time each year. The plants are tough, among the hardiest of the fruiting bushes, and have fruits that come in shades of red, black, and gold. There are enough early, midseason, and late raspberries so that you can have luscious fruit through much of the growing season.

There are raspberries that bear fruit once a year and those that bear fruit in early summer, then again in early fall. The latter are called ever-bearing. Like blackberries, the canes are biennial, growing vegetatively the first year and fruiting the second year. Raspberries can be easily grown within two parallel wires about four feet high.

Size: 6-10 feet.
Bearing age: 2 years.
Hardiness: -20-30° F. when established (Zones 4-5).
Pruning: Prune all diseased or damaged canes to the ground and all two-year canes in the fall when the fruiting season is well past.
Pollination: All are self-fertile.
Varieties: Some single-crop red raspberries include 'Canby', 'Hilton' and 'Taylor' and 'Washington.' Everbearing re raspberries include 'Heritage' and 'September.' Black raspberries that ripen in midseason include 'Bristol' and 'Jewel.' 'Fall Gold' is a popular everbearing yellow raspberry.

Strawberry

Cultivated strawberries (*Fragaria* x *Ananassa*) have a wider distribution than any other temperate zone fruit. They will grow throughout our country, including parts of Alaska, and in much of Canada. They need full sun for good productivity and perform best in a moist, fertile, sandy loam with a pH of 6.0. At the same time, they are tolerant of a wide range of soils and soil pH. Good drainage is essential.

Most strawberries produce one big crop. A few, called everbearing, bear a more sparse crop over a longer harvest period.

Winter mulches will prevent heaving due to freeze-thaw cycles. Summer mulches of straw will help keep weeds down and also will conserve soil moisture. Apply compost and well-rotted manure in the spring to encourage a good crop.

Size: 6-12 inches.
Bearing age: 1 year.
Hardiness: -20-30° F. (Zones 4-7)
Pruning: Maintain new young plant runners each year, eliminating older plants.
Pollination: Self fruitful.
Varieties: Among the hundreds of good strawberry cultivars are 'Garnet', 'Ozark Beauty' (an everbearing type), 'Stark Red Giant', 'Surecrop', and 'Veestar.'

Grapes

Grapes are marvelous! They are in a class by themselves in providing so many products—from sweet, juicy fresh grapes to juices, jellies, conserves, and wines of all kinds as well as brandies. It's no wonder that grapes have been enjoyed and revered for thousands of years. In addition to being the source of traditional beverages and foods, grapes can be used in the landscape for their ornamental value as well, twining over arbors, pergolas, and trellises.

Grapes (*Vitis* species), one of the oldest fruits known to civilization, are prized plants in the food garden. They grow vigorously in full sun with good drainage and highly organic soil that is fairly deep and has a pH of 5.0-7.5. Full sun guarantees that grapes will have a sugar content high enough for high-quality juice and wine, or for just enjoying as fresh fruit.

Grapes grown in this country include American and American hybrids (especially *Vitis labrusca* also known as the fox grape), French hybrids and Old World grapes (*V. vinifera*) and muscadine cultivars (*V. rotundifolia*).

Size: Vines may reach 50-100 feet with no competition. Vines usually controlled by pruning.
Bearing age: 3-5 years.
Hardiness: -10° F. (Zones 5-6)
Pruning: The fact that grapes are borne on first-year growth which arises from the previous year's growth is the key to learning how to prune these vines to their intended purpose. Prune for two rea-

sons, to fit the vine into available space and to balance the vegetative with the fruiting growth.

Pollination: Self fruitful, except for the muscadine varieties of the South.

Varieties: Check with your local Cooperative Extension Service for regional variety recommendations. American grapes and hybrids worth considering include 'Campbell's Early', 'Niagara', 'Ontario' and 'Romulus.' American seedless grapes include 'Canadice', 'Himrod', 'Remaily Seedless' and 'Suffolk Red.' European grape cultivars include 'Flame Tokay', 'Muscat Hamburg' and ''Thompson Seedless.' Muscadine grapes for the South include 'Carlos', 'Higgins' and 'Southland.'

Kiwis

Hardy kiwis (*Actinidia arguta* and *A. kolomikta*) are tasty fresh or in preserves. This vining fruit is becoming very popular in North America. These varieties can grow in climates that have temperatures down to -25 F. or less. Hardy kiwis are about the size of a large grape with slick skins that are edible. Mature vines bear large clusters of these small fruits. Fuzzy kiwi (*A. deliciosa*) are the traditional fruit found in grocery stores. The vines, which can be used ornamentally, may easily become tangled masses if not pruned regularly.

Kiwis thrive on rich well-draining soil in full sun although they can tolerate partial shade. Fertilize well.

Size: Vines 30-40 feet long.

Bearing age: 2-4 years.

Hardiness: Depends on variety but some are hardy to -40° F. (Zone 3)

Pruning: Kiwis fruit on current year's growth. Prune them like grapes. Prune new growth back to 8-10 buds to encourage branching and increased fruiting. Grow hardy kiwis on trellises, strong fences, or sturdy arbors—the mature vine with its fruit is heavy.

Pollination: Male and female on separate plants in most varieties. Plant one male for each 4-8 females.

Varieties: 'Blake' (*A. deliciosa*) is a fuzzy kiwi hardy to 0° and is self-fertile, others need a pale pollinator. 'Issai' (*A. arguta*) hardy to -25° is self fertile 'Arctic Beauty' (*A. kolomikta*) from Russia, was introduced to the U.S. by Jim Gilbert from Northwoods Nursery in Canby, Oregon. It is hardy to -40° and has a similar growth habit to (*A. arguta*).

Chapter Nine

Lawns & Ground Covers

About Lawns & Ground Covers

Lawns make a good foreground for ornamental borders. Turfgrass playgrounds and leisure areas are easy on the eye and provide soft footing as well as a lot of foot traffic. Turf areas reduce noise by up to 30 percent and they prevent erosion. Grasses, like all plants, exchange carbon dioxide for oxygen in the air. Lawns cool surrounding areas and keep the ground itself cooler than bare soil by 10 to 14° F. In areas prone to fire, lawns serve as effective fire-fighting buffers because they do not sustain fires the way that dense woody vegetation does.

On the negative side, lawns require a lot of time and energy for maintenance. Most turfgrasses must be watered during dry spells, not a good characteristic in droughty regions where water may be rationed. And for those homeowners who insist on an even monocrop of turfgrass with no other species, doses of herbicides and insecticides are used routinely.

For those reasons, a gardening trend has been to reduce lawn areas and increase the space devoted to gardens and other ground covers. The love for vast expanses of lawn traces back to the English garden designs of the eighteenth and nineteenth centuries.

The "New American Garden" promoted by the National Arboretum stresses a return to a more balanced landscape, with more equal emphases on hardscape, lawns, shrubs, and flowers. It promotes the use of native plants and drought-resistant plants in out-

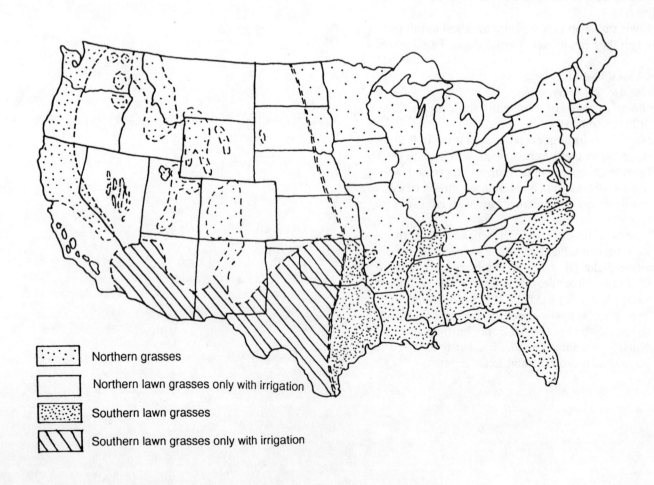

::: Northern grasses

☐ Northern lawn grasses only with irrigation

▦ Southern lawn grasses

▨ Southern lawn grasses only with irrigation

door-room designs in the front yard as well as in place of the usual backyard gardens. Thus gardeners are "taking back" their front yards, replacing front lawns with beautiful gardens that offer peace and privacy for outdoor relaxation.

An associated trend in turfgrass lawns is to follow practices that are water efficient and require less mainentance. This includes everything from native and disease-resistant grass varieties to reduced fertilization and increased use of automatic irrigation controls.

Philosophically, this trend includes a wiser attitude of not seeking perfection in lawn areas, of tolerating a few weeds, of using appropriate care techniques to eliminate treatments with fungicides, herbicides and insecticides. By following this philosophy, not only will you and your neighbors be exposed to fewer chemicals, you also will be saving money and time.

In designing your landscape, use lawns to serve appropriate purposes, for lawn games and play yards, for walkways between gardens and other parts of the yard, and as contrasts to set off or frame garden areas.

Ground covers, low-growing plants that blanket the soil, are excellent choices for many sites where turfgrasses would not grow well or would be difficult to maintain. Consider ground covers for shady places, rocky terrains, areas under trees and hillsides. Consider sturdy ground covers if you wish to cut down on maintenance.

While ivies, pachysandra, sedum, and myrtles are common and popular ground covers, don't be confined to these standard few choices. Ground covers need not be just low-growing, vining or clumping plants. Ferns make good ground covers for shady sites. Daylilies are good ground covers for sunny sites. Both, once established, are low maintenance.

Lawn Maintenance

Lawn maintenance is highly dependent upon the kinds of turfgrass you choose to grow. Select the grasses that are suited to your intended use of the area, and climate.

In general, turfgrasses are divided into cool-season (northern or boreal) grasses and warm-season (southern or sub-tropical) grasses. USDA Zones 6 and 7 represent the transitional areas between the cool-season and warm-season grasses.

Limited rainfall in areas west of Kansas is also a limiting factor in growing conventional turfgrasses. Normally it is best to plant a mixture of grasses. One grass matures quickly, producing a protected environment for slower-growing perennial grasses to mature. Bermuda grass thrives in warmer climates, and blue-grass-fescue combinations are best in the northern latitudes. Grasses suited to their climate are much less prone to fungal and other disease attacks.

Bluegrass and other cool-weather turfgrasses do better with fall fertilization, even though the growing season is limited. Fertilizing in fall instead of spring means that you will avoid encouraging the growth of annual weeds at the start of the season.

Bentgrass, a favorite for golf course tees, flourishes where winter rainfall is plentiful and grows poorly in hot arid regions. This grass forms a dense, vigorous carpet of turf that looks best when mowed at ½ to ¾ inch tall and the weather is cool. It goes dormant when the temperatures climb. This is not a grass for organic gardeners and is not used for everyday lawns.

A good grass for sunny drylands that will endure drought and compact soils better than most turfgrasses is buffalograss. This grass is native to and grown in plains from northern Texas to Nebraska. It needs less mowing than other turfgrasses and is a good choice where irrigation is not possible.

See the map that shows what types of turfgrasses will grow best in your area. See also the list of turf-grasses for different habitats in different Zones.

The key to maintaining turfgrasses is to realize that they try to grow to their natural height of, usually, about 18 inches. Keeping them just a couple of inches high is an artificial practice.

Organic lawn care is both easier and less expensive than using chemicals to weed and fertilize. The first order is to mow the grass often and let it stay about 3 inches high. Never mow more than one-fourth to one-third of the height of the grass at any one time.

Do not collect the clippings. By allowing the clippings to lie, you are returning the majority of the nutrients to the lawn. Keeping the turf taller than what was usually recommended in the past prevents many weeds from germinating because the grass shades the soil. Thick turf competes successfully against weeds.

Use grass varieties that will thrive in your climate. Substitute other ground covers if grasses do not thrive. Pull weeds by hand. They will come up easier after a heavy rain. Use biological controls for pests and diseases.

There are easy ways to tell when you should water lawns. Using a moisture probe is the easiest of all. When the temperature and wind are both high, plants and soil will lose moisture faster than usual. Watch the spots on the lawn that are higher and drier and so tend to dry out faster. They will turn bluish green, then yellow as soil moisture diminishes. If footprints remain after you walk across the lawn, the grass is losing its resiliency because of inadequate moisture.

Beware of overwatering turf. A general guide is to add 1-1 ½ inches of water per week during dry spells.

Place the lawnmower wheel on the edge of concrete and the other wheel on the grass.

Water enough so that the top six inches of the turf-grass root zone is moist but not soggy. Saturated soils can kill plant roots and cause shallow rooting.

A strong lawn has a deep root system that is promoted by deep watering and the addition of organic matter. Let the sprinkler run long enough to moisten the soil 6 to 12 inches deep. In hot weather, lawns may require one to two inches of water per week for good growth. In hot dry weather, cool-weather grasses go into a less active state, a kind of summer hibernation. They will green up again when cooler weather and rains return.

Mow the lawn in opposite directions each time it is cut to help keep growth even. Keep the mower blade sharp so that grass blades are cut, not beaten in two. Cutting the lawn too closely or scalping patches encourages bare spots.

Do not mow grass when it's wet. It's difficult to cut and ends up uneven with the grass clippings falling in clumps. Cutting wet grass tends to spread water-transmitted disease rapidly.

Increase the mowing height as the temperature increases to keep the ground cooler and slow evaporation. Mowing high causes more bushy growth of the grass. Set the lawn mower at 3-4 inches.

Scratch the sod hard with an iron rake and overseed bare and thin places in the lawn every spring and fall. When turfgrasses are mowed, natural reseeding does not take place. For a healthy lawn, over-seeding replicates the natural process.

Repair bare spots in the lawn with a piece of sod dug from another portion of the lawn, or lightly cultivate the hole, reseed and cover with a fine layer of compost. Keep the repaired area moist until it fills in.

Mow the lawn in opposite directions each time it is cut to help keep growth even.

To fill a gap or divot in the lawn, cut sod with a shovel and peel it back. Fill the hole with soil or compost and lay the sod back over the hole. Water the sod heavily and lay a wide board over the repaired area while still wet and walk over it until it's level with the lawn.

Improve drainage in compacted areas of established lawns by removing plugs of soil with a manual or power aerator. After aerating, let the plugs of soil dry, then rake over them to disperse into the lawn.

Feed established lawns in the spring and fall with compost, manure, sewage sludge or another slow-release complete fertilizer like blood or fish meal. For a quick green effect, apply dilute fish emulsion that is high in nitrogen. Activated sewage sludge and Milorganite are excellent top dressings for lawns.

Biological controls are being developed that are right in line with organic methods. Studies at Cornell University show that the application of composts and other well-rotted organic matter to turfgrasses will introduce large populations of microorganisms that interfere with disease development.

The Cornell researchers are working to better understand the microbiology of disease-suppressant composts. They also are working on microbial fungicides that occur naturally, can be grown and concentrated, then returned to the environment as an organic substance. Unfortunately, these turf-disease control products, including those known as Dagger G, Quantum 4000, and Galltrol-A, are not yet labeled for use in this country.

Many beneficial soil microorganisms can colonize both above and below ground to protect plants from infection and disease. The organic approach to lawn and garden care is proving effective and safe. Cornell researchers recommend using composted manure, sludge, or agricultural waste to topdress lawns. These materials are readily available and include natural disease suppressants.

Composts have been found to suppress gray snow mold, dollar spot, brown patch, red thread, summer patch, and necrotic ringspot. Apply composted materials by hand or with a drop spreader.

Many moths routinely fly and flit over lawns at dusk in the summer. Their presence does not necessarily mean that they are infesting the lawn with larvae. Large brown spots on lawns are more often caused by dogs, fungus, drought, or fertilizer deficiencies. See Chapter Five, Pests & Diseases for more information on lawn problems.

Thatch

Allowing grass clippings to fall back into healthy lawns where no chemicals have been used will not cause thatch problems. The clippings will decompose and return nitrogen and other nutrients to the soil. Now that lawn and yard trimmings are prohibited in landfills in many states, collecting grass clippings has become an environmental "no-no."

Only when the amount of old dead stems and roots exceeds the rate of decay does thatch become a problem. This can happen with unhealthy lawns with virtually no soil life and lawns that are mowed too short on a regular basis. Dethatching is not a necessary chore that needs to be done on a routine basis.

Only collect grass clippings if the grass, for any reason, has become too long. If you must collect the clippings, be sure to compost them so as not to lose the nutrients.

Lawn Restoration

Lawn damage can be caused by pests, diseases, contamination, excess traffic, weather, and neglect. The first thing to do is to get rid of the cause of the lawn damage. If the wrong species was planted, either replant or overseed with the correct one. Good fertilization, mowing, and watering techniques to encourage thick turf development and strengthen damaged grasses are the first things to do.

This calls for analysis of the condition. Diagnoses and discussions of pests and diseases are in Chapter Five - Pests & Diseases. Once the pests and diseases are gone, overseed the damaged area rather than replacing the sod. Use pest- and disease-resistant cultivars if possible. and certainly use the correct species for your climate.

Contamination by gasoline, oil, or chemicals is not uncommon. First, the grass yellows and dies. Then roots disappear from the soil for five years or even

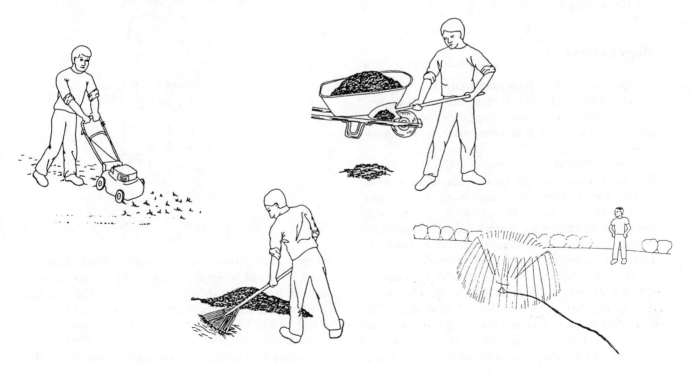

To restore a lawn, mow the grass very short. Rake up all the grass and thatch. Apply a layer of chicken or steer manure, sludge or Milorganite ¼-½" thick. Water heavily. The lawn will look like new in 2-4 weeks.

more depending upon the extent of the contamination. The solution is to dig and remove the top five to seven inches of soil, replacing it with new topsoil. Then use sod or seed to replace the turf.

Excess traffic will compact the soil, making air and water circulation difficult to impossible. Aeration or cultivation is regularly needed in such areas, followed by scratching the sod surface and overseeding. Resodding is a faster if more expensive way to repair compacted lawns. In areas of extreme compaction, you would be wise to give in to the traffic and build an attractive walkway.

Lawn damage from weather or neglect can be treated in much the same way. Begin a regular program of care—fertilizing, watering, and mowing. Long neglected lawns have been known to recover under wise and regular care.

In lawn areas with very poor soil where the grass shows little sign of becoming healthy and thick, the best solution may be to apply four to six inches of good topsoil, improve it with the addition of organic materials and then sod or seed over the newly improved area.

Under many trees, grasses will dwindle because of shade and competition for water and nutrients with the tree roots. When lawn grasses are under trees, the danger of mower or weedeater damage is high. Replace the lawn with mulch, ground covers or flowering plants. If plants are installed under trees, be sure to fertilize them.

Weed Control

The best way to control lawn weeds is to develop dense turf and let it grow three to four inches high. Mow high and often to encourage the development of long, thick turf which will compete successfully with weeds.

Our favorite solution to weeds in the lawn is two-fold. First, learn to accept a few weeds. Identify them and learn more about them. If the weeds are noxious and get out of control or become invasive, then formulate a plan to cause their demise. Second, those weeds that are unacceptable are easy to remove by hand or you can try one of the organic weed killers.

There are many tools made expressly for weed removal. They come in long-handled and short-handled types. They range from hoes of many shapes to Cape Cod weeders and dandelion diggers. Find one or two that fit your hand and your gardening habits, and weeding can become, if not a joy, at least efficient and easy. A few minutes a day is all you need to keep weeds out of the more obvious places near outdoor living areas. (See also Chapter Four, Weeds)

Planting A Lawn Step-by-Step

If you install a new lawn, which is better—seed or sod? Seed lawns are less expensive than sod, but it will be up to three months before they can handle foot traffic. Sodded areas are ready to use in only four to six weeks.

Whatever you choose, sod, grass, stolons or a ground cover, you will want to prepare the soil well. The better condition the soil is in, the stronger the grass will be. Make extra efforts in preparing the soil because it can only be prepared once. Take the same care preparing the soil for both seed and sod lawns. After roots penetrate the soil, they should not be removed.

Fall sowing decreases heat damage and weed growth. Lawns need at least six weeks of 50 to 70° F. weather for the grasses to get a strong start before killing frosts set in. Sow in the spring in the South.

Step One. Check the soil pH with an electronic pH meter or colorimeter pH test. The soil should be moist for the electronic tester to function properly. The pH should be in the range of 6 to 7. A soil test from the Cooperative Extension Service during spring or summer will provide answers about other nutritional needs of the soil.

Step Two. Till the soil, blending in finished compost, leaf mold, or garden debris. Add nutrient materials that the soil test indicates are needed. The soil of a healthy lawn should have a uniform structure to a depth of 8 to 12 inches. This even texture avoids an "interface" zone where two different types of soil meet. It promotes good drainage and root growth. If the pH is below 5.5 add 50 to 75 pounds of lime per 1,000 square feet. If the soil is very alkaline (above 7.5), add 10-30 pounds of sulfur per 1,000 square feet. The most important amendments to add are organic compost and manure. Incorporate up to six inches of organic matter.

Remember, you will only plant the lawn once and have one chance to amend the soil. A good option is to have the city road crew deliver enough leaves in the fall to cover the entire ground to be planted. Spread the leaves out across the new plot of ground a foot or two thick. Run the tiller over them to grind them into smaller pieces. Till the leaves plus lime and rock phosphate (if indicated by soil tests) into the soil. Wait two weeks to allow some decomposition of the leaves before sodding or seeding. Continue with the other steps for planting a lawn.

Step Three. Level and smooth the surface with a bow rake, filling low spots and scraping down high spots. Water the ground and let it settle for a day or two, then level again.

Step Four. Rent a roller, a large drum that is filled with water. Roll the ground first one way, then across

at a right angle to the first rolling. Roll it several times in several directions. This will bring out any high or low spots that need to be filled and leveled.

Step Five. Lightly cultivate the surface of the rolled soil with a bow rake.

Step Six. On a windless day, broadcast seed by hand or use an inexpensive spreader for more even coverage. Rake seeds lightly into the soil and cover with a light layer of fine mulch or straw. Apply a ¼-inch layer of straw (not hay) to the planted lawn. You can also use spun fiber held in place with pins made from coat hangers. Remove when grass is 1 inch high. The mulch will help protect the surface from moisture loss and keep birds from eating the seed.

Step Seven. Water once or twice daily, morning and late afternoon, so that the surface is evenly moist. Daily watering will be necessary for about a week. New lawns have shallow root systems and are vulnerable to dry weather. Make sure to water new lawns regularly with a sprinkler that produces fine droplets of water to reduce soil compaction during dry weather.

Step Eight. Let the grass get long enough, about three to four inches tall, so it bends over before the first mowing. Set the mower to one and a half to two inches for the first mowing.

Sod Lawns

Order sod from the nursery or discount store two to four days before planting. Do not accept sod that has been piled up for over a day or two, it may be sickly and yellow. Always inspect sod for insects and diseases before purchasing. Larger amounts of sod are delivered on a pallet. Small amounts can be carried home from the nursery, but remember it is very heavy.

Lay sod strips out straight and stagger the ends as bricks are staggered in a running bond pattern. Press seams together for a continual layer of grass. Cut sod where necessary with a large serrated knife or a sharp transplanting shovel. Roll lightly with a roller drum half-filled with water, then water the sod. Water regularly for the first few weeks.

Do not let sod lawns dry out before they are completely established. If allowed to do so before bonding with the soil, the individual patches of sod will shrink, leaving ugly gaps. Once rooted into the prepared soil, the grass will be greener and will appear more vigorous.

Bermuda & Zoysia Lawns

Since hybrid Bermuda and zoysia, both warm-season grasses, produce only small amounts of seed, sterile seed, or seed that is not true to type, they must be

Stolons of bermuda and zoysia lawns must be planted.

planted by plugs or stolons. Most of the warm-season grasses spread by stolons—above-ground lateral stems, or rhizomes—below-ground lateral stems.

. Broadcast stolons at the rate of 3-5 bushels per 1,000 square feet over the prepared soil bed. Next roll the planted area with a roller half-filled with water. Mulch the area with a ½-inch layer of compost, topsoil, peat moss or a combination of all three. Roll again after mulching, then sprinkle with a fine mist until completely wet. Water daily. Do not let the soil dry out completely for several weeks, until the lawn has become established.

Another method of planting stolons in a prepared seedbed is to make a series of parallel 2-inch wide, ½-inch deep trenches 10 inches apart in moist soil. Plant stolons in trenches so the white roots are completely covered and backfill with soil. Water the newly planted area after planting and keep moist for several weeks, until stolons have completely rooted.

The Better Lawn & Turf Institute recommends using a special tube with the same diameter as the plugs (2-4-inch rounds) to first remove a plug of bare soil, then place the sod plug in the hole. Place plugs in rows or randomly—the closer they are placed, the faster the grass will cover bare ground. Roll the area after placing plugs.

Water frequently with small amounts until the lawn is established. You can reduce weed populations between sod plugs or sprigs by seeding the bare area with fine fescues at the rate of 4 pounds per 1,000 square feet. Zoysia is usually planted as plugs. Bermuda grass is usually planted as sprigs.

Types of Grasses

The following page of turfgrasses for different Zones and habitats is adapted from a chart by the Better Lawn & Turf Institute. It provides grass choices for USDA Zones 1 through 11 and a variety of environments.

Ground Covers

Ground covers work well to hold soil on slopes and hillsides where they are far easier to care for than lawns. They also grow well around the base of trees where lawn grasses don't do well because of leaf drop or shade.

Most ground covers can be trimmed with a weed whip or rotary lawn mower. In the early spring, mow ground covers such as ivy, periwinkle, St. John's Wort (*hypericum*) and Virginia creeper back to four to six inches high to renew them and discourage pests such

Name	Habitat Preference	Remarks

Zones 1-3

Name	Habitat Preference	Remarks
Kentucky bluegrass	Best with full sun, but tolerates partial shade. "Likes" fertile, near neutral soils of good structure, but is broadly adaptable.	Probably the most versatile, widely-adapted, recuperative turfgrass; chief drawback in new plantings is slowness to sprout, especially in cool weather; fine fescue or perennial ryegrass in mixture hastens coverage.
Red, creeping, Chewings and hard fescue	Sun or dry shade; better adapted to poor soil and drought than is bluegrass.	Weakness is hot-moist weather, seldom a problem in the North. Good in mixture with Kentucky bluegrass, withstanding tribulations of dry, sandy infertile soils and shade
Perennial ryegrass	Not reliable hardy far north, but may be used for quick cover (nursegrass), and hardy cultivars in protected locations.	
Colonial bentgrass	Hardy but not at its best this far north, especially subject to snowmold.	

Zones 4-6

Name	Habitat Preference	Remarks
Kentucky bluegrass	In more northerly areas the same as for zones 1-3, but "enjoying" partial shade in zone 6.	Basically a boreal species with its zone of adaptation diminishing south of zone 6. Avoid over-zealous care in hot weather.
Red, creeping, Chewings and hard fescue	Useful in bluegrass mixtures, but planted alone often suffers summer die-back in zone 6.	
Perennial ryegrass	Does best in mild (maritime) climates, but newer cultivars are more broadly adapted and hardy.	The new "turf-type" cultivars are bred for lower growth, better looks and greater hardiness. Aggressive, will crowd bluegrass and fescue in seed mixtures if more abundant than about 20%. Often sown alone for quick cover.
Colonial bentgrass	Does best in climates that are at least seasonally moist; sun or partial shade; tolerates acid soil	The colonial bentgrasses can provide elegant turfs within the capabilities of homeowner care, but do require consistent mowing. Are best adapted to moist climates such as the West Coast north from San Francisco, leeward of the Great Lakes, and the misty highlands of New England.
Rough bluegrass	Moist shade or partial shade.	A very attractive cover for cool, moist shade, but wears poorly
Canada bluegrass	Colonizes poor soil; better species available for good habitat; stands shade well, and hardy into zones 2-3; broadly tolerant.	Use restricted to low-quality "maintenance" situations

Zones 5-7

Name	Habitat Preference	Remarks
Buffalograss	Adapted to drylands without irrigation; sun endures drought and compact soil better than competing grasses.	Native to and used in plains from northern Texas to Nebraska where irrigation is difficult.
Tall fescue	Broadly adapted; enduring poor soils that dry in summer; sun or some shade.	Useful where minimum care is required.

Zones 7-8

Name	Habitat Preference	Remarks
Bermudagrass	Demands full sun; does best on near-neutral, fertile soils, and when provided with amenities.	At its best in the upper South. Special selections and hybrids are finer-textured and more attractive, suggested for better lawns.
Zoysiagrass	Prospers in partial shade as well as sun; does best in good soil.	They Meyer strain of Zoysia is quite hardy even in the North, but has been a very short season (May-September). The finer-textured "matrella" strains are better suited to the South because of "tough" persistent tissues tends to thatch and merits mowing with a heavy-duty machine.
Tall Fescue	see zone 5-7	

Zones 8-9

Name	Habitat Preference	Remarks
Centipedegrass	Sun or moderate shade; well adapted to infertile sandy soils of the coastal plain.	An excellent low maintenance lawngrass, but tempramental about fertility and soul conditions, and some soil pests (e.g. groundpearl). Mainly suited to the coastal plain in the southern part of zone 8 and northern part of zone 9.

Zones 9-11

Name	Habitat Preference	Remarks
St. Augustinegrass	Widely adapted to hot, humid conditions, sun or shade.	Probably the most shade-tolerant of the southern grasses, mostly used in humid coastal climates, but often north ward into zone 8. Floratam, a SAD-virus resistant type, is best planted in Texas (where SAD is widespread).
Bahiagrass	Widely tolerant, enduring poor, sandy habitat such as roadsides, sun or partial shade.	One of the more economical southern grasses, not as elegant as the improved bermudagrass and zoysias, but attractive when cared for.
Carpetgrass	Adapted to wet soils, often volunteering in boggy situations; sun or partial shade.	Seldom planted except on difficult wet sites where growth of other species is limited.

as slugs and snails. After mowing, the ground covers may be unsightly for a month or so, but the bright green new growth soon will add resilience and life to the garden landscape. Use a lawn mower on level areas and a weed whip (string trimmer) on hillsides.

Fertilize ground covers heavily with a soluble fertilizer as soon as they are cut. Ground covers that will be used under trees should be low-growing and be able to stand some foot traffic. Good choices include perennial clovers, burnet, chicory, thymes, and prostrate yarrows. Look also for plants native to your area that are drought resistant.

A well-chosen ground cover, once established, gives garden borders a fuller, more finished look. Choose ground covers with different-colored foliage and leaf textures for more diversity. Make sure to prepare the soil well and remove all weeds before planting. Weeds, especially grassy ones, have a knack for hiding among ground covers as they are getting started, but once the plants have grown thick, weeds have a difficult time germinating and growing.

To plant hillsides, cut contours at a right angle to the slope with a rotary tiller. Drill or dig holes and plant ivy, labium, or other ground covers.

If ivy ground covers have gotten out of hand and climbed into trees where you don't want them, control is quite easy. Remove ivy from trees by cutting the stems around the base of the tree and letting the ivy dry out for a few weeks. Then it is easy to pull off the tree.

Meadow-in-a-can seed collections, available from several companies, can be used to grow mixed ground covers. There are special mixes of flowers to attract bees, birds, and butterflies. These seed mixes contain both annual and perennial native wildflowers. It takes more than just sprinkling the seed from the can. To grow these mixes well, you must prepare the soil just as you would for any garden bed. The better the soil preparation, the better the stand will be. You will also need to weed out unwanted plants.

As a general rule, wildflowers that prefer the shade of the forest floor grow best in filtered light with moist, rich humusy soil. The flowers that thrive in meadows or sunny locations, need drier conditions and well-draining soil that is less humusy.

It's perfectly possible and increasingly popular to use wildflowers as ground covers. Most native wildflowers require little or no supplemental fertilization but do require regular watering until they are established. Prepare the soil and keep the weeds down. Give the wildflowers all the natural help that they will tolerate. The entire area will need to be cut once a year.

Chapter Ten

Ornamental Shrubs, Trees & Vines

About Ornamental Shrubs, Trees & Vines

Once you have completed the hardscape of your garden—buildings, walkways, patios, decks, and general lay of the land—it is time to install ornamental and shade trees. These woody plants are the backbone, the strongest features and largest living structures, of the garden. Trees are the framework with shrubs and vines next in importance as long-lived woody plants for the yard.

Consider the roles that trees, shrubs, and vines will play in your landscape before choosing them. Landscaping can add 15 to 25 percent to the value of your property, according to experts. Landscape plants can save energy by shading the house in the summer and sheltering it from winds during the winter. Also study the needs and preferences of the plants for sun or shade, acid or alkaline soil, exposed or sheltered locations, and so forth.

When assessing your property for places to put trees and shrubs, remember that 90 percent of their root systems will be in the top six to eight inches of soil. Further, the lateral roots of these woody plants grow out much farther than the perimeter of their branches above, at least half again as far as the dripline.

In good soil, the roots can grow out three times the area farther than the area shaded by the branches. Some trees have deep taproots while others have taproots that stop going deeper when the lateral root system is large enough to gather sufficient oxygen, water, and nutrients. Taproots and lateral roots give trees and shrubs stability and support.

Fibrous feeder roots extend from the lateral roots. Only the tips of the feeder roots actively grow, burrowing through the soil as much as an inch a day. It is in the root hairs behind the growing root tip that moisture, oxygen and nutrients are taken into the tree systems. Each tree, even young ones, has miles of feeder roots and billions of root hairs that take in many gallons of nutrient-rich water solution each day.

When similar species of trees are near each other, their root systems will actually commingle, graft together and become, to a great extent, a single root system. They will share moisture, oxygen and nutrients. They also will share diseases. This underlines the importance of planting a variety of plants.

Vines are useful as vertical elements used to shade outdoor living areas, hide utility or other less attractive areas, and to buffer undesirable noise. Vines will grow on buildings, walls, trellises, or any other structure near them. Their vigor and aesthetic value to the landscape will depend on the variety, climate, and specific application. Before planting vines, or anything else for that matter, envision what the mature plants will look like in the chosen location.

Planting a wide assortment of plants that will attract an array of wildlife and beneficial insects should be one of the main rules for designing an ornamental garden. But beware of going to the other extreme, and planting just one of each different species and variety. Your garden will be more beautiful if you plant in amoeba-like patterns that include masses of smaller plants, and several larger plants.

When selecting trees, shrubs, and vines, remember that the hardiness Zones and ratings are meant to be used only as guides, not absolutes. They refer to the coldest temperature ranges that plants can tolerate. Very little has been done on hardiness to heat which also is a limiting factor for many plants. Locations near large bodies of water will have buffered temperatures.

Look around your neighborhood, talk to local nursery experts, check with your Cooperative Extension agent, and take notes at public gardens to learn what plants you like and how they will grow.

Raised or mounded beds around the perimeter of a lawn not only provide better drainage and early heat, they are easier to manage. And they are good sites for planting shrubs and small trees. Leave a four- to six-inch space between the lawn and mounded beds to fill with a mulch that will stop the grass from encroaching on the beds. When mowing, just set the inside wheels of the mower on the mulch and the other wheels on the grass.

Evaluating & Planting an Established Garden

If moving to a property with an established garden, the first step is to evaluate the plants and the hardscape. Make notes as you go. Are walkways, utility areas, decks, patios, the house and other buildings in good repair and as you want them to be? Are gardens of good design and well maintained? If not, what do you want to see done?

In some cases, properties become so overgrown that, even in winter when deciduous plants are bare, it's hard to see any method in the overgrown madness. If you can't make head or tail of the hodgepodge you've inherited, hire an expert to help you separate the good from the bad. Develop a long-range plan that you can execute over a period of time, perhaps even years.

Then and only then, begin clearing out the things you don't want. Rake and clean up flower and shrub beds, eliminating unwanted plants as you go. Prune dead growth and suckers from trees and shrubs. And, of course, pull the weeds. Start getting rid of stumps if necessary.

Work compost into the soil and top with mulch around perennials. Wait for a year so you can see where annuals, bulbs, and herbaceous perennials are planted. As you discover them, mark them with a stake containing their name, flower color, and when they bloom. Tender bulbs can be dug and stored in the fall.

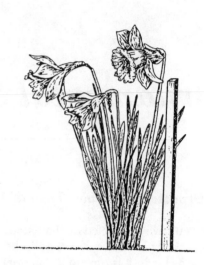

As you discover hidden plants in your yard, mark them with a stake containing their name, flower color, and when they bloom.

Add a thick layer of compost shrub beds to feed the soil and plants, to encourage earthworms, and to absorb moisture and protect the soil from temperature extremes.

Wait until the next growing season to replant the gardens if it is late fall in a northern climate. If you don't want to wait an entire year, start by digging beds with a spading fork, lifting and replanting bulbs and perennials as you go. And, of course, remove weeds. Provide consistent water to the transplanted perennials until they are established.

Transplanting Small Trees & Shrubs

Step One. In the spring, choose small trees, six to eight feet tall or less, or shrubs that are six feet or less in height with an equal spread or less. Anything larger would be too difficult to manage without professional equipment and help.

Step Two. Root prune the plants to be moved. Do this by using a sharp spade to cut a narrow trench straight into the ground 8 to 10 inches from the trunk. Fill this trench with compost and/or soil that has good texture. Prune back the branches by about one third. This will balance the root loss.

Step Three. By the next fall or spring, new roots will have grown into the narrow trench and the plant will be ready to move by digging the root ball an inch or two outside the narrow trench.

Step Four. Prepare new planting holes with sloped walls, so that the tops of the holes are about three times the diameter of the root balls of the woody plants. If the soil is heavy clay, do not improve its tex-

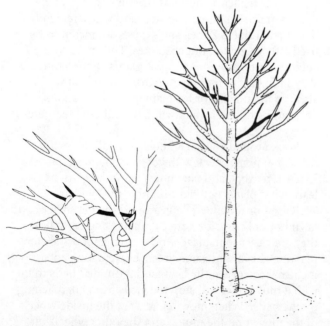

Prune out all dead and crossing growth from trees.

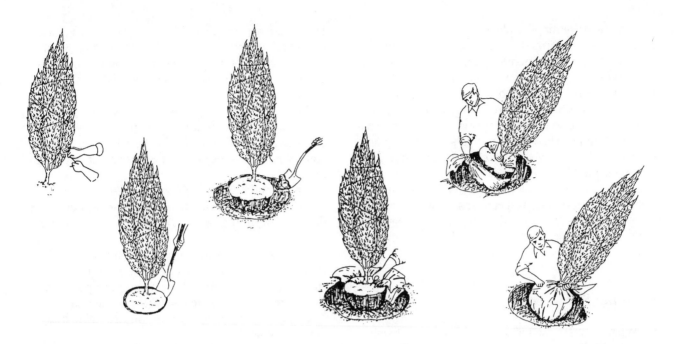

First, wrap a small rope around the shrub to protect the foliage. Next, cut the roots at the drip line. Then, dig around and under the root ball. Slip a piece of plastic or burlap around the root ball. Roll the root ball over and encircle the root ball. Tie the plastic around the base of the trunk. Now the shrub can be moved with a hand truck.

ture. If it is not heavy clay, add organic matter. If the soil is heavy and poor draining, plan to place the plant an inch or so higher in the new site than it was before. This will help ensure good drainage.

Step Five. Dig the plant and, before lifting it, roll some burlap, tarp or plastic under the root ball to support it. Tie up the root ball unless the move is a very short distance. The point is to hold the root ball together and to expose the feeder roots to the air as little as possible. This will diminish root injury and speed re-establishment. A certain amount of root injury is inevitable but you can keep it to a minimum.

Step Six. Before putting the plant in the hole, decide which way you want it to face. Then place the tree or shrub in the new planting hole, and carefully remove its covering as you begin to fill around it. Replace the soil and tamp it to remove air pockets, then water thoroughly. You may wish to mound up a soil saucer to hold water. Mulch around the tree or shrub and be sure not to let its soil dry out at any season for the next two years until it is fully recovered from transplanting.

Planting from a Container Step-by-Step

Step One. Before buying, check the condition of the tree, shrub or vine. Note that a one-gallon shrub planted in fertile organic soil will normally outgrow a root-bound five-gallon shrub in two or three years. Check the roots by knocking the plant from its pot and look-

ing for healthy, clean-white rootlets. Ask the nursery expert to do this for you. If all you see is roots, with very little soil showing, the plant is root bound. On root-bound plants, use a sharp knife to make several half-inch deep vertical slices on the outside of the root mass before planting. Or scratch and pull the sides and bottom of the root mass loose.

Cut the roots of a pot-bound plant before transplanting.

Step Two. Dig the new planting hole. Continue as in the process described above under transplanting, adapting to suit containerized plants. Keep roots covered and moist after they are removed from the container. Keep the time the roots are out of the ground as short as possible. Fragile root hairs easily dry out when out of the soil. Water transplanted shrubs heavily after planting. Then make sure to keep newly planted trees and shrubs watered well, not only during dry summers, but also in other seasons when rain is lacking. Two years of careful attention to newly planted trees, shrubs and vines will ensure strong, well-established root systems. Water the entire garden heavily before you go away for long weekend holidays or other vacations.

Choosing Shade Trees

When choosing shade trees, the maximum height and spread are two of the primary considerations. Consider where the shadow will be cast at different times of the year. An old-fashioned way to help you estimate where shadows will be at a given time of year is that the shadows cast by the full moon are about the same as those that will be cast by the sun in six months.

Once you know the two extremes, you can estimate where trees should go in order to provide the shade you want.

Trees are heavy feeders and will compete with nearby vegetation. Vigorous trees should be planted at least 30 to 40 feet from the house. This will help diminish problems that large trees can cause. Their leaves clog rain gutters. Branches may fall on the roof.

Roots may penetrate and block drains or even crack building foundations. If roots draw too much water from the soil around and under the foundation, it can cause soil shrinkage, which may cause the foundation to crack.

When shade trees are grown in lawn areas, fertilize them early in the year, about a month before the grass starts to grow. This way the fertilizer has more time to reach the tree's roots before the grass is actively taking up nutrients.

Shade and other ornamental trees do not need much pruning the first few years. Prune only crossing, diseased, or dead growth during the first few dormant seasons.

Shrubs and trees that produce fruit and are also attractive ornamentals include quince, pawpaw, persimmon, strawberry tree, loquat and pineapple guava. The evergreen pineapple guava (*Feijoa sellowiana*) is easily pruned, drops few leaves and the edible fruit does not splatter below.

Group together plants that have the same water, sun and soil requirements. Experiment with different plant combinations in different mini-environments in your garden.

Deciduous Trees

Trees are sold in several ways. Some are bare-rooted (as described under fruit trees), as they usually are from mail-order houses. The roots of bare-root trees typically are in plastic bags, with moist sphagnum moss to maintain humidity around the feeder roots. They are best planted when dormant, and should never be allowed to dry out.

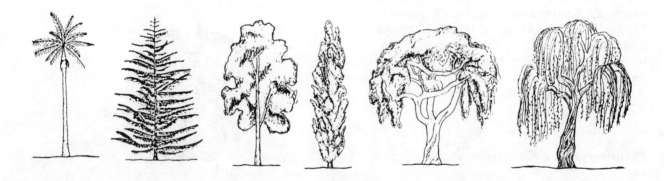

Trees come in all shapes and sizes that are perfect for most landscape needs. Trees left to right: palm, fir, dogwood, poplar, oak, willow.

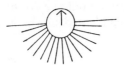

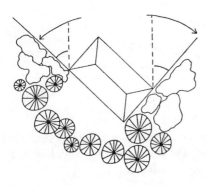

The upper drawing shows how just the end of the house receives sunshine. The house on the bottom is set at an angle and receives more of the sun's warming rays.

Another way trees are sold is in large pots or other containers. They may be grown in the containers or started in fields, then transplanted into containers. Container-grown plants suffer less transplanting shock. The exception is when they have been in containers too long and have become root-bound, also called pot-bound. Containers also limit the size of the plants. And those in containers larger than five-gallon will be heavy to manage.

Trees also are sold in a third way, as balled and burlapped (B & B) specimens. They are dug in the fields with a ball of soil and wrapped in burlap. They usually have been root-pruned and so are going to have comparatively little transplant shock. The negative side of balled and burlapped trees is the heavy weight, which makes the planting job hard to manage unless you hire lifting and moving equipment. However, the extra work may be worthwhile if you are purchasing an important specimen tree for your gar-

den or patio. Do not try to handle anything more than a five-gallon containerized plant by yourself.

Although containerized and balled and burlapped plants can be planted at any time of year, you usually will have greater success if you plant them in early spring or late fall when they are dormant. It's even more important to plant bare-rooted trees and shrubs while they are dormant.

After planting trees, do not stake the trunks, a custom that used to be popular, unless prevailing winds are extremely high. Trees will be stronger if their woody tissues are forced to cope with the stresses of wind. If staking is necessary, do it for only a year and stake the tree's trunk at a low level. Use soft webbing, not thin wire or any other thin hard material, to tie the trunks.

Consider mature size, growing habits, flowers and fruits, and other features, both good and bad. Most of all, consider how a tree will fit into your landscape and how well it will suit the role you want it to play.

Those who are seeking deciduous trees for city locations should note that the following trees, pin oak, willow oak, ginkgo, green ash, Norway maple, Japanese pagodas, thornless honey locust, serviceberry, and Grecian laurel, have shown tolerance to urban air pollution. Be sure to cross-refer these to the USDA zones to learn where they are hardy.

Evergreen Trees

There are both broad-leafed and coniferous evergreen trees. Citrus trees, figs, many of the magnolias, live oaks, and eucalyptus trees are examples of broad-leafed evergreens. Most are native to the warmer regions of the country. The coniferous, or cone-bearing trees, can be found in all regions. Many are native to colder, more northern climates. Typical coniferous trees are pines, cedars, firs, spruces and hemlocks. A number of coniferous trees also are available as shrubs and dwarf forms.

Shrubs

Most shrubs mature faster than the average tree, reaching full size in about five years. They need little care and will thrive in most locations for many years. Shrubs make good screens, sound buffers, and habitat for birds and other wildlife. If you plant flowering shrubs, you will find an even greater assortment of birds and butterflies in your garden.

The question often comes up as to whether a plant is a tree or a shrub. It is more a matter of growth habit than size since some shrubs easily reach the size of small trees. Most people, including nursery experts agree that shrubs have multiple trunks and do not grow more than 20 feet tall.

Shrubs often are used to hide ugly foundations and other unattractive features. They are the perfect shield for roads, highways, and garden utility areas that include compost piles and storage sheds. They are excellent choices for hedges used to define an area or to separate one area from another. Shrubs can make good windbreaks or background for flower beds. Shrubs are beautiful in ornamental borders designed to please the eye.

When planning to add shrubs to your garden design, think first of the role you want them to play. Are they to be screens, backgrounds, or sound buffers? Do you want them to define an area or separate several areas? Do you hope to attract birds and butterflies?

In designing shrub beds and borders, avoid straight-line designing unless you are trying to achieve a rigid, formal look. Plant odd-numbered groups of shrubs, placing taller ones at the back, shorter ones to the front. Use a number of different flowering shrubs that will provide a progression of blooms throughout much of the growing season.

Hedges

A hedge will buffer strong winds, slowing them down. Solid walls and fences retain frost-laden air by keeping it from flowing freely. Hedges allow cold air to pass slowly through them and so out of the garden. If you do not have room for a hedge, consider installing a wire fence that can be covered with climbing and vining plants.

There are two main categories of hedges: Formal, with shrubs trimmed tightly to create a manicured look; and informal, or relaxed, with the shrubs left to grow and flower naturally. A formal hedge can be trimmed back closely to reduce the space required for growth. Natural, informal hedges are very attractive, but require more growing space. Just about any tall-growing shrub is suitable for a hedge. In fact, even cactus family members make good hedges for arid regions. The thorns keep marauding pests from penetrating.

Even trees make good hedges if planted closer together than normal. Alders, hemlock, Chinese elms, yews, and cedars are among the trees that have been used successfully as hedges. They can be formally clipped or left to grow their natural way.

Bare-root hedge plants are less expensive than container hedge plants. However, bare-root plants are usually deciduous, that is, they lose their leaves in the

winter. Bare-root plants should be dormant with closed leaf buds when planted. Open, or opening,

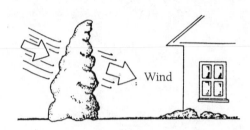

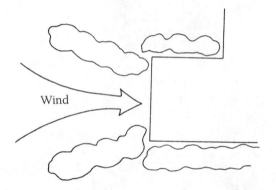

The upper drawing shows how a hedge will slow wind around a house. The lower drawing shows how hedges can be used to direct a breeze.

buds signify the plant is coming out of dormancy and may suffer more transplant shock. Plant hedge plants just as you would other trees or shrubs.

The distance between the plants will depend upon the plants used. If in doubt, get advice from the nursery expert where you buy the plants. Whether local or mail-order, there will be experts who can answer your questions and offer advice on specific plants when you tell them what you want the hedge to do in your landscape.

Maintaining Hedges

Treat a hedge like any other perennial shrub or tree. Fertilize it in the early spring with a balanced organic fertilizer containing all of the major nutrients. Mulch after the soil warms. Don't fertilize after July because late growth may be too tender to survive cold winter weather.

Fast-growing hedge shrubs such as eugenia, laurel, oleander and photenia need to be trimmed several times during the growing season to retain a well cropped, formal look. Be sure to make the top of any hedge more narrow than the base so that sunlight can get to all parts of the hedge. If you don't, you may have unattractive die-back at the base of the hedge. Privet hedges often show signs of improper trimming by having dead areas near the ground level. Trim natural, informal hedges after they flower in the spring, or in the fall if they are not flowering plants.

At planting time, prune or pinch branch tips of fast-growing shrubs to promote bushy growth. Some shrubs, like privet, eugenia, and photenia, need hard pruning after planting to encourage bushy growth.

Trim the top shoots of conifer hedges once they have reached the desired height. Prune both side and top growth of conifers and slow-growing shrubs in the late summer or early fall.

The area inside and below hedge shrubs tends to trap leaves and other debris. The extra rubbish also may trap frost-laden air and provide a hideout for pests. Clean the inside of hedges of debris and dead branches each fall. Remove this debris by hand and with a rake. Wash dust and small debris from foliage with a jet of water. If air circulation is lacking, prune out some internal growth to allow air and sunlight to penetrate the center of the hedge. You will be surprised what a difference cleaning the inside of hedges will make in overall vigor.

Pruning

Pruning is the art of making a plant grow into a certain shape or causing it to become more productive and vigorous by removing unwanted branches, buds, and flowers. Pruning will restore the balance between roots and tops of plants, following root injury from transplanting, or from nearby construction. Pruning also is to remove dead and diseased wood and can rejuvenate old trees, shrubs, and vines.

Pruning for shape and appearance usually follows the natural growth pattern of the plant, but may alter the natural shape as in hedges, topiary (sculptural forms), bonsai (miniaturized trees) and espalier (trees and shrubs pruned to grow flat against a wall or other vertical structure).

Wall shrubs are plants that are trained to grow against a wall. Train the shoots in a similar way as for espaliered trees—to grow horizontally to increase flowering and vertical stem growth from the lateral growth.

The timing of pruning is important, particularly when dealing with flowering plants. In general, they should be pruned after they bloom so that you do not prune away flower buds. Flowering shrubs can be constantly renewed by cutting one fourth of the old wood back to the ground each year.

Fruit trees and some other ornamental trees have regular growths of suckers often called water sprouts. These are rampant upright branches that will not bear fruit or flowers, are not in line with the main growth of the tree and will take nourishment that should go to the productive parts of the tree. Remove these as soon as possible. You can rub them from the main branches with your hand when they are still small.

When you prune, you affect the growth hormones and thus the growth of the plant. When you prune the growing tip at the top of a plant or end of a branch, more growth hormone will reach the buds below or behind and so new growth will occur there. Pruning the terminal tips of growth will cause branching. That kind of pruning is called cutting back.

The other main kind is thinning. When you thin plant growth, you cut branches all the way back to the main trunk or branch. This reduces the number of branches and opens up the center of the plant to light and air circulation while directly stimulating new growth.

Pruning can be done with simple tools. You will want pole pruners for high pruning jobs, lopping shears with long handles for leverage, a pruning saw, and a pair of good pruners.

Make pruning cuts in the order indicated and as shown in the diagram. Current wisdom is that you should not paint tree and shrub wounds. Experts believe that the plant will heal itself far better. Paint and other compounds may seal infectious agents next to the raw wood and so encourage rather than prevent disease.

Climbing & Vining Plants

The quickest way to achieve the dimension of height in the garden or to disguise an ugly wall or fence is to grow climbing plants. Vines also can serve as good screens without being impenetrable barriers.

A true climber has tendrils or curling, twining foliage that clings to supports. But many shrubs can be trained to climb by fastening the stems to a trellis or support with twine or plastic ties, or by weaving the branches in and out of a fence.

Climbers can also be trained to grow up a tree trunk or along branches. In fact, some undesirable climbers such as kudzu and the wild morning glory also known as bindweed can intertwine and choke out shrubs and trees.

Normally, climbing vines are purchased in containers and planted any time of year. Buy flowering climbers when blooming to ensure the color the flower. Choose sturdy vines with good branching.

Planting climbers along walls that are under the eaves of a roof provides extra protection from frost. But under eaves, plants will receive little or no natural rainfall. Also areas next to building walls can have poor soil because of building rubble that was never removed and because of lime that leaches out from a concrete foundation.

If possible, plant climbing vines far enough from the wall that they receive some rainfall. Plant next to a rain downspout if under overhanging eves. Like all plants, vines will grow most vigorously if fertilized and watered regularly.

Prepare a planting hole three times as big as the root ball. Follow the same procedure as when planting trees or shrubs. Plant to the same depth as before. You can tell where that is by the soil level in the container and the soil mark on the vine stems.

The exception to this is clematis which likes to be planted four- to six- inches below the level of soil in the container. Check with nursery experts when buying vines to learn if there are any special planting instructions or exceptions. Cover the soil with a two- to four-inch mulch to keep the roots cool, conserve moisture, and suppress weeds.

Vines with tendrils (thread-like fingers) should be kept away from house walls. The tendrils can get under and in-between shingles, planks or bricks and slowly separate them.

Train vines around windows to retain sunlight indoors or let deciduous varieties cover sunny windows to provide summer shade. They lose their leaves in winter to let sunshine filter through.

Prune climbers annually to improve flowering. A general rule is that vines can be pruned back after they flower, but check a book or ask an expert before you do so if you are not sure what your vine likes. Early-flowering plants should be dead-headed (flowers pruned after they've faded) and cut back soon after flowering. Mid- to late-summer flowering climbers should be pruned in the fall or the following spring.

Chapter Eleven
Container & Patio Gardens

About Container & Patio Gardens

Patios and decks have become very much a part of outdoor living. Since they are separate from the garden proper, it's tempting to bring the garden onto the patio through container gardening. Put favorite plants into attractive containers and use them to decorate outdoor living spaces. Annuals, perennials, trees, shrubs, or just about any plants are good choices for growing in containers. They will add new dimensions to the patio or deck.

The roof-top gardeners of New York City can provide inspiration to container gardeners everywhere. They have learned to garden in a motley collection of containers inspired by their imagination and promoted by their labors.

They cope with the original desert-like conditions of roof tops and miraculously transform this wasteland into green oases that create their own mini-environments. They construct these urban Edens with decking components, commercial potting soil, mix-and-match containers, and plants that arise from seeds, cuttings, mail-order plants, and trades with gardening friends.

Planter boxes and containers also can be integrated into the garden itself and used as features and focal points to accent plantings, pools, garden "rooms" and other design features. When including planters as garden or patio features, make sure that they are large enough to be important but not so large as to overwhelm their site. You can get help in making these and other esthetic decisions by visiting gardens with such features as well as by studying gardening magazines and garden-design books.

Round planters will echo the curves of a garden. Rectangular planters will repeat the lines of walls, fences and other garden features. Planters for the edge of decks and patios should be low and comparatively unobtrusive. They should define spaces beyond rather than obscure the view.

Containers can be clay, plastic, stone, wood or wire baskets lined with sphagnum moss. They can be old paint cans, wash tubs, waste baskets, wicker baskets or wooden crates. Anything big enough to contain plants can be a planter if you wish it to be.

The most important feature of garden planters should be adequate drainage. If containers do not have drainage holes, make sure to add at least one, good-sized hole for every gallon of soil. Roots will rot in soggy soils of containers with inadequate drainage. It's better to have too many drainage holes than too few. A heavy hammer and large nail or spike is useful for driving drainage holes into potential garden planters.

Most plants will grow better in well-draining soil and in the good-textured soils of raised beds than in soils with little or no drainage. If the containers do not have enough bottom clearance to facilitate drainage, set them up on a board or stones to provide free flowing drainage. Or cut drainage holes along the bottom outside edge of containers that sit flat on the ground.

Experts used to recommend putting pot shards or gravel in the bottom of containers and planters to improve drainage, but field experiments have proven that this actually makes drainage worse in containers. So, do not put gravel, stones or pot shard in the bottoms of pots and other containers. You can pack a few inches of old newspapers in the bottoms of large containers, simply to save on potting media. The newspaper will not improve the drainage so you should leave some room around the edges of the paper for planting medium to go to the bottom of the planter. Be sure that the potting medium is six to eight inches deep over the newspaper.

Large, inexpensive containers made from whiskey barrels that have been cut in half are popular and attractive. These oak barrels lend a natural, rustic look to the garden, breathe well and hold about 25 gallons of soil. The large volume of soil gives the roots more space and requires less frequent watering. The metal rings can be painted to prevent rust.

Whiskey barrels also are good containers for miniature water gardens. You can grow rushes, reeds, miniature water lilies, other submerged and surface water plants, and ornamental fish in these half-barrels. You can even install a small fountain or water fall if

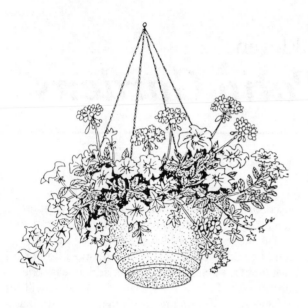

Hanging baskets are easy to plant and add new life to patios.

A whiskey barrel is an inexpensive large planter for decks and patios.

you wish. Remember though that water lilies prefer still water. Most nurseries that sell water garden plants and equipment can help you find plastic liners for lining barrels that will be used for water gardening.

New, large, inexpensive plastic containers on the market look like terra-cotta but are not heavy and do not dry out as quickly as clay containers. Five-gallon plastic buckets can be painted and given drainage holes to make attractive containers. These containers may not even need to be painted to be attractive if planted with cascading flowers that soon cover the sides.

You also may be able to find large used containers at the headquarters of contracting landscapers or wholesale nurseries. Try calling them first. Some landscapers will sell large used containers at bargain prices.

Chimney flue liners are rectangular and square, and open on both ends. They make excellent raised bed planters. Or you can put them on clay or plastic drain saucers to use them on the deck or patio. If they are too large for drain saucers, place them permanently on paved patios or on the soil next to the deck or patio.

These planters are great for heat-loving grapes or climbing vines next to a trellis. In areas where there are many winter freezes, these would have to be protected from the root-damaging freeze-thaw cycles during cold seasons. The additional heat provided by the raised soil in the flue tile gives the vines an early start and the soil does not dry out quickly because the bot-

tom is open and it wicks up moisture from the soil below. The moist soil also keeps the clay from getting overheated by the pounding sun.

Clay drainage and sewer tiles also come in many sizes, and are open at both ends. They can make effective planters. Combinations of clay flue and sewer tiles overflowing with handsome combinations of ornamental and useful plants will present a sculptural look, making an impressive large garden focal point.

Place heavy containers in their permanent locations before filling with soil and watering. They can be very heavy and impossibly awkward to move; a dolly or hand truck will make moving much easier. Large containers also can be placed on a permanent base with casters to facilitate moving.

To build planters, use soft wood that has been pressure-treated with a copper-based preservative, or paint the wood. You also could use cedar, or more expensive rough-cut hardwoods, to build planter boxes. Remember to include a minimum of one half-inch drainage hole for every gallon or two of soil. Big planters can serve a second purpose in the outdoor living area if they have seating spaces built like shelves around their edges. Raised planters also are easier on the back and knees for weeding and maintenance.

You can build planters of masonry and brick. There are masonry "stones" that will lock together and make durable permanent containers for garden plants. Many materials and plans offer a multitude of choices for getting started in container gardening.

Building a Planter Box Step-By-Step

Step One. To make a 4-foot square, planter box to place in the yard, purchase two 8-foot 2" x 8" pieces of lumber.

Step Two. Cut them in half to 4-foot lengths.

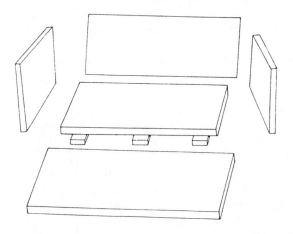

Step Three. Fasten the 4-foot long pieces together on the ends with 16-penny galvanized nails. Overlap each section of the boards to form a 4' x 4' foot raised bed 4 inches tall. See drawing above.

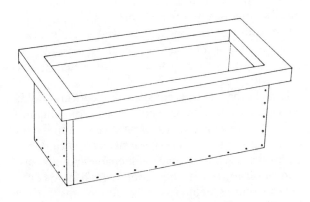

Step Four. Put 4" x 4" foot posts that are 4 feet in the inside corners. Fasten them to the corner walls of the planter with galvanized nails before backfilling and packing the soil around them.

Step Five. Place the planter in the desired location. Paint or stain both inside and outside to prevent rotting.

Step Six. Fill with soil or other planting medium and plant.

Small Spaces

Small spaces take more careful planning than larger ones. The overall plan for small spaces should provide as much room as possible for a table and seating, plus room to get around them easily.

In very small spaces, tables may have to be put in corners and accented by a couple of small chairs or a bench. The space will often dictate the design if you study it well.

Hanging baskets and vertically oriented containers and planters will not hog precious floor space. Hanging baskets of different sizes that are placed at varying levels will provide room for many plants.

Planters with trellises are ideal for vines. For twenty-four-hour beauty, plant moonflowers and morning glories in a planter with a trellis or near a tall fence.

Planters secured to the tops of walls or fences also extend the ground area of a small space. Flowering and foliage plants can trail off the sides, creating cascades of color and texture.

Sunny Decks & Patios

Use containers and planters to make an oasis of your sunny deck or patio. Container-grown trees, shrubs, ornamental grasses and some of the taller annuals and perennials will provide islands of shade, dappling the area with comparatively cool places to sit and enjoy the summer weather. You can also use hanging baskets or planters with taller, more vertical plants to shade your seating areas. For instant color, use the annual bedding plants that are so plentiful in the spring.

Shady Decks & Patios

Don't despair if your deck or patio is in the shade. To be sure, you can't grow as many brightly colored annuals and perennials in shady locations. But there are many beautiful shade plants that offer variegated foliage and a wide variety of textures. Shady decks are cooler and the greens of plant foliage are soothing and calming to the soul.

Try ferns and hostas for container growing in shady sites. Move house plants to the porch, deck or patio during summer months.

Impatiens are the most colorful of the shade-loving flowering plants. These annual bedding plants come in all shades of white through pinks to reds and, more recently plums, salmons and oranges.

Ideas & Suggestions for Container Growing

A marvelous advantage of container gardening is that you can move the plants around to create any illusion you want, and achieve the color and size relationships you desire. You can grow plants with diverse requirements side by side, yet each in its own specific nutrients and soil.

Containers of annual bedding plants add quick color to decks, patios or balconies in the early spring. The soil in the containers heats up faster than ground soil, and containers can be moved indoors during cool nights if necessary.

Early spring-flowering bulbs can kick off the gardening season with eye-catching color. They can be grown in containers if they are pre-cooled, or if the containers are protected from freeze-thaw cycles after fall planting.

Bulbs with shorter foliage and flowers may be better suited to containers on some deck areas because they are less prone to be affected by wind or rain common to cooler weather. Choose compact varieties of anemones, crocus, cyclamens, daffodils, hyacinths, irises, and tulips for the best results. Spring-flowering bulbs can be followed by prolific annuals such as geraniums, petunias, baby's breath, and lobelia that will bloom until nipped by hard frost.

A mixture of flowers will provide a dynamic display of color for summer and fall containers. Plant the center of the container with a tall plant, graduating to smaller plants as you move toward the side of the planter and finally end with cascading flowers around the perimeter. Before planting, take a stroll through local nurseries and public gardens to see which plants they use and in what combinations. Use their examples as models. You will see that they have two basic types of container arrangements, some for sun and others for shade.

The most popular annual flowers for container gardening include Pelargonium geraniums, zinnias, marigolds, and snapdragons for containers in sunny sites. Fuchsias, begonias, impatiens, and coleus are among the most popular choices for shady locations.

Small to medium-sized sun-loving plants for container gardening also include dwarf French marigolds, petunias, dwarf zinnias, and New Guinea impatiens. Shade-loving annuals include the annual forget-me-nots (*Anchusa* species),wax and rex begonias, the browallias, and the beautiful versatile impatiens (*Impatiens wallerana*) in its coats of many colors.

Trailing or cascading annuals for sunny locations include lobelia, ivy geraniums, baby's breath and many of the petunias. The multiflora petunia series are particularly carefree, blooming extravagantly as they tumble over the edges of their containers. Annual

flowering vines for shady places include the black-eyed Susan vine (*Thunbergia alata*) and the orange clock vine (*T. gibsonii*), both rather unusual and quite effective. Hundreds of annuals are available from which you can choose just about any color, texture, growth pattern, and size.

An excellent display for winter container plantings in mild to warm climates are hardy plants such as pansies, primroses, and ornamental kales and cabbages. Evergreens such as hollies, euonymus, miniature Alberta spruce trees or arborvitae will add life to a barren deck.

Plant to suit the environment of the container. South-facing decks and patios with no nearby sheltering trees, for example, bake in temperatures that could easily pass 100° F. on sunny days in many regions. Exposed containers receive much more wind than those in protected locations, such as the south or east sides of walls. Both south-facing sites and exposed sites will dry out plants quickly. Line the sides of large containers with rockwool insulation, vermiculite, or newspaper to help insulate them from heat and wind. This will help cut watering chores.

Always fill containers with a planting mix that includes 25 to 50 percent of well-rotted organic compost. The exceptions of course would be those plants such as the cacti which require sandy soils for top health. Organic compost holds moisture very well so that you do not have to water as often.

For plants that require an acid soil with low pH such as azaleas, camellias, and rhododendrons, mix acid peat moss half and half with well-rotted compost. For other plants, mix the rich garden soil with one-quarter compost and one-quarter well-rotted manure. Using growing media that has a high amount of organic matter will cut fertilization and watering to a minimum.

Most herbaceous perennials will grow very well in containers. Herbs also are good choices for container gardens. In areas with hard winter freezes, plunge the pots in the ground or transplant plants to a garden bed for the winter, especially if it enables you to have them closer to your kitchen door. A good large container-planting scheme might include several varieties of basil or tarragon in the center, surrounded by chives, dwarf sage, and parsley which in turn is ringed by low-growing thymes. Or you might group the herbs together in an assortment of kitchen containers such as colanders, peach baskets, egg baskets, and fruit crates.

If your garden space is limited, grow fruits and vegetables in containers. Dwarf apple, citrus, nectarine, pear and plum trees grow very well in containers. Check the nurseries for the miniature and dwarf varieties that have very compact growth and produce fruit a few years after transplanting. Blueberries and gooseberries grow exceptionally well in containers. All varieties of strawberries grow well in containers and they have the added advantage of cascading over the sides. For a sustained harvest, plant everbearing day-neutral varieties such as 'Tribute' and 'Tri-star'.

Vegetables in containers will need weekly feeding with liquid seaweed, fish emulsion, or a manure tea for sustained production. Grow beets, radishes, lettuce, spinach, and other leaf crops in the early spring, followed by crops such as cucumbers, peppers, pole beans and tomatoes. Toward the end of summer, plant the leaf lettuces, radishes, and spinach once again. This will provide a continual harvest.

Cherry tomatoes produce early and throughout the season. Determinate tomato varieties normally produce fruit for a short, more concentrated harvest while indeterminate tomatoes continue growing and setting fruit until the first hard freeze. Choose small determinate patio tomato varieties for small containers. Grow everbearing indeterminate tomatoes in five-gallon or larger containers with a stake or cage to help support them.

Look for miniature and dwarf vegetables that have been bred for container growing. They are becoming more and more common.

Crops such as cabbage, cauliflower, melons, potatoes, and corn take up too much space and only produce at the end of the season. If you want to grow these in planters, make sure that the containers are as large as possible in order to grow these long-season crops successfully.

Container Care

As with gardening in the ground, soil preparation is the single most important key to success in container gardening. Not far behind are correct watering and choosing the right plants. Know the requirements of the plants you are growing in order to provide them with soil that includes the right nutrients, pH, and moisture.

Most plants will grow well in a moderately rich soil that has good texture, is well-draining, and has a pH of about 6.5 to 7.0. The plants will grow best when the soil is kept moist but not wet. Although your garden plants will truly thrive under these conditions, you will find that many will tolerate less than ideal conditions.

Hanging baskets dry out easily, especially on long hot and windy days. Drip irrigation is an easy way to avoid this problem. See diagram on drip irrigation, for help in setting up a drip system for hanging baskets.

Shelter containerized plants from hot afternoon

Placing one container inside another prevents heat buildup. The outer container receives the heat and dissipates it before it affects the internal container.

sun in order to decrease watering requirements and also to keep heat stress to a minimum. Sun-loving plants will do well if they have six to eight hours of direct sun. Ideally, this might be from dawn until two or three in the afternoon. The sun is hottest in many regions from about three until shortly before sundown.

There are plastic polymer materials that soak up water and, according to the ads, will cut back on watering needs. Some of these, especially the ones with smaller particles, are useful if they are used with a good soil or other planting medium.

Once again, well-prepared potting media are the best solution for growing plants. Highly organic soils and artificial media will hold moisture very well.

When gardening on a rooftop, pick a spot out of the wind if at all possible. Otherwise, plan to make your own sheltered location with combinations of parapets, trellises, fences, and tall plants. Rooftops usually get a lot of sun so make sure the containers that you grow in are big so that moisture loss from evaporation is less.

Once you get a number of plants in a location, they create their own shade and mini-environments. They will make the area seem cooler than a bare rooftop and, indeed, it will be cooler. Plants in numbers affect the climate of a location, even a small environment.

With imagination and some hard work, you can have a rooftop garden that is as grand as those at ground level. Successful rooftop gardens create the illusion of a lofty Eden.

Chapter Twelve

Extending Growing Seasons

About Extending Growing Seasons

The easiest and most economical ways to extend growing seasons are to add warmth and shelter to protect plants from cold weather and high winds. Modern materials have greatly expanded the products available for protecting plants from early and late cold during spring and fall. These new products, in addition to traditional ones, such as cloches, and improvised ones, allow gardeners to grow vegetables earlier and longer than the weather would suggest.

In addition, these products make it possible to be able to grow desirable plants in a zone that is one or more zones farther north than the plants would grow if unprotected.

You can also lengthen the growing season by finding the mini-environments of your property where the soil warms up and stays warm longer. Some mini-environments occur because of orientation to the sun plus protection from wind. Other warm sites occur near buildings that are not very weather-tight. Still others occur next to brick, stone, and mortar walls, and fences which, by holding heat, buffer the surrounding climate and help prevent the very damaging freeze-thaw cycles so common in the Midwest and other parts of the country.

Dark walls will absorb and hold more heat than light-colored walls, another factor that may affect nearby growing conditions. Dark soil absorbs more heat than light-colored soil which is another factor to take into account when trying to extend growing seasons for useful and ornamental plants.

A body of water such as a lake, pond, or small creek will also moderate the air temperature. If your garden is near water, the winter temperature will be higher and the summer temperature warmer than the more distant surrounding area.

If untimely hard frosts threaten tender plants, an old-fashioned trick to avoid plant injury is to turn sprinklers or misters on the plants. This will work for tender trees and shrubs as well as smaller plants. One year, we saw tuberous begonias that were covered with thick ice after being sprinkled to avoid frost damage. When the sun came out, they were beautiful in a strange and sparkling way. When the ice melted, the plants were as healthy as before the frost hit.

Low spots will be colder than sites with a higher elevation. Cold air sinks. That's why an ideal site for an orchard is a slope. Cold air flows down the slope providing good air circulation to the orchard trees while avoiding the frosty air that flows down to the lower area below them.

In a pinch, if you have a cold-sensitive shrub, small tree, or smaller plant outdoors when early or late frost threatens, put a sheet or blanket over the plant and rig a low-wattage electric light bulb under the covering. Make sure the bulb is not near the fabric, which might catch on fire. The bulb under the cover will keep the temperature 10 to 15° above the ambient temperature in the rest of the garden.

Dark plastic mulches, which also shade weeds and prevent moisture loss, are an inexpensive way to increase the temperature of the soil 5 to 15° on sunny days. As plants grow, the leaves shade the dark soil, gradually stopping the warming affect. Clear plastic is more efficient in warming the soil than black!

Placing dark rocks strategically is a simple way to moderate temperature in small areas of the garden. You can create your own mini-environments with these rocks which will absorb and hold heat over a long period, slowly releasing it in its own immediate vicinity.

In the Northwest, where the winters are cloudy, you need to maximize what light is available. Greenhouses need to be glass or very clear plastic to transmit light well. Southern climates, with more light, can use less expensive plastic or double-walled greenhouses that do not transmit as much light.

Cool-weather plants need the opposite kind of shelter. You must protect them from too much heat and sun in order to extend their growing season. If you shade these plants, including lettuce and cabbage family members, from afternoon sun when the hot season arrives, you can extend their harvest time and keep them from bolting. Thick organic mulches help hold moisture and keep the soil cool.

Covers, Tunnels & Cloches

Spun fiber such as Reemay™ will protect plants from cold weather and the elements while letting air circulate freely.

A Wall-O-Water™ is the most efficient way to keep small plants protected from freezing weather.

Covering plants with row tunnels, covers, and cloches will protect them from extreme cold and freezes. They make it easy to plant earlier in the spring and have harvests far into the fall.

Spun fiber coverings, including the brands Agronet™ and Reemay™, will protect plants from late and early frosts if set over young plants and anchored around the perimeter with soil or rocks. Plants will support the light spun-fiber row covers and no super-structure is needed.

When using flexible row covers, you may need to buy the large staples that are available for securing row covers and plastic mulches in place. Or you can make your own from old coat hangers by cutting off the two curved ends. Staples that are one-inch-wide and four to six inches long are handy.

Row covers can be made of clear corrugated fiberglass that is bent into an arch and secured in the garden. The size of this kind of row cover is limited only by the size of the fiberglass panels.

There are commercial row covers that combine polypropylene with hoops to make season extenders that will protect garden crops to temperatures as low as 25° F. These come in sizes large enough to use on dwarf fruit trees and mature tomato vines. They also come in smaller sizes for pepper plants, eggplants, and rose bushes.

Cloches—made of plastic, glass, or wet-strength waxed paper—protect individual plants. Plastic milk jugs with the bottoms cut out make the simplest of cloches. And who does not remember rose fanciers who used Mason jars to protect small rose cuttings that they started in their garden beds?

There are commercial cloches in all sizes. Typical are the cone-shaped caps made of rigid transparent plastic or wet-strength waxed paper that are easy to use and will stack conveniently.

The water-filled teepee known as Wall O' Water™ is a season extender for protecting plants from cold at night and shielding them from excess heat during the day. They are ideal for extending the season for individual plants and, although most often used during spring months, also have potential for extending the fall season. Each water teepee holds three gallons of water and will last from three to five years if given proper care.

During the day, the water absorbs the heat of the sun and moderates the temperature inside the teepee. When night falls and the air becomes colder than the water in the teepee, the water slowly releases its heat. If the water begins to freeze, it will release more heat. These teepees will protect plants down to 20° F. or less. Each one can release as much as 900,000 calories, according to the product literature.

Cold Frames

A cold frame is a rectangular plastic- or glass-topped container about 3 x 4 feet that is placed on the ground to protect plants from climate extremes. The heat inside is provided by sunlight. A cold frame will slow soil-moisture evaporation, warm both soil and air, and also protect plants from pests.

A cold frame will extend the spring season from six weeks to two months. If you plant tomatoes in a cold frame two months earlier than recommended, you will have fresh fruit two months to six weeks earlier than everyone else. This big a jump on the growing season may be possible in mild climates such as the Pacific Northwest, but not in more rigorous climates such as the Upper Midwest.

Open a cold frame or simple greenhouse during the heat of the day to provide cooling and air circulation. Fancier cold frames have wax-filled vents that operate automatically. When the heat rises in the frame, the wax expands, opening the vent. When the temperature cools, the wax contracts closing the vent.

Cold frames come in many forms, the simplest of which is old window sashes laid over a rectangle of straw bales. This simple cold frame is as effective as more expensive ones.

Half or three-quarter-inch galvanized metal conduit pipe bent into an arc makes a great superstructure for a cold frame. Many local hardware stores or electrical supply companies will bend the pipe for you or loan you the pipe bender for a day to bend it yourself. Half-inch Schedule 40 PVC irrigation pipe also works well and can be bent by hand.

A piece of plastic is simply stretched over the dome-shaped conduit or PVC pipe. It is held in place with clamps so that it can be easily removed on warm days or completely covered at night. The ends are easy to open to form a breezy tunnel on medium warm days.

PolyWeave, made of 8-mil polyethelene reinforced with woven nylon mesh is a typical new plastic fabric. It transmits up to 90 percent of sunlight, can be sewn or taped, and has a life span of up to five years.

Hotbeds

Hotbeds are cold frames that are heated and have insulation. As such, they also can be made of anything appropriate. They, too, can be simple like the straw bales and window sashes mentioned above or they can be made more elegantly. Either way, they will work fine in the garden to extend growing seasons at both ends, spring and fall.

Convert your cold frame into a hotbed by placing heating cable or heating mats, available in most garden centers and hardware stores, on the soil below. Over the cable or mat put a two-inch layer of soil, newspaper or a two-inch thick piece of Styrofoam to distribute the heat evenly to the bottoms of the containers and flats.

Most heating cables or mats come with a built-in thermostat that is set at 72° F. As with all electrical equipment, read and follow the directions in order to use the heating cable or mat safely. Heating cables or mats will not heat the entire hotbed volume well, but

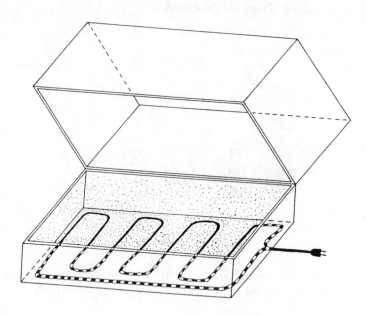

An inexpensive heating cable warms this hotbed.

will maintain the bottom heat needed for strong seedling growth.

You can also provide heat in a hotbed by digging a 2-foot deep pit the length and width of the frames that will be placed on the soil surface. Fill the pit with a blend of straw and fresh manure to within 6 inches of the surface. Then put down a layer of straw and 1-2 inches of topsoil. Place the hotbed frame over the area and you are ready to plant or put your seedling flats inside.

Greenhouses

A multipurpose solar greenhouse attached to the home can be used to grow plants and will also help heat and humidify the home. It is a nice place for afternoon tea or happy hour, and a bright and cheery spot for a winter picnic.

At night or on cloudy days, greenhouses are expensive to heat. To solve this problem, one grower in Portland, Oregon, heats his greenhouse with compost. He stacks organic matter up on the sides of the greenhouse to a height of about five feet, both inside and out. As the piles decompose they give off heat which keeps the greenhouse warm. This also might be a good solution for a home greenhouse on a large property.

Greenhouses are made of many materials and can function in any climatic conditions, if you're willing to foot the bill. The most economical way to use a green-

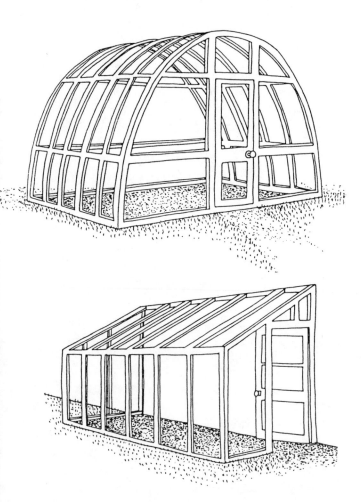

Greenhouses will allow you to garden all year long. They will also allow you to start plants much earlier in the season.

house is as a kind of large cold frame. Use it mostly to extend the growing seasons and its utilities won't amount to much. But if you live in a cold climate and want to grow exotic tropicals, be prepared for high heating bills. In sunny regions, solar heat can help reduce heating costs.

Solar grow frames hold their heat by using insulation. Solar (or any kind of greenhouse) also benefits from insulation and, in larger units, heat-retaining materials such as drums filled with water to serve as thermal mass.

Commercial growers use greenhouses in hot climates to shade plants and keep them cooler than the ambient air. Shade cloth and whitewash are the two classic ways to shade greenhouses in the summer. The home greenhouse can be shaded in summer in those same ways, or you can plant deciduous trees which will provide shade in the summer and allow the sun through their branches in cold months.

If you plan to add a greenhouse room onto your home, consult with experts and talk to someone who already has this kind of an addition. Double- or even triple-glazed coverings on greenhouses, although expensive, will be effective in cutting utility costs.

Before laying out time, money, and energy to build a greenhouse, analyze the project carefully on paper. List what you want to use the greenhouse for. Be very specific and figure in the square footage that you would need. Study the possible sites for a greenhouse and list the pluses and minuses of each. Then and only then, you are ready to begin discussing the project with an expert or developing plans to do it yourself.

It may be that you want a simple free-standing work area with a potting bench where you can start plants from seed and grow them into transplants. If that is the case, you could probably get away with having a temporary plastic cover like a tent over the area during the late winter and early spring months. This, combined with heating cables, and a heater in case of unseasonable freezes, might be all you need.

Protection From The Elements

Windbreaks protect plants from heat and water loss. They also can increase the average temperature from one to five degrees on the downwind side of the windbreak.

Traditional windbreaks in the prairies and plains where prevailing winds are strong and quite constant, are poplars and other fast-growing deciduous trees combined with tall evergreens such as Norway spruce. The evergreens are staggered along the windward side of the windbreak, with the deciduous trees arranged in random rows on the lee side.

Windbreaks for homes and home gardens need not be on such a heroic scale. They can include smaller trees and shrubs. They can also function as sound and sight barriers. Irregular rows of tall plants also can protect outdoor living areas from summer sun, often a very important function.

The best windbreaking hedges are not orchard trees and bushes, but woody plants chosen for their foliage and growth pattern as wind buffers. The flowers and fruit of edibles are damaged by high winds. There are a few exceptions, such as carob, mulberry, olive, and nut trees.

Arbors, Shade, & Lath Houses

Arbors, shade houses, and lath houses are excellent ways to protect people and plants from too much heat and sun. A shade structure can be used over both the patio and garden beds, especially when the vegetable varieties are chosen for their ornamental appeal and arranged in an artistic way.

Arbors and pergolas, ornamental structures built to support plants and create pathways and sitting areas in the garden, are classic solutions to providing shade in an attractive way. They are ideal for grape vines.

Arbors and pergolas are well-suited for climbing roses and clematis. And, they are also interesting challenges for growing the vining vegetables—the squashes, cucumbers, beans, and peas. Once the vines are growing well, use the shade inside or on the north side for growing shade-loving plants. Leaf lettuce will do better in the shade during the hot months, and it also makes a beautiful border plant.

Shade houses are created by attaching shade cloth to a frame. They may be used for a picnic area or also provide protection for potted plants during the intense heat of summer. Shade cloth is a synthetic material available in a range of sun-blocking ability. Homeowners and gardeners are just beginning to discover the many uses for shade cloth. It can be found in any horticultural supply store.

A lath house built from thin, narrow strips of wood can provide 25 percent shade, 50 percent shade, or even more, depending on how close you place the laths. Lath houses can be simple, stark structures to fulfill a practical function only or they can be built with aesthetics in mind so that they are handsome as well as utilitarian.

Chapter Thirteen
Garden Talk

About Garden Talk

Local gardeners, especially old-timers can be a wealth of knowledge. If they have lived in an area for a long time, they possess a fountain of knowledge about local weather, soil, and gardening practices. Older gardeners often can tell you about the blooming sequence of flowers and fruit trees in your area and which varieties do best.

Recent newcomers to this country may grow unusual plants from their homeland, many of which bear delicious fruits.

Remember to ask them what plants they grow as well as how to grow them. You might be surprised at what you learn.

Some of the common terms used in gardening may be confusing if you are a beginner. Here are the definitions of some of the words and phrases used most often.

Agricultural lime. Agricultural lime, also called ground limestone, is calcium carbonate, one of the most common forms of lime. It will not burn plants, is slow-acting, and will remain in the soil for years.

Annual. A plant that completes its life cycle within one growing season. This is a relative term in many cases as there are perennials that are tender and so must be treated as annuals in northern climates.

Anti-companion plants. Anti-companion plants are those which exude chemicals that discourage the growth of other plants within proximity. Allelopathy is another word used to refer to this ability to compete with neighboring plants by stunting their growth.

Bacterium. Any of a large group of microscopic plants that includes both helpful and harmful members. Some bacteria cause diseases while others are important to us, especially those responsible for fermentation.

Biennial. A plant that completes its full life cycle in two growing seasons. Typically, a biennial develops foliage during the first growing season, then flowers, fruits and dies during the second growing season.

Bordeaux mixture. Bordeaux mix is an effective fungicide that includes copper, sulfur, and lime. Its name comes from the fact that it was first developed and used in the Bordeaux vineyards of France during the last half of the nineteenth century. It was first used to discourage theft, but vintners soon discovered that the material, when painted on grapevines, would eliminate powdery mildew, a serious fungal disease of French vineyards at that time.

Chelation. Refers to the formation of bonds between organic compounds and metals, some of which are insoluble, as in humus. Soluble chelates are used in fertilizers to help keep nutrient metals, such as iron, mobile in the soil and thus available to plants rather than locked up in insoluble mineral salts.

Chlorosis. A word that simply means the yellowing of leaves. It can be caused by nutrient deficiencies, lack of light, light that is too bright, or high temperatures. If leaves are pale yellow while leaf veins are green, it is most likely an iron deficiency.

Cold frames. An enclosed unheated area, usually comparatively small with a plastic or glass cover used to protect plants from climate extremes. The only heat source for a cold frame is the sun.

Companion plants. Plants that, when grown together in close proximity, improve the growth and health of one another in some way. Although little scientific data gives specific examples, many gardeners have experienced good results by experimenting on their own..

Compost. The rich organic material that results from the natural process of decomposition of plant and animal waste. When compost has thoroughly decayed into a dark matter in which no original pieces of plant are discernible, it is called humus. Composting turns yard waste into a product to improve garden soil.

Corm. A thick underground stem base with scaly leaves and buds. Crocus and gladiolus "bulbs" are actually corms.

Crop rotation. Simply, this means that planting of different annual crops in a particular site each year. Different crops have different nutritional needs and are likely to have different diseases and pests. Crop rotation prevents a build-up of disease while allowing different nutrients to be utilized.

Deciduous. Refers to those trees and shrubs that lose their leaves in the fall. Maple, oak, and hickory trees are examples.

Diatomaceous earth. DE is the naturally-occurring, mined material that includes a high proportion of fossilized silica shell remains of tiny one-celled creatures called diatoms. DE includes 14 trace minerals in a chelated form and the sharp silica crystals are fatal to most soft-bodied insects, slugs, and spider mites.

Dolomitic lime. A soil amendment used to raise soil pH, calcium magnesium carbonate, includes the two important nutrients, calcium, and magnesium. A slow-acting material, it should be purchased in the finest available ground form so that it begins acting soon after application. It will remain in the soil for up to five years.

Double digging. A labor-intensive method for improving the quality of the top two feet of garden soil. It involves deep digging of garden soil while incorporating organic matter and fertilizer.

Drip irrigation. A system of small tubes, larger hoses, and emitters used to provide precise amounts of water to precise root areas of target plants. Because the water is not sprayed in the air, less is lost to evaporation. This system conserves water in droughty regions.

Ecology. The study of the interrelationships of organisms to one another and to their environment.

Environment. The total of all the external conditions that act upon an organism or community to influence its development and life.

Erosion. The wearing away of land surfaces by water, wind, ice, or other agents, including gravitational creep and plowing.

Espalier. A plant, often a fruit tree, trained through pruning and tying to grow flat against a flat surface, fence, trellis, or wall.

Evergreen. Having leaves that remain green and on the tree throughout the year. Hollies are good examples of broad-leafed evergreens; firs and pines are good examples of coniferous evergreens.

Fertilizer. An organic or inorganic material added to the soil, that is important for its nutrient value to plants.

Forb. A herbaceous plant that is not a grass, sedge, or rush. Typically used to refer to flowering plants of the prairie, many of which are good choices for drought-resistant gardens.

Fungus. Any of a large group of lower plants that lack chlorophyll. This plant group includes bacteria, mildews, molds, and mushrooms. Some fungi cause

disease which, if spotted and identified early, can usually be controlled with cultural practices and organically acceptable fungicides such as baking soda solutions and Bordeaux mixture.

Garden beds. Prepared sites with improved soil texture, structure and fertility that are used for growing ornamental or useful plants.

Green manure. A leguminous cover crop that is tilled under to enrich the soil. It is effective and inexpensive, but takes longer than directly adding compost or fertilizers and other soil improvers.

Ground Cover. Although grasses are in reality ground covers, other plants are usually thought of in this category. Ground covers are low-growing, spreading plants that are good in combination with or instead of with lawns. Ivies, myrtles, pachysandra, epimediums, low-growing sedums, the temperate gingers, and lamiums are examples of low-growing ones.

Taller examples are daylilies, fall-blooming sedums, and ornamental grasses.

Hardiness. A quality measured by a system of zones developed by the United States Department of Agriculture. The hardiness zones indicate the amount of cold that plants will tolerate. As yet, there are no hardiness zones to indicate how much heat plants can tolerate.

Hedge. A barrier of small trees or shrubs planted to act as a fence, a sight and sound barrier, a windbreak, or an ornamental background.

Herb. In the true botanical sense, an herb is any plant that is not woody and dies back to the ground at frost each fall. In the culinary and medicinal sense of the word, an herb is any plant valued and used for its flavor, fragrance, or medicinal qualities.

Hotbeds. Cold frame structures that are heated and insulated.

Humus. The dark organic matter in soil that results from decomposed plant and animal waste.

Hybrid. An offspring of two closely related but different species.

Inorganic. Term used for any material that does not derive from plant or animal sources. Chemically, the term means anything that does not have carbon molecules in its makeup.

Integrated pest management. IPM is a conservative way to control pests by first identifying them and understanding their biology, monitoring the population and, if pest population goes beyond a tolerable level, using mechanical and non-toxic methods to control them. Pesticides that are targeted to the specific pest are used only if the loss of the crop is possible without intervention. Pests are monitored and the effects of controls are evaluated.

Irrigation. The practice of supplying water to crops and gardens in addition to natural rainfall.

Leaky pipe hose. These hoses, made from recycled tires, release water slowly through thousands of tiny pores.

Mulch. A natural or artificial layer placed on the soil surface, consisting of plant residue or other materials such as sand, paper, or plastic. In gardening, mulches are used to buffer soil temperatures, suppress weeds, conserve soil moisture, and reduce erosion by rain and wind.

No-till gardening. This practice calls for no cultivation of the garden soil after the initial tilling. Instead, regular mulches are added and plants are planted through the mulch. This saves on labor and eliminates weeds which might germinate as a result of tilling the soil to expose weed seeds to sunlight.

Nutrients. Substances needed for plants and animals to develop, grow, and reproduce.

Open-pollination. Plants that are simply grown and allowed to freely pollinate by natural means produce open-pollinated varieties. Peas, beans, and lettuce all are open-pollinated species. This is in contrast to hybrid plants which are pollinated artificially to ensure that the offspring are from the chosen parents.

Organic gardening. A method of gardening that is based on building a healthy, living soil through composting and using supplemental nutrients from naturally occurring rock, mineral, or ocean deposits. The basic principle is to feed the soil and the soil will feed the plants. Healthy plants are better able to resist pests and disease. If control is needed, cultural and mechanical methods are used first. A selection of acceptable naturally derived pesticides are used only as a last resort.

Parasites. A plant or animal that lives on or in another plant or animal, usually to the detriment of the host organism.

Perennials. Plants that die back to the ground each fall and regrow from the roots the next season.

Pesticide. Substances used to kill pests. Most common subdivisions of pesticides are herbicides for killing weeds, fungicides for killing fungi, and insecticides for killing insect pests.

pH. pH refers to the number of hydrogen ions in the soil. It is expressed on a scale in terms of acidity and alkalinity with 7.0 as neutral, 0-7 acid, and 7-14 alkaline. Most plants prefer a pH in the range of 6.2-6.8. Lime is used to raise soil pH and sulfur is used to lower it.

Plant health care programs. PHC is a newer, more encompassing program than integrated pest management. PHC calls for addressing the entire garden and maintaining this larger view rather than concentrating on "managing pests." Know the plants. Learn what they need for good health. Provide those necessities to have healthy plants. Use only environmentally conscientious pest management programs.

Prairie. A tract of level to hilly land with growth that is dominated by grasses and forbs. Prairies are treeless and have very few shrubs. The natural plant communities of prairies consist of various mixes of tall, medium, and short native species, respectively known as true prairie, mixed prairie, and *tortures* prairie.

Predator. An animal, insect, or spider that lives by preying upon other animals.

Pruning. The practice of trimming branches and foliage of plants to improve their health, to control their shape, or to direct a tree's growth away from traffic areas or buildings.

Rhizome. Thick, horizontal stems with roots growing down and foliage and flowers growing up. Cannas and bearded irises are typical of plants that grow from rhizomes.

Salinity. The level of salt in the soil. Areas with low rainfall are inclined to have saline soils.

Season extender. Techniques and equipment used to extend the growing season in both spring and fall. Examples include greenhouses, cold frames, hotbeds, row covers, cloches, and products such as Wall O' Water™.

Seeds. Ripened plant ovules that under the right conditions will develop into new plants. They are the products of male and female plant parts.

Seedlings. Young plants that must be tended carefully if they are to mature.

Sheet Composting. The practice of spreading organic garden waste, grass clippings, and animal manures over the garden soil and allowing it to decompose in place.

Soaker Hoses. Hoses that leak water at the soil level through small openings along the length of the hose.

Soil tests. An analysis of the soil that gives information on pH, nutrient levels, organic matter content and, if needed, other important soil characteristics. Gardeners use soil tests to find out what amendments are needed to raise or lower nutrient levels.

Species. Refers to a natural population or group of populations that transmit specific characteristics from parents to offspring. Species are reproductively isolated from other populations with which they might breed. The word is used as both singular and plural.

Stolon. A plant runner that is actually a stem growing along or under the ground and takes roots at the nodes or joints to form new plants. Zoysia grass is typical of plants that spread by means of stolons.

Transplanting. The process of moving a plant from one location to another. Transplanting usually damages roots, therefore gardeners should perform the process as swiftly and efficiently as possible to minimize root damage and thus speed the re-establishment of the plants.

Thatch. The collection of old dead stems and roots at the soil level of turf grasses. This collection is normal and returns nutrients to the soil as it decomposes. Only when the amount of old dead stems and roots greatly exceeds the rate of decay should some of the thatch be removed. This rarely happens unless a lawn has been over-fertilized, cut improperly, or if the soil life has been destroyed by overuse of pesticides so microorganisms are not present to decompose the thatch.

Tuber. Fleshy underground stems that have buds from which new foliage and flowers will grow. Irish potatoes are an example of a tuberous plant.

Tuberous roots. Thick fleshy roots that grow roots from the bottom and foliage and flowers from the top pointed bud. Dahlias have tuberous roots.

Virus. An actively infectious agent that is small enough to go through a filter too fine for bacteria to pass through and too small to be seen with a light microscope.

Weed. A plant that is growing where you don't want it to grow.

Windbreak. Plants, usually combinations of trees and shrubs that shield home, buildings, and other living areas from strong prevailing winds. Windbreaks are common in the Plains states where northwest winds are an everyday occurrence.

Xeriscaping. A water-conservative method of gardening that emphasizes such water-saving practices as increasing organic content of garden soil, limiting lawn areas, mulching and using native plants and other plants that require little water to thrive.

Index

Organic Gardener's Composting
by Steve Solomon

Steve Solomon has been composting for more than twenty years and writing garden books since 1976. Steve also tells how to make powerful compost that is fortified with nutrients that *grows* the garden. Solomon is not a "hard-line" compost fanatic pushing humus as *the* solution for every and all garden problems. He scientifically explains compost's roles in soil fertility in a way any layperson can understand.

8 ½ x 11", 144 pages, illustrated
ISBN 1-878823-06-X - **$9.95**

Organic Gardener's Basics
by Barbara P. Lawton & George F. Van Patten

This comprehensive, practical manual is packed full of basic "how-to" examples that make organic gardening fun, simple, safe, and easy. Lawton and Van Patten, two expert gardeners, share more than 30 years of professional writing between them, in This priceless easy-to-use guide covers all aspects of basic home organic gardening.

8 ½ x 11", 208 pages, illustrated
ISBN 1-878823-01-9 - **$12.95**

Organic Gardener's Annuals
by Peter Loewer

This book teaches you "how-to" paint your yard with picture-perfect arrangements of these colorful plants, then change the look of the garden from month to month and season to season. The book gives you everything you'll need to know about planning and planting the ultimate annual garden. You'll find descriptions of more than 300 annual varieties and tips on how to grow them.

8 ½ x 11", 144 pages, illustrated
ISBN 10878823-08-6 - **$9.95**

Organic Gardener's Edible Plants
by Rosalind Creasy

This easy-to-use guide is alphabetically arranged guide of attractive and delicious edible plants, including suitable varieties for all North American climate zones. More than 130 plants included range from such popular, familiar edibles as apples and plums, with special mention of outstandingly attractive or delicious varieties, to ethnic and regional favorites. For each edible, the internationally acclaimed author includes: Effort scale, Geographic range of cultivation; Thumbnail description of the edible; Sources of the edibles; and Recipes.

8 ½ x 11", 224 pages, illustrated
ISBN 1-878823-07-8- **$12.95**

Organic Garden Vegetables
by George F. Van Patten

This book is packed with exact information that gives all gardeners quick answers to difficult problems. The easy-to-reference facts on climate, soil preparation, planting, crop care, harvesting, kitchen ideas and exact details on growing more than 300 varieties of vegetables make this book one that you must have in your gardening library.

8 ½ x 11", 144 pages, color cover, b/w text, illustrated
ISBN 1-878823-02-7 - **$9.95**

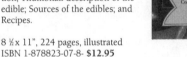